Praise for Priscilla Stone Sharp and
Langhorn & Mary

"An engaging, well-researched book that demonstrates the heartache and the strength of two courageous people. Ms. Priscilla Stone Sharp has written a book with care, love, and an abiding faith in humanity. She illuminates another piece of African-American history."
  —**Jewell Parker Rhodes, Author of *Douglass' Women***
    and *Voodoo Dreams: A Novel of Marie Laveau*

"Langhorn and Mary is a clever and creative epic that should not be missed. The compelling story is full of intrigue, richness, and depth that is relevant to any time and culture."
  —**Terrie Williams, author of *A Plentiful Harvest: Creating***
    Balance & Harmony Through the Seven Living Virtues

"Priscilla Stone Sharp brings history alive. Anyone who liked Alex Haley's Roots will love Langhorn and Mary."
  —**Daniella Monetta, Librarian, Collection Development**
    and Genealogy, Arizona State Library

"A haunting tale of forbidden love that crosses racial lines. Chillingly turned murder mystery, set in historic Bucks County, Pennsylvania, based on the author's exhaustive research and historically accurate themes—from the abolitionist movement to the struggle for freedom. Highly recommended.
  —**Roland Barksdale-Hall, Managing Editor, Black Caucus**
    American Library Association Newsletter; Founder and
    Former Executive Director, Western Pennsylvania
    African-American Historical Genealogical Society

"A compelling tale of race, slavery, and an interracial marriage."
  —**Ann Burns, Editor, *Library Journal***

Langhorn and Mary

A 19th Century American Love Story

Langhorn and Mary

A 19th Century American Love Story

PRISCILLA STONE SHARP

Ambrosia Books
Phoenix
New York   Los Angeles

Langhorn and Mary
A 19th Century American Love Story
by Priscilla Stone Sharp

Published by:
Ambrosia Books
A Division of Amber Communication Group, Inc.
1334 East Chandler Boulevard, Suite 5-D67
Phoenix, AZ 85048
amberbk@aol.com
www.amberbooks.com

Tony Rose, Publisher/Editorial Director   Samuel P. Peabody, Associate Publisher
Yvonne Rose, Senior Editor   The Printed Page, Interior & Cover Design

Library of Congress Cataloging-In-Publication Data

Sharp, Priscilla Stone.
  Langhorn & Mary : a love story / Priscilla Stone Sharp.
     p. cm.
  ISBN 0-9727519-0-4
  1. Pennsylvania--History--Civil War, 1861-1865--Fiction. 2.
Interracial marriage--Fiction. 3. African American men--Fiction. 4.
Bucks County (Pa.)--Fiction. 5. Trials (Murder)--Fiction. 6. White
women--Fiction. 7. Uxoricide--Fiction. I. Title: Langhorn and Mary.
II. Title.

PS3619.H3565 L365 2003
813'.6--dc21

                                          2002045411

Printed in the United States of America

Contents

Dedicated with love to

Aunt Mary and Uncle Langhorn

and to

Samuel P. Peabody—A Great Friend
—T.R.

Acknowledgments

First and foremost I give praise and thanks to God and to His Messengers and Prophets, especially Bahá'u'lláh, Prophet-Founder of the Bahá'í Faith (1817-1892), who brought to world the principles of Oneness—Oneness of God, Oneness of Religion, Oneness of Mankind.

To my parents, Oscar P. Stone and Eleanor Clara Samuels Stone, for giving me an appreciation of the Word of God and an understanding of my purpose in life: To know and to love God and to strive to carry forward an ever-advancing civilization.

To my wonderful husband, William H. Sharp, his parents and family. To my daughters, Michelle and 'Nice, and granddaughters, Megan and Yasmin; my brother, Steve, sisters, Virginia and Lynna, aunts, uncles, nieces and nephew, and cousins, especially: Alice Wilkinson Donner and husband William Donner (in memoriam), Jackie Hunt and husband Jerry Scezny, Richard Welch and wife Liz Welch, Louise Rorer Rosett and husband Walter Rosett. To my former husband, Michael Chunowitz, his wife, Lottie, and parents, Gert and Sam.

To all my Bahá'í and secular friends who have been so supportive, especially Terry Agahi, Maxine Bell, Sandra Bufford, Virginia Dindy, Michael Freisinger, Bahia Gulick, Fereydoon Hakimi, Michelle Holte, and Debra Momon.

To my fellow Board members on the InterFaith Action Coalition of Arizona, people of all faiths who have helped me understand that the spark of Divine truth is inherent in all people and all religions—all we have to do is open our hearts to see it—especially Rev. Kyra Hines Baehr.

To the Church of Jesus Christ of Latter-day Saints for its wonderful teachings on the importance of families and its blessed dedication to preserving the pieces of the past regarding our ancestors and making the information available, at no charge and with a great deal of assistance and encouragement, at its Family History Centers located around the world.

To the staff of the Phoenix Public Library's Interlibrary Loan Department.

To the staff of the Arizona State Library, Archives and Public Records.

To the Bucks County Historical and Bucks County Genealogical Societies, with special appreciation for Beth Lander and the wonderful resources of the Spruance Library attached to the Bucks County Historical Society in the Mercer Museum at Doylestown, Pennsylvania, Joan Fitting and the staff at the *Bucks County Intelligencer*, and to fellow historians and researchers Walter Jacobs, Frances Waite, Cyndi Henry, Nancy C. Janyszeski, Rev. Joseph DiPaolo, and Jack Frye. Thank you Jewell Parker Rhodes, Terrie Williams, Roland Barksdale-Hall, and Daniella Monetta.

Finally, and most importantly, my special gratitude to Tony Rose and Yvonne Rose of Ambrosia Books. Were it not for their recognition of the great potential this story has, their investment of finances, publishing expertise, hard work, optimism, and unfailing encouragement, the extraordinary history of Langhorn and Mary Wellings would have remained hidden in obscurity.

Introduction

It all started with an interesting, albeit somewhat disconcerting, dream I had in April 2000. It was the night before I left for a visit to the Spruance genealogical library in Doylestown, Bucks County, Pennsylvania. In the dream, a woman in an old-time dress—I got the impression her name was Elizabeth—was encouraging me to take in my hand one of those big, antique door keys.

"Here," she pleaded as she covered the key in my hand with both of her hands. "Please take this. It will open the door. Tell my story."

By that time, I had been doing genealogy research for almost a dozen years. My husband, Bill, and I had always been curious about our family histories and had been meaning for years to look into it. Finally one day in 1988, we went out to the Family History Center of the Church of Jesus Christ of Latter-day Saints in Mesa, Arizona, about twenty-five miles from our home.

"Here, get a life," he said, jokingly. He figured that my background working as a secretary, paralegal and investigator for lawyers for thirty years had uniquely prepared me for researching our family trees. Armed with only the names and barest facts about our grandparents and a couple of our great-grandparents, I plunged into the records.

Twelve years and twelve thousand individual lives later—grand-parents, aunts, uncles, cousins—I think it's safe to say I "got a life." In the meantime, we have spent thousands of dollars and traveled thou-sands of miles back and forth across the country on trips foraging into old county courthouse records, graveyards and libraries for sometimes the tiniest bit of information.

In the course of this research, I learned that my third great-grand-parents, Jacob Stone and Mary Trullinger Stone, German-Americans of Bucks County, Pennsylvania, had seventeen children from the period

1809 to 1835, and I continued doing more research on the lives and descendants of those seventeen.

And so it was that I came to be in the Spruance Library at the Mercer Museum in Doylestown, Bucks County, Pennsylvania, on a Thursday afternoon in April 2000 looking through the drawers of 3x5 cards containing extracts of obituaries printed in the *Doylestown Democrat* newspaper over the course of almost two hundred years of continuous publication.

I pulled a card out.

Wellings, Mary, it read.

I remembered that Mary, one of Jacob and Mary Stone's daughters had married a Mr. Wellings. I only knew that because after her mother died in 1862, she had signed the Release of Dower as "Mary Wellings." I read further.

Died Jan 3 1865, aged 55, murdered by her husband, a black man.

What?!

Oh, my God! I had to sit down on the library stepstool to think about this for a few minutes.

First thing next morning I hurried back and continued to search. My findings were confirmed by the obituary in the *Bucks County Intelligencer*:

WELLINGS, MARY, w. of Langhorn, dau. of Jacob and Mary Stone, Solebury

I read the newspapers and found the outcome of the case, which gave me a great deal more information, including his full name— Langhorn H. Wellings—and the fact that they were married for thirty years, an incredible feat considering the interracial aspects and living in that time and place.

In fact, I didn't know of any other legally-married, interracial couple who lived at that time and place, and I still haven't found any working-class folks, only one or two couples who were high-profile and rich and could afford to live unconventionally, apart from society.

I came home and wrote a report to the Stone cousins, fellow researchers, who were all as astounded as I was. We were still unsure what to do with all this information except to dutifully record it in our respective family histories. I began thinking and talking about the possibility of writing a book, but at that point did not have enough information; there was a lot more research to be done.

In August 2000 I started working at a new job. Before I even accepted the job, I had to ask for two weeks' unpaid leave since we had previously planned a family trip to Vermont in late September to celebrate my father's eighty-seventh birthday. And, well, as long as I was within a thousand miles of Pennsylvania, I just had to go over there for a few days.

Makes sense to me, probably not to anyone else who's not infected with genealogy fever. But, in the process of learning more about these people, I had fallen in love with them and become consumed by a passion to learn as much as I could about them and their story.

Probably because of this compulsion, it turned out to be a frustratingly wasted first two days. I found nothing of any significance. Finally, one day after the library closed, I drove east on Route 202 to try to find the Canada Hill Baptist Cemetery where Langhorn and Mary are buried. I found the graves easily enough, and I was thrilled to be able to visit them. At the same time my depression was deepened when I saw that the little cemetery was becoming overgrown with bramble bushes and piled with brush and dead leaves.

I sat on the steps and literally cried.

What the heck's the matter with me? Why am I so consumed in this? It's old news, a hundred and fifty years old. I need to go home and get a life, get back to work, pay off some of these horrendous bills I'm piling up.

That's it.

I got up and walked back to the rental car, confirmed in my decision to just pack it up and go home, forget this nonsense and get back to work. The next morning, I checked out of the bed and breakfast that, incidentally, was directly across the road from the little Tinicum Union Church where Mary Stone Wellings was baptized in 1810 and where my fourth-great-grandma Elizabeth Barntz Stone and her son, my third-great-granduncle Henry Stone, are buried. I went for a ride through the beautiful countryside in Bedminster Township and found the area that fifth-great-grandfather Philip Stein farmed in 1760. Part of it is now a lovely manmade lake and reservoir called Nockamixon State Park.

Still undecided, I walked around the lake and pondered and prayed. *What should I do? Should I forget all this and just go home and get back to work? Or should I keep on researching and do something with all this information?*

Back and forth.

Finally, I decided to start driving back to Connecticut to visit my brother Steve and his wife, Anne, before flying home to Phoenix. I drove down Route 611 to Doylestown and toward the freeway. Don't ask why I didn't just go north from Bedminster a few miles to the turnpike at Easton. I don't know why. Driving down Main Street in Doylestown, at the last minute I veered off toward the Spruance Library.

I've got some time. I'll just give it another couple of hours.

At four-thirty that afternoon, I received my answer and more inspiration. I found the trial transcript. Armed with this information, I was confirmed. I could go home *and* tell their story. Not *or*.

There was still a lot of research to be done, and I had no doubts that the commitment of time, energy and money would be increased significantly. I immediately ordered microfilms and began reading at lunch, nights, and on weekends almost fifty years of the weekly *Bucks County Intelligencer* newspaper from 1838 to 1880. I began compiling stacks of research about slavery, anti-slavery movements, the Underground Railroad, the Civil War, racism, the Society of Friends, the Baptists and other churches of Bucks County, interracial marriage, Pennsylvania laws, the history of Bucks County and Doylestown, right down to minutiae such as the actual streets of Doylestown and the real people who lived and worked in Bucks County at that time.

In March 2001 I began setting keystrokes to computer bytes and it started flowing. Every once in a while I would look up to the empty air behind me. "Who's writing this?" I asked aloud.

Just be quiet and keep typing.

We went back to Bucks County in June 2001 for a delightful "Stone Cousins Reunion and Grand Tour" where I got to meet Cousins Jackie and Rich and their spouses for the first time and renew acquaintance with Cousins Alice and Louise. I did another day's research at the Spruance and found pictures of Joseph Fell, Quaker educator, Henry Darlington, publisher of the *Intelligencer* for almost twenty years, William H. Johnson, abolitionist/educator/founder of the Temperance Society, and Rev. Silas M. Andrews, Presbyterian pastor in Doylestown for nearly fifty years. The pictures are taped to my computer. These men are my inspiration. I have not yet been able to locate pictures of Langhorn and Mary or, in fact, to learn if any even exist.

I've come to realize a great many things in the process. Foremost, I understand why my family was drawn to the Bahá'í Faith three generations ago. The Bahá'í Faith, founded in Persia in the 1840s, has always, against sometimes insurmountable odds and at the cost of over twenty thousand lives martyred, carried aloft the banner of oneness—the Oneness of God, of Religion and of Mankind—and the elimination of all forms of prejudice, especially racial. Indeed, even purging the word "race" from our vocabulary when speaking about our fellow human beings.

"There is only one race, the human race."

Being raised in a Bahá'í home, I cut my teeth on these principles. Even so, if I were to tell you that I was completely free of prejudice, I'd be lying. Everyone has prejudices of one kind or another. For example, I asked myself, with all my professions of oneness, would I have married a black man like my Aunt Mary did a hundred and fifty years ago. When she never knew from one day to the next if her husband might be kidnapped and never come home again? If the forces of slavery might overtake the north at any time? When she couldn't even walk down the streets of a strange town with her husband, go into a shop, sit in a restaurant, or be given a hotel room? When it was highly likely her children, outside their neighborhood, would be subjected to the worst manifestations of racism—indeed, even be kidnapped and sold into slavery themselves?

In writing the story, I had the choice of just giving the facts or enriching the reader with the greater picture of the events of that day and the involvement in them of Langhorn and Mary. At a minimum, we know they were affected to some degree by everything going on in the world around them.

With the exception of four people—Mahlon Riegel and his wife Nancy Evans and her parents—who are the only completely fictional characters, everyone who has a first and last name actually existed at that time and in that place and had a role in the events, in varying degrees of minor to major, such as Messrs. Fell and Darlington and the District Attorney, Henry P. Ross. Even Old Jakey Yothers was a real, live produce peddler in Doylestown in 1865. On the other hand, although someone by the name of Tamar Lacy actually lived in Buckingham in the

1830s and '40s, I have completely fictionalized her relationship in Langhorn and Mary's lives.

I hope you enjoy reading *Langhorn and Mary* and learning about these incredibly courageous people and the significant events in their history, and that you will grow to love them as I have, with all their "warts" and "beauty marks." I think it's important that their story is told, their triumphs and sufferings acknowledged, and their spirits honored.

Most importantly, I think Aunt Mary and Uncle Langhorn would want the lessons we have gleaned from their lives to help future generations—in how we treat each other within our families and in our other personal relationships and with the way we face the inevitable trials of life and as we make health and lifestyle choices. I know they have provided me with a tremendous amount of personally insightful reflection.

Priscilla Stone Sharp

Phoenix, Arizona
January 2003

Chapter I

Doylestown, Bucks County, Pennsylvania
May 12, 1865

CHARGED WITH MURDER—On Saturday last, Langhorn Wellings, of Solebury, was committed to Doylestown Jail by J.B. Pugh, Esq., charged on oath of H.P. Ross, Esq. with the murder of his wife, Mary Wellings, by poisoning her with strychnine. His wife had been unwell for a long time and had been treated by Dr. Cernea for apoplexy. On the third of January last she became much worse, and died that night. Suspicions of foul play becoming excited, the body was disinterred on Saturday last, from the burying ground of the Canada Hill Baptist Church, near Lahaska, the stomach taken out by Dr. Cernea, and sent to Professor Rogers, of Philadelphia, for examination, and Wellings committed to jail to await further developments. Wellings has two children living. He is willing that the matter should be investigated and is confident of having his innocence established. When the body of Mrs. Wellings was taken up, the brain was also taken out and preserved by Dr. Cernea. We learn that it presented the appearance usual in cases of apoplexy, clotted blood being collected under the skull. It does not appear that the woman exhibited any symptoms of the operation of an active poison like strychnia previous to her decease. The fact that Wellings had poison in his possession is admitted, but he says that he purchased it and used some of it for killing dogs. It is not likely that the case will be tried in this term of court.

[*Bucks County Intelligencer*, Wednesday, February 7, 1865]

2 Pricilla Stone Sharp

It took much longer than the estimated five minutes for Mahlon Riegel to walk the six short blocks from his home on York Street in Doylestown to the *Bucks County Intelligencer* offices on East Court Street, not only because the chilly humidity made his leg ache more than usual and made walking more difficult. It was also because of the many friendly and well-meaning townsfolk—shopkeepers and neighbors— who greeted him with warm handshakes and pats on the back, welcoming him home from the war, and inquiring beyond mere politeness about his life in the past two years, and especially asking after his bride, Nancy.

It was the first time he had been back at his home in Doylestown since serving for a year and a half with the 163rd Regiment, 18th Pennsylvania Cavalry, attached to the Army of the Potomac, and being wounded at the Battle of the Wilderness a little over a year ago.

Truthfully, it was the second time he had come home within a month, but today was the first time he had been able to get out of the house and into the public eye. The first homecoming was followed within days by the National Tragedy—the Assassination of President Lincoln—and Mahlon and Nancy immediately hurried back to Washington to be with her parents where her father, George Evans, served under Secretary of the Navy Gideon Welles.

As he walked toward the center of town, Mahlon noticed some of the changes that had taken place since he was last home in 1863, including a huge American flag stretched across Main Street in the summer of 1864 by the *Intelligencer's* rival paper, the *Doylestown Democrat*, as a show of loyalty to the Union cause. The red, white and blue decorations that hung from nearly every window along Doylestown's major streets during much of the war were replaced by black mourning buntings for the President.

During his walk, Mahlon was particularly delighted to see old Jacob "Jakey" Yothers, the nearly-blind farmer who pushed his handcart up and down the streets of Doylestown almost every day with his little dog always by his side. There was Widow Remmey, whose husband, John Remmey, the railroad conductor, had just died. And John S. Brown, the former publisher for many years of the *Intelligencer*. And Jesse Armstrong. One after another, he greeted friendly neighbors working in their gardens and shops or walking back from the store and post office.

He saw Abraham Garren sweeping the steps and sidewalk in front of his oyster and ice cream establishment, which he apparently started in the basement of his home on Main Street last year. And S.S. Overholt, Superintendent of Schools, Mahlon's former supervisor when he was working as a teacher in Doylestown.

Mahlon saw, walking on Main Street near State, Moritz Loeb, Jewish publisher of the German Whig paper *Der Morgensterner* (Morning Star) since 1848, who had, Mahlon remembered, received a substantial inheritance from a distant relative in Germany a couple of years ago. Mahlon stopped at the post office and greeted Mrs. Sherer, Doylestown's long-time postmistress and paused briefly to speak with Henry Sands, who had been in the lightening rod business in Doylestown for several years.

Some of the folks in Doylestown had known Mahlon when he was a young boy, since his family had lived and farmed in Bucks County practically as long as there had been a Bucks County, and others he came to know since moving into town seven years ago. The Riegels were among the first German families to settle the area. Mahlon's father and grandfather and great-grandfather had sowed, plowed and harvested the same land near Cross Keys off the Easton Road northeast of Doylestown for more than a century.

Bucks County—the beautiful, verdant, hills of Eastern Pennsylvania. Bucks County—the "bump-out" into New Jersey, or, as the locals preferred to think, the "nose leading the rest of Pennsylvania."

"So goes Bucks County, so goes Pennsylvania; so goes Pennsylvania, so goes the Nation," they were fond of saying.

Bucks County, one of the three original provincial counties founded by William Penn in 1681 under a land grant from King Charles II in payment of a substantial debt. Its name was a shortened honor for Penn's beloved home in Buckinghamshire, England.

Farming was the predominant way of life during the almost two centuries that Bucks County had been founded. Mahlon, however, like so many other men born in the antebellum period at the dawn of the Industrial Revolution, broke the long-standing farming tradition. He preferred the library and classroom—studying, learning and teaching. Books were his favored pastime; in fact, he would much rather read a book than be among people. He described himself, like Charles Brockden Brown,

the eighteenth and early nineteenth century author whose family origi-
nated in Bucks County and whose books and manuscripts were among
Mahlon's favorites, as being particularly shy—indeed, "mute among
strangers."

Being an only child of an economically-comfortable family, his
parents indulged him and were eager to encourage whatever pursuits
were most interesting to him, and his father was not unduly disappointed
that Mahlon showed no inclination to follow in his footsteps on the farm.

Mahlon chose instead to attend college at Princeton across the Delaware in New Jersey. Shortly after graduating, he accepted a teaching
position at Mt. Vernon Boys' Grammar School in Philadelphia, where a
fellow Bucks Countian, George W. Fetter, was principal.

He lived and taught, and continued his studies, in Philadelphia for
one year, until the summer of 1858, when his father was killed in a terrible accident on the farm, and his mother, who was always frail of health,
both emotionally and physically, was unable to care for herself or the
farm. Mahlon found a tenant to rent and continue operation of the considerable property.

Then, he went about the business of finding a teaching position. On
September 13, 1858, he went to the home of N.P. Brower in Doylestown
to meet with Abiah J. Riale, one of the school directors, and was hired as
a teacher for a five-month school term at twenty-five dollars per month.
With the rent from the farm and his teaching salary, Mahlon was able to
find a comfortable home for himself and his mother in Doylestown. His
contract was renewed each term for the next four and a half years.

Then came the War—that horrific conflagration that set brother
against brother and nearly consumed the young American Republic in
its own blood. The first shots on Fort Sumter in April 1861 signaled
more than the beginning of war; it meant the end of government and
society as Americans had known it and a profound change in the character of the United States of America forevermore.

"War! War! WAR!" The posters sprang up on walls and fences all
over town, exhorting the "Young Men of the Lower End. Your Country
Calls, 'Tis Duty to Obey."

Mahlon struggled with his conscience; he felt compelled to go
along with the many young men from Bucks County who eagerly joined
up, following Capt. William Watts Hart Davis, one of the first enlistees

in the volunteer companies. Yet, at the same time he was torn with loyalty to his mother, not comfortable leaving her on her own, and not having anyone to help with her care.

At first, the men were signed up for only three months' service. No one thought the insurrection would last as long as it did. When it became apparent it was not going to end so soon, the draft was organized.

The first draft pick came in 1861 and included all able-bodied white male citizens aged twenty-one to forty-five, except those who had lost a limb or eyesight, ministers, preachers, college professors and school directors, judges, telegraph operators, train engineers, ferry pilots, marines and stage drivers.

No one other than those in the listed occupations was exempt, not even Henry Gallagher of Doylestown, forty-five years old, who left a wife and nine children when he was killed in Beaufort, South Carolina, on November 19, 1863, a member of Co. A, 104th Regiment—one of a total of five hundred and one casualties from the 104th over the course of their three-year tour of service. Others, such as Levi Stone of Tinicum, forty-two years old, bent over and ill with rheumatism, whose only child, Emmeline, died in 1862 just before Levi was called up, were not exempt. The list was endless. One by one they came forth to serve, and Bucks County gave up its sons, many of them forever.

By 1862, over twelve thousand Bucks men were enrolled for the draft. Draft Marshall Cadwallader and his clerks dutifully recorded the names—an incredible job in itself, made increasingly difficult by having to track down and sometimes forcibly bring in the men who were chosen. Eventually, of that total, a little over two thousand served in Pennsylvania regiments, and another two hundred joined companies formed in other states.

Many brothers and cousins went together—in most instances, the parents felt it was more important that the boys be together to keep an eye out for each other, if they could not stay home to work and take care of the farm and family.

Conscientious objectors, it was said, should not be compelled to serve, but should offer to pay an "equivalent" for "personal services." Those who decided on that route had to choose carefully the agents they dealt with so as not to be taken advantage of by the pervasive recruiting swindlers who, for a fee, promised to provide an able-bodied substitute but failed to deliver and were long gone with the money at sun-up. Even if a soldier found a substitute, he was still liable for a later draft.

By November 1862, Bucks County had filled its draft quota and local homeowners began advertising rooms for men from other areas who could claim to have moved to a Bucks County address and thus be excused. This was particularly attractive to men who lived along the borders of the county. And, since the schools and businesses were rapidly being depleted of workers, it was also a way to lure teachers and laborers.

Mahlon's name was among those called in the first draft pick of 1861, and, after several nights of soul-searching before he was to report to Camp Lacey outside of Doylestown, he decided to legally "dodge" the draft since he fell under a rather obscure exception as the only son and sole support of a widowed mother.

By the fall of 1862, due to a change in circumstances when a recently-widowed aunt came to live with Mahlon and his mother, he decided to join the fight. He resigned his teaching post and went to see Mahlon Yardley, Captain and Provost Marshall for Doylestown, who signed him up with the 18th Pennsylvania Calvary for a three-year stint. Within a year, Mahlon was given a field commission as lieutenant.

He managed to come through eighteen months of heavy fighting, including Gettysburg, until May 7, 1864, when he was wounded in the right leg during the Battle of the Wilderness near Spottsylvania Court House, Virginia. He was taken to a hospital in Washington, D.C. and there met Nancy. After a few months courtship, they were married in a quiet Christmas ceremony.

In April, when they were back in Washington for the funeral of the President, as Mahlon and Nancy and her parents were walking toward the Capitol Mall one day, he heard his name called.

"Mahlon!"

He looked up and saw with delight Henry Darlington, publisher of the *Bucks County Intelligencer* weekly newspaper, coming toward them.

"Mr. Darlington! What a wonderful surprise! How are you?" Since he had come to know Darlington in 1858, Mahlon admired him immensely and valued his mentoring; he always felt privileged when the slightly older man showed almost big-brotherly affection and interest.

Mahlon introduced Nancy and his in-laws and briefly filled Darlington in on the last year away from home—his war activities, wounding, hospitalization and marriage.

"Have you decided where you will be living?" Darlington asked.

"We're planning to come back to Doylestown. Mother is still in the house with my aunt and the housekeeper. She's not doing well and undoubtedly would wish to have us home with her. I suppose I should see Principal McReynolds about my teaching position."

"Oh, you haven't heard, then," Darlington said. "Tom McReynolds resigned last year, and Henry Hough was elected principal. But, before you do that, Mahlon, come and see me. If you're interested, I could use some help on the paper. You know, my partner, Enos Prizer, passed away last November."

"Yes, I heard. Allow me to offer my condolences. He was a fine man. You've been friends and partners for many years."

Darlington nodded sadly. "Almost our whole lives. We were friends in childhood. So much has happened in the last few years. The war, the President…" His voice trailed off as he looked away briefly. Then he smiled slightly. "But, we must go on. There are so many incredible events happening these days I don't have time to indulge in lamentations. There's a particularly interesting murder case I want your help on. A colored gentleman accused of poisoning his wife—a white woman."

Mahlon was immediately taken aback and intrigued with the story and pleasantly surprised at this new prospect for his future. He had not thought about the possibility of writing or reporting beyond the few letters he sent home from the war that Darlington and Prizer published in the *Intelligencer*.

"That sounds very interesting. With your permission, sir, I'll come and see you as soon as we get home in a couple of weeks."

"Be sure you do that. I'll be waiting for you."

Darlington turned to Nancy and the Evanses, tipped his top hat and bowed. "Pleasure to meet you all. Best wishes, Mrs. Riegel. This is a wonderful young man you have here. Mrs. Darlington and I will look forward to seeing you both in Doylestown."

Mahlon thought over Darlington's offer as he walked through town along with greeting folks and noticing the several changes over the past few years. As he came to the intersection of Main and State, he noticed the historic Brower's Hotel with its well in front, the site of the original crossroads of the town.

Then, as he turned east onto Court Street, there immediately was the 1812 Court House with its odd little white cupola atop the two-story building and directly across the street to his right was the *Intelligencer* building, one in a row of two-story wood frame buildings, and next to it the rival *Doylestown Democrat* office. Both buildings shared a large community water trough along the curb of the wooden sidewalk, in front of which several buggies and horses were tied.

The large *"Bucks County Intelligencer"* sign emblazoned across the front of the building that was put up by artist and sign maker J.R. Torrence in 1856 was looking none the worse for wear.

The *Intelligencer* had been operating continuously since July 7, 1804, when twenty-six-year-old printer Asher Miner came from Connecticut to Doylestown to found the *Pennsylvania Correspondent and Farmers Advertiser*. Miner printed the paper, at first a four-page weekly, in the back room of his log cabin and distributed it around the county through taverns and general stores. He must have been a man of great vision, since in Doylestown at the time there were less than a dozen dwellings, and the County seat was in Newtown about thirty miles to the southeast. Doylestown did not become the county seat until February 28, 1810, almost six years after Miner began publishing his paper.

For almost sixty years before Miner came to Doylestown, the place was known mainly as "Doyle's Tavern" and was nothing much more than a crossroads and "publick house," founded by William Doyle in 1745. One of the reasons given by Mr. Doyle for building his dining and drinking establishment was that there was none other for five miles around—"a rather long time for a gentleman to suffer between refreshments!"

The earliest mention of the word "Doylestown" was in 1777 in maps made by the British army. The town was not officially named Doylestown until 1818, when several citizens petitioned the legislature, saying "they reside on the extremity of the townships of Buckingham, Warwick, New Britain, and Plumstead, and that it would be to the interest and advantage of the said petitioners to have a new township, making the courthouse the centre thereof, or as nearly so as may be convenient."

In 1816, Lewis Diffenbach started the rival *Doylestown Democrat*, which was sold to Benjamin Mifflin of Philadelphia, then to Samuel Johnson Paxson in 1845; finally to Gen. John Davis, father of then Capt. (later Col.) W.W.H. Davis, in 1858. The rivalry and vitriol, especially during election campaigns "was at times decidedly spicy," as the *Intelligencer* noted in Paxson's obituary in 1864. In spite of—or as a result of—the heated competition, both papers generally thrived. Other papers came and went over the years, but none so successful as the *Intelligencer* and the *Democrat*.

Miner ran the *Intelligencer* successfully for twenty-one years and expanded the office into a two-story building with huge bins on the ground floor for the patrons to pay for subscriptions with corn, flour and oats. He also took other items in trade, as in later years an 1816 receipt for payment by Shipley Lester in calf skins was found, Lester presumably being a tanner.

In 1825, he was succeeded by publishers Edmund Morris and Samuel Kramer, then, in 1827, by Elisha Jackson and James Kelly, who were the first to name it *The Bucks County Intelligencer and General Advertiser*. After another few ownership changes, John S. Brown took over early in the 1840s and continued publishing the paper "devoted to political, literary, agricultural, scientific, morality and general intelligence." He eventually sold it to Enos Prizer and Henry Darlington in 1853.

The present *Intelligencer* offices were built by Brown in 1843 to replace the rudimentary log cabin that had housed the presses since 1804. The little lane to the left of the building was always known as Printer's Alley. Mahlon remembered fondly as a young boy, on the few occasions when his parents came to town, being treated to ice cream at Mrs. White's next to the *Intelligencer* offices.

As Mahlon entered the office he was immediately struck with the commingled scents of fresh paper, ink, wood and machine grease. The place was bustling with activity. He liked it immediately. *I could easily get used to this*, he thought. In the front room was a long wooden counter on which several lawyers and trades people seemed to be writing advertisements, other patrons appeared to be paying for subscriptions or placing orders.

"May I help you, sir?" the clerk asked politely. Mahlon noticed that he wore cuff protectors and a printer's apron over his starched white shirt, and a little cap that seemed to consist of only a visor with headband attaching it around his head, and he had a nervous habit of putting his pencil behind his ear and taking it down every time he spoke.

"My name is Mahlon Riegel. Mr. Darlington is expecting me, though not specifically today. Is he in?" Mahlon asked.

"Yes, sir. I'll ask if he can see you now." The clerk disappeared into the back room. Through the back of the front office, Mahlon could see the presses and workmen. Around the corner he noticed an enclosed wooden staircase leading to the upper levels. The clerk reappeared moments later.

"Come with me, please. Mr. Darlington will see you."

Mahlon was led up the stairs to the second floor to Darlington's office in the front of the building facing the street. Everywhere was wood—flooring, shutters on the windows, a very large wooden "partners' desk" in front of the windows, some cabinets and bookshelves, a couple of chairs. On overcast days like today, the dim light coming into the room necessitated the gas lamps being lighted. Doylestown had been fully modernized with gas works since October 1855.

Darlington stood up. "Mahlon! 'Pleasure to see you. Come in, come in," he said as he moved stacks of paper from the chair beside his desk.

"Here, sit down."

Mahlon sat in the chair and looked around the room. There was an unusually great amount of clutter. Stacks of old *Intelligencer* papers on the floor, piles of letters, bills, and notepapers on the desk.

"Quite a mess, I'm afraid," Henry offered. "Since Enos died, I've been trying to do most of the work myself. So many men gone off to the war, not many left behind to do the work."

Mahlon nodded. "Yes, I know. They are having a terrific time trying to find teachers all over the County. But, frankly, Mr. Darlington…"

Darlington smiled. "Please call me Henry."

"…Henry, yes, thank you. I've been quite intrigued with your offer. I'm not sure I want to go back to teaching. And there's my leg…" He bumped his right leg gently with his cane. "It is doubtful I would be able to stand at the blackboard all day, not to mention chase those little urchins around the playground."

The men smiled at the memory of a hundred little children running about the schoolyard, yelling joyfully. It had been such a long time since anything joyful was heard.

"Then you would consider my little proposal? I'm so glad." Henry reached over the desk, searched through the papers and brought out a clipping and some notes written with pencil on heavy, tan newspaper stock.

"Here's the first case I want you to look into. As I said, a very interesting murder—or, I should say, 'alleged' murder—considering the source."

"What do you mean?" Mahlon asked.

"H.P. Ross is the source, and others of his ilk." He stroked his chin thoughtfully and shook his head. "Mister District Attorney Henry P. Ross, brilliant lawyer—or so they say. Princeton educated…. Say, didn't you go to Princeton with him?"

"Well, yes…and no. I went to Princeton at the same time as H.P., but certainly not *with* him. I was never much for all the political meetings or social folderol, parties and balls. I lived in a boarding house in the town. I didn't even have my own horse like so many of the other boys there."

Henry nodded approvingly. "In my opinion, much smarter. Live simply, my boy, and you'll never be sorry! On the other hand, H.P.'s certainly made a name for himself since he's been home. He's become the most notorious Copperhead in the County."

"However did he get elected?"

"Believe me, I've been wondering about it myself. The only answer I can come up with is that all the good Union men were away in the war and unable to vote. The only voters left were draft dodgers and rebel sympathizers like Ross himself! Enos and I watched it happen in astonishment. H.P.'s open, public speeches against Lincoln and the Union. It's shocking, absolutely shocking. Did you know, they had a meeting back in July of '63 up at Ahlum's tavern in Haycock and all the men suspected of being Union were ejected. But there was one who snuck in and told us all about it. He said the speeches made could have been spoken with safety in Richmond and would doubtless have afforded Jeff Davis unbounded satisfaction."

"That's terrible! Was there nothing you could do about it?"

"We asked ourselves and our readers over and over how these people could get away with it and still be elected year after year. They've even been so audacious as to wear Copperhead badges conspicuously on their shirt bosoms since '62."

"I remember at the beginning of the war, in the year or two before I left, there were a few problems, but they seemed to die down."

"Yes, at first several sympathizers who dared to speak up in support of the secessionists were roughly treated. One was even tarred and feathered early in the war. Enos and I named several of them publicly in the paper," Henry said with a satisfied nod of his head.

Mahlon nodded in response, then hesitated for a second before asking, "Henry, please excuse me for changing the subject somewhat, but I've always wondered about this. I thought as a Quaker, you were a 'conscientious objector' and opposed to war."

Henry had fielded this type of question for years and was ready with the answer. "Yes, you're right. That's true. Quakers are pacifists and abhor any kind of violence and war, but Quakers are not traitors. We are loyal to the government of the land and obey, to the dictates of our conscience, a call to service. I, myself, joined up during the emergency—remember when the Rebels were at the borders of Pennsylvania in the summer of '63?"

"Yes, I do. I was with the 18th by that time."

"Many of our men have volunteered and have specifically requested ambulance and hospital service rather than taking up arms against another man, no matter how he has shown himself to be our enemy. As you know, our Quaker women have been sending supplies to the troops and hospitals all along."

Mahlon raised his eyebrows in sudden reminder and nodded at the memory of the baskets that arrived at the camps and the hospital almost daily, filled with quilts, shirts, socks, pillows, blankets, combs, underclothes, handkerchiefs, sheets, moccasins, canned and dried fruits, jellies, and more. Mahlon also knew that the Quaker women especially were most recently busy making winter clothing for the destitute slaves who were seeking refuge with the ever-advancing Union troops.

"You know that most of us became Hicksites back in the eighteen-thirties," Henry continued explaining," and did away with a lot of the old bonds of structure and rigidity. But perhaps most importantly, I personally feel a Quaker should never judge or speak against anyone who, in good conscience, has chosen to take up arms in defense of their religious convictions, their country or family or land. Now, mind you, 'defense' is the key word in my mind."

Henry shrugged. "Now that may get me in trouble with my fellow 'brethren' but I feel it's important that we stand up for what we believe in."

Mahlon nodded his understanding. "Thank you for clearing that up. You know, getting back to the Copperheads, you just reminded me about Isaac Thomas in Solebury Township back in the very beginning of the war. Do you remember, he was engaging in outright disloyal talk and discouraging his fellows from enlisting, and Ross refused to prosecute?"

"Do I ever remember! Enos and I railed about that case for weeks. Despite our constant badgering, Ross refused to do anything. Finally, U.S. Marshalls from the City came and took Thomas to Mayamensing Prison. But, nothing came of it. They couldn't do much without Bucks County witnesses and support. Thomas was eventually released on a writ of habeas corpus in the fall. And, then, you know, he ran for Clerk of the Orphans' Court in '63 on the Democratic ticket and won!"

"Amazing! Again, all the loyal voters off in the war?"

"Undoubtedly. So, this is what we're living with. In the last few years, H.P. and his fellow prosecutors, like J.M. Vanartsdalen, have become bolder in their public statements in support of Jefferson Davis and the South...."

Mahlon interrupted at the mention of 'Vanartsdalen'. "Is he of the same family Vanartsdalen from Bensalem and Southampton?"

"I don't know. I think they're all related. Why?"

"Interesting. A couple of years ago I ran across a document when I was doing some research at the Court House. A list of slave owners in Bucks County in 1790. The Vanartsdalens were on it. The name stuck with me for some reason."

"Hmm. Any other names pop out at you?"

"Well, I did notice there were no Germans. And no Quakers." He smiled at Henry.

"I should hope not!" Henry laughed.

"Yes, I was particularly relieved there were no German names! And, let's see if I can remember...oh, none in Solebury Township. I remember thinking at the time that's where a great many of the county's

Quakers live. There were several in Bensalem, which I found most curious since I understand the name 'Bensalem' is Hebrew for 'son of peace'—Ben sholem."

"That so? Most interesting. We'll have to do a story on that some day." Henry made a mental note and returned to his listing of District Attorney Ross's offenses. "You know, they even use the *Democrat* newspaper for their vitriol, and I've heard, but cannot prove that they let slip vital information about the movements of our troops to the *Democrat*."

"No!" Mahlon was genuinely shocked that such traitorous activities could go on in Bucks County of all places.

"All too true, I'm sorry to say. I've given Col. Davis no end of grief on the matter, despite the fact that he was off with the 104th. No excuse. He should pay attention to what's going on with his paper. Although I will concede that after he came home for a few weeks in July eighteen sixty-four…you know he was wounded in the hand at Hilton Head?"

"No, I didn't. Is he all right?"

"Oh, yes, back with his troops right away. I'll give him credit, and a lot of it, for that. When he was home, he must have made a few changes, including installing Mendenhall as publisher. That's also about the time the huge flag went up over Main Street. Just before that, I'd pretty much had it up to my ears, and pointed out that they *hang* men in a minute in the South for expressing sentiments not one-tenth so traitorous as what we have had to put up with from these damnable Copperheads for years!"

Henry's face became red with anger. "It's near enough to give a man apoplexy!"

"Yes, I heard that they—not Ross in particular, but other Copperheads here in Bucks County—went so far as to threaten President Lincoln's life and person."

"Indeed, they did. Last fall before the elections, I heard them say myself that means would be found to put Lincoln 'out of the way' if he were elected again, that he would not finish out a second term. I guess they've come true with their foul warnings."

Mahlon asked, "Isn't Ross the least bit unnerved by this turn of events? I mean that he could be held accountable in some way, for example, by stirring up sedition?"

"H.P. embarrassed? I doubt it. Now he's talking nonsense that slavery is justified by the Bible and even called for in the Constitution, that Lincoln was the traitor by emancipating the slaves and President Johnson will restore the institution, and the measures adopted by Congress will be counteracted. Ross even tried to run for Congress against Thayer twice, but lost, thank God. Can you just imagine that kind of voting in Congress," he said shaking his head. "But, still, he lost by only three hundred votes out of thirteen thousand."

Henry suddenly remembered. "Did you see that open letter Joseph Fell sent to H.P. through the *Intelligencer*? You may not have. It was last fall, and you were in hospital in Washington."

"What was it about?"

"It was fantastic. Apparently H.P. had been giving his typical speeches about Negro equality—or, I should say, the lack of and justification for not granting it—and he was railing about Fell having invited a black man to address the Ladies' Aid Society in Buckingham. Fell wrote that this same freed slave was invited to address Major General George McClellan himself—the Democratic candidate for President—H.P.'s own party!"

Mahlon was suitably amused at the irony.

"But the best part is that old Judge Ross himself—H.P.'s father— was down to Buckingham Township about three or four years ago looking for a maid and specifically, mind you, asking for—let's see, how did he put it? Looking for one 'with a skin not colored like my own'."

"In other words, an African woman." Mahlon smiled. "How ironic."

"Exactly. Fell wrote that old Judge Ross preferred a girl with an 'ebony hue' over a 'buxom lass from the Emerald Isle' to do his chores and cooking. And that's the audience, the Irish immigrants and others, H.P. and his cronies are now trying to stir up with their frightful stories about the tidal wave of newly-freed slaves streaming north to take all of their hard-fought and dearly-won jobs and homes away."

Mahlon shook his head. "If it weren't so tragic, it would be funny."

"Oh!" Henry suddenly said, "there was something very funny. I'll never forget it. I was at the post office one day and some of the people were discussing Mr. Ross and his friends, and a little five-year-old boy was standing with his father. I leaned over and asked, 'Do you know what a Copperhead is?' He answered, 'A man that takes the *Democrat* and likes the rebels and don't go to the war.' And then I asked him, 'What do you think of a person like that?' and he replied, 'The sure cure for that cur would be to cut off his tail close behind his ears!'"

The two men laughed. "A five-year-old boy!" Henry shook his head and repeated.

Mahlon asked, "So, tell me, now that the rebel cause is lost, I can't believe H.P. isn't at least a little discomfited?"

"Hardly! The pompous little jackass...." Henry stopped himself and rubbed his hands together quickly in a nervous motion as if to wipe away the source of his disturbance. "Oh, what's the use. I just get myself worked up into a lather. And then I feel guilty like when I heard last fall he had some sort of mishap and has been off work. And apparently his father, old Judge Ross, is not doing well."

"I'm sorry to hear that."

"On the other hand, we can't help but wonder if arresting this Negro man Wellings wasn't some sort of retaliation. The case looks pretty slim to me. Apparently he's got some witnesses who say, although the woman was sick for some months, she died suddenly after Wellings ordered some poison, ostensibly to take care of dogs running around the neighborhood. Fear of rabies, you know."

Mahlon cocked his head at that news. "Well, that's certainly true enough. I know that's been a terrible problem for years, especially in the lower county and rural areas."

"Yes, just so," Henry agreed. "But, they also had witnesses at the inquest who claimed that Wellings was complaining that his missus had not been a proper wife for many years, that he was tired of her being sick and would be sure to remarry shortly. In all fairness to my not-so-worthy nemesis, H.P. had to convince the grand jury, and apparently there was enough evidence for them to issue a bill of indictment. And we'll see soon enough. They cut the woman's stomach out back in February and sent it to Professor Rogers at the University in Philadelphia."

Mahlon smiled. "Good old Professor Rogers. Rather a mainstay here in Bucks County of late testing stomachs for poison."

"Yes," Henry said, "and not a few of them colored folks. H.P. almost seems to me to be on a 'witch hunt'."

"Then there's the matter of the property," he continued. "Wellings and his wife owned a little piece of land at Canada Hill which apparently

Wellings stands to inherit on her death—at least that's one of the motives they've attached to him."

"Who is defending the man?"

"Fell, Johnson, and some of the others in Solebury have hired George Lear to defend him, but don't count on Lear for any information. When I asked him about the case, he just shrugged and said he was eager to have the matter investigated and was confident—you know, all the usual, nothing of substance."

"I read in the *Intelligencer* that Mr. Lear has been a prominent speaker in support of the Union. Is that one of the reasons he was chosen, do you suppose?" asked Mahlon.

"Could be they asked a certain newspaper publisher in Doylestown who he thought a good defense attorney would be," Henry said with a wink, then "No, that's not why. Turns out Joseph Fell's son Bill is clerking with Lear. But, if I were you, I would start with your 'old college pal' Ross…"

Mahlon grimaced and laughed.

"…then perhaps Mrs. Wellings' family. She was a Stone, daughter of Jacob and Mary Stone."

"Don't think I'm acquainted with them."

"No, you're too young to remember them. Most of them left the area before you came to town. I understand old Jacob died in the late '40s. They came originally from Tinicum and were living in New Britain. Big German family, originally 'Stein'. She had some fifteen or sixteen brothers and sisters, a couple of them still left around. Amos Stone, who lives here in Doylestown—he's got a store over on West State where it intersects with Court—he's one of her brothers."

Mahlon jotted notes as Henry spoke.

"Then, of course, you'll want to talk to the witnesses—you can get the names from the record of the coroner's examination—and especially Dr. Cernea."

Mahlon asked, "Is that the same Arthur D. Cernea who is on the Doylestown Bank board?"

"Yes, the same."

"Didn't I hear he bought the Pickering farm in Buckingham a couple of years ago?"

"Yes, he did," said Henry. "A pretty sum, too, over four thousand, as I recall."

Mahlon's eyes widened as he whistled. "Very nice." He couldn't help but briefly calculate the value of his own land in comparison.

"But he's not living there," said Henry. "I think he leased it out and, come to think of it, I recall he sold it last fall and, instead of moving as he was planning, he's attached an office and surgery on his old house in Centreville."

Mahlon dutifully noted the location.

"Frankly, Mahlon, I'm a little envious that you will be doing this story. I think it's a fascinating case. But, I'm off almost immediately to Washington and Virginia for a 'grand review' of the victorious Grand Army of the Republic. My head pressman here will receive whatever you wish to send in, and he is proficient at editing."

Henry turned serious for a moment. "My foremost and firm rule for anyone who wishes to write for the *Intelligencer*: Be sure, whatever you do, check your sources. Don't write anything you can't prove later."

"Yes, sir. I'll certainly remember that. As a teacher, I know that accuracy is utmost."

Henry smiled and nodded remembering some of the teachers who had tried to thump accuracy into his young head, literally.

"We haven't talked about a very important matter," said Henry, now looking downright dour, "and it all hinges on this. I'm afraid I can't afford to pay you much."

Mahlon was visibly relieved that money was all that was bothering Henry.

"No need to worry, sir. I don't expect much, at least not at first. I have a good, steady tenant on the farm, and perhaps I can take in some students for private tutoring. What do you expect of me?"

"Well, this story to begin, a couple of articles and then, of course, the trial, which we expect in September. Perhaps gradually you can add on some other pieces. In fact, there's a Bucks County Teachers' Institute coming up you can attend for me. Yes, you'd definitely be the one for that." Henry smiled at his recognition of the perfect fit.

"I can offer you half-penny a word to start," he continued. "If you average twenty articles a month of about two hundred fifty words each, that will almost equal your salary as a teacher."

"That is most acceptable! Really. And, if you like my writing, I am confident you will give me more responsibility."

"Yes," Henry agreed. "And I already know I like your writing. The letters you sent home from the war were very impressive, very descriptive. I wish I could pay you for them, for your service...."

"Not necessary, really. It was my pleasure." Mahlon's face turned sad and thoughtful. "Writing allowed me to relieve the stress and tension during the quiet moments."

Henry clearly wanted to continue this discussion and hear about Mahlon's war experiences, but he was distracted by one of the pressmen who suddenly appeared at the door with a proof for him to examine. Henry introduced the man to Mahlon, and briefly explained what he would be doing, then turned his attention to the proof.

As Henry was thus occupied for several moments, Mahlon gazed around the room. He noticed on the desk amid the clutter a tintype photograph of Henry's wife, Susan, a typically plain, 'no-nonsense' Quaker lady with a pleasant face, wearing a dark, heavy dress with high collar, hair parted in the middle and pulled back into a bun. She seemed to Mahlon to possess a calm self-possession, an emotional repose not typical for one so young, yet found in most of the Quaker women he knew of every age.

Henry, who was born in 1832 in Chester County, Pennsylvania, son of Edward Darlington and Hannah Sharpless, had married his cousin, daughter of Abraham Darlington of Thornbury in Chester County, in a Quaker ceremony in September 1857. Shortly after, a somewhat indignant article appeared in the *Intelligencer* lambasting the practice of the "calathumpian serenade."

> A Great Nuisance.—The practice of treating a newly-married couple to a "calathumpian" serenade, as tolerated, encouraged and sustained in many sections of our county, by persons who ought to know better and set a better example to the rising generation, is becoming a nuisance almost beyond endurance. It is a crying evil. A reform is needed. Who will commence the good work? Clergymen, Justices of the Peace and all others are largely interested in this matter. In fact, if this nuisance is allowed to go on, it will

> seriously interfere with the institution of marriage itself.
> —Timid persons who do not relish a boisterous parade on
> such a momentous occasion, will be afraid to approach the
> hymenial alter, preferring to waste their days in single bless-
> edness. Others, in order to escape the vociferous clamor of
> the "calathumpians," are obliged to resort to a clandestine
> marriage. A Justice of the Peace, sending us a marriage
> notice a few days since, accompanied it by a remark that its
> publication had been suppressed some weeks in order to
> cheat the calathumpians.

Mahlon smiled at the memory. Though not signed by Henry, Mahlon always suspected the article was a result of the practice having been inflicted on him and Mrs. Darlington, probably on their wedding night.

"How is Mrs. Darlington?" Mahlon inquired when Henry finished his perusal and turned his attention once more. "Well, I trust?"

"Yes, thank you. She's busy with the children, unfortunately not able to travel with me. But, then, the South is not an appropriate place for a lady. There's still much disease and deprivation, even among the victorious Union armies."

Mahlon nodded in agreement.

Henry continued. "I do hope you will have Mrs. Riegel call on her while I am gone. I'll have Mrs. Darlington send a note around."

"That is so kind of you. It would be wonderful for Nancy to meet some of the ladies of Doylestown. She's been rather cooped up in the house with mother and me. I'm going to take her over to meet Reverend Andrews soon." Silas M. Andrews was long-time pastor of the Presbyterian Church in town, as well as secretary of the Bible Society for over twenty years and Director of the Doylestown Library, among other civic organizations.

The men stood and walked to the door. Henry smiled as he put his hand on Mahlon's shoulder and took his right hand in a warm handshake.

"So it's settled, then. How delightful. Come, let me introduce you to my head pressman before you go."

Leaving the *Intelligencer*, Mahlon walked across the street to the one-and-a-half story building that housed the office of District Attorney Henry P. Ross in a row of buildings in front of the Court House on East Court Street called "Lawyers' Row." The small, compact building was a curious mixture of Federal-style and New England saltbox.

From the sign on the front door, Mahlon learned that Ross had recently taken into partnership his younger brother, George. They were the sons of Thomas and Elizabeth Pawling Ross; the elder Mr. Ross was himself a long-time judge in Bucks County and the son of a judge. Both of the Ross brothers attended Princeton, Henry graduating in 1857 and George in 1861.

As he walked into the office, Mahlon noticed an open room on one side that ran the full length of the building, with several tall, slanted wooden desks at which sat on high stools young men who appeared to be painstakingly writing on long sheets of good quality paper, every few seconds dipping their pens anew into the inkwells.

For several seconds, Mahlon watched the men with their heads bowed intently over their work before anyone noticed or cared about him standing there, so deeply involved were they. He knew these were the clerks who wrote the deeds and wills and court papers. And several copies of each paper had to be made. If he ever needed a reason not to enter the practice of law, this certainly was enough to provide him ample. He frowned unconsciously as he thought about being closed up all the daylong hours, six days a week, with only Christmas off, and bending over a desk writing all the time with nothing but dim light coming through the windows or gaslight on overcast days.

Finally, one of the young men looked up. "Good morning. May I help you?"

"Yes. I wonder if Mr. Henry Ross is available?"

"No, sir, I'm sorry, he's not here today," came the reply. "Would you care to see someone else or would you prefer to leave a card and try back another day?"

"Yes, yes, I'll do that." Mahlon reached into his jacket pocket, brought out his wallet and gave the young man a calling card.

"Lieutenant Mahlon Riegel," the clerk read aloud. "Thank you, I'll give this to Mr...."

At the sound of the name, one of the other clerks suddenly raised his head, stood up and called out, "Why, Lon, old man!"

Mahlon looked up at the direction of the voice and recognized a younger schoolmate from Princeton, a particularly odious little fellow whom he had never much cared for who was a freshman when Mahlon was a senior. Mahlon was also embarrassed that he could not immediately recall the man's name. His struggle to remember was compounded by the fact that he detested being called "Lon" or "Lonnie" or any diminutive other than his full name.

He tried to recover. "Well, hello there," he said amiably enough. "I didn't know you were clerking here."

By this time, the two men were face to face.

"Yup. Been here 'bout two years. Knocked about for a couple of years and decided to go for the bar. Managed to escape the draft. See you weren't so lucky. Lieutenant, no less. Impressive."

Mahlon, trying desperately to remember the man's name, nevertheless was struck by the fact that in his rambling the fellow began every sentence with a verb. *That's odd for a college-educated man*, he thought.

"So, what brings you to see H.P.?" the clerk inquired.

Mahlon filled him in briefly on his immediate concern.

"You're going to work as a reporter?" the man asked incredulously. "And for the *Intelligencer* no less? Honestly, Lon, those damn Quaker nigger-lovers are going to be the ruin of this country yet."

There he goes, true to form, thought Mahlon. *Now, how the heck can I tell him what I'm here for?*

He tried to throw the man off from continuing that diatribe. "Well, with the leg and all, I've got to find another occupation." He tapped his leg slightly with his cane. "I can't stand at a blackboard and teach all day. I don't even think I could clerk for the bar. It seems you have to sit a great deal of the day on those hard stools."

"Yes, true enough. So, what are you writing about?"

Mahlon decided to jump in feet first. "The Wellings case. I understand H.P.'s prosecuting it."

"Oh, no," the fellow screwed up his face. "See, already Darlington's got you wasting your time on nigger wife-killers! Guilty he is and hung he'll be soon enough."

"Are you familiar with the case, then?"

"You bet I am, old man," he said and moved closer to Mahlon in a conspiratorial manner with his arm on Mahlon's shoulder. He was so close Mahlon could smell the chewing tobacco on his breath. He tried to mask his repulsion and suddenly got the idea of taking out his handkerchief and pretending to sneeze, thus breaking the man's hold on his shoulder.

"Don't you know," the fellow continued, "that this is what them niggers do when they want to get rid of a spouse? This has been going on for years. Why, there's been three or four cases in the last few years, far as I've heard."

Mahlon didn't dare say what he thought: *And there's never been a conviction, either.*

Which was true. The Bucks County District Attorney's Office had never won a conviction in a murder-by-poison case.

"You mean the Sanders-Rico case," said Mahlon.

"For one, and more besides!"

The most famous Negro poisoning case in recent memory was that of Joseph Sanders, of Buckingham Township, who died in 1858. Sanders and his wife, Susan, were living in the tenant house of Robert P. Ash. Sanders had been suffering a lingering sickness for some time, and finally died on the 24th of February, a Tuesday evening.

At the inquest, called by Coroner Shepherd, Dr. Cernea, assisted by Dr. Samuel Scott, testified on his post-mortem of the body. The stomach and contents of the deceased were sent to Dr. Rogers in Philadelphia.

While the coroner's jury adjourned to await the result, it was determined prudent to place Mrs. Sanders in jail, along with a Negro man by the name of Alexander Rico, who was said to have been frequently intimate with Mrs. Sanders over the past several months. The *Intelligencer* described the accused as "degraded wretches, leading an abandoned life for years."

Within weeks Dr. Rogers reported finding a large quantity of poison—enough to kill two or three men. The results were given to the coroner's jury, and an indictment was returned against Mrs. Sanders and Rico.

Shortly after, the paper reported that while Mrs. Sanders had the reputation of being somewhat of a "loose character," Rico, on the other hand, had always borne a good character and was known as "an honest and well-behaved man in his neighborhood."

Mahlon remembered there was a great amount of talk generated in town about the propriety of publishing information about the case, such as the character of the accused and the amount of poison found in the body, before the trial, but the *Intelligencer* stood by its principle to print all of the facts, and leave it to "every judicious man [to] suspend his opinion in regard to the innocence or guilt of the prisoners until the facts are presented in Court."

Witnesses who testified before the coroner's inquest included Annie Trusty, a colored lady, who said she was in the house a few days before the death when Rico came from Dr. Cernea's with some medicine powders that he said were to be given to Sanders immediately. Trusty watched Susan put some of the powder in a baked apple, which Sanders ate, but immediately threw up.

Seipio Willett said he was well acquainted with the three-some; that Sanders did not like Rico much. Rico had been "too thick" with his wife. Willett saw Rico at George Maris's barn where Rico procured the medicine ordered by Dr. Cernea. Rico ordered Willett to leave the bottle alone, that it would cure Sanders' disease "or kill him in four-and-twenty hours."

The next witness, Silas Johnson, told about Sanders coming to him and complaining that he had found a couple of vials in his wife's possession that were "damn curious." Johnson was also present when Sanders and his wife, Susan, had a terrible argument about her hanging around Rico.

Perhaps the most damaging of all the testimony was that of Catharine Willett, the wife of Seipio. She testified that she heard Rico say he wanted Susan Sanders and "if he did not get her by fair means, he would get her by foul, for he intended to have her this spring at the risk of his life." At the time he said this, they were walking through the Paxson's limekilns area coming from a quarterly Quaker meeting. Rico pointed out that Susan was wearing a new shawl that he had given her.

Another witness to Rico's claim to "have her by fair means or foul" was Stephen Sands, who also heard Rico say that Susan Sanders was "the best-looking woman in Bucks County." He told about another incident in which Rico accosted him while on his way to an apple dumpling party at Hannah Sutton's in New Hope.

"Go back and tell Joe [Sanders] that I'm going to the party, so's he'll go too and leave Susan alone," Rico said. He told Sands he actually had no intention of going to the party, but intended to go back to the house after Sanders left.

Instead, Sands testified, he "took Joseph Sanders back home, so as he might see for himself that Rico was there." But Rico spied them coming back and hid in the cellar and waited until Sanders left again. Susan later told Sands that after he and Joe left for the party, Rico stayed with her until one or two in the morning.

Finally, Dr. Cernea testified about his role in the case. He remembered being at Maris's barn, talking with Mr. and Mrs. Maris, when Rico came up to him and said that Sanders was sick and asking for him. Cernea was not able to go to Sanders at that moment and asked what the symptoms and complaints were. Rico said Sanders was complaining of nausea and could not retain anything on his stomach.

"Being urgently engaged on my way to a distant case," Dr. Cernea testified, "I told him I would prepare some medicine for him to send to the patient."

Rico immediately objected to carrying the medicine, saying that if anything went wrong, everyone would accuse him of having brought poison.

Dr. Cernea laughed and told Rico the medicine he was preparing was harmless and not about to kill anyone. He testified: "Having frequently met with the prejudices of the blacks respecting their poisoning each other in several cases, and not having heard of anything respecting this case previously, or any report bearing upon it, I told him I would go security for the poisoning, and for him to take the medicine and give the directions which I gave with it to the wife or family."

Dr. Cernea went to visit the next day, examined Sanders and gave him some additional medicine. By the time he could get back two days later, the patient was dead. He said Mrs. Sanders exhibited considerable sorrow, "as is usual upon such occasions."

As to the post-mortem examination, Dr. Cernea did not believe that the body presented signs of poisoning. However, he and Scott found many adhesions in the liver, lungs, and intestines indicating an illness of long-standing, perhaps one or two years, and more recent violent inflammation of the stomach and bowels caused, in Dr. Scott's opinion, contrary to Dr. Cernea's, by arsenic. This was confirmed by the report from Dr. Rogers.

When the trial came up originally in April 1858, an immense crowd was collected in the Court House and packed into the courtroom, every passageway being crowded with people anxiously listening to the proceedings. The prisoners looked very well, apparently in buoyant spirits, and appearing not the least worried about the terrible, mounting evidence against them.

But the case was not to be heard at the April term, owing to a problem in the way jurors had been drawn, and was postponed to the September term.

The trials of the two defendants were separated, and the case against Rico finally came to trial at the December term 1858, again exciting much interest in the County and great crowds in the small courtroom. After all of the testimony and evidence, the jury came back within a relatively short period of time with a verdict.

As the jury filed into the box, Rico literally shook with fear, and a wild stare on his face betrayed his prior bravado. The crowd silenced, and stillness reigned throughout the courtroom, many of the spectators seeming to hold their breaths in eagerness and anxiety.

The judge asked the jury if they had come to a verdict.

"We have, Your Honor," the expected reply. "Not guilty," *not* the expected verdict. That Sanders had been poisoned was not denied, but there was no proof that Rico was the one who administered it.

While a smile immediately lit up the face of Rico, the crowd erupted into loud whisperings, almost ear-deafening noise so that the judge had to bang his gavel several times to bring the crowd into order.

Rico was discharged by the District Attorney, O.P. James, and the judge. As the Sheriff opened the gate, Rico advanced out of the prisoner's dock, slowly at first, on wobbly legs as if just learning how to walk again, but after having taken two or three steps, he immediately picked up his speed into a run and disappeared from the Court House, followed by a crowd of colored folks, leaving the people in the packed courtroom dissolved into surprised laughter.

As was generally anticipated after the Rico verdict, Susan Sanders was acquitted following a short trial in February 1859. She and Rico were married by June of that year and living in Trenton, and Susan was pregnant.

The attorney for the defense was Henry P. Ross.

The next case occurred in 1861. When Virgil Maxey, a colored man of Quakertown, died very suddenly, it was learned that he had been living very unhappily with his wife, Catherine, and it was suspected that poison was employed to get rid of him.

District Attorney Gilkyson and Coroner Mannington proceeded to Quakertown, had the body disinterred and called upon Drs. Carey, Meredith, Bradshaw, Linderman and Green to examine the stomach. A coroner's jury was impaneled and listened to the findings of the physicians.

The stomach and its contents were placed into a glass jar and sent to Dr. Rogers in Philadelphia for chemical analysis. Turned out to be no poison found, and Mrs. Maxey was released from suspicion in her husband's death.

Catherine's troubles were not over forever, however; she was later arrested and brought to trial in August 1863 for severely beating a little colored girl in her care. She was convicted of aggravated assault and battery and sentenced to fifteen months in the penitentiary.

"You know as well as I do that just because there weren't no conviction don't mean to say they didn't do it," the law clerk insisted.

Mahlon shrugged. "It just seems the esteemed District Attorney is, shall we say, concentrating a little too much on the ebony-hued people."

"Not true, old man! And not fair," came the protest in return. "Why there's a couple of Irish—a brother and sister—from Southampton who were arrested last month."

True enough. James Anderson and Dorothy Miller were detained in the Bucks County jail briefly, having been suspected of poisoning Julia Ann Willet. Anderson and Miller were living with Willet and had been ordered to leave the house. Shortly after, Willet died under mysterious circumstances. Again, no poison was found, and the suspects were quickly released.

"And in this case," the informant continued becoming agitated, "there's even more reason to suspect foul play. Why, H.P. has witnesses lined up left and right to testify about Wellings' poor relations with his wife. And the man ordered enough poison to kill off two persons just a week before she died!"

"You're sure of that," Mahlon asked cautiously.

"Absolutely! This case is not going to slip away. I have no doubt that poison will have found its way into Mrs. Wellings' stomach… *If you know what I mean*." He lowered his voice and leaned toward Mahlon.

Mahlon dared not bring out his notebook, instead made a mental note. *Poison to kill two persons*.

"So, when will H.P. be back?" he asked. "Will I be able to talk with him?"

"I don't know, old man. He's not feeling well. You know he was injured quite badly in an accident last fall?"

"Yes, Mr. Darlington told me something like that. I'm sorry to hear it. What happened?"

"He was getting off the train at the Old York Road Station and fell down from a high wall about twenty or twenty-five feet. No bones broken, but he was knocked unconscious for a short time and hasn't been feeling his old self since."

"Really. I'm very sorry," Mahlon repeated. "I do hope he will recover."

"Oh, I think he will." He cocked his eyebrows, looked around to see if anyone was listening and said, "Between you and me, old man, I think he was imbibing a bit too much, if you know what I mean." He snickered, then became serious and said in a grave tone. "But, another concern is their father, old Judge Ross. He's not expected to live through the summer."

"Oh, that is a shame. Really, no matter my political opinions, my concern for a fellow man…"

"Sure, sure, old man, I understand." The clerk put his hand on Mahlon's shoulder. "Sure you don't want to join us in reading law?"

"Oh, quite sure, quite sure," Mahlon said as he turned to leave the law office. "I think I'm going to like this newspaper business."

Chapter II

County Jail, "Fort Wilkinson," Doylestown
May 12, 1865

Langhorn Wellings awoke at precisely four-thirty in the morning, as he had done just about every day of his fifty-three years that he could remember, whether it was a workday or not. As he rolled over on his cot to sit up, the muscles and joints of his large body protested with dull aches, unused to the cold dampness of the stone walls and floor of the jail and already beginning to atrophy from the lack of exercise of even a modicum of everyday work.

It was still dark. Lang closed his eyes, rubbed his face awake and bowed his head, realizing again, for the ninety-fourth day since he had been arrested and taken to jail, that the very thing he had most feared (and expected eventually) all his life—the loss of his freedom—had happened, according to his jailers and accusers, by his own doing.

He shivered in the cold, musty morning and pulled his blankets closer around him. Pennsylvania had still been deep in winter on February 4 when Langhorn first arrived at the jail, called "Fort Wilkinson" in honor of Sheriff James M. Wilkinson. On February 11, there was a severe snowstorm and the Fort was extremely cold. He asked the jailer for another blanket or something to keep him warm.

"A second blanket you want, is it?" the guard sneered. "We got boys fightin' and dyin' for *you people* who need 'em more."

Langhorn looked at the man and thought, *I suppose I'm guilty of that, too,* but kept his mouth shut, instead turned his face toward the wall. It was the "you people" that offended him most, as if he, simply because of the color of his skin, was the sole summation and cause and effect of it all—slavery, the war—and the primal point for every member of the Negro race. But he said nothing. He had learned over the past six months that it was not prudent to speak even if one thought he was among friends.

"I'll see what I can do," the jailer muttered contemptuously and shuffled off. In the end, though, Lang had received another blanket.

After relieving himself in the "honey pot" and washing his face and hair in the cold, stagnant water in the wash basin, Lang propped the thin mattress of his cot against the wall, wrapped his blankets around him and sat back to wait for breakfast. If one could call the just-warm tin of coffee and cold biscuits he received each morning a breakfast. Once in a while he would get a piece of bacon or ham, and he hadn't yet figured out a pattern, so each time was a pleasant surprise.

As he had done every waking hour, every day, since February 4, Langhorn Wellings spent May 12, 1865 thinking about "freedom." He had managed to live his whole life until that day in February as a free black man. Ironically, he was incarcerated just five days after the Constitutional amendment outlawing slavery was passed by Congress and affirmed by President Lincoln.

His friends, especially Quakers Joseph Fell and Bill Johnson and his fellow Negroes and mulattoes Mahlon Gibbs and Andrew Hartless, had all rushed to the jail and tried to ease his anxiety.

"They can chain thy hands," Joseph had said, slipping back into the old "Quaker speak" of years gone by, "but they cannot chain thy spirit. Thou art a free man forever through our Lord, Jesus Christ. He it is Who hath taken thy heart, and no mortal can enslave it."

The words were comforting, but difficult to remember in the small, dark hours as he sat alone in his cell and waited for the days to begin—especially with so much happening on the outside of the prison walls.

In these first months of 1865, one by one the last bastions of Southern insurrection fell. As he sat in Fort Wilkinson, Lang could hear almost daily the ringing of Doylestown's 1812 Court House and church bells to celebrate the increasing Union victories.

On April 11, the bells rang to celebrate the fall of Richmond and Lee's surrender to General Grant. Then, just five days later, word came that President Lincoln had been shot, and the bells rang again in an entirely different, somber tone and again for Lincoln's funeral services and memorials on April 19.

There was nothing much for Lang to do but sit and think. He had never learned to read, even if there had been anything to read. He was separated from the other prisoners, not that he wanted much to do with most of them—forgers, burglars, horse thieves, and worse. Even the occasional overnight drunk protested sharply about being locked up with a "murderer." What they meant, but what most didn't voice, was "Negro." If he'd had his say, Lang didn't much like being locked up with *them*, either, knowing what he knew about the propensities of most of them for drinking to excess in public and beating their wives and children in private.

And he was just as glad no one else wanted to be locked up with him when he watched in amazement one evening as four young ruffians, who had been arrested for robbing a safe at Quakertown, surrounded old drunk Frances Haskins, stole all of his money, then calmly threw the empty *port monaie* back to him. He saw no evidence of "honor among thieves" that evening!

There had hardly been a day in his life that Lang hadn't worked, as far back as he could remember since he was just a little fellow helping his mother in the kitchens and laundry rooms of some of the big houses of Bucks County. Then, when his mother died, he'd had to fend for himself by doing odd jobs for farmers. Later he worked as an indentured servant for Joseph Carver, and finally for the past thirty years out on his own as husband and father trying to provide for his little family.

His only occupations since he had been incarcerated were eating and sleeping, varied occasionally by spells of scrubbing and whitewashing and working a little in the prison garden an hour or so each day that the weather was clement. Lang would not be going to work today or any day soon—or ever again if his accusers had their say about it. Even though his friends from Buckingham and Solebury had reassured and encouraged him, Lang had heard talk of "hanging" and knew there was more than a few who would rather not wait for the judge to pronounce it.

Lang was somewhat reassured that it had been a long time since the last person was hanged in Bucks County, about five years ago, and that was Old Man Armbruster, a crazy, white man who had stabbed his wife to death.

More recently, Thomas P. Dilworth, a white man who shot his wife in May 1862, he claimed by accident, was sentenced to only eighteen months in prison. The story told was that his wife, Urania, wanted to go church, and he didn't approve. He took the gun out, he said to frighten her, but it went off, striking her in the leg. She recovered and, at least in public, made protestations of his innocent intent.

Then there was poor, crazy Matilda Frost. The unmarried colored woman was charged with smothering her illegitimate son during the same month Dilworth shot his wife. She was a loony, Matilda was, some said brought mad from poverty and disease. Matilda found herself pregnant, and her fiancé, Edward Foster, died before they could get married. She was about to have this baby and had no place to live, so George Frost (no relation, apparently) and his wife, also named Matilda, took her in, but they were just about as destitute as Matilda. The only place for her and her other son, a seven-year-old boy, was a small, unheated loft reached by a ladder from the outside. There was no bed for them, just a pile of old clothing in the corner.

The child was born sometime during the night, unknown to George and his wife, and when it was produced at their request, it was dead, wrapped tightly in a quilted skirt. Matilda claimed the baby boy had been born dead, but the medical examiner said, no, it was born alive and smothered sometime in the hours after his birth.

Matilda was arrested and languished in prison for two terms of court before the case was finally brought to trial. The Commonwealth, through District Attorney Gilkeyson, failed to prove that the child had been born alive or that, if so, Matilda had suffocated it intentionally. Within minutes, a verdict of not guilty came from the jury for the defendant, Matilda, who was represented by none other than Henry P. Ross. Matilda and her older boy spent some time in the Almshouse, then dropped from sight.

On the other hand, Lang remembered all too vividly thirty-five years ago—he had been a servant working nearby for the Carvers at the time—when Aaron LaRue of Solebury had killed a Negro for allegedly insulting LaRue's mother. The grand jury ignored the bill of indictment and refused to do anything, thereby condoning the murder of the black man.

Langhorn was also acutely aware that the Negro population in prison, and the number of those executed for capital crimes, was considerably larger compared to the general population. The abolitionists said this was because there were no Negroes allowed on juries, and no black lawyers and judges, also that the Negro was not financially able to hire lawyers to defend them. Others, however, used the population figures of blacks in prison as what they considered "proof of the inferior character of the Negro."

Surely, Langhorn had many friends in Bucks County, but it was doubtful any of them would be sitting on the jury, and there was just no way of predicting how things could go for him—a black man accused of killing his wife, a white woman—before a white jury (his "peers"?), with white lawyers and judges.

As the light gradually permeated the darkness of the jail, through the bars of the cells Lang could make out more of the features of his fellow inmates. Some of them, he knew, were here for very serious offenses. There was Paul Hess, charged with committing violent assault and battery on his wife, Sarah. So bad was Hess' temper and the severity of his attacks, either drunk or sober, that it was suspected he was insane.

Another repulsive tenant was Asbury Boring, charged with rape upon his 14-year-old niece. Lang had heard the story from one of the other prisoners during yard time. The informant had been in the courtroom and eagerly imparted the details.

"Old man Boring, see," he said through the cigarette clenched in his mouth, "he's had this little girl Mary living in his house for a coupla years. Her father's dead, and the mother's working in the city. She's such a little thing for her age. She sure didn't want to testify at the trial, and the judge sez she didn't tell 'em enough to get a conviction, but they got 'im anyway, the bastard. Got him for somethin', I think they sez 'assault or *attempt* to rape,' somethin' like that."

"So, is he guilty?" Lang asked.

"Yeah, sort of. He got all of six months, though. Sure would like to get my hands on 'im. He won't last six months."

What must you think of me, accused as a wife killer? Lang thought, but dared not voice, even though this young man was particularly friendly. He was one of three—Strickland Knight, Joseph Knight, and Warren Ferris—charged with cheating one James Opdyke out of a falling top carriage. It all had to do with a horse trade that went bad. The details were so confusing that no one could make hide nor tail out of it, and the defendants were all eventually released. It was nothing but a lark for them, and Lang was somewhat envious of their flippancy at being jailed.

Another youthful offender and all-around *bon-vivant,* David Kramer, was so intoxicated the night he was brought in he could not even remember having done what he was accused of doing—taking a slouch hat of Alexander Kirkpatrick's, a pair of gloves belonging to Samuel Rufe, and an overcoat and a pair of gloves belonging to John Buck from Hartzell's Hotel on the night of a fancy dress ball. *Just a kid out with others celebrating the end of the war and having gotten through it with his life and limbs intact, not quite so lucky as some of his friends*, Langhorn mused.

Lang's celebration of the end of the war and slavery was certainly ruined, not to mention his ability to appropriately mourn his wife's death. All of that had been replaced by anger and fear.

One almost funny incident—if *anything* about being imprisoned could be humorous—was young Samuel Lear, who was brought into jail accused of robbing the store of Hugh Warford of Tinicum. One Thursday morning early in April, just before Samuel was to be brought up for trial, he came up as Lang was doing some perfunctory clean-up work in the yard.

"Hey, old man," he whispered. "Wanna make a break with me?"

Lang leaned on his rake and stared at the fellow in amazement. "What're you gonna do, you foolish boy?"

"I'm headin' over the wall this afternoon," he said. "I got too many things to do to sit around here!" He chuckled half to himself, crazy-like.

"What?!" Lang could hardly contain his surprise. He looked without thinking at the fifteen-foot walls that surrounded the yard. "How're you gonna do that, right out here in the open?"

"Shhh!" the boy admonished, "you'll call attention to me. I've got it all figured out. The guard goes to the outhouse every afternoon. Takes his time about it, too. I'll have me a good five minutes. You comin'?"

Lang shook his head. "No way, son. You're on your own." He resumed his raking.

Sure enough, the guard went to the "john," and Samuel went over the wall, quick as a rabbit. Crazy thing was, no one even noticed he was gone until it was time to go in for the night. Over the years, jail breaks like young Lear's were so common that it became a great joke in the

County. It was the "paper Fort," the newspapers would jibe when up to four and five men escaped at once.

Lang knew also there were two colored women incarcerated upstairs. He had seen them in the yard from time to time. Francena Rice was one, from Bristol. She had stolen a letter from Elizabeth Darrah, also Negro, and destroyed it. *Silly, jealous females*, Lang thought. *Prob'ly a 'cat fight' over some fella off in one of the colored companies in the war.*

On the other hand, he felt very badly for Jane Wilson who had been sentenced to two months in County jail for stealing a chicken from Samuel Allen of Morrisville. *No doubt just trying to feed herself and her kids 'best she could. I'll bet her husband's in the war. They got all kinds of relief societies for the families of white soldiers, but not much for our boys.*

As long as he lived, Langhorn would never get over the absurdity of this poor woman serving two months in prison for stealing a chicken, and a white man receiving a sentence of only six months for raping a child.

And, what are they likely to do to me, a black man, accused of killing a white woman? he worried every time he thought about it.

Lang had a lot of time to think and worry over these months. He thought about his children, Elizzie and Jonas, and their little half-acre and house at Canada Hill in Solebury Township. He knew twenty-two-year-old Elizzie would take care of things around the house and see to her little brother, Jonas. Mahlon Gibbs and Andy Hartless and some of the neighbors would check on them, as well. The neighbors. Neighbors took care of each other out in the country.

'Cept some of 'em. Some of 'em turn on you and accuse you of the most unspeakable things….

By the time Mahlon Riegel came around later in the day on May 12, 1865, to talk with the prisoner, Lang was fast asleep, having fallen thus more out of boredom than from any tiredness, although his muscles and joints had not ceased their persistent aching.

"He looks like he's sleeping the sleep of the innocent," Mahlon remarked jovially.

"Ha!" the jailer laughed, "more'n likely the sleep of the guiltless!"

The sharp bark of the jailer's laugh woke Lang.

"Good day, sir. My name is Mahlon Riegel and I would like to ask you a few questions on behalf of the *Intelligencer* newspaper."

Lang sat up and turned his head away from the intruder.

"Don't have nothin' to say to the newspaper."

"I see. All right. Ah, well…sorry to bother you. Perhaps I'll come back another time."

Lang didn't answer. After a few seconds, he heard Riegel's cane tapping on the stone floor and turned to watch the young man's back as he left and struck up another conversation with the jailer, who was sitting just outside the cell block. Lang couldn't hear what they were saying, and he felt more than heard they were talking about him.

What do they know? They don't know about me. They don't know nothin' 'bout my life and what I been through.

He began to relive in his mind, as he had done countless times since being jailed in February, his childhood and teenage years, meeting Mary, their marriage and life together, the children. He tried not to think about the bad times, but he couldn't help it. It's that old misery loves company thing: When you're down, sometimes sad things are all you can think about.

Langhorn H. Wellings had come into this world in December 1811 in the Bucks County Almshouse. The Almshouse, also called the Poor House, opened on May 4, 1809. Originally called Spruce Hill, the land was purchased by the County Commissioners from Gilbert Rodman on December 20, 1808.

His mother gave her name as Mrs. Wellings and would not tell the Almshouse keepers any more about herself or the father of the child. Mrs. Wellings' teeth were in fairly good condition and her chocolate-brown skin was unwrinkled, thereby making it impossible to guess her age. She could have been as young as twenty or as old as thirty or thirty-five, for all the Almshouse staff knew.

Since she was a dark-skinned Negro, the keepers figured it was possible she had been a slave on the Wellings plantations of Virginia and New Jersey and had run away, although, if that were the case, it was unlikely she would give the real name of her plantation.

Or, she could have been descended from Cudjo and Joe, the famous black men, manumitted slaves of Jeremiah Langhorne who bequeathed to them in the late 1600s a great deal of land, including all of the property on which the town of Doylestown now stood. Cudjo and Joe somehow lost the property, through shady dealings and political maneuverings, some have said, on the part of white settlers. The whole affair had been shrouded in mystery for almost two hundred years, but several blacks in the area traced their families back that far.

Since the Almshouse was particularly busy at the time, they did not press for details, but took her in and helped her through the birth of her baby. It was apparently not her first child, although she had no other children with her and did not mention anything about having another waiting somewhere. A few days later, they gave the woman some clean clothes, a warm coat, and new shoes, and sent her back into the world with her infant son.

In fact, what we don't know is often more fodder for the human imagination than pure, hard facts, and for several months after Mrs. Wellings left the Almshouse, the staff spent many hours in the evenings sitting around the fire entertaining themselves by making up stories about the origin—and fate—of Mrs. Wellings and her baby son.

The name Langhorn was rather well known in the area, stemming from Thomas Langhorne of Westmoreland, England, who had arrived in Bucks County in 1684. His son, Jeremiah Langhorne, became a chief justice of Pennsylvania and came to own much of the land in the County including the land on which Doylestown was built, and Langhorne Park, now the town of Langhorne (formerly Attleborough and, before that, Four Lanes End).

Justice Langhorn also owned a number of Negro slaves. When he died, his nephew Thomas Biles inherited Langhorne Park along with several of the Negroes, some of whom had houses built for them under the terms of the old man's will. The property was sold in 1794, and the mansion declined into ruin. The last of the slaves was Fiddler Bill, who lived in the ruins of the mansion for many years and was eventually taken to the Almshouse where he died.

Thomas Biles named one of his sons Langhorn in honor of the uncle, who had no children, and thus the name began to gain popularity down through the years.

It was even possible that Mrs. Wellings might recently have been a slave of a Bucks County farm, since at the turn of the nineteenth century, there were still a number of slaves in the state. By the Emancipation Act of 1780, there was a gradual manumission, meaning anyone born a slave before 1780 would be a slave forever, unless willingly freed by their masters. A male slave born after 1780 would be automatically freed on or before his twenty-eighth birthday and a female on her twenty-first birthday, thereby gradually abolishing slavery by 1808.

The English and Dutch settlers of Bucks County in the late 1600s and early 1700s had brought slaves purchased in the markets of New York and Philadelphia. For many, without slave labor, it would have been virtually impossible, physically or economically, to cut the vast forests and tame the wild land into productive farms. Among the original slaveholders was William Penn himself, and many of the other early Quaker (Religious Society of Friends) settlers had owned slaves.

Except the Germans—the original German settlers of Pennsylvania, the Krefelders, in 1683 settled the area now called Germantown, led by Francis Daniel Pastorius, and were among the first to protest slavery. The Krefelders, skilled experts in the arts of carpentry, weaving and tailoring, unlike their farming counterparts, had no need of slave labor and found it easy to eschew the practice on the moral grounds that it was barbarous and beneath the dignity of civilized people. Pastorius and his people felt slavery was incompatible with their Christian doctrines and protested against importing Negroes as slaves as early as 1688.

While it would take another hundred years for the majority of their fellow Pennsylvanians to come to the same understanding, it did set the tone for most German religious communities in and around Bucks, Berks, Philadelphia, Lancaster, Montgomery, and Northampton Counties and the counties farther west as the State expanded, including the Catholics, Lutherans, Mennonites and Dunkards. It is nearly impossible to find a Pennsylvania German (or Pennsylvania Dutch, as they came to be erroneously called) who ever engaged in slavery; on the other hand, they were consistent in speaking out against the practice.

In the late 1700s, Quaker John Woolman and others began taking up the banner of anti-slavery, speaking out publicly against it and ordering their parishioners to divest themselves of slaves or face being "put out of meeting"—excommunicated. Many of the Quaker families of New Jersey and Pennsylvania split, with one or more brothers taking their slaves and setting up plantations in South Carolina and other more hospitable Southern areas. The families who stayed in the North found themselves in many instances less than a hundred years later seeing their grandsons off to fight their own cousins in the Civil War.

Quakers also actively participated in the organization of abolition societies, in the raising up of schools for the education of Negro children, and in championing the rights of free blacks who were kidnapped and sold into slavery. Lawyers were hired for the hapless blacks who found themselves spirited away from farms and even off Northern city streets.

The first treatise against slavery was published in Philadelphia in 1729 by Ralph Sandiford; it would take another fifty years before the idea became majority sentiment in the State.

Up until 1780, Vermont was the only state to have abolished slavery in its constitution in 1777. Then, on March 1, 1780, the Pennsylvania legislature, called the Assembly, passed the Gradual Emancipation Act, the first such statute in the United States. In this incredible document, adopted well before the general acceptance of its radical ideas, with a vote of thirty-four to twenty-one, the Assembly began by acknowledging the recent throwing off by the young American Republic of the yoke of oppressive British rule. Since the Americans had gone to war to preserve their freedom and civil rights, they reasoned, the same rights and freedoms should be extended to those who were imprisoned in the abhorrent system of slavery. It was particularly "odious and disgraceful" for people claiming to idolize liberty.

The writers, finding their "hearts enlarged with kindness and benevolence towards men of all conditions," went on to say that "all are the work of an Almighty Hand," that God "had extended equally his care and protection to all," and the Pennsylvania Assembly considered it "a peculiar blessing...that we are enabled this day to add one more step to universal civilization, by removing as much as possible the sorrows of those who have lived in undeserved bondage, and from which...no effectual legal relief could be obtained."

In 1790 the Pennsylvania Society for the Abolition of Slavery, organized in 1775, undertook an ambitious plan to assist the Negroes to assimilate into society. The program became famous especially in the areas of education, trade schools, and instructions in morals and "general comportment in polite society." Regularly included in educational materials were appeals to those of African heritage to show moral, upright behavior by attending worship regularly, reading the Holy Scriptures, acquiring education in the fundamentals—reading, writing and arithmetic—and teaching their children useful trades.

Blacks were further encouraged to be honest, diligent, faithful, civil and respectful in their relations with society (whites), to conduct themselves with virtue, sobriety and hard work, to abstain from alcohol, marry legally, avoid lawsuits and expensive amusements, and to refrain from noisy or disorderly conduct on the Sabbath. By doing thus, the Negro was told, he could effectively counteract the negative stereotypes which had plagued "the ebony-hued people."

The Pennsylvania Society was by no means victorious in this audacious plan, yet by 1821 the directors could report that despite the Negro's general degraded condition—"excluded from most of the respectable and profitable employments of life, confined to the humblest and least gainful occupations, with strong prejudices to surmount, and labouring under every species of difficulty"—there was still a smaller proportion of poor blacks in Pennsylvania than whites.

Still, by 1835, when Langhorn and Mary were married, not one State except Pennsylvania recognized as legal an interracial marriage and there only because the law provided that whatever union was permissible to the church was acceptable to the Commonwealth. The pervading sentiment and law seemed to follow Virginia, which, when it outlawed interracial marriage in 1691, labeled their children as "that abominable mixture and spurious issue." In the ensuing thirty years, this law was duplicated by Massachusetts, North Carolina, South Carolina, and eventually Pennsylvania.

Leaving the Almshouse that cold December day, Mrs. Wellings, with her infant son swaddled underneath her coat, went straight to Buckingham where, she knew, there were Quaker families who would take her in, especially seeing that she had an infant and was so close from parturition.

And she was right. She found shelter and work among the Friends for several years. But, even with all of their kindness and Christian charity, simple, clean living and abundant food, they could hardly protect themselves and their children from the many prevalent diseases, let alone Mrs. Wellings who still was forced by poverty to live in the worst of conditions. She died in the winter of 1819, in a cold, unheated shack on a farm in Buckingham.

Langhorn never knew his father. "He's gone, son. Best not to think about it," his mother would say the couple of times he tried to ask. And she spurned any men who came a-courtin'. "Just want to be lef' alone," she insisted, distorting her face in disgust. "Don't need no man."

Then she would smile lovingly at her young son and say, "Got me a little man to take care of me by the name of Master Langhorn H. Wellings!"

He heard, as well, plenty of stories about the proud heritage of his name.

"Why, there's a big, fine mansion not twenty miles from here down County bears your name, son," his mother used to say. "A fine name for a fine boy."

"Master Wellings, be a kind sir and fetch me a cup of water to make these biscuits."

During the last year of her life, as she became obviously ill and weakened and her body was wracked with cough, Mrs. Wellings was not able to get work in the kitchens, even doing the washing and ironing. The housewives would hear her coughing and send her away.

"Thee needs to rest, Sister Wellings. Thee mustn't be working," they would say, thinking more about themselves and their children than about Mrs. Wellings and without thinking about how was she ever going to get better if she couldn't earn enough money to put bread in her stomach. They all feared contracting whatever disease was wracking her frail body, and none wanted to be saddled with the responsibility of taking care of a sick Negro woman and her young son.

"They jus' don't want me around coughin' on their food and childrens. Whatever am I to do, Master Wellings?"

"I'll take care of thee, Mama!" Langhorn said, mimicking the Quaker-talk of the children. "I'll go get a job."

In the final few months, she got so bad she lay on her cot practically unable to move. Little Langhorn, not quite seven, would do his best to clean his mother and bring her porridge and soup. He found odd jobs on the farms around Lahaska and even up to Centreville and begged bread, eggs, and milk from the kitchens as part of his pay.

Despite all of his efforts, ministrations and pleading with his childish concept of God, his mother did not live out the winter and was buried in an unmarked shallow grave in the woods near the Buckingham Friends Meeting House.

At the urging of the elders at the Meeting House, Langhorn went to live with an old Negro lady who took in some boys working in the neighborhood, but it was basically a flop house where he could hang one of his two shirts on a peg over the bed he shared with two other boys. This was not a family to him by any sense of the word, foster or otherwise.

He learned to keep his mouth shut and his nose clean and managed to board with the woman for several years, working on the nearby farms. But he had to turn over almost all of his wages. There was nothing left for himself, and this made him angry. It was made worse by the fact that some of the other young boys living with him at the home were engaging in activities that were not, shall we say, conducive to a chaste and honest life.

Not having received a good moral grounding, by the time he was eleven and just coming into puberty, Lang was beginning to mimic their behavior. He neither knew nor, in his ignorance, cared about the consequences of his actions. Nor, if you were to have asked him, would he have realized, or cared, that he was gradually becoming angry at the world and hardened to society at a very susceptible age for entering a life of crime and anti-social behavior.

He was angry with his mother for leaving him alone. He was angry with God for taking her. And he was gradually becoming aware of racial differences and their importance in his life. He was angry with the whites for treating him as an inferior—even with kindness in the case of the Quakers and other socially-conscious Christians. He was angry at his fellow blacks for taking advantage of him.

Langhorn was beginning to learn negative lessons about life at a critical age in his development that could have caused him to go either way—a pious, fruitful life or a life of crime and dissolute behavior. Unfortunately, all he saw was the latter behavior; there was no one to show him the benefits of the former way of life.

One day in late spring in 1823, he arrived home to discover that the Sheriff had raided the shack and taken away several of the boys. The old woman hollered at him through her toothless mouth. "You get on outa here, too, 'fore you get the Sheriff comin' back here! Don't need the lot o' you. More trouble'n you're worf'!"

Lang grabbed his few belongings and headed out as fast as he could. He had no way of knowing that going with the Sheriff would undoubtedly have been much better for him, since it turned out the other boys were not incarcerated, as they had feared, but were taken to the Quaker school in Philadelphia where they eventually learned useful trades.

Lang high-tailed it out into the woods. *I don't care*, he thought, hurting and angry and so very much alone. *I can fend for myself. I'll hunt and fish and live in the woods. Don't need nobody.*

Which wasn't far from the truth. Bucks County was filled with large, rugged wooded areas where, if one knew even the rudimentary rules of survival, he could hide out seemingly forever. The streams and rivers—from the mighty Delaware to the smaller creeks—Neshaminy, Cuttalossa, Tohickon, Paunacussing, Pidcocks, Phillips, and Tinicum, the hills and valleys—especially the breathtakingly beautiful Buckingham Valley—were filled with fish and wild game.

There were, in addition to shad in the Delaware in the spring and summer, trout, pike, herring, and sturgeon in the smaller rivers and brooks. There were ducks, deer, pheasant, wild turkey, pigeons, rabbits, and squirrels. There were hundreds of big frogs in the ponds, and Lang knew that the legs were very good eating.

There were turtles, as well, but they were hard to kill and harder still to crack the shells. Once, Lang found a large turtle with a number etched into its shell. He didn't know how to read, and knew little about numbers, but he could plainly tell the "1–7–8–6" marked forever on the turtle's back presumably by some boy who had wandered these woods in the previous century.

Lang quickly decided it was much easier fishing and trapping small game than hunting large animals. He lacked the appropriate equipment for that and, besides, he couldn't eat a deer all by himself. Even if he had meat morning, noon and night, he realized, the carcass would have quickly rotted unless he built an elaborate smokehouse. It was just too much trouble, and small game was so plentiful and easy to trap.

Lang knew, from forages into the forest with his mother when he was young, which wild flowers and roots were suitable for eating, and it was an easy matter to sneak onto the fringes of an orchard and collect all the fruit he could possibly eat, or at the farthest reaches of the fields—as far away from other humans as possible—to take some corn. *Besides,* he justified himself, *if I don't get 'em, the deer and raccoons will.* He was able to steal a few bits of clothing from wash lines, a piece here, a piece there, so it wouldn't be so noticeable.

By summer and early fall, wild berries of all kinds were everywhere for the picking, especially raspberries, strawberries, and blackberries. Rounding out his diet was a plentiful variety of seeds and nuts, and he even found a cow out in a field, with its calf close by, that let him squirt her milk directly into his mouth. He came back several days after that, but as the weather got colder, the cow stayed closer to the farmhouse, and Lang was afraid to venture close to people.

If anyone saw him and challenged him, he had learned what to say. He chose a name of someone he had done an odd job or two for over the years and would say, "I work for Mr. Reeder over t'Solebury. He sent me down here on an errand, and, 'scuse me, sir, I gotta get back home now." That worked the two or three times anyone saw him on the road and cared to ask who he was and what he was doing in this neighborhood.

By this time, Lang was already a large boy, bigger than most grown Caucasian men. His mother, if she was not able to see her boy into manhood, had at least prepared his body as best she could. Working in the kitchens, she was able to slip her son an extra biscuit or two almost every day, along with fresh vegetables and the first cut of meat.

Thus Lang was prepared physically, if not emotionally and spiritually, for life alone in the wilderness. He was able to survive and maintain good physical health throughout the summer and fall. Whenever he craved the company of human beings, he would steel himself by remembering the bad things he had seen people do all his young life. There was hardly a person in the world who had cared for him other than his mother, and she had died and left him.

It's doubtful he realized it at the time, but what Lang experienced that summer and fall alone in the wilderness was not only a crash course in survival, but in a sense a spiritual awakening to the beauty of nature, a joy of life—an epiphany of sorts.

Lang particularly liked an area on Buckingham Mountain close to Centreville known as Wolf Rocks, which stood like a sentinel overlooking the valley. He could sit up there and look right down the valley and see everything without being seen himself. He would watch the big, red stagecoach with its four horses and spare going down and coming up the

Durham Road every day, the farmers coming and going to markets, the fancy coaches and carriages of the rich landowners driving to the County seat in Doylestown for some important business, and the farriers and commission drivers in their huge wagons loaded with goods from the docks on the Delaware River in Philadelphia and Bristol.

But mostly he enjoyed watching nature, wandering through the woods admiring the trees and flowers, listening to the chirping of the birds and the chattering of the squirrels and chipmunks. Several times he spotted foxes and envied their beautiful red coats and long, fluffy tails, but was unable to catch one. And once he could swear he saw a wolf—at least it was big and gray and looked like a large dog.

Or, maybe it *was* a dog! Lang hated dogs from the time he was a child, when he had seen some cows and other dogs bitten by a rabid dog. It was a horrible sight. The animal was foaming at the mouth and snarling. It had to be shot, and every animal it bit was shot. It nearly frightened Lang out of his little life.

Lang thought many times that summer and fall that he could stay in the woods forever. He kept pushing thoughts of winter—cold, freezing rain, wind, snow, iced-over brooks and rivers—to the back of his mind.

Several times he felt he was not alone, that there was someone else, another human, around, and one morning in late fall this was proven true. Lang awoke and found that it had suddenly turned cold sometime during the night. But, very mysteriously, there was an old, well-worn blanket laying over him and a little pile of parched corn by his head. There was no one else nearby. He called out several times, "Hey, who's there?" but no answer came back.

Years later in the 1850s, when he was living in Solebury, some strange events were to occur that would cause him to remember this incident in the woods when he was a boy of almost twelve in the fall of 1823. It began when a very old-looking, decrepit man, with a beard a yard long was found on a cold October morning laying on top of one of the lime kilns of William H. "Bill" Johnson.

Bill thought the man dead, since the kilns had been burning at full blast all night and emitting noxious gasses very close to the old fellow's nose. His eyes were completely closed and the face had a livid pallor. Closer examination revealed the man was still breathing, though intermittently and lightly.

Even in his dilapidated, disheveled, more-than-half-dead condition, Bill recognized him as Albert "Bert" Large, someone he had known from childhood who would be out of the neighborhood for months and years on end, then suddenly reappear as mysteriously as he did this morning on the lime kiln. He always had been a good worker in the limestone quarries when he did work, but was also known to have a propensity for drinking whiskey.

Bill picked him up and brought him quickly in a wheelbarrow to a nearby house and laid him upon the kitchen rug. A phial of hartshorn was applied to his nostrils, which brought him around somewhat. Bert began coughing and sneezing, and the spirits of ammonia were administered several more times, with improved results each time.

"It was not long before the whole body gave increased signs of animation," Bill wrote in a reminiscence of the event twenty-five years later in the *Intelligencer*. "He sat up, and preparations were soon making for a cup of coffee and some other refreshment."

However, when Bill went to get the doctor, and the lady of the house stepped out of the room, Bert seized the opportunity to "beat a hasty retreat." He disappeared once again without telling anyone where he had been or what he had been doing over the years.

Several years later, in April 1858, William Kennard was up on Wolf Rocks looking for stray sheep one day, when he saw smoke issuing from the Rocks and heard a strange noise like the rattling of tinware, or as Kennard described it, "like the dragging of a kettle by a chain." He ran for Moses Allen, who was close by on the mountain and together they searched further and eventually discovered Bert's cave.

They were unable to convince Bert to come out, however, and feared venturing further, as Bert called out that he would "put a ball through you both" if they came nearer. They ran for help at Aaron Ely's limestone quarries and obtained other men from the neighborhood, who had been searching for the source of mysterious smoke emanating from the massive pile of rocks for some time. They were finally successful in extricating Bert from his mountain aerie. What they discovered was a complete apartment of rooms under the rocks, which made very comfortable and cozy living quarters, though apparently lacking in cleanliness or tidiness, as was its tenant.

By then, Bert looked, in Bill Johnson's words, "like the last remnant of humanity. He was dressed, not covered, in a ragged dirty suit, and the appearance of every part of his body that could be seen showed that no attention had lately been given to cleanliness." His beard hung almost down to his waist, and his gray hair fell in profusion. Bert claimed he had been living in his "rock mansion" for most of the past forty years, that he was driven to do so from grief and loneliness caused by the death of his mother. Bert was just a teenager himself in 1823.

Whenever Lang thought about old Bert Large, later dubbed the "Hermit of Wolf Rocks," he wondered if that would have been his fate if he had not met Joseph Fell. He honestly thought, if only he could find shelter, he could have lived in the woods forever, but it was becoming increasingly obvious to him that he must have human assistance if he was to get through the winter alive. He was big for his age, but he was still just a boy not quite twelve.

One morning, as he was bending over in a garden collecting a pumpkin and some squashes, he heard a voice behind him. "What art thou doing here?"

Startled, he looked up and saw a white boy a little older than himself, a Quaker with the characteristic black pants, suspenders, white shirt with no collar, black jacket and short hat with wide brim.

He stammered. "Uhm, ah…I work for Mr. Reeder over t'Solebury. Uhm, he sent me on an errand…"

"And how does that errand bring thee into our garden?" the boy asked.

Lang did not have an answer. He had not thought that far. He froze for an instant, then began to run for the garden gate.

The Quaker boy started after him and called out, "Pray thee, don't go! I didn't mean to upset thee. Thee can have whatever thee needs from our garden."

Lang stopped and, remembering the characteristic generosity and kindness of the Quakers, turned around to see if it was still true.

"You sure it's all right? 'Cause I'm powerful hungry."

"Better than a raw pumpkin and squash, come with me into the house, and we will give thee a proper meal. My name is Joseph Fell. And what art thou called?"

"Langhorn…Langhorn H. Wellings."

"What does the 'H' stand for?"

Langhorn cocked his head and thought for a second, "I don't know. Just 'aich'. Was it s'posed to stand for something? My mama never told me."

Joseph laughed. "Well, we'll just have to think something up." He took Lang's arm and began leading him toward the house. "How about 'Horatio'? Or 'Heathcliff' or…?" Both boys began laughing.

Langhorn would forever bless the day he found his way into the Fell garden. He later learned his new friend Joseph (never "Joe") was born on April 12, 1804, at Lurgan, in Upper Makefield Township, Bucks County, to Dr. David and Phoebe Fell. Dr. Fell was one of the earliest graduates of the University of Pennsylvania. His certificate to practice medicine was signed by Dr. Benjamin Rush, signer of the Declaration of Independence and founder of the school.

Since before anyone could remember, the homes of most all of the Fell family in Bucks County and beyond were well-known as sanctuaries for the oppressed and downtrodden, especially escaping slaves. Dr. and "Mother" Fell immediately took Lang into their home and allowed him to stay with them for two years working for his room and board. He lived with several other blacks in a small, comfortable house on the farm and spent as many hours as he could with Joseph who would practice his love of teaching on this eager and willing young pupil.

Unfortunately, Joseph was never able to teach Lang to read or do more than write his name. "I just can't get them letters and numbers," Lang protested. "I'm too old and I don't have a head for it." Joseph did, however, teach him somewhat about the Religious Society of Friends and the history of slavery and how the Quakers were fully engaged in battle against the abominable practice.

Joseph also tried to instill in his young charge a sense of the Christian virtues with which he himself had been raised by his parents and the Quaker community—especially the concept that each human being is born with the "inner light" that will enable them to understand the Word of God and lead a righteous and pious life.

Joseph's ancestors had been Quakers from the very beginning of the movement. Margaret, the wife of George Fox, the founder of the Society of Friends, was a Fell by her first marriage. She and her children became staunch defenders of the Reverend Fox, standing by his side through imprisonment and persecution, having his lands and property taken from him and even to his death.

Members of the Fell family were among the original settlers of Bucks County in the early 1700s and were with William Penn when he came in 1684 to claim the land grant given to him by the king of England in payment of a debt. They became solid supporters of Penn, who was perhaps the most famous member of the Society of Friends, in his Holy Experiment to build a community in this new world dedicated to religious freedom and tolerance.

The Religious Society of Friends was founded in England in 1652 when Fox began preaching against the practices of organized religion, especially the Church of England. Rejecting the concept of a clergy class which had power and authority over the common people, Fox taught that the inner light possessed by every human being enabled each individual to offer opinions, in other words "preach," on any subject that moved them to speak. Every member of the community, man and woman, was thereby eligible to become a spiritual leader, and ordination was not necessary.

Yet, many Seventh Day services were passed in complete stillness and silence whenever only the inner voice was heard by each individual in the congregation.

Even if they did not speak out in meeting, every member was capable of and expected to show forth the Divine virtues, such as kindness, peace, love, and charity, in their daily lives. The outward testimony which the Friends gave against war and violence, they felt, had no value unless the true peace it represented was manifested in their daily lives by the exercise of piety, charity, forbearance and Christian love.

There are two theories as to how the name "Quaker" came about: One that a person quakes or trembles when moved to speak and, two, because George Fox was known to have preached, "Tremble at the word of the Lord." The term was basically derogatory in its original use by their critics, but over the span of a hundred years, the Friends took on the name reverently, like a symbolic crown of thorns, and gave it dignity and respect.

The Quakers were devoted to plain living, were plain in their dress and entertainments, and in every aspect of life practiced democratic concepts and equality. Quakers were not forbidden from drinking alcohol, but were not allowed to manufacture it or drink to excess. A Quaker was required to marry someone from within the Society and according to its traditions. Perhaps most important, a Quaker was expected to be a committed pacifist in both public and private affairs and not allowed to bear arms, even to hunt.

Anyone breaking the stringent rules faced punishment ranging from being reprimanded by the entire community to the final judgment of being put "out of meeting."

The characteristic "thee," "thou" and "thy" of their speech stemmed possibly from two things: An English reminder of the different manner of addressing plural and singular, familiar and respectful, as in the German "du" and "sie" and the French "tu" and "vous," and as a symbol of the commonness of all, as one Quaker said it, "We are not respecters of persons." People were not addressed, and thus elevated somehow in station, by titles such as "Mr." or "Miss"; instead, everyone was called "Friend" or, in some cases, "Brother" or "Sister." These principles of speech gradually died out as Quakers assimilated into evolving American society.

As Philippe Suchard, founder of a famous chocolate factory in Switzerland and a visitor to Philadelphia in 1824, wrote of the Quakers: "There is a certain hardness about them, a stiff unrelenting fanaticism. No Christian sect has, at the same time, so much gentleness, humanity, unselfishness, devotion, and love of truth. They mete out the same affability to all mankind while standing aloof from its follies and passions. They apply the precepts of Christianity literally and strictly, to everyday life, thus appearing odd, uncouth and even ridiculous to those who have been brought up in other ways. They do not argue about forms and dogmas like other Christians; their faith shows in their daily conduct. As a result of childhood training, these habits become an essential part of their lives. Their upbringing, as a result, is certainly very different from most people's and is perhaps unduly strict in many ways; but this very strictness is the surest defense against a light-hearted acceptance of dishonesty and vice in later life. Dancing, music, hunting, gambling and the theatre are forbidden.

"…Here are none of the hypocrisy, vain piety and hidden pride to be found in comparable European sects, but firm conviction, borne out in daily conduct, and soundly based on education and habit. It seems to me that the simplicity and truthfulness, the modesty and honest dealing of the Quakers have had, and continue to have, a great influence on the think-ing and conduct of American society, as well as upon the laws and Consti-tution of the United States. I saw traces of Quaker thinking wherever I went. They deserve the high esteem in which they are everywhere held.

"Within the Society of Friends there is complete equality. Wealth and poverty make no difference. The headmen at their meetings receive no salary, and are accorded no special mark of respect. Nor do they force their opinions upon other people. Women have the same position as in other sects; they receive the same consideration and enjoy the same respect. Their charming modesty, simplicity and housewifely virtues no less than their cultivated minds make their company much sought after by the first families of other religious groups. When a Quaker fails to carry out his duty conscientiously he is privately warned by one of his nearest relations or by a close friend. Should this warning go unheeded it is renewed from several quarters. Should it seem impossible to bring him back to the path of duty he is excluded from the Society of Friends. This all takes place quietly, without fuss."

As one of the speakers at the opening ceremony of Swarthmore College in November 1869 summed it up, "The Society of Friends chiefly aims by its system of training to develop the innate genius of truth and goodness implanted by the Creator in every soul. As these are cultivated and grow, their effect is to choke out the weeds which would otherwise mar and deface the garden of the heart."

Joseph Fell also taught his young charge about the evils of slavery, how three million people, the vast majority of whom were Africans, had became the property of other human beings who felt privileged to do so simply because their skin was a lighter color—as if that denoted a higher station in life and an inherent superiority over every other creature. He told him that undoubtedly Lang's own ancestors had come to this coun-try after having been captured, sometimes by other tribes, sold to the slavers, literally packed into ships and transported to America.

More than half never completed the trip. Once they were in New York or Baltimore or Philadelphia or, after 1780 when the selling of human beings was banned in Pennsylvania, in one of the friendlier ports in the South, they were put up on the auction block in chains and sold to the highest bidder. Families, if they had managed to stay together after all that had preceded the sale, were most often torn apart, sometimes young children taken directly from their mothers' breasts.

"For generations thereafter," Joseph concluded, "from the moment they were born, these human beings, just like thee, Langhorn, became the chattel—property, like our cows and horses—of other humans and forced to work heavy labor and live under deplorable conditions their entire lives."

He explained to Lang that sometimes slaves managed to break free and run away, more and more were thus coming to Pennsylvania now that slavery was outlawed here and they could escape northward out of reach of their pursuers.

"We are beginning to see an increase in the number of these poor, wretched souls, so much so that we have had to organize ourselves into a system of transportation and way stations northward from Chester, York, Adams and Lancaster Counties. Some also from Philadelphia, but more from the outlying counties."

What Joseph was describing were the beginnings of the Underground Railroad. The name came about because of a slave catcher who, coming to the town of Columbia, in Lancaster County on the shores of the Susquehanna River, and finding all traces of his prey vanished, cried out bitterly, "Why, there must be an underground railway somewhere's in the neighborhood which spirits these slaves away!"

"That's exciting!" Lang cried out. "Can I help thee?"

"Oh, no, dear friend!" Joseph said. "'Tis much too dangerous for thee, Friend Lang. First of all, thou art much too young yet. Then, too, thee would be the first to be suspected. And, if thee were caught, assuredly thee would be carried back to the South and sold into slavery thyself!"

"How do they do it? I mean, how do you spirit these slaves away?"

Joseph started to tell Lang everything, then thought better of it. "I probably shouldn't tell thee too much, in case thou art questioned at some time, but most often farmers and merchants will hide the people, usually no more than two or three at a time, in their wagons. Some very ingenious methods have been devised, such as fake bottoms in the wagons. Then they travel short distances from one farm to another or to churches, and sometimes factories and businesses, in the night."

Joseph's eyes lit up with excitement as he described it. "Why, thee wouldn't believe it if thee saw it, but there are some houses right here in

Bucks County that have elaborate underground tunnels and whole rooms with false fronts in the basement!"

"Really!" Lang was suitably impressed. "Tell me more!"

Joseph described the efforts of, but did not name their names, some of their Bucks County neighbors—the Atkinsons, Browns, Tregos, Blackfans, Smiths, Simpsons, and Paxsons; John E. Kenderdine, Jonathan P. Magill, Jacob Heston, Bill Johnson, Richard Moore, and Edward Williams, in addition to his own large family, the Fells—to save as many slaves and send them as far north as possible, all the while understanding their homes and neighborhoods would be subject to constant surveillance and invasion by Southern agents and bounty hunters.

From the moment of his enlightenment by Joseph, Lang became more interested in the plight of his fellow Negroes. As his teenage world expanded beyond the confines of his immediate vision, he began to understand the suffering that his mother and, undoubtedly, his father's people had endured from the very inception of their lives.

Instead of being aloof and shy and withdrawn, as he had been his whole life, and particularly since his mother had died, Lang began to listen more acutely to the stories the people told as they passed through the Fell farm. They told him many instances of the degraded conditions of the life of a slave, the beatings, the humiliations and other inexpressible horrors some had experienced. He learned of their anguish at being separated from their families, traveling hundreds of miles on foot or hidden in wagons, and always the fear of being caught by the ever-present slave agents.

Over the years, Lang came to hear and understand the songs the slaves would sing, within hearing of oblivious slave masters and overseers, as they worked in the fields and houses of the South. The lyrics passed on from plantation to plantation included *Wade in the Water, Steal Away* and *Follow the Drinking Gourd*—all instructions for keeping in the direction of the stars which formed the Big Dipper, the "Drinking Gourd."

> Follow the Drinking Gourd
> Follow the Drinking Gourd
> Follow the Drinking Gourd
> The riverbank makes a very good road,
> The dead trees will show you the way.

Left foot, peg foot, traveling on.
The river ends between two hills.
There's another river on the other side
When the great big river meets the little river,
Follow the Drinking Gourd,
For the old man is a-waiting for to carry you to freedom,
If you follow the Drinking Gourd.

Another means of giving directions was by the use of "coded quilts" that told in picture form sewn with fabric when escapes were planned, how to survive in the wilderness and avoid detection, whom to trust on the route, and other valuable information that was easily understood especially by illiterate people.

Lang began to realize truly how lucky he was, even if he had been orphaned at an early age and had to fend for himself for the greater part of his life. If truth be told, he had previously avoided these miserable creatures in part because their mere presence had created in him some innate, unspoken fear and repulsion. Not only was he afraid of what they represented, he did not understand their speech, their manners of behavior or dress. It was as though they were from a foreign country, and the only thing he had in common with them was the color of his skin and the shape of his nose.

He now realized how several of these former slaves—perhaps even his own mother—had stopped their running in this neighborhood, had settled down with jobs and families around the county, and had begun to take on the mannerisms and speech of their hosts.

Eventually, however, Joseph told him sadly one day, it was time for Lang to move on. He was, of course, welcome to stay at the Fell farm and work, but Joseph wanted more out of life for his young friend.

"I am going away to college soon," Joseph said, "and it's time we made a plan for thy future, too, young Langhorn. Father and I have come up with an idea that we believe will suit thee well."

Lang sat on an overturned bucket in the barn, leaned the shovel with which he had been mucking the stalls against the wall and looked with "all eyes and ears" to his friend.

"First of all, Lang, we have concluded that thou art unusual in thy size and strength for a young man of only fourteen years. We are afraid for thy safety because thou would be very attractive to the slave catchers who are kidnapping Negroes right off the streets and farms and selling them into slavery."

Lang's eyes widened as he unconsciously looked around him, fearing perhaps there was a slave-catcher under the very bucket on which he was sitting.

Joseph smiled. "No, no, Lang. Thee musn't let me frighten thee! 'Tis not as bad as all that. But," he continued, "we must also be concerned for thy future, as I said. We have found someone who is willing to take thee for seven years as an indentured servant and teach thee the art of limeburning."

"Limeburning? What's that?" asked Lang.

Joseph explained that the process of limeburning was to take the quarried limestone and burn it into an ash, which was then used for fertilizer. Later it became useful as an additive to plaster, mortar, white-wash and paint and as a spread over the waste in outhouses, among other things. When added to the soil and compost piles, it allowed the soil to maintain alkalinity and assisted the microbes to do their work of turning dirt into rich soil. Joseph didn't say it, but Lang found out later, that lime was also spread over bodies in preparation for burial.

"Limestone is found all over the county," Joseph told him. "It takes a big, strong man such as thee to mine it, but the making of lime ash is very necessary. Thee would, no doubt, be in great demand and have a steady source of income for as long as thee cared to work."

Lang thought for a few seconds, and then asked, "Why would I have to be a—what did thee call it, 'indentured servant'? That sounds like slavery to me."

"In truth, it is for thy own protection *from* slavery that we even suggest it. As I said, thee would be very attractive, since thou art so big and strong. If there is a piece of paper stating that thou art an indentured servant, these vile slavers could not touch thee. Friend Carver—that is the man we have chosen for thee, Joseph Carver—would protect thee and claim thee immediately. In this way, hopefully, no harm shall come to thee because of the curse of thy having been born a Negro and always susceptible to the slavers."

Joseph explained that not only would the slavers openly kidnap blacks, sometimes they would try to lure their victims with false promises of lucrative work. And because of the Fugitive Slave Laws of 1793, it was extremely difficult and expensive to do anything to assist those who had been taken. Judges and other authorities considered every black to be a slave until proven otherwise. On the other hand, the slavers were paid handsomely for their evil work and very rarely questioned as to where they obtained their captives.

The most famous Bucks County fugitive slave capture was that of Benjamin "Big Ben" Jones in 1844. Big Ben, called thus because of his unusual height of six feet ten inches, had been a slave of William Anderson of Little York, Maryland. Fearing they were about to be "sold South," Ben and four of his fellow slaves made their escape in 1833 and succeeded in reaching Buckingham where Ben decided to stay, working for Jonathan Fell of Mechanicsville, Thomas Bye, William Stavely and others for eleven years. During that time, he earned a reputation of mildness of disposition, honesty and uprightness of character. He bought a lot and built a little house on it.

One day in the late spring of 1844, when Ben and a few other black men were out chopping wood near Forestville, William Anderson, his former master, suddenly appeared with four men to assist him in capturing Ben and bringing him back to Maryland. Ben's fellow workers fled, but Big Ben stood his ground and defended himself with his ax. At one point in the ensuing fight, he had all five on the ground. But, his attackers succeeded in cutting his suspenders so that his pants fell down about his legs and he was tripped up.

When people began to gather and protest this treatment of their neighbor and demand the authority of his ambushers, Anderson retorted, "This man is a runaway slave. We'll take him to a judge in Doylestown, where you can join us at ten o'clock tomorrow, and there and then we will show you our authority."

The neighbors finally agreed, and Big Ben was calmed with this promise of justice and lulled into peaceably getting into the carriage. His captors set off toward the county seat but instead went south through Bridge Valley by Laurel Hill to the Philadelphia turnpike. It was said later that Big Ben's anguished wails could be heard by people all along the road after he realized the carriage had passed the turnoff to Doylestown. Many asked, "How is it possible a human heart could fail to be moved by his plaintive cries?"

Big Ben was severely injured in the fight, so much so that when he was eventually taken back to the infamous Slater slave prison and market in Baltimore, his wounds made him unsalable. He languished there, suffering with his injuries, until shortly after June 6, 1844, when a meeting was held at Forestville, presided over by George Chapman, at which seven hundred dollars was raised for his release. Chapman and Jonathan K. Bonham rushed to Baltimore to bring Ben home.

After his return, however, his health and physical strength were so much diminished that he could no longer live and work as he used to. He stayed for a time with Charles Cope in Buckingham, then in Solebury. He married with Sarah Johnson of Norristown. But his physical and emotional health continued to deteriorate; he and Sarah moved to the Almshouse where Ben eventually died sometime after 1860.

Joseph Fell wrote to the *Intelligencer* about one such incident, which very well could have been the capture of Big Ben in 1844:

OUTRAGEOUS.

About 4 o'clock this afternoon, three men, one of whom was Nathaniel Hubbard, ex-high constable of Doylestown borough, made their appearance on my farm in the vicinity of the buildings very suddenly, having secured their horses quarter of a mile to the north, and followed a ravine to within a few rods of the house. I inquired of Hubbard if he were hunting negroes? What is that your business, said he. I told him it was my business to know what men were doing on my place, and stepping up towards him, ordered him off. He then put his hand into the breast pocket of his coat and drew a pistol part way out, stating at the same time, he'd be damn'd if he would go off till he was ready, and that he would come when he pleased. I then told him if he ever came here again it would be at his peril, that he was a notorious coward, and dare not even pull his pistol out, much less shoot; that he was steeped to the dregs in infamy, and had now openly hired himself to the 'hunters of men' to catch human beings and send them to the land of 'chains and scourges,' that he need never expect to be employed in any decent business hereafter, for decent men would not employ him.

I followed them to the place where their horses were hitched, all of them swearing they would have the negro they were in search of before sunset, and that somebody would be killed if there was any attempt made to aid or rescue him, as they were all prepared. Their preparation for the diabolical deed was manifest enough, for their frock coat pockets appeared distended with pistols, dirks, 'manacles and gyves.' I detained them in conversation some time, when Hubbard directed my attention to the sun, evidently anxious to be off. I told him I saw it, that God made it, and he also made him and the negro, 'out of one flesh and one blood.' He said that God did not make me—that if it had not been for my 'ingenuity' he would have got a black man from me before, which was all the evidence he gave of the truth of his assertion. I asked him if in his soul he was sorry Henry Miller made his escape. He said he 'didn't make a practice of crying for spilt milk.'

I told him he would have to die some time, and asked him if he ever prayed, and what would be his death-bed reflections for such conduct? One of the strangers then spoke in this most horrid and awfully blasphemous manner, 'What the hell did God make negroes black for if they are not for slaves?' I asked him if he believed a negro had a soul, which question he would not answer. * * *

I then told him it was a most pitiful, mean business he was engaged in, and asked him what he would take to bind himself never to assist again to catch a negro. What will you give, said he. Fifty dollars, said I. He replied, 'You think I would be damned easy bought off?' One of the strangers fearing perhaps I might increase the offer till it would be accepted, told this champion of the oppressed that he would give him much more than that to aid the 'hunters of men.' The strangers were in a two-horse wagon. Hubbard in a sulkey. They separated at Greenville, the former going towards New Hope, the latter towards Doylestown.

I think it proper that the material facts of this case, without comment, should be made public, that our citizens may be on their guard against the prowling desperadoes that are lurking in our borders, ready and willing to snatch from among us, without the shadow of law or authority, whomsoever they claim as their 'chattels personal.'

JOSEPH FELL.

Buckingham, 4th month 22d, 1844.

In the spring of 1826, Langhorn began the next phase of his life, learning the trade of limeburning as an indentured servant for seven years to Joseph Carver of Solebury, along with another, slightly older, mulatto boy, Andrew Hartless, with whom he was to form a lifelong friendship. These two men were never thereafter separated more than a few miles for almost fifty years. For those first few years, they lived together in a small cabin in back of Carver's house.

Another, younger man who later was to become a lifelong friend and companion was Mahlon Gibbs. Mahlon's father was black (perhaps a descendant of 82-year-old Richard Gibbs, listed as a slave on the 1782 slave census as being owned by Peter Vansant of Lower Makefield), and his mother was one of the last Indians in Solebury Township. He was raised by Moses "Old Mosey" Eastburn, who took a shine to the boy and made sure he was well-educated. Annie Pearson Darrow, in her remembrances of her family contained in the book, *Crispin Pearson of Bucks County*, published in 1932, wrote that Mahlon, "had a better schooling than many a white boy of his time." She remembered him well and described him as having "many Indian traits and was tall and straight and walked like an Indian. He married a Negro woman and lived near Burn Bridle Hill most of his life and raised a large family of children, fifteen, I think.

"He often worked for my father at butchering times and often came in on an errand and would stay to dinner, so I saw much of him while I was a girl. The last I saw him was some fifty years ago (1880); he was then living on Bainbridge street, Philadelphia. He looked old and worn out then and probably did not live many years. His descendants are the last ones I know of to have Solebury Indian blood in them, at least of those who roamed Burn Bridle Hill."

Lang's relationship with Carver was quite different from the friendship he had known with the previous white family, the Fells and their son Joseph. Mr. Carver, son of Joseph and Hannah (Cary) Carver, was much older than Lang. He and his wife, Cynthia Kirk, were married on April 13, 1815 at Plumley's Tavern in Newtown. He entered public service several times, and in 1848 was elected Bucks County Register. He was described by the *Intelligencer* as "a miller and farmer—a plain, industrious, honest man—well qualified for the important office for which he has been nominated—not proscriptive in his political opinions."

As a married man with children and several servants to look out for, a large farm and mill with its constant labors and concerns, as well as his position in the community, Mr. Carver's relationship with Lang was a straightforward one of master and servant. Although Lang missed the many hours listening to and learning from Joseph, his new friendship with Andy and Mahlon made the loss somewhat easier to accept.

It also meant his separation from the Quaker faith.

"I just can't. It's too strict," Lang told Joseph when he inquired whether Lang would continue attending services. "Honest, I thank you…I mean, thee for everything thee has done for me. But I like music and dancing and hunting."

Lang was a normal child for his age—a restless teenager, eager to explore and experiment. He could not bear being confined in worship service sitting on hard benches for hours sometimes in total silence, if no one in the congregation was moved to speak. He was too young to understand the concepts of sacrifice and self-denial.

Life and society had already done a good job of denying him most everything, especially the basic human rights of "equality" and "liberty" accorded to all men in the Preamble of the Constitution of the United States. He didn't know about the Constitution and probably never thought about it in those terms, but something inside him held back, and that was, he was damned if he was going to give away his "life" and "pursuit of happiness," too.

Something else that made Lang uneasy about going to the Friends meeting house, though he would not have been able to put it into words, was the fact that even at Quaker services, where the high-minded principles of freedom for all mankind were expounded, Negroes still had to sit segregated and apart in the balcony or in the back of the room.

As Joseph went away to college and lost touch with Langhorn, he could only hope the old saying, "Give me a child for seven years, and I'll have him for the rest of his life," was true, that during the past little over two years he had managed to instill in him at least some of the Christian virtues which would guide him through his life and work.

And, oh! the work was so hard, so strenuous, so taxing of strength. On the other hand, the exercise was probably what kept Lang's body in good shape for most of his life.

Before the general practice of using dynamite to blast the limestone rock into manageable pieces began, Lang had to do it alone by hand, one piece at a time. In one hand he held a steel drill, while in the other a small hammer, with which he struck the drill, loosening the rock into pieces that were then loaded into the wagon and carried to small kilns at the farms built to hold about three hundred bushels of rock.

Later on, large stone-and-mortar kilns were built closer to the quarries that were rented out to the limeburners, and the finished ash was then bagged and hauled to the jobsite to be spread in the fields. One of those was the giant "Three-Eyed Kiln" built in 1824 on Aquetong Road just east of York Road in Solebury, close to Canada Hill where Langhorn lived from 1845 to the end of his life.

Since a belt of limestone about a mile wide extended across Solebury township from Lahaska to Centre Bridge, the lime workers were furnished with an almost inexhaustible supply, yielding approximately five hundred thousand bushels of lime annually.

Limestone had been quarried in the Buckingham-Solebury area of Bucks County as early as 1703. In a deed from Lawrence Pearson to his brother Enoch, for one hundred acres dated March 8, 1703, is the following notation: "Except the privilege of getting limestone for the said Lawrence and his children's own use with full egress and regress for fetching the same."

The kilns were fired in the early years with wood, so expeditions to the forest to replenish the wood supply were frequent. Later on, when coal was made readily available via the Delaware canal from the mines in northeast Pennsylvania, it became a popular fuel. Either way, it meant loading and unloading tons of materials, day after day—backbreaking work outdoors in all weather.

The kilns were always nestled against a hill or into a steep bank, which was sometimes manmade, to enable the rock to be shoveled into the top and the lime ash to be raked out at the bottom. Kilns usually faced in a westerly direction to provide a draft, which was crucial to efficient firing. After packing rock and wood alternately in layers, the kilns were fired with brushwood at the lower entrance, enough to heat the contents to a temperature of nine hundred to eleven hundred degrees centigrade. The burned materials would then settle to the bottom, and Lang had to rake it out, "slake" and sift it before it was ready to be spread or bagged.

Slaking consisted of adding water to the hot ash, which caused extreme chemical reactions in the resulting steam and produced, when dried, the powder that was eventually spread.

Two tons of limestone had to be burned to produce one ton of lime ash, or quicklime, and it then took ten to fifteen tons to lime two to five acres. Average farms in that day consisted of thirty and more plantable acres. Joseph was quite correct in his estimation that there would be work for Langhorn as long as he wanted.

There were many dangers associated with the work, however. Sometimes the workers would take the quicklime straight from the kiln to the field, which, if it began to slake could cause a fire in the carts and wagons. The fumes released in the steam of slaked lime were extremely caustic and toxic, and asphyxiation was a very real hazard. If a man inhaled the powder or gasses, he could burn his lungs beyond repair.

In April 1853, the *Intelligencer* reported that thirty-year-old Washington Kimble had fallen asleep on top of a limekiln where he had gone to warm himself. He apparently got too close to the kiln and suffocated to death. "The kiln was filled to within two or three feet of the top, and was on fire," the paper stated. It further pointed out that Kimble "had been for some time laboring under an aberration of mind," speculating that his death could have been deliberate.

Two men, Simon Crouthamel and John Messer, died in 1876 when they put their beds between two burning kilns to keep warm during the night. Crouthamel left a wife and four little children.

As if the danger of inhaling fumes was not bad enough, along came the dynamite and the resulting deaths and disfigurements. In May 1844, Daniel Kelly of Buckingham was killed by powder kegs exploding. He was badly burned and lingered in agony for twenty-four hours before death released him.

One of the earliest deaths was James Jamison, who was generally credited with being the first to bring coal into practical use in lime-burning. He rented the quarries of Aaron Ely below Greenville and was setting a charge one day along with his son, Robert, and a hired man, Mark Wismer, when a premature explosion occurred, burning them all. James was fatally injured, and the others were terribly crippled and disfigured for the rest of their lives.

In September 1859, another Irishman, Hugh McGowan, who was employed at Cope's limestone quarry at Limeport, was, mercifully, instantly killed by a premature blast. He was thrown into the air by the explosion and his body terribly mangled. He left a wife and six children.

Seneca Fell, Jr., a distant relative of Joseph Fell, was badly injured about the face in May 1864. His face was blackened by the powder and his eyes so much injured that it was doubtful for a while he would ever see again. He did recover his eyesight, although he was scarred for the rest of his life. After Seneca had improved somewhat, and it was known he would not be blind, Lang was able to joke with him, "You whites're always trying to become black and handsome like me, but that ain't no way to go about it, my friend!"

The joking hid the fear that it could happen to him, too. Beyond the brave posturing, a man had to be mighty careful indeed.

Just before the lime business began dwindling in the late 1800s another serious accident occurred at the lime quarries of Joseph Reeder in Solebury. Thomas Conners and Thomas Harrity were engaged in "popping," a term used to designate the operation of blowing the larger rocks that had already been loosened by a previous blast. They were supposed to swab the hole to extinguish any remaining fire before putting the new powder in, but they were in a hurry and failed to do so. The result was an explosion that immediately shattered Conners' hand so badly that it had to be amputated just below the elbow. Harrity, who was standing nearby, was severely burned in the face.

Although lime was used in several products year-round, the liming of fields was generally seasonal, and Lang was free for several months to vary his work and supplement his income by hiring himself out to help with jobs such as plowing, sowing, harvesting, house-building. Even in wintertime, there were a myriad of chores around the farms. In addition to chopping ice and restocking the ice house, there was plowing and turning the stiff clay soil, thrashing and cleaning grain, shoveling surface drains on wheat fields, chopping wood, mending fences, cleaning and refurbishing stables and animal pens, and reconditioning implements, wagons, carts, and tools.

Once the obligations of his indenture to Joseph Carver ended in 1833, Lang was a free man who could work where he chose. As a big, strong man, he was in great demand, and quickly gained a wide network of farmers who were eager to have Langhorn Wellings working for them. He continued to live in the house behind the Carvers, but now paid rent for his room and board. And he had managed to save enough money from his extra wages to buy a horse and wagon.

So it was that he found himself in August 1835 working as a hired man on the farm of Jacob Stone at Wormansville in Tinicum Township, a medium-sized place of a little over seventy acres of a large German family.

Jacob was a small man of about fifty-three years; his wife Maria, Mrs. Stone, looked to be about ten years his junior. Lang learned from one of the boys that the couple had seventeen children living, the youngest, Emma, having just been born in May.

Lang had not had much interaction with the German families of Bucks County, so this was quite a new experience for him. So many children. Everyone so light-colored and so small. He had never seen such a large family before and, it appeared to him there also numerous neighborhood children, who were probably related in some way, running around the place, all chattering in German, which Lang did not understand.

Lang hired himself out for several days to Mr. Stone, working in the fields. At night he slept in the barn curled up in a blanket on the soft, clean hay. He didn't need his wagon, so he had left it at home and come on horseback.

The food was abundant—more than he had ever seen. If the weather was nice, the morning and evening meals were served outside under a huge tree at large tables set end to end; during rainy weather, the tables were set up in the great room of the large farmhouse. The noontime meal was delivered by Jacob's older daughters to the men working out in the field.

One day, as Lang was working in a far corner of the property, one of the girls came with a lunch pail filled with fried chicken, bread, cheese and fresh fruit. Lang put down the shovel he had been using to dig the weeds out of a ditch, took the pail, nodded "thank you" and sat down in the shade of a tree at the edge of the field to eat.

The girl, who appeared to be about twenty or so—it was hard for Lang to guess, she was so petite—stood silently waiting for him to finish his meal. Her blond hair was braided in the German style and curled tightly into rolls just behind both ears. A sunbonnet shaded her head and face. She wore a plain, blue cotton work dress over which was a full-length white apron. She was barefoot, as in the summer she only wore shoes to go to church or visiting.

"Sit down," Lang motioned to her. She shook her head no and continued to stand demurely a few feet away.

"You speak English?" Lang asked.

"Ahf course, I do," she replied, in a sweet voice with a slight German accent, which came out sounding like "off course" and made Lang laugh a little to himself at the cuteness of it.

"My name is Langhorn, Lang for short. What's yours?"

"Mary," she replied cautiously, seeming almost frightened of him by the way she stood back.

"What's the matter, never seen a black man before?"

She blushed. "Yes," she said, slightly indignant. "I haff even been to Doylestown and once to Newtown. I have seen many schwartz…black people…I mean, Negro." She became embarrassed for not being able to remember the appropriate English word.

"You white folks, I feel sorry for you," Lang teased her. "You can't hide your blush like I can."

"I am not blushing!" she protested, but her face reddened all the more in the process.

In fact, it almost felt to Mary that Lang could read her mind, and she was mortified that he might find out she was just that second thinking that this was possibly the most handsome man she had ever seen in her life. *His skin looks like rich, dark honey. Not one blemish on his face. So smooth. His hair is so black. His teeth are so white and even. And he is so big, such strong arms.* Subconsciously, as she was examining him, she leaned toward him as if to touch him, immediately became embarrassed, and brought herself back up with a start.

Lang had been around enough girls to realize something was up with this little Mary. He knew he was attractive, he had a good, steady income and every prospect for doing well in life. He was almost cocky about being seen as "a good catch." But, all of the other girls who had shown this kind of interest in him had been Negro girls or mixed. Most white girls, in fact, were indifferent, except the Quaker girls who were polite, but downright stern—all business, no nonsense. So here was a unique, almost heady experience.

He wasn't quite sure what to make of it, but decided to venture a little further.

"Come, sit down. Don't be embarrassed. I won't bite."

She shook her head. "I really should be getting back. My mother…"

"Oh, you can take a few minutes. Surely they won't miss you so soon. Tell them you couldn't find me for a while." He reached over and took her small, white hand and gently bade her sit. She pulled her hand back quickly, but kneeled where he directed her, sat back on her heels and folded her hands self-consciously in her lap, with her head bowed shyly.

"So, talk to me," he said. "Show me how good you speak English."

"What do you want me to talk about?"

He thought for a second, then laughed. "Tell me about what it's like with all these children! I've never seen such a big family in my life!"

"Did you not have brothers and sisters?"

Lang told her about his early life, his mother dying and leaving him an orphan and how he had worked as an indentured servant for Mr. Carver. Mary's heart was melted with compassion for him. "I am so sorry," she said sincerely. "I guess I have been very fortunate—we all have. There are seventeen of us, and we are all very healthy, 'knock on wood,' as are Mama and Papa."

"What does that mean—'knock on wood'?"

She told him about some of the German sayings, and the German community and stories about life with her family, mostly humorous incidents about how the children—the boys, especially—ran her parents ragged with their antics. She told him about Papa, how he was a strict disciplinarian who would be beside himself sometimes trying to keep his brood in line, and Mama, how sweet and loving she was, in temperament almost the complete opposite of Papa.

Lang nodded and laughed at the thought. "Oh, I can certainly see your father's temper. He's been courteous to me, but not friendly. He doesn't dislike blacks, does he?"

"Oh, no! I don't think so. I've never heard him speak about it, really. But I know he wouldn't have hired you if he felt that way."

They talked a little about Mary's love of books, how her brothers had taught her to read, and Papa had a small library that she would read from whenever she had a few moments. She especially loved the German poet and novelist Goëthe and the English playwright Shakespeare, whose works had been translated into German. In fact, at this point in history, Shakespeare was far more popular in Germany than he was in his own country.

Mary explained that her father had been given a book with some of Shakespeare's plays many years ago, and it was truly a prized possession. "Sometimes we divide up the parts and put on a play amongst ourselves," she said, becoming animated as she talked. "Some of us have even memorized the lines, and it is in very difficult 'high' German. Would you like to hear?" Without waiting for a response, she rose up on her knees and began to recite passionately a passage she had learned from *Romeo and Juliet,*

> Drey Worte, liebster Romeo, und dann gute Nacht, im Ernst Wenn die Absicht deiner Liebe rechtschaffen ist, und auf eine geheiligte Verbindung abzielet, so laß mich durch jemand, den ich morgen an dich schiken will, wissen, wann und wo du die Ceremonien verrichten lassen willst, und ich bin bereit, mein ganzes Glük zu deinen Füssen zu legen, und dir, mein Liebster, durch die ganze Welt zu folgen.[1]

Suddenly she realized, even if this boy could not understand the German, the content of this passage was about doomed love and marriage intent. She sat back and blushed.

"That's nice," Lang smiled and said. "I never could learn how to read. Maybe you could read a book to me some day." He looked in Mary's eyes, and she closed them immediately for fear he could see right through to her innermost thoughts.

"Oh, I must go!" She jumped up and gathered up the pail and napkins.

He reached out and touched her hand. She stopped short and froze.

"Maybe you could read to me tonight, after supper."

---

1   "Three words, dear Romeo, and goodnight indeed.
    If that thy bent of love be honourable,
    Thy purpose marriage, send me word tomorrow,
    By one that I'll procure to come to thee,
    Where and what time thou wilt perform the rite,
    And all my fortunes at thy foot I'll lay,
    And follow thee my lord throughout the world...'

Mary felt her face burning. Realizing he was correct, indeed, that she could not hide it, she laughed in embarrassment. "Perhaps. We'll see. I have to help Mama clean up and put the children to bed."

"Come and see me, then, when you're finished with your chores."

Mary practically ran all the way across the field and had to stop for a few moments to refresh by the brook. She arrived home right after Elizabeth and Rachel came back from delivering lunch to Papa, their brothers and the other men.

She did not go out to meet him after supper that night, but she thought about it a great deal all night and all the next day, mostly trying to justify her attraction to him. *After all, opposites attract*, she reasoned. *That must be it. He's like no other man I have seen in my life.* And she firmly resolved not to pursue her inclinations any further.

However, when the men came in for supper and were gathered around the washtub, her eyes met Lang's for an instant, and she felt a shock—almost as if a bolt of lightening had passed between the two of them. Mary was so unnerved, she handed her father one of the boys' small shirts.

"Ach, so you think I am shrinking?" her father asked in German, laughing.

Then, as she was serving supper that evening, she had to reach between Lang and her little brother Reuben. It was a warm evening, and she had rolled her dress sleeves up to just above her elbow, leaving her lower arm exposed. As she extended her arm to put the bowl of corn on the table, Lang unconsciously lifted his hand from under the table and ever-so-gently and quickly stroked the underside of her forearm.

No one noticed. They were busy talking and eating, and the gesture only lasted for a second. Mary was stunned. She had never before in her life felt anything like the effect it had on her. It wasn't a chill, it wasn't a shiver, nor a fever. It was as if she had turned into one of the numerous fireflies flitting around the yard. Every single cell of her body had been electrified and waves of thrill passed up and down. It had taken hours to build her resolve, and a millisecond for it to crumble.

But, how to see him was a very real problem. She was always busy and surrounded by people from early morning until after supper. She shared a bed with two of her sisters, and they would wonder where she was if she tried to slip out.

As it turned out, after the dinner dishes were cleaned up, she happily noticed her mother was occupied with baby Emma, and all of the other children were either running around outside or in the great room reading books, playing games and busy with various activities. The men and older boys were still sitting at the tables outside smoking their pipes and talking. Lang did not smoke then and did not understand German, so he wandered off to the barn, he said to take his horse out for some exercise.

Mary took a clean pail from the kitchen and called out in German, "I'm going to get some raspberries, Mama, before it gets dark."

"Zehr güt," her mother called back. "Danke, liebschen."

They met on the far side of the barn where the woods began and where there were, indeed, raspberry and blackberry bushes. Mary didn't know what to do or what to say. She only knew she wanted to be close to this man. Lang felt exactly the same way.

They walked and talked, as Mary absentmindedly picked berries with Lang beside her leading his horse. Just in case anyone came around in back of the barn and saw them, they kept a respectful distance. Lang told her more about his life, living with the Fell family, having been indentured to Mr. Carver for seven years. They talked a little about slavery, and Lang told her some of the stories he had heard from runaways and freed slaves. Mary's heart was melted even more with compassion as she listened to his accounts of their suffering. He told her about the work of the abolitionists and the Underground Railroad.

Then he began talking about his dreams for the future, how he was ready to find a wife and make a home of his own. As soon as she heard the word "wife," Mary became curiously filled with the same thrill she had felt earlier. Embarrassment and shyness made her mute, but, she thought, *He must be giving me a message of his intentions.* Her face glowed and her whole body smiled.

As it grew darker, she said, "I must go. Mama will be looking for me to help with the children."

"Come and see me tomorrow at noontime. I'll arrange to be away from the others again." She smiled shyly at him, but said nothing.

As she started to go, he put his arm out, touched her shoulder and turned her gently toward him. Then he bent down and softly kissed her mouth.

At twenty-five, Mary had never been kissed, at least not like that. She melted into the softness of his lips and instantly her body became all jittery inside. She felt as if her legs were going to buckle from underneath her. She stumbled a bit, and Lang instinctively tightened his hold on her.

She broke away and, filled with uncertainty mixed with exhilaration and a faint lightheadedness, began walking quickly back to the house.

"Come and see me tomorrow," Lang called in a loud whisper. But, even as he watched her disappear into the dark and he began walking back to the barn, he was filled with doubts. Conflicting thoughts plagued him all night as he tossed and turned on his hay bed. *What am I doing to this girl? There can never be anything. We cannot possibly have a future. Why not? I've seen plenty of evidence that other blacks and whites have been together. Look at all the mulatto people. But, you fool, this is a good, Christian girl, not one of the harlots, the 'yaller girls' in New Hope or Bristol.*

The next morning it was Lang's turn to vow an end to pursuing the attraction. And his resolve lasted until about noon when he saw Mary coming across the field with his lunch pail.

Her love had blossomed overnight and was reflected in her beautiful, light blue eyes. She had taken extra care with her dress and hair to make herself presentable. Her adoring eyes reflected her thoughts, *Du bist mir ein lieber Man, so bald ich dich gesehen hann.*[2]

He sat and tried to eat his lunch as she gazed at him. The conversation was somewhat stilted and staccato until Mary said, demurely, "When do you think we should ask Papa for permission?"

Lang halted in mid-bite, "Permission?"

"Of course," she said, "we need his permission to marry."

This time he nearly choked.

"Marry?"

"Well, of course, I assumed…. I mean, you kissed me. A man is not permitted to kiss a woman unless…."

Oh, my God! What have I done? Lang was not familiar with that little rule. Then, again, he had never had any experience with German girls.

---

2   Thou wast dear to me as soon as I beheld thee.

He thought quickly for a second and stammered, "I…I wonder…I mean, it just occurred to me, with the situation the way it is…I mean, with my people, ah, if it is even legal, for…us. To be married, I mean."

"Oh! There is something wrong with it? You mean because you are Negro and I am German? But my friend married an English, and another boy I know married an Irish girl." Lang quickly realized this girl knew next to nothing about the world outside her little village. She was meant to be some man's wife. That was all she knew. That was her purpose in life, whomever God sent to her.

And apparently she thinks He's sent her me!

"I know!" Mary said brightly. "We'll go to see Reverend Miller. He will tell us. He is just down the road. I'll go see him this afternoon!"

She jumped up, gathered up the lunch pail, kissed a startled Lang on the cheek and went back across the field toward the house, this time practically dancing all the way.

Lang watched her go with feelings of shock and dismay—*What have I done?*—mixed with twinges of tenderness and love—*She certainly is a darling little thing!* He was definitely attracted to her, that was no lie. *She sure would make a man a fine wife. And, by golly, why shouldn't I have a fine wife?*

By mid-afternoon, when Mary came running back across the field to tell him the good news that Reverend Miller had said the marriage was legal and acceptable to the church, Lang had graduated to daydreaming about what their children would look like, and about the clean, comfortable home she would keep for him, filled, in his mind, with plentiful food and happy, healthy babies.

And, just like Mary, he had succeeded in shrinking his vision so that it enveloped only the two of them. The rest of the world didn't exist. They were in love and happy together, and that's all that mattered.

Chapter III

The Stone Family Farm
Tinicum Township, Bucks County
August 1835

The yelling, the pounding of his fist on the table—if there was anything Mary Magdalena Trullinger Stone was unable to get used to in over twenty-five years of otherwise reasonably contented marriage to Jacob Stone, it was his fits of impotent rage, the infamous "German temper."

When he was upset and at the point of utter frustration—and that was understandably often with seventeen children—Jacob would pound the table and yell in German, "Bei Gott! Donner und blitzen...!"—"By God! Thunder and lightning will strike this house! The demons of hell will ascend to this place and all of its inhabitants will be consigned to fire and brimstone!"

Short in stature though he was, at barely over five feet four inches, his voice was powerful enough to carry throughout the house. And, although he would not hesitate to use the strap if he had to, he rarely had to hit any of his children. The mere look on his face, the yelling and pounding his fist on the table were enough to make them scatter, if not immediately obey.

His temper and dictatorial manner, however, created an ever-widening gulf between Jacob and his children. In his efforts to mold them to his perception of acceptable behavior, he managed to push them further away. As the years passed, and the children grew, they would indeed scatter, not just around the house and neighborhood, but far and wide away from Bucks County.

Jacob had also taught his children to be independent thinkers and not "follow the crowd," had impressed on all of the boys the importance of education and the need to find worthwhile employment away from the farm. As early as 1830, Jacob could see the beginnings of the Industrial Revolution and a shift away from an agricultural base to the cities.

"Working with the soil and bringing forth fruit and vegetables and wheat for flour has been the proud occupation of this family for centuries," he would counsel his boys—Jonas, Mahlon, Aaron, Amos, Chillian, Reuben, John, and Hiram—sitting in the evening in the great room of the old farmhouse or at lunch in the field leaning against a haystack and smoking his pipe. "But I can see the writing on the wall. There's not enough farmland for everyone."

Jacob, himself, had learned as a young boy the art of tailoring, and during the winter when the fields were covered with snow and in the summer when all they could do was wait for God to ripen the crops, he would sit for hour upon hour in the great room fashioning handsome, well-cut and fitted clothing by hand. His suits were of such fine quality they would be passed from one son to another throughout the years with only the slightest worn-look. And it provided the large family with an extra income over the years.

Shortly before Jonas, the eldest boy, turned fourteen, after careful consideration, Jacob suddenly decreed at dinner one evening that every one of his sons would become shoemakers.

"Shoemakers?! Why shoemakers, Pop?!" the boys protested, as teenagers are likely to react when first presented with a new idea. Shoemaking was hardly the exotic, romantic future they had envisioned for themselves after reading stories of swashbuckling seamen, well-to-do merchants who traveled the world, and respected diplomats.

"Because there will always be a need for shoemakers," he told the boys. "And you will all have a worthy profession to fall back on no matter what happens. A farmer can never know when the crops might fail."

He scoured the weekly *Intelligencer* for advertisements seeking shoemaking apprentices, wrote letters in response, and began sending his boys, one by one over the next fifteen years to learn the trade, some as far away as Philadelphia. Although a few of them balked like little boys being forced to attend violin or piano lessons, most willingly agreed and obeyed.

The girls—Elizabeth, Mary, Sarah, Eliza, Rachel, Harriet, Camilla, Rebecca, and Emma—were all trained in the household arts from the time they could stand at the dough trough and knead bread dough or churn butter hour after hour or scrub clothes against a washboard in a big tub in the back yard. It was expected they would find husbands and spend the rest of their lives engaged with housekeeping and bearing and raising children.

Mrs. Stone was generally a contented woman. "What is happy? A woman's happiness is in her children." Jacob was basically a good man, a considerate and attentive husband, even if outwardly stern and over-bearing, and a successful farmer. She had seventeen healthy children whom she loved with her life, and the home was always filled with their precious chattering and laughter. That is, if Jacob didn't manage to drive them off with his temper. She sighed unconsciously at the thought.

On this beautiful, warm evening in August, Mrs. Stone, glancing out of the window, saw her daughter and the young black man, the hired man Langhorn Wellings, coming toward the house, and knew instantly with a mother's instinct and a sudden catch in her throat what was happening.

The last she knew, young Mary had called out, "Going for a walk, Mama!" after supper. Now she saw the two young people approaching the house in the twilight. She noticed first that they were walking alone—not appropriate for a well-bred young German lady. Then she saw how they were walking a little too closely to each other up the path and how their eyes had met for just an instant that spoke volumes: This small, blonde German woman and this large, dark African man were in love.

Mein Gott, mein Gott, nein, nein! she thought and looked around the great room. *Where's Jacob?* She quickly handed baby Emma to Rachel and told her and the other children gathered in the kitchen to leave the house immediately.

A schwartz! A Negro! How could I have missed this? This was too much! It might have been easier if Mary was going to announce that she was leaving for Arabia to join one of the harems she had read stories about, or go to Philadelphia to become a "lady of the evening," which, in her young innocence, she knew nothing about. At least that news would have given her father instant heart failure, and it would have been done and over with. This!—this was going to be prolonged torture and it was not going to abate any time soon, if ever.

Mother Mary ran to the kitchen entrance off the long porch that covered the entire front of the house along the east side. There were two doors—the entrance directly into the kitchen area and the other for guests into the great room. She reached the top of the porch steps just as Mary and Langhorn approached the bottom.

"Mary!" she whispered strongly down to her daughter.

"Mama, Langhorn and I want to see Papa."

The mother bowed her head slightly and closed her eyes. "Young man, please go avay," she said in English in her heavy German-accented voice. "I don't vant to be disrespectful to you, but I tink you know vhat ziss vill lead to."

Langhorn, appearing nervous and uncomfortable, started to speak, but the mother turned to the daughter. "Mary, don't do this," she said in German. "You can put a stop to it now and not upset your father. You know…"

"I don't have a choice, Mama."

The mother was instantly stricken. "What do you mean? Are you pregnant?!" she asked, immediately thinking the worst at the same time remembering that she had been almost three months pregnant with Elizabeth when she and Jacob married in 1809. She had tried to keep her girls pure and innocent, but still, those things did happen, she knew, especially on the farm. There was something earthy and down-right erotic about life on a farm. It's no wonder they had seventeen children.

Her face reddened at the thought, and the young woman mirrored her blush. "No, Mama! That's not what I meant. I mean Langhorn and I are in love." She took the young man's hand. "We want your permission and blessing to be married."

Mother Mary sighed deeply, closed her eyes and raised her hand to cover her eyes. Her other hand clutched her apron. Though small in size, she was a strong-willed, strong-of-body woman whose tears did not come often. She had borne seventeen children without flinching, and she ran her house and family with the famous German military-like precision that her immense responsibilities required. She had watched, with a benevolent smile that masked her inner anxieties and fears, as her oldest sons left the farm to begin their new lives in the city as apprentice shoemakers. She had cried happy tears as two of her daughters had married and left home to start families of their own.

But on this August evening the anguished mother's tears flowed freely into her palm and through her fingers. This was certainly not what Mary Trullinger Stone had, in her wildest imagination, ever envisioned for her second child or, indeed, for any of her children.

Suddenly, she heard her husband's voice behind her on the porch. "Hullo, what is this? We have visitors?"

Young Mary Stone's great-grandfather, Johannes Philip Stein, had been the original immigrant of the Stone family. Philip, as he was known, was born July 15, 1716, in Germany. He came to America in the mid-1740s and worked for years as a brewer to pay his way and save up to buy a farm.

On January 13, 1760, Philip settled his family on a farm of one hundred fifteen acres and thirteen perches in the beautiful rolling hills of Bedminster Township, to the northwest of Tinicum, which he bought from Isaac Tettemer, one of the original patentees.

The Germans were uncanny in their ability to find the best, most productive land, and in the 1700s, before the Midwest—the "Heartland" of America—was opened to migration and settlement, most of that land was in Pennsylvania.

Early German immigrants would often join together in cooperatives to pool their resources and assist each other to buy farms. In Philip's case, he gave a mortgage of £100 for the purchase to Philip Herbel, "yeoman," Henry Ketter, "weaver," Georg Schwartz, "yeoman," and Jacob Gehrling, "yeoman."

On July 15, 1765—his forty-ninth birthday—Philip, along with his brother, Sebastian, took the Oath of Naturalization, becoming citizens of England and subjects of the British crown. In May 1778, Philip and his brother again gave an Oath and Affirmation, but this time to the new government of the United States of America.

Philip and his wife, Elizabeth, had ten children: Christian, Anna Barbara, Elizabeth, Anna Margaret, Anna Catherine, Maria Margaret, Philip Jr., Magdalena, Anna Maria, and Anna Dorothea, born between 1750 and 1768.

He quickly became a prominent citizen of Bedminster. In 1765, he was one of three trustees, along with Frederick Solliday and Christian

Fretz—Mennonite, Presbyterian, and Lutheran, Philip being the latter—
for the receipt of property from Hartman Tettemer to form the Tohickon
Union Church, school and graveyard in Bedminster, where he was
buried in February 1791.

His prominence, however, did not go so far as to be involved in politics or even to volunteer to fight in the Revolutionary War. In fact, in the
insular German community of the time, most of the behaviors and attitudes of the cultural heritage of many centuries in their homeland were
carried over for several generations in America. Among those was an
almost vehement aversion to armies and war, since many of these
German men had fled conscription into the army of whatever duke, king
or emperor happened to be in power during the years of almost constant
warfare in Europe throughout the seventeenth and eighteenth centuries.

As a result, another German immigrant trait was antipathy toward
government. A German was not likely to know anything about the democratic form of government, having lived for centuries as subjects of a
strict, almost feudal monarchy, and would be unlikely to engage in politics or run for office, nor even go to the secular court to settle disputes.

And, being a good Christian—Lutheran, Catholic, Mennonite, or
other denomination—certainly *never* would a man drink to excess, lie,
cheat, steal, break the law, or otherwise come under public scrutiny in
any manner whatsoever.

"There's only three times in his life a man should get his name in the
newspapers," Philip Sr. used to say, "and that is when he is born, when he
is married and when he dies, and, by golly, he'll lead a good, pious life in
the meantime if he knows what's good for him!"

If a man or woman shamed the family or community in any way,
they were very often treated from that day forward as if they were dead.
There have even been a few instances recorded that tombstones were
placed over empty graves with the person's birth date and "date of
death" fixed at the time of their disgrace.

This attitude, known as "shunning," would continue to be carried
out in later centuries in German Amish communities and was quite final
in most cases, as "no one can return from the dead." In Jewish families, a
father would often figuratively or literally "rip the lapel" of his coat, thus
signifying that his son or daughter was dead to the family from that point
on. Another form was the Quaker "out of meeting"—excommunication.

Being barred from the church or synagogue and home was just part of the practice; it carried over to the secular world, as well, in that no one of that family or religious company would speak to the miscreant or even look at them in public. They were as if invisible from that moment on.

Unfortunately, Philip's son Philip Jr., born December 30, 1759, did not listen to these warnings and experiences or to his father's sage advice. Philip Jr. began adult life well enough, marrying Elizabeth Barntz, daughter of prosperous tavern-keeper Jacob Barntz, whose tavern was on the road to the Delaware River from the Christ's Evangelical Lutheran Church, also known as the Lower Tinicum Union Church, and later becoming known simply as the "Brick Church."

On April 6, 1778, Philip Jr. bought from Valentine Marsteller the farm to the immediate southeast of his father's place, consisting of ninety-four acres and twelve perches. About ten years later, the family, including children Jacob, Elizabeth, John, Henry, and Mary Magdalena, moved to nearby Tinicum Township, presumably because Elizabeth wanted to be closer to her family and expected that Philip would take over the tavern some day.

But, sometime in the late 1790s, something went wrong. Philip simply took off one day, left the farm and the family and the church and a potentially lucrative future as a tavern-keeper.

As to exactly what happened, whether there was an argument, another woman, no one knows. Neither Elizabeth nor the children would ever speak of it, and as far as they were concerned, he was as if dead from that day on.

There was some speculation and gossip in the community that he had gone west to the new Northwest Territories—the future Ohio, Indiana, Illinois, Michigan—and that Elizabeth had refused to go with him. Whatever the cause, he was never heard from again, and when old Jacob Barntz made his will on June 27, 1799, it read: "I also give to Phillip Stone, husband of my Daughter Elizabeth, *and has left her*, the sum of five shillings and no more of my Estate." Five shillings being the equivalent of five pennies, bequeathing such a small amount to a family member in one's will was intended as a deliberate insult and also served to preclude the particular legatee from contesting the will.

Because of the cloak of silence over the family, Jacob's seventeen children never knew about their great-grandfather, Philip Sr., that he had been among the earliest German settlers in America, precipitating a veritable tidal wave of German immigrants over the next two hundred fifty years.

When any of Jacob's children asked, "Where are we from, Papa?" the answer was simply, "We are from Germany, and you should be very proud of it." Therefore, that is what the children told their children and grandchildren—that Jacob was the original immigrant—and two generations of rich history on American soil were lost because of the real or perceived wrongdoing of one person. One "rung" in the family history ladder was simply removed.

German life during the eighteenth and nineteenth centuries in Pennsylvania revolved around the church and the farm. Almost without exception, Germans until the mid-1800s, were farmers, mechanics and laborers.

The German language was spoken almost exclusively in the homes and churches, although children were also taught Latin and enough English to get along in the greater, English-speaking world. By 1858, of the little more than eight thousand pupils being taught in Bucks County schools, over three hundred were still being taught in German as their primary language in the small communities of German culture that remained.

No American German, male or female, went without education of some type. If the older children went to school—mostly boys, since the girls were needed to help in the home—they were expected to teach their younger siblings in the evenings at home.

Religion was as important as education, if not more important and, until the early 1800s, most of the schools were directly tied to the churches. As public schools began to be established around the county, many Germans hesitated sending their children because they feared religion would be neglected and the children would lose their moral compass. They were also wary that the establishment of state schools might signify somehow a union of church and state. As soon as they were convinced such was not to be the case, they became ardent advocates of a free, public school system.

Almost every family had a Bible, a Psalter, Stark's *Gibet Buch*, and Arndt's *Wahres Christenthum*, as well as the classics, such as the poetry and other works of Goëthe, which were read from every night, as well as on Sundays. If the family was prosperous enough, each child was given his or her own Stark's *Hand Buch of Prayer, Praise & Worship* upon confirmation at age seventeen, some of them beautifully bound in dyed leather with brass closure clips.

So well were the children taught about religion and urged to join a church that in the mid-1800s scarcely an adult could be found without church membership. If a minister heard of anyone in his community who was not a God-fearing church member, very often he would consider it his duty to make a public example of them and hold them up as a warning to others.

When Jacob died in Doylestown in 1848 he lived on a typical 1800s Pennsylvania Dutch farm (originally "Pennsylvania Deutsch"—meaning German—this phrase was somehow changed to Pennsylvania Dutch and mistakenly used ever since to describe these people). Jacob's property, in the New Britain Village of Doylestown, consisting of fifty-two acres and one hundred twelve perches, was described as having "a stone dwelling, two stories high, with two rooms on the first floor; the second conveniently divided; out kitchen, with a well of water at the door; spring house over a lasting spring of water; good barn; hog house; wagon house; wood house, and other out buildings; apple orchard, and other fruit trees; ten acres of timber; the residue divided into convenient sized helds."

The barns were most often huge—almost twice as big as the house—well-built, painted bright red and festooned with beautiful designs called "hex signs." No one is quite certain how or why the practice began. Originally it was thought they were placed on the barns to ward off evil spirits or witches. But, perhaps it was for no other reason than that they were pretty decorations.

The German farm was supplied with all of the modern conveniences. For example, as soon as the steam engine was invented, and in the mid-1800s converted into service for plows and harvesters, nearly every German farm had one. The latest and best machines and inventions, introduced to the farmers at the yearly "Sanitary Fairs" and "Agricultural Fairs," were quickly welcomed. The farmers would scrimp and save and help each other one-by-one to procure the machinery.

Almost every neighborhood had at least one farm that would specialize in dairy cows, with a creamery that produced the finest quality and freshest products—milk, sweet and sour creams, cheeses, and butter.

The animals—pigs, chickens, geese, sheep, and especially horses and cows—were scrupulously kept clean and well fed. The German farmer treated his beasts with the greatest consideration, foregoing at times his own comfort. He took to heart the verse of the Book of Proverbs in the Bible—"The righteous man regardeth the life of his beast." (Proverbs 12:10)

Nearly every German farm had a great variety of fruit trees, with several acres devoted to orchards of apples, pears, peaches, and plums. Draping over arbors, fences and gates in and around the small flower, vegetable, and herb gardens close to the house, it was not uncommon to find ten or more varieties of grapes.

German men enjoyed smoking pipes, and many farms raised tobacco and made handsome profits. In the mid-1800s, commercial cigar-making factories sprang up all around Mumbauersville in Northern Bucks County, where both men and women could earn a good wage, and, as Jacob predicted, the young people began leaving the farms in droves for this and other industrial-type labors.

Life for most German girls consisted of helping their mothers tend to the younger children and doing housework—cooking, baking, cleaning, sewing—everything by hand until 1857 when the sewing machine was generally introduced—washing, ironing, gardening, as well as joining in the work of the farm on occasion—raking hay, binding grain, hoeing and husking corn, milking cows, tending chickens, "slopping" hogs. Their lives were by no means easy. It is estimated that the average farm wife in that day lifted and carried a ton of water a day.

Their medical care consisted of midwives for births, sulfur mixtures, herb teas, molasses and, later in the nineteenth century, castor oil for "whatever else ails you." There was no protection against diphtheria, consumption (tuberculosis), smallpox, typhoid, hydrophobia (rabies), scarlet fever, yellow fever, or rheumatic fever. Families often lost three or more children at one time as diseases ravaged cities and towns.

Because of their early training, German girls were always highly prized as servants, since it was the responsibility of every mother to educate her daughters in the art of housekeeping before they were permitted to leave the family home to either work or marry and set up their own houses.

The house, yard and flower garden of nearly every German home were beautifully arranged and immaculate. Most housewives adorned their homes with colorful décor, with houseplants and flowers in pots in the windows. The doors, floors, walls and windows of the house were washed several times a week and swept and dusted daily, except on Sunday. It was rare to find a house where the beds were infested with bugs or the clothing was moth eaten.

Personal cleanliness was very important, as well. Like most German farm wives, Mary Trullinger Stone kept a tub of fresh water and clean, ironed shirts by the back door for Jacob and the boys to wash up after working in the fields. The Germans, by their actions, if not by their words, coined Charles Wesley's sermon on "Cleanliness is, indeed, next to Godliness."

Perhaps the most exciting times in a German farmwife's life were going to the yearly Sanitary Fairs and Agricultural Fairs, where her husband would exhibit his cattle, swine, sheep, poultry and produce—fresh fruits and vegetables.

The women would enter their foods—jellies, preserves, butters, canned fruit and vegetables, wine, bread, cakes, pies, pickles, sauerkraut, mince meat, sausages and scrapple, dried fruits, and more. They could show off their flowers and crafts in pretty displays. And they would exhibit their needlework—rag carpets, clothing and underclothing, bed quilts, sheeting, pillowcases, stockings, gloves, homespun and homemade fabrics, as well as knitting and crocheting.

Among the prizes offered at the Bucks County Fair in 1864 were a blue ribbon and eight dollars for showing the best six butter cows of any breed, and four dollars for best mules. "Best knit bedspread" earned one dollar, "Best display of Hand-made Shirts, Bosoms & Collars" two dollars, and so on. (No premium was offered for fruit canned in liquor.)

Frakturs—hand-painted mementoes of births, marriages and sometimes deaths—were an important part of German life. The term "fraktur" describes the "broken letter" style of calligraphy that provided a means for teachers and ministers to supplement their incomes. There were many itinerant fraktur painters who would travel about the country and prepare frakturs for several families at a time.

In their spare time, the boys worked with wood to make chests for storing clothing, bedding and blankets. These were often embellished with lovely designs, the initials of the young man and his sweetheart and the year of their marriage. The men would also make chairs, tables, bedsteads, and more than a few took on the more complex work of clock making.

Music was very important in the German house, with an organ and often a piano, violins and other instruments found in almost every home. The young people would gather around the piano "of an evening" or on Sunday afternoons happily singing for hours.

As neighbors, the Germans were extremely kind and friendly. They would frequently assist each other with loans of money without interest and without requiring written promises of repayment. "Your word is your bond." In sickness and misfortune they would help one another and never accept compensation. When a family was visited by death, the neighbors would assist with food, money for burial—whatever was needed for however long it was necessary to get them through the crisis.

Before the days of insurance, when a building was lost, most frequently to fire, money was collected by the neighbors, often more than sufficient to cover the costs of replacement. No repayment was expected, only that the recipient would help another. "What goes around comes around," they would say. "You'll do someone else a good turn some day."

The German families epitomized the word "hospitality." No one, not even a beggar, was allowed to go from their gates without having their hunger appeased. No farmer would think of accepting payment for meals or lodging. As a result, no section of the county was so much infested by tramps as the German areas.

Germans were very sociable and given to visiting. In winter, entire weeks were devoted to visiting, and no visit was complete without a meal. Foods of all varieties and description were served: Several kinds of meats, vegetables—fresh when in season, preserved in winter—followed by pies and pastries. It was not unusual to have six to eight different kinds of pies at table and frequently as many kinds of cakes. It was expected that everyone must at least taste every dish that was passed around. "Helf dir duch selver," they would say. "Help yourself!"

A German was expected to be sober, modest, honest, and humble. The men were not abstainers from alcohol, mostly beer and wine, but seldom were they ever drunk. The Germans abhorred drunkenness or, indeed, any public display of bad character. For a German, "A good name is rather to be chosen than great riches." (Proverbs 22:1)

Perhaps most important, a German worked—and worked heavy labor and long hours—his or her entire life. "Hard work won't kill you," they would say, "but slothfulness will. It's one of the seven deadly sins." While work was elevated to prayer—"labour is worship"—laziness was simply not tolerated. If anyone, including a child, was capable of performing even the most minor chore, they were expected to do so. "In the sweat of thy face shalt thou eat thy bread." (Genesis 3:19)

Rarely would a German become a beggar or tramp, and it was shameful to ask for or accept public assistance. They would suffer denial, deprivation and poverty proudly before intruding on others and would never accept public charity. These firm principles carried even into the twentieth century among the Amish people who, despite paying their taxes willingly and cheerfully, still refuse to accept Social Security benefits, farm subsidies or government welfare of any kind.

On his farm, in his home, and in all matters of his household, the German man was the absolute monarch. "A man's home is his castle," Papa would frequently remind the inhabitants. "Papa" was the boss, and his will was not to be crossed, especially by the girls who would have a very difficult time indeed if they willingly left or were banished from the home because of a dispute or wrongdoing. If they were removed from the protection and benevolence of even a despotic ruler, it was assumed they would be lost to iniquity forever.

Knowing all of this, generations of the Stone family since have wondered in awe at young Mary's boldness on that August evening in 1835, bringing as she did, for her father's approval and blessing to marry, her beloved Negro man, Langhorn Wellings. It must have been true love indeed, for nothing else can explain her heroic insanity.

Mary looked up at her father. "Papa, we would like to talk with you."

"Vee?" he asked, somewhat confused. Who was the "we"? Mary and her mother? The colored man Langhorn and…?

"Yes, Papa. Langhorn and I—Papa…." She didn't have to say any more.

If Jacob had received a musket ball in the middle of his stomach at that instant, he probably would have registered much the same look. His breath immediately drew in. His eyes opened wide in astonishment. His mouth opened and his pipe fell clattering to the porch steps.

It took only a few seconds, which seemed like hours for everyone around him, for his surprise to turn into anger.

"Mary! Come into the house this instant!" Turning to Langhorn, he said, half in German, half in English, "Du! You! Go away from my house! I vill not haff ziss. You are not velcome here no more."

Langhorn looked immediately to Mary for guidance. Unspoken. He did not want to go. He did not want to stay. *How did I ever get myself into this? Am I crazy? Get the hell out of here! No, I love her. I can't leave! My God, they kill blacks for less than this! I'll get myself shot. No, stay. I don't care what happens. I love her.* All these thoughts and more jumbled his mind in those confused seconds.

"Wait for me, Lang," Mary said calmly and smiled, though her lower lip quivered ever so slightly as she did so.

"No! You get going," Jacob shouted.

Mary repeated. "Wait for me." She raised her head, straightened her back to her full five feet two inches, lifted her skirt slightly, walked up the stairs and went into the house.

Jacob picked up his pipe, gave a look of fierce anger to Langhorn and went into the house behind Mary. Mrs. Stone, still crying softly, now with her apron covering her face as if to hide from the shock and shame, followed and sat at the kitchen table at the far end of the big room.

"Sit down, young lady, and explain yourself!" he said in German. Mary obediently sat in her mother's sewing chair next to the large round table in the middle of the great room, but would not look up at her father at first.

"There's nothing to explain, Papa. Langhorn and I are in love and want to be mar…."

"That's not possible!" Jacob roared.

"Why, Papa?" Mary cried. "He's a good man. He's hardworking…."

"He's a Negro! Dear Jesus! Don't you understand?! His people are slaves not a hundred miles from here! He's liable to be kidnapped and sold into slavery himself at any moment! What would become of you, of your children? Children!" Jacob was instantly filled with aversion at the thought. He raised his hands heavenward. "Have you completely lost your mind?"

Mary shook her head, "No. Things are getting better. Slavery won't last for long. We've heard about the abolition groups. Mr. Fell has told Lang about the meetings in Philadelphia. They're going to abolish the evil…"

"You're a naïve child! You are stupid! Slavery is so entrenched in the South, they will never give up their slaves. You have no idea what you're saying! Those damn Quakers are putting crazy ideas into people's heads, giving them false hopes!"

Mary regained her strength somewhat. "I think they are wonderful people, and they will prevail. Besides, Lang says we could go to Canada, where there are laws against slavery, and we could find a…"

"You'll never find anything! You can't be married, black and white! It's not even legal. He has no citizenship rights anywhere but Pennsylvania. I'm not even sure he can own property…"

"It is, Papa!" Mary said and sat up brightly, hopefully. "We asked Reverend Miller, and he said he would marry us. He said, 'The law states that whatever is acceptable to the church is legal in the Commonwealth.' Those were his words."

Up until now, Jacob had been pacing the room. At the news that Mary and Langhorn had already talked to Reverend Miller, the family's pastor since 1823 at the St. Luke's Evangelical Lutheran Church—the successor of the Reverend John M. Mensch, who had married Jacob Stone and Mary Trullinger in the little church on January 1, 1809—he stopped short.

"You've what? How dare he interfere in my family business! By God, I'll not have this!" He pounded his fist on the large round table so hard that the glass oil lamp jumped and the pretty red glass beads tinkled. "Now it's a conspiracy, you say."

"Oh, no, Papa!" Mary cried. "We didn't mean to go behind your back. But Langhorn wanted to make sure of these things before we asked you. Please, Papa…"

"No!" Jacob yelled. "It's just not right. It's not natural. They are not the same, these blacks." Slightly, almost imperceptibly softer and slower he repeated, "It's not in the natural order," as if not completely sure of what he was saying.

Indeed, Jacob was an educated man. He was also a normally kind-hearted and generous Christian man, not given to prejudicial or bigoted attitudes and statements. He absolutely abhorred slavery, as did most every German he knew. It was contrary to his Christian values. "One cannot be a Christian and enslave another human being." "Every man is created equal in the sight of God."

He publicly espoused the principles of the anti-slavery movement. He had unreservedly hired Langhorn and other colored workers, and invited them to his table. One can only suppose that his now violent reaction was because everyone knew the races were separate, and it simply never occurred to him that they would be mixing in marriage, in his own family, no less.

Working beside and sharing a meal with a Negro was one thing. Giving your daughter in marriage—the commingling of your "blood"— to a man of another race was a different matter altogether.

Jacob regained the strength of his argument. "No! They are different!"

Mary, remembering her father's love of the classics, suddenly seized upon an opportunity. "But, Papa, remember what Shakespeare wrote about the Jews, 'a different race.' 'Hath not a Jew eyes? Hath not a Jew hands, organs….'"

"No!"

"….If you prick us, do we not bleed? If you tickle us, do we not laugh…."

"No!"

This time Jacob slammed his fist down on the table so hard the sound produced was almost as loud as a gun report. "Don't you quote Shakespeare to me, young lady! Are you to be this Othello's Desdemona? Tell me, will he be the ruin and death of you?! You are agreeing that you love not wisely but too well? 'Oh, ill-starred wench'!"

Oh, no! What a fool I am! Mary had completely forgotten about Othello, Shakespeare's play about the Blackamoor king who eventually kills his Caucasian wife, accused unfairly of adultery.

Mary lowered her head and began crying.

Jacob never could bear to see his beloved wife and daughters cry. "Go upstairs, Mary," he said gently. "I'll tell the young man to go away. We'll forget about this nonsense. You'll find a nice husband. We'll go and visit your cousins up in Northampton…."

"Please, Papa, don't be cruel," Mary sobbed. "I know I'm not a pretty girl. Ich hab geward schone in manger dag, und mich doch kein but nicht haben mag," she said sadly. "I have waited already for many a day and yet no fellow comes my way. Eliza's married. Sarah is married. Rachel's Mr. Vansant is already courting her."

"Your older sister is not married yet, and no prospects," Jacob retorted. "You should be happy with the position God gives you—we must 'bloom where we are planted'."

"Elizabeth is not inclined as I am. I want my own family. I'm twenty-five years old and I'm going to be an old maid helping Mama take care of *your* children for the rest of my life! I want my own children. I want Langhorn!"

Realizing that he could no longer reason with this headstrong girl, Jacob shouted, "By God, I'll have it out with him, then!" and started to walk to the door.

Mary jumped up. "Oh, no, Papa, please don't hurt him!"

It didn't occur to either of them that Langhorn towered over and far outweighed the small German man. At that moment, Jacob was like a cat, which, when backed into a corner, could become twice its size in defense, and Jacob's castle was being assailed by this Blackamoor.

He walked out to the porch. Langhorn was still standing on the path, with his hat in his hand, twisting it through his fingers nervously. It seemed an eternity. Several times as he had heard Jacob yelling and pounding his fist, Lang would start to walk toward the house. But he could not enter another man's home from which he had been forbidden.

At the sight of Jacob, he perked up expectantly.

"Please, sir. We didn't mean to upset…."

"Du, you! Go avay from ziss house. Ziss cannot be. You haff betrayed my trust und dizgraced my family."

"Papa, please!" Mary came out of the house behind Jacob on the porch.

"Sir…" Langhorn started to walk toward them.

"Bei Gott, I'll get my gun," Jacob shouted and turned to go back in the house.

The next few seconds will remain as a prime example of one of those events that occur in everyone's life where actions are taken, things are said and done that take in reality only a few moments, but every detail of which remain imprinted in our memories forevermore. And very often the decisions that are made in a split second, especially in the impetuosity of youth, will profoundly affect everyone around us, in ever-widening circles, for the rest of our lives.

So it was on that August evening in Wormansville, in Tinicum Township, Bucks County, Pennsylvania, in the year of our Lord eighteen hundred and thirty-five that Mary Stone made her decision. She suddenly sprinted past her father, ran barefoot down the steps of the farmhouse, down the flower-bordered path to her beloved—this man Langhorn Wellings—took his hand, and began running.

Before Jacob had time to react and could call for his sons, who had been waiting a respectful distance from the house, Langhorn and Mary had reached his waiting horse at the end of the road.

By this time, too, it was growing dark, and Jacob knew he could never find them, indeed, if he even *wanted* his daughter back, so great was his disgrace, rejection, anger, and fear all rolled into overwhelming, stunned disbelief.

Mahlon, Chillian and young Reuben ran up. "Do you want us to go get 'em, Pop?" "Should I get the horses?" they shouted at once.

"Nein…no," Jacob said sadly. His shoulders suddenly became hunched, his body deflated to such a degree that he looked very small and pitiful indeed.

"She is gone. Your sister is gone."

The reverberations of Mary's impetuous decision began immediately. So great was his shame that within months, Jacob left his farm in Tinicum and moved his family, "lock, stock and barrel," to Doylestown. After having it out with Reverend Miller the next day, Jacob never spoke to him again or returned to the Lutheran church, or any other church, until his conversion to the Baptist faith on June 6, 1847.

Jacob would not allow his daughter's name to be mentioned in his presence. He began calling his wife "Maria" or "Mütter," German for "mother". And, even though he lived for the rest of his life within ten miles of Mr. and Mrs. Langhorn Wellings and their family, it would be eleven years, when he was making his last will and testament, before Jacob would finally inquire, at the urging of his wife and his friend John Riale, about his second daughter's whereabouts and welfare.

Chapter IV

Doylestown
May 13, 1865

LANGHORN WELLING, a colored resident of Solebury, was arrested on the 4th of February last, on complaint of the District Attorney, charged with having caused the death of his wife by poisoning. Since that time he has been confined to county prison. The body of his wife was disinterred, and the stomach taken out and sent to Professor Rogers, of Philadelphia, for examination. We understand that the District Attorney has received information from the Professor that the stomach of the deceased woman contained poison enough to kill two persons. Whether there is any evidence to show that Wellings administered the poison or not, we are unable to say.

[*Bucks County Intelligencer*, Wednesday, May 16, 1865]

Nancy Riegel hurriedly pulled off her apron as she pushed through the swinging door from the kitchen into the dining room of her home in Doylestown. Because she had given the housekeeper the morning off to attend a funeral, in addition to her practice of sitting with her mother-in-law for a few minutes, this morning Nancy had to cook and serve breakfast to Mahlon, and she was anxious to hear the details of his new assignment.

She sat fascinated as Mahlon related the facts of the Wellings case as he had learned them from Henry Darlington and his contact at the Prosecutor's office.

"So, what do you think so far?" Mahlon asked his wife.

Nancy was a little surprised, and delighted, that her husband would seek her opinion. Her own mother was never included in her father's business affairs or the men's conversations. She sat thoughtfully for a moment.

"I don't know what to make of it," she said finally. "I suppose if he is found guilty, he will be punished, and rightfully so, probably hanged. But, what is puzzling me is why would he poison his wife if she were already sick and dying? If he was so unhappy, one would think he would simply wait."

"Precisely," Mahlon replied. "But the fact that they found enough poison to kill two persons—those were the exact words I heard—and that Wellings purchased poison just a week before his wife died, it's just too much to ignore. Even if Mr. Ross is the most infamous Copperhead in Bucks County."

"Really!" Nancy was astonished. "But, how could that be? A Southern sympathizer who is a public officer in Pennsylvania?"

"Incredible, but true. All during the war, Mr. Ross was constantly stirring up trouble in his speeches and articles in the *Democrat* newspaper."

Nancy shook her head. "That is amazing. How could the people tolerate it?"

"Not only did they tolerate it, my dear, but they continued to re-elect him. In the midst of all this 'Grand Army of the Republic' patriotic rhetoric, there must've been an unseen majority. Either that, or all of our voting men were off fighting the war. At least, that's Mr. Darlington's theory.

"But, getting back to Wellings. Tell me, what do you think about the intermarriage of white and black?"

Nancy replied, "Well, again, I'm divided. I must admit, half of me is repulsed. I've never seen such a union or even heard of it. Is it legal?"

"Apparently, only here in Pennsylvania. I'm not aware of any other place in the country they could have wed at that time—1835. Although there is certainly plenty of evidence of the races mixing, I don't know if one could consider it a *legal* union or valid in the eyes of God."

"What do you mean?" Nancy asked.

"Why, all the mulatto people—light-skinned." Seeing the puzzled look on his wife's face, he continued. "The light-skinned Negroes are the product of Negroes and Caucasians mating, usually slave owners and overseers and slave women or sometimes prostitutes..."

Nancy suddenly looked stunned and flushed and sat up straight in her chair. "Mahlon!"

Too late, Mahlon remembered his twenty-two-year-old bride had been completely innocent about "familiar relations" when they married. Her mother had apparently not even told her about the wedding night, except to give her some vague indication that it was something unpleasant a woman had to endure in order to have children. It took almost a week of patient tenderness and constant wooing on Mahlon's part to convince her that it was—could be—one of the more pleasurable aspects of marriage. She was still not convinced, though otherwise a perfect wife. Mahlon vowed that when he and Nancy had children who married, they would certainly be better prepared.

"Oh, I am so sorry! I didn't mean to embarrass you," he said quickly. "I forgot..."

She sat for a moment. Until this time, she had honestly thought that the variations in color among black people were the same as different skin tones, color hair or eyes among white people. "So, you are telling me that, that...these slave owners...forced themselves on these poor, wretched creatures and...." It was all too repulsive. She could fathom it no further.

"Yes, my dear. I am truly sorry to have offended you with this sordid fact, and it is one of the most unpleasant aspects of slavery. And then to know that these despicable men actually sold the product of their own seed." He glanced at his wife. "Do you wish me to desist?"

Nancy got up from the table, picked up her fan from the sideboard and thoughtfully fanned herself. She sat back down and looked at her husband.

"I want to be a part of your life in every way. I want to be a true wife and helpmate. I'm tired of being an ignorant and coddled baby who knows nothing of the world and is constantly shocked by what she learns. I'm absolutely furious with my parents for not having better educated me about life."

Mahlon patted his wife's hand gently. "Your parents love you and wanted to protect you. We'll probably want to do the same for our children some day. I'm just sorry that I have to be the one to educate you. If I begin to tell you something you don't want to hear, just stop me. I'll understand."

Nancy nodded. "What you have just told me has made me detest slavery all the more. I hated it from the very moment I heard about it when I was a child in Connecticut. Of course, we had no slaves there. The cruelty and depravity of it. I shouldn't be surprised by anything you tell me. What more evil could they have inflicted upon fellow human beings, I cannot bear to imagine."

"Well, you seem to have hit on the right key, then," said Mahlon, "—'human beings'. You see, there are, unfortunately, a great many people who do not accept that Negroes are human or at least not on the same par with whites. They justify what they do by claiming that Negroes are a subspecies of human beings, and thus inferior and liable to be subjugated."

"Yes, I've heard father say, especially after the Dregg...something Scott..." She looked at Mahlon questioningly.

"Ah, he was undoubtedly talking about the infamous Dred Scott Decision of the Supreme Court back in eighteen fifty-seven which basically stated that blacks have no inherent rights to freedom even if they are residing in free states."

"Yes, Dred Scott. Anyway, father was just livid. I was only fourteen or so at the time, but I remember him and the other men talking about it. I listened to them talking in the parlor through the closed doors. They were yelling and very upset, saying things like 'What an abomination this Court is'."

"Quite so," Mahlon agreed. "It set the anti-slavery movement back twenty years or more and, actually many people think, made the Civil War inevitable as it further entrenched both sides of the issue. And it's no wonder that men like John Brown became so disillusioned that they resorted to violence. But, in the end, unfortunately, it did nothing more than inflame the fires of Southern passion. You do know about John Brown?"

"Oh, yes! I learned about him in school. Let's see, he was an abolitionist who formed a small army, some of them from right here in Pennsylvania, I think..."

"In Chambersburg, as I recall. You're right."

"…and they raided Harper's Ferry in Virginia in October eighteen fifty-nine, hoping to arouse the slaves to form an army to free themselves. And I learned about Nat Turner, as well. He was a slave, wasn't he, who led an insurrection in Virginia somewhere in the early eighteen thirties and killed several white people?"

"That's right," said Mahlon. "Unfortunately, though, Turner killed many innocent women and children and was viewed as a madman even by most abolitionists and thereby raised no sympathy in his efforts. Well, at least your father has been diligent in educating you about social and political issues."

"Oh, yes! Daddy made sure my brothers and sisters and I were on the right path of thinking as to the evils of slavery—or, I should say, *some* of the evils of slavery…" She blushed and smiled at her husband, "…and the efforts to restore freedom and equal rights to the colored people."

"Mrs. Riegel, I'm afraid your family has been very unusual in their liberal political views. I was raised in that persuasion, as well. Unfortunately, we are much in the minority. Even our dear Mr. Lincoln was not a believer in Negro equality."

Nancy frowned and thoughtfully tapped her cheek lightly with her fan. "I am astonished you say that, really. While I don't remember hearing father say anything about it, the President seemed to be such a kind and decent man. I have difficulty believing he would not extend that compassion to the dark races."

"That may well be, and you certainly knew him better than I, since I never had the privilege of meeting the great man, but I followed his campaigns and presidency carefully, and I know for a fact in '58 he gave a speech at a political rally and said that he had never been in favor of social and political equality, nor allowing Negroes to vote or hold office, nor to intermarry with white people.

"He said—let's see, how did he put it. He said as long as both races remained in the United States, there must be the position of superior and inferior and he, as much as any other man, was in favor of having the superior position assigned to the white race.

"Now I suppose it could have been as much for political expediency—to garner the middle-of-the road voters who would not, under any other circumstances, go to a Republican agenda. But, still, it did set the tone of race relations."

Nancy looked thoughtfully at Mahlon and nodded reluctantly in agreement. "I do remember when the Emancipation Proclamation was signed in sixty-two, father said the President did it more to keep England out of the war than to free the slaves."

"That's right. Because of their investment in and dependence on cotton, England was threatening to join with the South, and through the Proclamation the President was able to change the perception and focus of the war from states' rights to slavery. And since England had long ago abolished slavery, it could not very well join the war in its defense."

Mahlon took a drink of coffee and continued. "Now that the war is won, though, there is still a great deal of work to be done. Freeing the slaves was simply the beginning, I'm afraid. Now we shall have to educate them, find work—or try to persuade them against leaving the farms. The Negro still cannot vote or own property, as far as I know. The country will have much to fix."

He suddenly sat up. "I just thought of something."

"What's that, Mahlon?"

"Well, it is said one of the motives for Mr. Wellings to have murdered his wife was inheritance of the property at Canada Hill. But, if he cannot legally own property—or could not when she died—they cannot ascribe that motive to him. Interesting. Well, I'm anxious to learn more about them and what their life was like. I'll be taking some trips out to the country to talk with the neighbors and witnesses. Perhaps you would like to come along, to see some of our beautiful Bucks County. We could go over to New Hope, and you can see the canal."

"Oh, I would so love that, Mahlon!" Nancy exclaimed and sat up.

Mahlon smiled at his wife. "I thought so, Mrs. Riegel. I can just as easily rent a carriage at Brower's as well as a horse. Now, for today, we are scheduled to see Reverend Andrews this afternoon. You will be prepared to go?"

"Oh, yes," Nancy replied eagerly. "I'll be ready."

Mahlon had sent a note to Reverend Andrews by yesterday's post with their intentions of calling the next afternoon to present Nancy's removal letter from the Washington church to the Doylestown Presbyterian Church, which asked that the Doylestown congregation extend "the right hand of fellowship to Mrs. Riegel." It was a formality, but where one attended church spoke a great deal about one's acceptance into society, and Nancy was eager to be accepted. Mahlon had not seriously attended any church since college, but, because he had known and worked with Reverend Andrews for several years, it was his intention to now join his wife's denomination.

"Do you mind if we walk to the church?" asked Mahlon, "Or would you prefer that I hire a carriage?"

"Oh, let's walk," said Nancy, "that is, if you think your leg will stand it."

"I think so. I did fine yesterday. We'll just take it slowly."

Nancy was reassured. "Good. It's such a lovely day. And I want to show off my new parasol that matches my linen dress perfectly." Prior to the war, cloth manufacturers developed a process of turning flax into a fabric called linen, and, because cotton was such a scarce commodity during the war, linen had become a popular substitute. And, Nancy was well trained that it was improper for a lady to leave her home without a hat, gloves and parasol.

"Very well. There's a shop on the way I would like to stop and visit. It's a toy and candy store, and the owner is Mrs. Wellings' brother. About the only member of the family left in Doylestown, apparently."

That afternoon, they walked leisurely the three blocks to Amos Stone's store, meeting several neighbors along the way. Mahlon was proud to show off his bride. Several people stopped to greet them, and many promises of "come to call" were exchanged.

Mr. Stone's store consisted of the front room of a small, two-story house at the lower point of an "X" intersection of West Court and West State. As Mahlon and Nancy entered the shop, a little bell over the door rang, and a lady came out from the back room and greeted them.

"Is Mr. Stone available?" asked Mahlon.

"Just a moment," she replied. She went back to the door. Mahlon and Nancy could hear her speaking to someone, obviously Mr. Stone. "There's a gentleman and lady here asking for you. No, I don't know who they are."

She came back immediately and said, "He'll be right with you."

Presently, a man emerged from the back room, a short, stout fellow with light-colored, receding hair. As he put his jacket on and pulled a napkin from his collar, he nodded at Mahlon and said, "Good afternoon. I am Amos Stone. May I help you?"

Mahlon extended his card, and introduced himself and Nancy. "I've been away in the war for two years. I don't recall this shop being here when I left."

"It is new. We moved up from Newtown in '64."

"Well, let me tell you what I am here for. May I speak freely?" Mahlon asked.

Amos nodded and replied, "This is my wife. You may say what you have to say in her presence."

"Very well, thank you. I'm here about your sister, Mrs. Wellings, and her husband."

Amos sighed and frowned. He looked away and closed his eyes for a few seconds. "Are you a lawyer or something? Am I compelled to speak to you?" he asked.

"No, no. I'm working for the *Intelligencer*. Mr. Darlington told me of your relation to the deceased and asked me to call on you. See if you could fill me in on any of the details of the case."

Mr. Stone was visibly not happy. "Really, Mr...." He looked at the card. "Lieutenant Riegel, we really don't have much to say about it. I've already told the lawyers everything I know. 'Far's I'm concerned, my sister 'made her bed' and she's been lying in it ever since, may she rest in peace." He looked down at the floor thoughtfully.

"So you didn't approve of her marriage?" Mahlon asked

"It doesn't matter what I approved or not. Our father did not approve. It created a terrible upheaval in our family for many years and has been a source of embarrassment for us ever since. I would truly appreciate it if you would kindly leave us in peace."

Mahlon nodded. "I understand. I won't trouble you further." He suddenly noticed the black cloth armband sewn on Amos' jacket. "I'm sorry, did you have another death in the family, sir?"

"Our son—our only child, Thomas, was killed in the war." Amos pointed up to a small display on the wall with a young soldier's picture arranged with a small flag and military mementoes. "He was...at... I'm sorry, it's still difficult for us to talk about it."

"Please, sir, I understand."

Amos smiled. "Maybe you knew him. Thomas Chapman Stone. He was in Company C of the Fifth U.S. Artillery almost from the beginning—August sixty-one. He fell at Spottsylvania Court House, Virginia."

"No, I was with the cavalry. I don't think I knew your son. Please accept my condolences." Mahlon suddenly remembered, "Oh, that was in May last year, wasn't it? I was wounded just before that battle. We were on our way to Spottsylvania when I got hit at the Wilderness."

"I'm sorry," Amos said. He looked at the card again. "But my brother was with the Eighteenth! Surely you knew him—Reuben Stone."

"Private Reuben Stone from Newtown? He's your brother? I didn't make the connection. For goodness sake. But now that I look at you I can see the family resemblance."

Amos nodded. "We were all living in Newtown when the war started. His wife, Emily, took the children to live with her family in Mount Holly, New Jersey, when Reuben joined up, and then he went there when his service ended. You know, he took sick with the fever pretty bad, lost the use of an eye. He was just released from the hospital recently."

"I didn't know. Mount Holly, you say," said Mahlon. "I have cousins over there. Perhaps I'll take Mrs. Riegel to visit and see your brother while I'm there. Are there any other family around?"

Amos shook his head. "No, my wife and I are about the last of the family left here." He thought for a second. "Well, there is another matter you're undoubtedly going to find out about, so I mind's well be the one to tell you. My brother Hiram had two wives. His first wife, Sarah Closson Stone—we call her 'Sally'—and their child Susan Augusta still live here in Doylestown. Sally is housekeeper for Reverend Andrews over at the Presbyterian parsonage."

Mahlon was visibly taken aback. "Why, another coincidence! We are just this moment on our way to call on Reverend Andrews. Do you think she will speak to me?"

Mrs. Stone, who had been standing quietly at the counter a few feet away from her husband, suddenly spoke up. "Oh, no! Please, sir, I wouldn't even ask her, if I was you. She's real sensitive on the subject of the Stone family. She's friendly with us and all, and we've come to care for Augusta a great deal, but don't talk to her about the rest of the family."

"I understand," said Mahlon, respectfully. "I won't even let on that I know of her connection to the family."

"We appreciate that," said Amos. "You and the missus will have to come back. Do you have children?"

Nancy blushed, and Mahlon said, "No, no children yet. We were just married last December. But I have no doubt we will patronize your establishment when we do."

The two men shook hands. Mahlon thanked Mr. and Mrs. Stone for their time and offered his condolences again as they left the shop.

The walk to the Presbyterian Church and parsonage took Mahlon and Nancy east on Court Street across Main Street, as Mahlon pointed out to Nancy some of the sights—Brower's Hotel, the old Magill Mansion House, now a hotel, the Court House, the lawyers' offices, and the *Intelligencer* and *Democrat* buildings. Everywhere fruit trees, flowering bushes and little yard gardens were in spring bloom. The grass on the Court House lawn was a lovely, bright green surrounded by a short wrought iron fence that had within the last few years replaced the original white picket fence.

From the crest of the hill that forms Doylestown, Nancy could catch glimpses of the farms stretching out as far as the eye could see to the north and west. She was enchanted with the delightful little town and felt right at home.

Mahlon told her that the Presbyterian Church, built in 1815 by Reverend Uriah Dubois, was perhaps the oldest church in Doylestown still in use, although quite certainly there were other Quaker, Lutheran and various denominations around the county, built as far back as the late 1600s, still in service as houses of worship.

Reverend Andrews greeted Mahlon and Nancy warmly and welcomed them enthusiastically. They sat in his study and sipped tea that Mrs. Stone served from a tray.

After the housekeeper left the room and closed the sliding doors that led from the study to the entry hall, Reverend Andrews turned to Nancy and inquired about her family and where she had grown up, what schools and churches she had attended. He was obviously impressed with the position of her father in Washington and told her he was delighted to have her in his congregation.

He then turned to Mahlon and they began catching up on some of the activities of the past two years of the Library Committee, which he and Mahlon had worked on before Mahlon left for the war. Several moments after Mahlon began to tell Reverend Andrews about his work for the *Intelligencer* on the Wellings case, Mrs. Stone slipped into the room and bent down to whisper something to Nancy.

Nancy smiled, sat up and set her teacup down on the tray. "Mahlon, Mrs. Stone has just informed me that she has some shopping to do and has kindly invited me to go with her. Is it all right?" She turned to the Reverend. "Would you mind?"

"How kind of you, Mrs. Stone," Mahlon said. "That would be very nice." It was very perceptive of Sally Stone to know that Nancy would undoubtedly soon become bored with the men's conversation, if she had not already become so.

Reverend Andrews indicated his approval. "I have another appointment at three. I'm sure you'll be back by then."

Mahlon told Nancy, "If you find anything you would like to buy, just tell the shopkeeper I will settle the bill later." He was confident in making the offer that Nancy would not spend much; his wife was not an extravagant person.

"Mrs. Stone has been a God-send to me and the children since my wife died," Reverend Andrews said after the women left. Mahlon remembered that 1863 had been an eventful year for the pastor. Mrs. Andrews, Martha Matilda DuBois by birth, whom Reverend married in 1833, passed away in April. Their son Robert was in the second Battle of Fredericksburg in May, then went to Denver to take charge of the operation of the new mint established by the government to coin the gold from Pike's Peak.

Mahlon asked, "Did you know she is related to the Wellings woman?"

"Yes," said the pastor, "she told me her husband is…was brother to the deceased. But they were not close. Mrs. Stone and Mrs. Wellings had never met, as far as I know."

"Do you know anything about the case?"

"Not much more than what I read in the *Intelligencer* and the *Democrat*."

"You read both papers?"

"Oh, yes, believe it or not, I have members of my flock on all sides of the political debate! It makes for some, shall we say, 'highly charged' meetings at times." The reverend crossed his arms in front of him palms out as if to ward off an unseen attack, and the men laughed.

"Do you think Wellings is guilty as charged?" Reverend Andrews asked.

"I haven't gotten much into the case as yet. But I heard an extraordinary thing at the District Attorney's office—that there was enough poison in the woman's body to kill two persons. I've written it up into a small article which will be published on Tuesday."

"Really. Well, I guess that shuts it tight, then," said the pastor. "It doesn't matter what I think."

Mahlon nodded. "Sounds like it, from the way Ross' office tells it. I'm going to write up one or two more pieces on the subject, then Mr. Darlington has asked me to cover the trial. He's just thrilled that I know some shorthand from college days."

He paused for a few seconds, then asked. "Can you tell me anything about the Wellings' woman's family? Did Mrs. Stone talk much about her in-laws?"

The reverend frowned a bit and said, "Not much I can talk about. There's some that's public knowledge, but, of course, I can't share the private information."

"Oh, no," Mahlon said immediately, "I certainly wouldn't ask you to betray confidences."

Reverend Andrews told Mahlon a little of the background of the large Stone family, including the fact that Mrs. Wellings' marriage had caused quite a rift in the family for some years. "And, too, Mrs. Stone's own situation."

"How so?" asked Mahlon.

"Well, it seems her husband Hiram had two wives…"

"Yes, I heard that from Amos Stone."

"…at the same time."

"Oh! That's a bit of a predicament. And this Mrs. Stone was the first?"

"Yes. He and Sally were married in eighteen fifty-three by the Reverend McMichael. They then moved out to Illinois, where he apparently abandoned her late in fifty-four, but not before making her pregnant. His second wife, Hannah Roberts, whom he married in August eighteen fifty-five had already had a child in March of that year here in Pennsylvania—no proof it was Hiram's, but he took responsibility. Susan Augusta was born to Sally in August eighteen fifty-five in Elgin, Illinois. Then Sally shows up here from Illinois with the baby expecting to rejoin her husband, and finds him married to another woman who has had a child."

Mahlon was visibly confused. "My goodness, what a mess! How did it turn out?"

"Sally came to us in pitiful condition, and we took her and the baby over to Wilhelmina Morris, who took them in, and Mrs. Stone worked for her for some years. At one point, in, I think it was fifty-eight, she went and saw a lawyer who filed a divorce petition on her behalf. But I don't think it was ever finalized. Either the court could not get jurisdiction, as Mr. Stone was living by that time in New Jersey—just across the river, actually, in Lambertville—or because Mrs. Stone dropped it. She did say to me at one time that she considered him a bigamist and she wanted criminal justice, not a civil divorce."

"Fascinating," said Mahlon. "So where is he now, do you know?"

"From what we hear, he's back in Illinois—in Kane County—living with the second wife, Hannah, and their children. I think they've got four children now."

"And did she ever share with you how it all happened?"

"Well, yes, and it's confidential. Suffice it to say that about five years ago Mrs. Andrews and I welcomed her and little Augusta into our home and they have a home with us for as long as they desire. Augusta is almost ten years old now and a star pupil at Linden Academy. She's a wonderful child, almost one of our family. Hiram will no doubt one day have to face our Maker and confront the facts of how he's neglected and mistreated these two."

"I see," said Mahlon. "That's very kind of you, I must say, to take them in. You know what suddenly struck me. Wasn't Illinois where the Mormons were so strong back about that time? And didn't their leader sanction polygamy? I'm thinking maybe Hiram got caught up with them and got illusions he was going to have himself two wives!"

Reverend Andrews laughed. "Well, again, I can't comment on that. But, you're right that's where the Mormons were before they went out to Utah *en masse*, but it was somewhat before Hiram and Sally arrived in Illinois. And that reminds me, the subject of the multiple wives has come up rather frequently recently in the *Intelligencer*. There was just a funny story the other day, in fact, something to the effect that their correspondent in Utah was dispatched to take a count of how many wives Brigham Young really has. He wrote back that he'd run out of multiplication tables trying to count all the ladies bloomers' on the laundry lines at Young's home!"

Mahlon laughed. "I think that's somewhat of an exaggeration."

"Oh, undoubtedly so, but, all the same there are some fellows out there with ten and more wives. I just don't know how they can keep up…. Oh, pardon the pun!" Reverend Andrews unconsciously blushed, and the men chuckled at the unintentional risqué humor.

"Well, seriously, though," Reverend Andrews continued, "you know the Mormons—or Latter-day Saints, as they prefer to be called—were part of a tremendous religious fervor that was going around the country—indeed, the civilized world—at that time."

"How's that?"

"Well, I've done something of a little study—a time line, if you will—about religion over the last forty years or so and have found a number of interesting things. The Mormons began in the early eighteen forties, like the Millerites—do you know about the Millerites?"

Mahlon shook his head no. "I've heard the name, but I don't know much about them."

"It was a very large group of people—I've heard estimates of anywhere from fifty thousand up to a million, which I find hard to believe—who followed the teachings of William Miller, a Baptist lay preacher, that the world was going to come to an end in eighteen forty-four and Jesus would return. He convinced a great many of them to sell their property, and I believe they went up on a Mount Carmel in New York State all decked out in white robes to await the arrival of the Messiah—or maybe it was here in Pennsylvania. Anyway, of course, no such thing happened, and they call it 'the Great Disappointment'. It was quite tragic, actually. Some of these people had sold or given away everything, believing that money and possessions were no longer necessary when Christ came to rule again. But this was quite typical of the religious fervor of the time. I've just recently heard about a group of Germans called the Knights Templar who are preparing to go to Mount Carmel in the Holy Land to await the return of Jesus."

"That's absurd, don't you think?"

"Yes, of course, but I can certainly see their point, yearning for our Lord to return to us—it's been over fifteen hundred years since He made the promise. And there is some validity of how they came up with the calculation of the year, but obviously it didn't happen, or perhaps not the way they expected it. And each had his own opinion as to how it would happen. Some said He would come standing on a cloud and appear to everyone around the earth at the same time. Others said there must be a horrible conflagration accompanying his return—Armageddon. There's a few die-hards in all of these groups who still cling to the prophecies, though have had to adjust the timing. The Miller group was transformed into what they call the 'Seventh-day Adventists' about two years ago."

Reverend Andrews caught Mahlon's sight squarely to give his next point more emphasis. "Did you know, there was even a mention in the Congressional record back in eighteen forty-four that, the return of our Lord being imminent, Congress would most definitely want to invite Him to speak to a joint session."

"No!" Mahlon was astounded. "Don't say. I never heard of such a thing!"

"Oh, yes. It's in the books. You can read it for yourself. In our own community, there was a religious 'renewal', if you will, back in the thirties and forties, especially among the Baptists and the Methodists. Even the Quakers went through a tremendous commotion with the teachings of Mr. Hicks. The new Hicksite denominations took over most of the Friends' meetinghouses and the former, what they call 'Orthodox', were forced to build new facilities. It really became quite heated and challenged the pacifist nature of the sect for a time."

Mahlon nodded. "Henry Darlington just told me a little about the Hicksites."

Reverend Andrews continued, "You know, old Jacob Stone—Hiram's and Mrs. Wellings' father—and his wife were caught up in that religious fervor, too. Almost the whole family became Baptists in the late 1840s. Old Jacob himself was baptized, along with hundreds of others, by Reverend Heman Lincoln, a particularly charismatic preacher at the New Britain Baptist Church. He doubled the size of the church during his pastorship, and when he left around eighteen fifty—to go to Providence, I believe—I remember the house was packed for his last sermon, with more waiting outside. Several people were openly weeping." The pastor took on a look in his eyes that meant he was lost in thought momentarily.

"What was the family before?" asked Mahlon, bringing Reverend Andrews out of his memories.

"Pardon?"

"I say, what was the Stone family before they became Baptists?"

"Oh, undoubtedly Lutherans, like most of the early Germans here—Lutherans or Catholics. Well, and then the Mennonites and Dunkers, but they generally keep off to themselves. A great many of the other Germans and Swiss have drifted to other religions, like yourself.

"By my own estimate, Reverend Lincoln was known to have baptized and converted hundreds," Andrews continued, obviously in awe of his Baptist counterpart. "I would love to know how he did it, what his secret was. He would have these mass baptisms in the Neshaminy. It was an incredible sight. The buggies were lined up and down the roads. The new converts were in white robes standing in the creek waiting to be touched by Pastor Lincoln and immersed. And he could certainly 'preach up a storm', as they say. It spawned a rather funny joke at the time." Andrews looked up to see if Mahlon was interested in hearing the joke.

"What's that?"

"Well, it was said that during one of these mass baptisms, Reverend Lincoln was preachin' and quoting the Bible with the converts standing nearly waist deep in the creek when suddenly one of them started hoopin' and hollerin' and jumping all about.

"'Praise the Lord,' Pastor Lincoln cried. 'Good Brother Johnson's been moved by the Spirit today.'

"'No, sir,' came the reply, 'been bit by a snappin' turtle!'"

Mahlon laughed heartily at the joke, picturing this poor fellow jumping out of the creek with a turtle on his toe.

"So you say that Mrs. Wellings' father, Jacob, was one of these converts?"

"Oh, yes, it made quite a difference in his life, as well. One can say he was figuratively 'born again' as Jesus says in the Bible, 'Except a man be born again, he cannot see the kingdom of God.' It was his wife, Mary, who first began going to the church. Old Jacob was not happy at all about religion of any kind for some reason. Mrs. Stone was a heartsick woman, who desperately needed the solace of the Lord. You see, Jacob had a terrible temper..."

"Probably just like my father," Mahlon interrupted.

"Undoubtedly," Reverend Andrews said. "Quite common among the German men." He smiled at Mahlon. "Before that time, he had managed to alienate almost every one of his children—there were seventeen of them, you know..."

Mahlon nodded. "So Mr. Darlington said."

"Mrs. Stone, as I said, missed her children and by then there were several grandchildren she had never seen. She had one of the elders of the church, John Riale, come and talk with Jacob. It took some time, but Mr. Riale was able to effect a tremendous change in Jacob's heart."

"That's wonderful," said Mahlon. "I'll bet he died a peaceful man."

"Yes, one can only hope so. I understand he wrote letters to as many as he could reach asking for their forgiveness and forgiving them—'Forgive us our sins, as we forgive our sinners.' Mr. Riale and Reverend Lincoln helped him understand the relationship of forgiving and being forgiven and going to our Lord cleansed of any defilement on our hearts."

"And Mrs. Stone? What became of her?" asked Mahlon.

"Well, let's see. Jacob died in about forty-eight. Mrs. Stone stayed on the place for a while. In fact, one of her daughters, I can't remember which, married their next-door neighbor, Owen Swarts. He was somewhat older than she, a widower with several small children. They moved out to Illinois."

"Like so many thousands have left Bucks County, it seems," Mahlon observed.

"Yes, yes, quite so," said Reverend Andrews. "I've often thought that just about everyone in this country has passed through Bucks County at one time or another on their way to somewhere else. Why, I'll venture that my congregation has done an almost complete turnover in my years here, so many have moved away and migrated west.

"Anyway, to answer your question about Mrs. Stone, after her children moved on and married, she went to live with several of them in turn—a few months with this one, a few months with another. Mrs. Stone—Sally—told me that her mother-in-law just passed away a couple of years ago."

Reverend Andrews reached over to the tray and poured fresh tea for himself and Mahlon.

"So," Reverend Andrews continued. "Are you ready to talk about your experiences in the war? Do you want to tell me about it?"

"If you don't mind listening," answered Mahlon. "I've never really talked about it except with some of the other fellows in the hospital."

Reverend Andrews nodded and sat back to listen.

"Well," Mahlon began at the beginning, "as you know, I joined the Eighteenth with several other men from Bucks County, some from Philadelphia, and several other counties. We initially rendezvoused at Camp Curtin, where we trained briefly. They gave us horses but no equipment. We then moved to a camp near Bladensburg, Maryland, where we were partially armed, unfortunately with outdated and inferior weapons, and commenced drilling. Our first duty was to picket the long line covering the defenses of Washington on the Virginia shore. We were constantly harassed by Confederate soldiers at night who then fled back to their farms and posed as 'innocent' civilians during the day.

"Let's see—yes, it was at that time that the regiment became associated with a brigade of Michigan troops under the command of Lieutenant Colonel George Custer. I remember him particularly because of his incredible head of blond hair and his particularly meticulous and flamboyant manner of dress. We were employed with his troops for a time in guarding the gaps of the Blue Ridge.

"By the summer of sixty-three, we joined the Army of the Potomac under the command of General Kilpatrick and were assigned to Hanover, Pennsylvania, to search for the rebel General Jeb Stuart who was known to be moving through Pennsylvania attempting to locate and reunite with General Lee since they had become separated some months previous. It was then that we were surprised by a rear attack from Stuart who drove us almost through the town before we could find room to turn and face him. We managed to hold the center of town, while Kilpatrick mounted a line of battle on the hills south of town. We kept this up all day, until Stuart eventually retired."

Reverend Andrews said, "I understand that engagement had a significant impact on Gettysburg."

"Yes, I heard the same thing. Apparently because we were successful in stalling Stuart at Hanover, he was unable to join General Lee at Gettysburg. In the Hanover engagement, I remember there were four killed and several wounded, and the horse I had been given in Maryland was shot. I found out later that when the town was cleaned up, the camp cook butchered the carcass for the men to eat."

Reverend Andrews wagged his head sadly. "I'm sorry to hear that."

"Oh, I had long before stopped asking what dinner was or where it came from. We were lucky to have any meat at all. But, still…"

"You had become attached to this horse?"

"Yes, for a while there, I had become very attached, almost as if he could magically protect me somehow from harm. I spent a lot of time grooming him. I even gave him a name, which they told us not to do…. Anyway, from Hanover we headed to Gettysburg. The heavy fighting had already begun by the time we got there, so General Kilpatrick moved the troops to the extreme left of the field around Round Top. We struck the rebels' right wing and were hotly engaged in that battle for the entire day. We managed to drive the rebels in upon the main line, but were unable to dislodge them from behind stone walls and rocky, wooded heights. As night fell, the bombardment and rifle firing died out, and the rain began pouring in torrents. It was incredible. The creeks and streams were literally running with blood. I remember thinking it was as if God Himself was weeping for the fallen and trying to wash the scene of man's inhumanity to his fellow man. There was no sleeping that night. We could hear the screams and groans of the wounded all night through the rain."

Reverend Andrews closed his eyes and grimaced at the thought of what Mahlon was telling him. "I'm so sorry," he whispered.

"That's not the half of it, Reverend," said Mahlon. "In the morning I witnessed something that will stay impressed in my memory for the rest of my life. One of the Confederate boys had apparently fallen wounded near a spot in a meadow where there was a small patch of violets growing. The poor fellow, probably no more than sixteen or seventeen years old, had been crawling around the dead littered about him gathering violets and had already made a beautiful bouquet when we found him.

"By this time, I was getting so sick and fed up with this damnable war! It was as if the souls of a million men were hounding me day and night. It really came to a head in the following days. Can I confess to you that there were several times when I just felt like jumping on a horse and running as fast as I could—as far as I could—away from the insanity?"

Reverend Andrews nodded. "I understand, son, and, believe me, I don't blame you."

"Well," Mahlon continued, "I was beginning to think I was a coward."

"What happened next?"

"After Gettysburg—I remember it was early on the morning of July 4—Kilpatrick ordered us to follow Lee's army who were attempting to retreat south through Maryland. We found the flank near Monterey Springs, as the rebels were crossing South Mountain, and charged. They were pretty worn out, too, and we managed to scatter the train guard and capture a couple of pieces of artillery, a thousand prisoners, and two hundred wagons and ambulances. But, somehow—and I still can't figure out how this happened—the main body of the retreating forces came in close behind us on the narrow, steep mountain road, and Kilpatrick, thinking perhaps they were going to charge us from the rear—which was ridiculous, since they were beaten and exhausted—ordered us to race headlong down the mountain with the captured supply wagons and ambulances at break-neck speed. In the middle of the night! Can you imagine? Several of the wagons plunged over the edge to the gorge below, along with horses and occupants. When we finally reached the bottom of the mountain at morning, and the full extent of the carnage was revealed to us, I literally broke down in tears. Captain Ulrich Dahlgren himself came and sat right down beside me on the ground."

Mahlon sighed. "I was crying like a baby. And so ashamed at the same time."

"You mustn't be," said Andrews. "I'm sure it happened to a lot of men."

"Yes, that's what Captain Dahlgren said. I told him I didn't feel very soldierly at that point. He reassured me. 'You're a good soldier,' he said, and that I was undoubtedly suffering from exhaustion and a culmination. It had all built up to that point—like a dam filled to overflowing."

"Sounds reasonable," agreed Reverend Andrews.

"But, I haven't been able to figure out why I would mourn these Confederate soldiers out of all of them that I had seen killed."

Reverend Andrews thought for a few seconds, and offered, "Perhaps because they were wounded and lying in the ambulances, they were defenseless and helpless. They were 'out of commission'—not the fierce rebel fighter you were accustomed to looking at down the barrel of your rifle. And, do you remember thinking at all that perhaps the boy with the violets might be part of the train?"

Mahlon considered this idea. "You could be right. I hadn't thought of that before or put the two together, but after seeing the boy with the violets, I was in danger of seeing these men not as soldiers, but as flesh and blood men with feelings, a lot of them just scared young kids. If I had indulged that thinking, that probably would've finished me off, but good. Finally, with Captain Dahlgren's help, I was able to compose myself. At least he convinced me I was not suffering a nervous breakdown, and after a few moments of rest, I got up and joined the other men laying out the dead. We then burned the wagons, which were surprisingly still in moving condition, so that the rebels behind us could not use them."

Reverend Andrews quietly offered a thin cigar to Mahlon, which he refused, and lit one for himself. "My only vice," Reverend Andrews said with a mischievous wink.

Mahlon continued, "Let's see, next we moved on to Boonesboro where we delivered the surviving prisoners to General French's infantry and then to Hagerstown, where we found the head of the enemy's column. Two battalions were ordered to charge and we succeeded in driving them through the town, but we suffered some terrible losses by having to fight with sabers, in a narrow street, while the enemy was using pistols. Captain Lindsey was killed, and Captain Dahlgren was wounded in the leg and later lost it. But he came right back and kept on fighting. Amazing man.

"At Hagerstown, one of my most vivid memories of the fighting was seeing the color bearer of Company A shot dead, yet still in death he managed to hold the standard aloft, so tight was his grip on the staff.

And Sergeant Brown of Company B was shot in the back by a woman who fired on him from a window."

Pastor Andrews lowered his head and sighed a great sigh. "The depravity of these people using a woman to fight," he said.

"I could have shot her easy enough," said Mahlon, "but I hesitated just long enough for her to duck back into the house. I was angry with myself for wanting to shoot her, then for not doing it when I had the chance!

"During the fight, Companies L and A were ordered to charge into the center of the town to test the enemy's strength. Unfortunately, they discovered that the rebels held two major cross streets, and few of our men returned. Kilpatrick had ordered that the rebels be held at all cost until the pontoon bridge at Williamsport could be destroyed, thus holding up their retreat, but we were not successful and the main force was able to cross the river back into Virginia. The rest of the summer and fall was spent chasing them down, scouting and skirmishing. During that time, Major Van Voorhis, three lieutenants and about fifty men were captured. I was the only one with a college education who had been with the unit from the beginning, so they made me a lieutenant."

"Now, Mahlon, I can't believe that's the only reason you were chosen," Reverend Andrews interjected. "Surely you had displayed some leadership capabilities."

Mahlon shook his head. "I don't think so. In fact, in November, scouting across the Rapidan River, we were surprised by a large rebel force. Lieutenant Sellers was killed, and Captain Kingsland, who was in command, was severely wounded. A number of officers and men were captured, and the camp equipage and regimental colors were lost. It was a horrible humiliation for us—for me.

"We withdrew to winter quarters near Stevensburg, until the end of February last year when the regiment was called out by General Kilpatrick to accompany him on the most hair-brained scheme you ever heard of. He had it in his head to raid Richmond—the rebels' capital city—to rescue the Union prisoners being kept there, we had heard under the most dreadful conditions."

"Richmond!" Reverend Andrews said somewhat dismayed. "Why, not even Grant would venture that until this year."

"Precisely," said Mahlon. "Of course, the plan failed. We were miserably defeated, and it was a tremendous personal loss for me that Dahlgren, who was still commanding on horseback despite the loss of his lower leg, was among those killed."

"I'm sorry," the pastor said sincerely.

"Well, as you can imagine, General Kilpatrick was relieved of command and succeeded by General Wilson. We were allowed to camp and rest for a while. It was fairly quiet during the spring with the exception of a skirmish near Fox's Ford in April... Oh, and terrible weather—all I remember is rain, rain, rain all March and April. Everything sopping wet for weeks. In early May, we formed up with the remnants of a couple of other regiments and were ordered to lead the advance from Germanna Ford to Wilderness Tavern in the general direction of Orange Court House. On May 5 we met the Confederate forces—we learned later commanded by General Tosser—and were able to drive them back into their infantry supports, which were commanded by General Longstreet."

Mahlon sat up and moved his hands on the desk to illustrate the scenario. "Apparently, the way we've been able to reconstruct it, the combined rebel force, attempting to retreat and reconnect with the main body of General Lee's army, moved down a side road that intersected in a 'T' the one on which we were marching. We didn't realize it and continued right on by thinking they were still ahead of us on the same road.

"General Wilson then ordered the division to fall back, with the exception of the Eighteenth. Colonel Brinton was left in charge, and we were directed to hold the ground in case the Confederates recouped and came back. Then we were to rejoin the main force in half an hour. We waited and watched, and at the appointed time began our march back up the road and quickly realized the rebels were indeed returning, but between us and the rest of our division, not down the road, as we had supposed. We were cut off from General Wilson and the main body."

Pastor Andrews sat up. "What did you do?"

"Well, Colonel Brinton saw that the odds were overwhelming, that if we stood and fought we would assuredly be killed or captured. He realized our only hope of escape was through the pine forest to our right. But, it was so thick and overgrown with shrubs that the horses could not press through and had to be abandoned. He passed the word and, at a given signal, we plunged into the woods, hacking at the dense brush with our sabers and knives. The Confederates were close behind us, and managed to kill or wound a few of the stragglers. It was the most terrifying thing I had ever experienced. I felt as if every branch of every tree was enfolding me somehow. It was like I was tied down and couldn't move fast enough."

Mahlon paused for a moment and shivered slightly as the memories came flooding back.

"As if that wasn't bad enough, when we came out of the pine thicket, we found a swamp directly ahead. We had no choice but to continue on or surrender, and the latter was just not in our realm of reasoning. Several of the men became entangled in the muck and mire. Others lost their balance and their weapons got wet. It was awful difficult slogging through."

By this time, Reverend Andrews was so thoroughly engrossed in the story that he almost failed to notice the live cigar ash ready to fall on the carpet. Mahlon motioned to him and he cupped his hand under the ash over to the ashtray.

"Go on. I'm sorry," he said.

"Well, we finally reached the far bank, took cover in the woods and from that vantage point were able to hold our pursuers in the swamp until dark when they decided that going back was the smarter plan than coming towards us. We were able to make our escape minus thirty-nine men killed, wounded or captured, and one officer—me—wounded. Sometime during the fighting in the swamps of the Wilderness, I caught a bullet in the thigh, which nearly shattered my leg, then went through the head of Private Jenkins, killing him instantly."

"Good God!" Reverend Andrews exclaimed. "That must've been at some close range."

"Oh, yes. The rebel just seemed to pop up from nowhere. I looked him right in the eyes. I don't think I will ever forget his face as long as I live."

"How did you get out?"

"Well, apparently as evening came on, and the rebels fell back, Colonel Brinton had time to make out some directions, and he realized we had come through the pine thicket, the swamp and the woods on a diagonal to within half an hour's walk from the division, which was camped near Old Wilderness Tavern. When we straggled into camp that night, I recall vaguely we were received with shouts of rejoicing. Because we hadn't shown up at the appointed time, and they could hear the guns firing all afternoon, apparently our entire regiment had been reported lost or captured. I heard later that a bottle of wine was sent to Colonel Brinton on which was attached a note, 'To the Eighteenth Pennsylvania Cavalry, which knows how to fight into and how to fight out of a hard place.' Now, mind you, I was told all this later. I don't remember much after coming out of the swamp.

"The camp doctors tried to dress my wound as best they could, but apparently they had few supplies and pitiful equipment at their disposal. There was no medicine left by that time, but some whiskey to dull the pain. The next morning they put me in a train of ambulances with some forty or more other wounded. We started on the road across Ely's Ford, but were attacked and turned back. We then went to Fredericksburg, where I understand almost every house had been converted to a hospital. Within a day I was placed on a train and taken to Armony Hospital in Washington. I found out later there were 1,600 other soldiers in just that hospital alone. They had beds lined up in hallways, mostly just make-shift cots."

"I know, the numbers are staggering—killed, wounded..." Reverend Andrews said sadly.

"So, the doctors managed to repair my leg somewhat, but infection set in and I became inflamed with fever. The doctors were not sure I would survive, let alone save the leg. It was touch-and-go for two months. I remember coming around once in a while, and I would know a lot of time had passed because there were all different fellows in the surrounding beds and sometimes I was in a different place in the hospital altogether.

"Finally, I began to recover, very weak and slow for a long time. The fever seemed to have robbed me of my senses, but the doctors say it turned out to be the best thing since it allowed my leg to heal."

"Are you completely healed? I mean, will your leg..." the reverend asked.

"Oh, I don't think it will be one hundred percent healed, ever. There was quite a bit of bone shattered, apparently. But, I'm alive. I can walk. I've still got all my limbs. A heck of a lot luckier than most, I suppose. They're still not sure I can ever have children though."

"Oh?"

"It seems a piece of bone penetrated one of my testicles, although they were able to repair it. And then, too, there's the fever. The doctors are not sure what affect that would have."

"I see. We will certainly pray that you are healed in that respect. And, praise be to God that He has brought you through," said the pastor. "Now, with time, we can hope to heal your spirit which has undoubtedly been sorely wounded, as well."

"Yes," Mahlon agreed. "I still wake up in the middle of the night sometimes apparently dreaming about something that's still tormenting me. Nancy says at times I talk and cry out. But, I am so immensely grateful to have her. I am a very lucky man in that regard."

"Tell me, how did you meet her?"

"Oh, she was a miracle in my life. You talk about a God-send—that was Nancy. One morning—I remember it was a warm, Indian summer day in September—as I lay on a chaise in the sun porch, drifting in and out of sleep, I opened my eyes and blurrily focused on a beautiful face. I was instantly awe-struck. I thought she was an angel come to collect me to heaven!"

Reverend Andrews smiled. "She is indeed a lovely girl."

"She spoke to me. She said 'Good morning' or something, and without waiting for an answer, she continued, 'Would you like me to read to you, or is there someone to whom you wish to write a letter?' She bent a little closer as she spoke, and in the warmth of the sunroom, I could smell her fragrance—roses—and for an instant thought I would swoon right where I lay!"

"Sounds like Cupid got you with his arrow right then and there!" Reverend Andrews smiled.

"It must've been so," Mahlon said, "as I had never before been the least interested in a female, I was so shy. Well, there was one lady— Lizzie Aldrich—a fellow teacher, do you remember her?"

"I do," Andrews said. "Didn't she end up with consumption? She passed away in New York State somewhere a couple of years ago?"

"Yes, an ill-fated attraction at that."

"That's a shame." The reverend wagged his head. "So, back to Nancy. What did you do?"

"Well, you can imagine, I was so stunned, about all I could manage was a deep sigh and moan, which apparently sounded to her very much like a groan of pain. 'Oh, I'm so sorry, Lieutenant!' she said. 'You seem to be in pain. Please forgive me for disturbing you.' And she started to walk away. I cried out 'No, please stay!'—in time, thank God."

Reverend Andrews chuckled appreciatively at the description.

"From that day on, she came to the hospital as often as possible. As soon as I was well enough, she arranged for me to meet her parents. I found out later that when Nancy declared her intentions to her father, he made a discrete investigation into my background and financial prospects, so that when we asked his permission, he was ready with his approval. We were married in a quiet Christmas ceremony in the home, with just her family present. And that's it."

"That is really sweet," Reverend Andrews smiled. "I'm so very happy for you that God has singled you out for this special girl."

"Oh, and I, too. Believe me, every moment with Nancy has been heavenly, a complete dichotomy of the horror I experienced for the past two years. I am beginning to believe I can push away the nightmares and look with hope to the future."

"We will pray so. We will certainly pray so for all of us—that our entire country can be healed, as well. It's going to be a long, hard struggle."

Nancy and Mrs. Stone returned a while later, after Mahlon and Reverend Andrews talked for a few more moments about Mahlon's work for the *Intelligencer* and activities at the church and Doylestown Library Committee, in which Andrews hoped Mahlon would again become involved.

As they were preparing to leave, Rev. Andrews said suddenly, "Oh! I just remembered. I knew another one of the Stone family—Harriet. I performed the marriage ceremony for her and John Hoff, I believe her husband was, oh, way back a number of years, eighteen forty-five or so."

"Are they still around?" Mahlon asked.

"No. I haven't seen them or heard anything in a number of years. They were not members of the church, but his family had attended." Rev. Andrews looked reminiscent. "You know, I've performed over six hundred marriages since I was ordained and installed in this church in eighteen thirty-one."

"Congratulations," Mahlon and Nancy both commented sincerely.

The pastor nodded and smiled. "Yes, I counted them up the other day, and when I report them to the paper, I'm going to begin numbering them."

On their way home, Mahlon asked Nancy, "Did Mrs. Stone mention anything about the family?"

"No, she just pointed out interesting sights and shops to me. She asked me about life in Washington. And she did tell me a great deal about her daughter, Susan Augusta—they call her Augusta. She's a very devoted mother. That always makes me a little uneasy."

"How's that?" asked Mahlon.

"Well, in the back of my mind, I'm always a little frightened that something might happen. You know I had a brother and a sister who died young. I remember mother was nearly devastated with grief each time. I just can't imagine how she could have gone on if she hadn't had us to comfort her. But it occurs to me that, while she has always been loving and caring, she has also been somewhat reserved in her relations with us. Not especially affectionate." She looked up at her husband. "Do you know what I mean?"

Mahlon looked questioningly, then pictured his own relationship with his mother. "Yes, I see what you mean. I had always thought my mother's detachment was because of her frail health. But, you say it may have been because she was afraid? That something could happen to me and she could not bear to…"

"Yes," Nancy said. "Just like I can't bear to think of anything happening to you." She looked lovingly into his eyes. Mahlon wanted to enfold her in his arms right there in front of God and everybody, but managed to restrain himself. Instead, he placed her petite, gloved hand in the crook of his arm, and they slowly walked home.

Chapter V

New Hope and Lahaska
1835-1838

The first night of Langhorn and Mary's life together was spent hidden in the woods between Wormansville and the Delaware River. Jumping on his horse, Lang pulled Mary up behind him and started first down the road toward home to Carversville, then changed his mind, thinking they would be sure to search for them first at Carver's, and headed instead down the road leading to the Delaware River.

Unable to see very well in the growing darkness, he finally decided to veer into the woods and found a small clearing with a soft, moss floor and some clean grass for the horse.

"We'd better stay put for now," he said, "and start out early in the morning. They're bound to be out looking for us."

"No, they won't." Mary spoke softly, sadly, yet with confidence. The gravity of what she had done was beginning to sink in. She knew about the practice of shunning, had seen it occur often enough in her twenty-five years, although she was unaware it had happened in her own family with her grandfather forty years before.

Lang sat on the ground and leaned against a small tree. Mary curled her body next to his, and covered her legs with her skirt and petticoat to protect against the mosquitoes. Lang cradled her and tried his best to protect her face with his shirt and large hands. She cried quietly and slept fitfully all night.

She thought about her family, Mama and Papa, her siblings, especially her beloved baby brother and sisters—Rebecca, five, Hiram, three, and Emma, just barely two months old—whom she had helped her mother deliver and cared for since they took their first breaths. Gradually, she came to understand during the night that it was quite possible she would never see them again. *Mein Gott, what have I done?*

There was Grandma Mary Magdalena and Grandpa Peter Trullinger, who lived nearby on their farm. Grandma Elizabeth Stone who lived with Uncle Henry Stone and Aunt Sarah and their family, also in Tinicum. Aunts, uncles and cousins in the Barntz, Trullinger and Stone families lived in just about every farm in this part of Tinicum. She was related, even if distantly, to almost everyone who attended the Lutheran services at the Tinicum Union Church.

She was leaving them all behind. In this one moment of impetuous passion—like a bird flinging itself through the door of its cage, not knowing what is outside the cage yet not wanting to stay inside another second—she had flown and, at the same time, shut the door on everything and everyone she had known her whole life.

She could not go home with Lang, and she could no longer go home without him. She knew she was as if dead to them all forever, and she cried the grief appropriate for the deceased.

All of this mixed with more than a little apprehension about the future, but since it never once occurred to her that her future would be without Lang, whenever she felt anxiety about the unknown, she was able to push it away with thoughts of him. *Lang will take care of me. I am safe with him.*

In the morning, Lang, thinking for the wrong reason she was crying because she was sorry for what she had done, asked if she wanted to go home.

"No. It's done. I can never go home again."

They went out onto the road just after dawn and, indeed, saw that no one was out looking for them. Mary experienced opposing feelings of relief and disappointment upon the realization, filled as she was with conflicting emotions.

Lang at the same time was concerned with his own thoughts all night—worry, fear of the unknown future and the consequences of what they had done, and even exhilaration as these emotions produced adrenalin—all overwhelmed with such love and physical attraction for this small, light-skinned lady that he feared even hugging her, lest he might crush her with his clumsy attentions.

Mary tried to make herself presentable by smoothing her hair back into a bun and straightening her dress. When they arrived at the River Road next to the Delaware Canal, Lang had the presence of mind to get down from the horse and walk ahead, while Mary sat demurely side-saddle to cover her bare feet. One never knew how these canal men would take to seeing a white girl sitting so closely on a horse with a black man. It was best to be safe.

They went at once to a "safe house" that Lang knew about in New Hope in one of the alleys off Mechanic Street, a boarding house for colored canal men and servants run by a mulatto woman who immediately took them in and supplied Mary with clean clothes and shoes.

The landlady had a rather eccentric habit of wagging her head from side to side and murmuring "Uhn, uhn, uhn," always three times. She did it when she was happy with her head up and a big smile lighting her face and with her head down when she was sad. And when she looked at Lang and Mary, she couldn't help but be sad for the young couple, thinking of her own unhappy life as the child of a slave mother and the white overseer rapist.

"Don't nobody dare call *that* man my 'daddy'!" she would vehemently insist. Her mother, clutching her baby to her breast, had escaped from the plantation in Virginia and made her way eventually to Pennsylvania before dropping dead from disease and exhaustion, leaving an orphan daughter to fend for herself. She didn't want to ever think about what she had had to do in the brothels of Bristol and New Hope to make her way in the world before she was able to rent this house.

"You chil'ren just don't know what you're askin' for, that's for sure," she would shake her head and sigh. "Life is hard enough when you're of the same color, for heaven's sake. Ain't nowheres in the world you're gonna be safe, you mind my words."

But Lang and Mary didn't care and would not listen to any negative remonstrations. They were in love, and whenever they were alone together in their room, the rest of the world didn't matter in the least bit. As long as Langhorn's arms were around her, Mary was safe and happy.

Within a few days, they went back up to Tinicum where they were quietly married by the Reverend Miller in the parlor of his small parsonage near the church. He had insisted, when Jacob came storming over to confront him the day after Mary fled, that the marriage was legal and valid in the sight of God—indeed, Mary had been baptized in this church in 1810 and, by God, if Reverend Miller had any say about it, she was going to be married fitting and proper a Christian girl.

So insistent was Mary—twenty-five years old and old enough to make her own decisions—that she and Lang would be together, Reverend Miller told Jacob, "I will not have her living in sin with any man, no matter what his color!" This only infuriated Jacob more and caused a permanent rift between the two men and between Jacob and the church.

"You have destroyed my family and condemned my daughter to God-knows-what kind of life by this terrible, stupid thing you've done!" he shouted at the pastor. "If this is what you call 'religion' I'll have no use of it—ever!"

The couple was not seen by anyone in Tinicum, but it wouldn't have mattered if they were. They had become invisible. Their wedding was celebrated with a little extra cake and wine at the boarding house that night, while the landlady cried happily, at the same time wagging her head sadly. "Uhn, uhn, uhn. You just don't know what you're askin' for," she moaned over and over.

By the time Mary and Langhorn arrived in New Hope in the late summer of 1835, it was a bustling town of paper, fabric and sawmills, canal barges, shops, farmers' markets, inns and travelers. It was first settled in 1710 when Robert Heath, a Scotsman, received a grant of one thousand acres from William Penn and built a gristmill on Ingham Creek.

In the 1720s, John Wells chose the spot to run his ferry across the Delaware. Over the years, it was known by several different names, including Wells' Ferry, Canby's Ferry, and Coryell's Ferry. When a fire destroyed several mills in 1790, Benjamin Parry, one of the owners, decided to rebuild and called it "New Hope Mills." The town was known as New Hope Mills and, eventually, just New Hope from then on.

In the 1820s, New Hope was caught up in the almost frenzied development of Pennsylvania. Canals, turnpikes, bridges, and roads were begun by the hundreds. In 1822, it was estimated that one hundred forty-nine turnpike construction companies, forty-nine bridge companies and eighteen canal companies were in operation. As early as 1818, roads between Philadelphia and other major cities were macadamized.

The sixty-mile long Bristol-Easton branch of the Delaware Canal, passing right through New Hope, was begun on October 27, 1827 with construction on the first eighteen miles from Bristol. The canal was fully opened to New Hope in 1831 and completed to Easton September 1832. It was eventually built in a series of twenty-three lift locks with several aqueducts by which the canal and its traffic crossed small rivers and streams and carried coal, timber and other raw materials from the Lehigh Valley down to Bristol, thence through a tide lock and out into the Delaware.

By 1835, there were hundreds, if not a thousand or more, boats passing each year through the locks at New Hope, the only spot where the barges could pass four-abreast. The canal brought with it to New Hope a booming economy, with its bargemen, called "swampers," mule tenders, businessmen, and travelers.

It also brought with it the usual assortment of hostlers, hustlers, hucksters peddlers, opportunists, thieves, and their ubiquitous retinues, prostitutes.

Lang found New Hope to be a good central base from which to continue his work as a limeburner and hired man on the farms. He was within convenient distance to the quarries and lime kilns that dotted eastern Bucks County. New Hope was an ideal location, being the center of an arc stretching from Yardley to the south, through Newtown, Wrightstown, Wycombe, Buckingham-Lahaska-Holicong, Cross Keys and the farms east of Doylestown and Plumstead, but not quite up to Tinicum. He dared not venture into that vicinity, no matter how often Mary assured him that she and Lang were invisible.

"Maybe you're invisible," he would say, "But they're going to see my black face comin' from miles away!" Lang was probably more accurate than he knew. Just five years after he and Mary ran off, the census in 1840 showed not one Negro living in Tinicum Township, Bucks County, Pennsylvania.

Unfortunately, traveling meant he very often had to be away from Mary for days at a time. Once becoming involved in a job of liming fields, harvesting crops or helping to raise a barn, it was not possible for him to come home each night.

In addition, it was not safe for him to be out alone; it was better that he wait for someone like his friend Andy Hartless with whom to travel. Since the Underground Railroad had begun operating right through Bucks County, the slave catchers and bounty hunters were not far behind.

Mary immediately found work in one of the many mansions and inns that were beginning to be built almost overnight all over New Hope with the advent of the new prosperity brought by the canal. Because she was a German farm girl, she was highly prized as a worker. They knew without asking that she was well trained and accustomed to farm labor. They did not ask the particulars of how she came to be in New Hope.

She often wondered how her employers would feel about her if they knew to whom she was married and where she lived. Undoubtedly, these well-bred, powdered and pampered, indolent ladies of the manor would have opened their eyes wide in astonishment and fluttered their fans with shock at hearing the gossip.

"No! You don't say! Tell me more!" But, it probably would not have mattered much to them, Mary being so much appreciated as a hard worker. And work hard she did—laundry, ironing, sewing, cooking, baking, polishing, dusting, cleaning, primping the ladies, bathing the children—still taking care of other people's children!

On chilly fall days, she had to get up well before dawn, bundle up and walk to her work, and take up whatever chores the live-in help had not begun—stoke up the fires, start the water, bake the bread, prepare the breakfast, start the dough for pies and pastries.

By the time she dragged herself home at night, she was exhausted, almost too exhausted for Lang. More often than not, Lang himself was tired, but on Sunday mornings, whenever he was home, they would relish the time together and the few hours of rest and quiet.

Mary loved to lay in bed with the window of their room open, despite the ever-present stench from the smokestacks of the paper and cloth mills. She wanted to listen to the bells on the bellybands of the mules as they trudged up and down the canal bank hauling the barges. And the cries of the swampers, "Yo, mule! On mule!" in a cadenced sing-song.

She very quickly adapted to and delighted in their intimate relations, much to Lang's happy surprise. She was a virgin when they married, but having grown up on a farm observing literally hundreds of animals conceived and born, Mary was certainly no stranger to sexual relations. Her sensual nature was well developed and well past ready to bloom by the time they married.

However, having been nurtured and protected on her cloistered family farm not twenty miles from the bustling, cosmopolitan town of a thousand people in which she now lived, Mary was an innocent and knew nothing about the "ways of the world." After a few weeks of being around the landlady and the other tenants of the boarding house, and hearing the stories of their travels and experiences, she learned quickly and after a while ceased to be shocked or blush at their rowdy tales.

If the men were not out drinking and gambling, they would wile away the hours of the evening taking turns telling stories. Although she never really became comfortable listening to their bawdy talk, she did grow to enjoy hearing and was not frightened by as she had been initially, their tales about the haunted houses and inns of New Hope.

Mary asked once why it seemed so many of the people never stayed around for more than a day or two.

"Mary, my dear, we thought you knew, this is a jumping-off place"—a station on the Underground Railroad.

"Oh!" Then, "Of course! That makes sense."

She learned the fugitives, called variously "flying bondsmen," "baggage," and "travelers," could usually stay for only a day or two before being "forwarded" to New Jersey and into New England or up through New York State to Canada.

She also learned a great deal more about slavery and the Negro experience in America and was constantly amazed that, while not one of them had a happy story of life to tell—indeed, each one had a heart-wrenching tale of hardship and suffering—nearly every one of them was cheerful, optimistic, kind-hearted and even-tempered, and amazingly accepting of their "lot in life." They firmly believed that, by passing through and enduring the crucible of this life, they would be rewarded and welcomed to heaven, and all of their songs and stories alluded to "the Promised Land bye and bye."

They were also, every one of them, completely taken aback and awed at Mary. "Now, why would a white girl want to associate herself with a colored boy and take on these troubles? This is strange, mighty strange indeed. Must be somethin' wrong with this girl in the haid."

There was some misconduct among them, most often arguments that evolved into fights or petty thefts, and, like their Caucasian neighbors, it was usually associated with bad liquor, fast women and money—or the lack thereof. Lang went "out with the boys" a couple of Saturday nights, while Mary sat home and waited and worried—by this time she had heard some of the stories—but shortly he came to realize that he much preferred to be with Mary over a bunch of boozy men.

One Sunday morning in late September, a beautiful "Indian summer" day, Mary jumped up suddenly and said to Lang, "I want to go out! Let's go over to New Jersey."

She ran to the window. "I'm sick of smelling paper mills and oil lamps and smoke. Let's find some flowers! Lang, get up!"

Lang was not in the least excited by the prospect. They had thus far not been out in public together. His wife had never experienced prejudice and "white fright," had never been the object of staring eyes filled with venom or, worse, bullying and "young-gun" bravado. In the company of her father and brothers, she had been free to go anywhere a lady was allowed, undeterred and unchallenged.

Besides, he was out all the time and wanted to stay home for a change.

"I don't know, Mary," he said cautiously. "I don't think it's such a good idea."

"Oh, what's the harm, you old stick-in-the-mud!" She pounced on him and playfully tickled and wrestled with him.

Eventually, Lang reluctantly agreed they could try walking over the footbridge to Lambertville, even though the toll cost two pennies per person each way. Besides, there was someone there he knew he could talk to about the possibility of getting work on the farms of Hunterdon County.

Mary braided her long hair and wound it into a large bun. She washed herself all over at the wash basin and dressed in her "other" dress for special occasions, complete with a shawl, bonnet, gloves and parasol, the latter two articles being gifts from the landlady, who had come to adore the petite German girl and her handsome husband. She still couldn't help, however, constantly sighing, shaking her head and murmuring, "unh, unh, unh" whenever she saw the couple together.

Out on the street, Lang and Mary were swallowed up in the bustle of people coming and going across the river to church, to visit, and to shop, and were not noticed. Lang thought he saw a flicker of puzzlement cross the face of the toll-gate keeper, but they were quickly through and the gatekeeper was forced to turn his attention to other customers.

Once in Lambertville on the New Jersey side, they turned northward and walked away from the village and into the farmland and woods. Mary was invigorated with the fresh air, the smells of late-season, newly-mown hay, fallen leaves already beginning to form a new blanket on the forest floor, and little streams bubbling toward the Delaware.

The few people they met on the road and paths were alone and, if they were inclined to say anything, apparently declined to do so without the power of numbers behind them.

By mid-afternoon, they had reached Lang's destination, the farm of a Quaker acquaintance of Mr. Carver. Mary waited at the gate while Lang walked up to the house. She could see him talking to the farmer, and then he turned and waved to her to come up.

"Good afternoon, Sister Wellings," the farmer greeted her warmly. "Thee and thy husband are welcome here. Please come and partake of the Seventh-day meal with our family."

The farmer brought them into the main room of the large house. "Good wife," he called. "We have visitors. Please come and make them welcome."

The farmer's wife hurried in from the kitchen, surrounded by an assortment of red-cheeked, tow-headed and barefooted young children, and stopped short at the sight of Mary and Lang.

Her eyes ceased blinking and her mouth opened in shock as her husband continued, "Good wife, this is Friend Langhorn Wellings from across the river and his wife, Sister Mary. He is an apprentice of Brother Carver, and they are friends of Brother Joseph Fell." He spoke calmly, stressing the words "wife," "Carver," "friends," and "Fell."

His own wife understood immediately and recovered her poise. She came toward Mary and taking her hands in a friendly gesture, said with a smile, "Thee are welcome at our table. Please come."

Although the farmer's wife protested, Mary insisted on helping her set the table and bring out the meal, a dizzying assortment of ham, roast beef, chicken, potatoes, carrots, and corn, and freshly-baked bread, followed by just picked berry pies and milk. More members of the large, extended family drifted into the house for dinner.

Lang and the farmer talked throughout dinner about things agricultural and industrial and, after dinner, went out to the barn and outbuildings with some of the other men to look over the stock. Mary and the women chatted for hours during dinner and cleaning up afterwards. Being with the family, and especially around their little children, reminded her of home and eased the pain somewhat of her separation from her own family.

It was a wonderful afternoon, and the time raced by too quickly. Finally, a half-hour or so before the sun went down, Langhorn motioned to Mary that it was time to get back home to New Hope.

By the time they crossed back over the Delaware on the footbridge, it was dark, and they were so tired and relaxed and happy they failed to pay attention to the three men who staggered out of the saloon just behind them on South Main Street. Mary had let her bonnet slip off her head and was too tired to pull it back up, so that her face and hair were visible.

"Well, what have we here?" one of the men said in slurred words. "Why, it's a pretty little German girl and her nigger man. Hey, nigger! C'm'ere, I wanna talk to you!"

"Whaddya you talkin' 'bout? German girls don't have niggers," said another.

Lang stopped short. He felt a flush in his face and the "hairs on the back of his neck stand up." Mary took his arm, "Lang, come on. Don't mind them." They began walking on, but heard the men still behind them.

"Hey, you! Nigger! Din'ju hear wha' I said? Turn 'roun' and look at me when I'm talkin' to you."

Lang gently pulled his arm away from Mary and took a half step in front of her as he turned around to face the men.

"This is my wife. We are legally married," he said. "Kindly let us pass in peace."

"Whoa! Did you hear what I think I heard?" The first man looked at his companions in astonishment.

"This nigger says they's married?" said another. "I don't think so!"

They began advancing toward Lang and Mary in a puffed up, arrogant manner.

"Tha's too much to swallow," said the first man. Never heard'a anythin' so…so…Why, I can't think of what it's so, but I never heer'd of it."

"Tha's fer damn sure!" one of his companions agreed.

Lang stepped fully in front of Mary in a protective motion just as the fist came toward his face. He dodged his head aside, and the drunken man staggered and fell on the pavement. As he struggled to his feet, another man came toward Lang. He raised a powerful arm, caught the man's wrist, twisted his arm slightly, and easily brought him to his knees.

By this time, Mary had backed up several feet and was leaning against the wall, as if trying to crawl inside the bricks, crying, "Lang! No! Stop it!" A crowd began gathering outside the saloon.

Lang was somewhat thankful, yet at the same time filled with dread, when he saw a couple of other Negro men approaching on the east side of Main Street, attracted by the shouts. *Oh, no! Stay away,* he thought to himself. He knew, with these drunken Irishmen itching for a fight, it could easily turn into a "donnybrook," and he had no illusions about which of them would be taken to jail. He lifted his hand ever so slightly to signify stay away, I can handle this.

Fortunately, with Lang's large size and sobriety, he was able to out-power and out-maneuver his smaller, drunken opponents, who began staggering and blustering to such a degree that even their own friends began laughing at them.

"What're ya doin' now?" they cried. "Sure'n you're daft to take on such a big nigger!"

"C'mon. Come 'n have another drink. Calm yerself down."

"You'll be givin' yerself heart failure, you will."

The first man still wanted to fight, yet in his drunken haze was aware enough to understand that he was far out-matched, while his friends had given up much more easily, so that he was deprived of the combined strength of his companions. He still had to express his revulsion at the pair.

He turned toward Mary, who was standing back against the building. Swaying almost to the point of falling, he called out, "Hoorrr!" and spat in her direction. He turned and staggered back into the bar.

Lang straightened his clothing, nodded silently to the black men on the other side of the street and turned to Mary, who was by this time shaking and sobbing with fear. She had never seen any violence like that, had only read about it in books. She knew that men would engage in fist-icuff matches at the county fairs in a separate tent to which the ladies were never admitted, and her brothers were always wrestling and tus-sling, but never with nastiness or anger intent.

Mary didn't know what the words "nigger" and "whore" meant. Lang had to explain for her, since she had never heard of them nor even read them before, but she knew by the evil and hatred in the face of the bearer that they were not meant in kindness.

Theoretically, she should not have been surprised by the behavior of these men. Lang had tried to warn her, yet he resisted saying, "I told you so." Instead, he said resignedly as they started for home, "We'll have to cover you up or go out separately from now on, as long as we're in New Hope."

From that moment on, Mary began to detest New Hope. Every day she found something more to complain about—the people, the stench, the crowded conditions, hard work twelve hours a day, six days a week, for little pay—everything but what was really making her heart ache. Her world was narrowing into the little boarding house off Mechanic Street.

Despite all the obstacles and troubles in the outside world, Mary had always felt comfortable and accepted in the boarding house, until one day, within weeks after the incident with the drunken Irishmen, she overheard a conversation between two colored girls newly arrived from Baltimore.

"Who she think she is, anyway, white girl, struttin' herself, takin' our man?"

"They so few of 'em, 'n she go 'n take the cream o' the crop. He shor is a fine-lookin' man!"

"You said that, sister! Good man, hard workin', too. No lazy bones in that fine man. I'd shor like to get my hands on them bones!" The girls bumped together playfully and giggled behind their hands as they walked down the hall.

Langhorn laughed it off as silly girl talk when Mary told him about the incident. He'd been used to that reaction from girls since he was a teenager, but from that day on, Mary became convinced that these girls—indeed, *all* girls, colored or white—were determined to take her husband away from her. And because her survival was so inextricably tied to him, she became almost unreasonably jealous and afraid. Now her world had narrowed to the small room inside the little boarding house on Mechanic Street, and Mary became more withdrawn and morose.

In November, she suffered a miscarriage that, while quite early in the pregnancy, still knocked her down for several days. It was confusing to her, as well. It never occurred to her that she would not be able to have babies one after another just like her mother had done. She blamed herself that it must have been something she had done to cause the pregnancy to fail.

For the first time since she had left home, Mary longed to be with and talk with her mother. The landlady did her best to comfort and care for her and tried to reassure her that there must have been something wrong with the embryo, since "Good fruit doesn't fall from the tree." Mary was somewhat comforted by the words and kind ministrations, although still tired, sad and crying much of the time.

The cold, gloomy weather certainly didn't help Mary's mood, and it forced her to stay indoors at her work and in the rooming house, thereby giving her no exercise or fresh air to speak of—that is, what little fresh air was available in New Hope. Her life that winter of 1835 was basically reduced to work, eat and sleep.

Lang's worry and concern grew steadily; he felt he had to do something. While he would not have been able to put his finger on the exact reason, still he felt a nagging sense of responsibility for Mary's situation. He tried to talk about it with his friend Andy, who himself now had a wife, Margaret.

"Heck, Lang, I don't know what to tell you. I can't figger out my own wife!" he protested helplessly.

Lang did not want to share too much of his troubles with Andy, since he had not been at all enthusiastic about his marrying a white girl. His initial reaction had been incredulousness. He and Mahlon Gibbs, who had just started to work and pal around with the older men, came over to the boarding house at the first opportunity when Lang told them about the marriage, not so much to *meet* Mary, but to *see* and wonder at this white girl who had married their black friend.

They were polite and circumspect and friendly enough in the house in front of the women, but expressed their apprehension later.

"What're you, crazy?!" Andy hollered at Lang when the men went out to the barn to get their horses. "I'm serious! You got somethin' wrong in the head you been hiding from us all these years?!"

Young Mahlon agreed. "Now that ain't too bright, Lang. What d'you think them 'patter rollers' are gonna do if they get hold of you?" A patter roller was slave slang for a bounty hunter hired to capture runaways. The patter rollers, very often frustrated in their endeavors, had been known to kidnap or beat up any black they happened upon just for spite.

Lang shrugged. He didn't expect his friends—or, for that matter, anyone—to understand. How could he explain that, in an instant it seems last summer, Mary had become not just his wife, she was his life. He had run away with her and had brought her to New Hope and married her. Now he was responsible for her for the rest of his life. It said so in the vows.

His emotional state of mind was so intertwined with Mary's that as Mary's mood darkened, so did his. Finding it difficult to face the source of his concern, he often found excuses to stay away from the little room in the boarding house. He never said it, but sometimes he wondered if his friends were right.

Unfortunately, the bars of New Hope saw more of his company that winter than did Mary, and this only gave Mary more to be upset about, as she was a sober, hard-working girl who was determined to save money so that they could buy land of their own some day.

Work hard, buy land, have children, work harder—that was the pattern of life from which Mary had been molded. She simply could not understand why Lang would fritter away their money in bars and gambling houses. His behavior was so completely abhorrent to her vision of life that it caused several arguments between them.

"Lang! How could you waste our money with liquor and gambling? We have so little and you throw it away!"

"Be still, Mary. Don't be ordering me about. I work hard, and I deserve a little entertainment, and I'll do with my money as I please."

She began to wonder if her father had been right, but, in the end, Mary kept still and tried to maintain a brighter mood, with the landlady's wise counsel: "That's a young buck with some wild oats left in him to sow. He probably wasn't prepared to settle down when you two run off together. That's just the way men are. It's harmless, you'll see. Mind my words, you make sure he's got someone sweet and warm to come home to."

Finally, in the spring, it occurred to Lang that a change of scenery might brighten Mary's mood. As soon as there was a fair-weather Sunday afternoon, Lang took her out to the countryside again, to Buckingham to meet Joseph Fell. Joseph had himself recently taken a bride, Harriet Williams, in March of 1835 and had begun some years ago teaching at the Buckingham Friends School in Lahaska in addition to helping on the family farm.

The Buckingham Friends school had been originally built from logs as a meeting house in 1706. A stone addition was made in 1720. In 1768 the entire building had burned down, and the existing structure was built in its place.

Buckingham was a place Langhorn had always subconsciously associated with safety and friendship; perhaps it would be true for Mary, as well. Indeed, Joseph and Harriet welcomed Mary in a very friendly manner, yet privately Joseph expressed his disappointment and uneasiness to Lang.

"I do wish thee had come to me first, young Langhorn. Thee has become like a brother to me, and I would have counseled thee against such a marriage for thy own well-being. I have heard of one or two other marriages between the races, but they are wealthy people who have the means to live against convention. I fear thee has 'bitten off more than thee can chew,' as the saying goes."

He stroked his chin thoughtfully. "Still, the deed is done in the eyes of God, and we must do all we can now to take care of Mary and to protect and preserve the sacred union of man and wife."

He put his hand gently on the large man's shoulder, "Know thee can come to me at any time, and there is always work for thee on our farms."

Lang knew Joseph spoke for most all of the Quaker farmers, and he felt greatly relieved that some resolutions might be found to their problems. If he had thought about it at length, Lang would have also admitted that he loathed New Hope—the noise, the smells, the saloons and houses of prostitution, so many different people coming and going. No doubt, there were fine places in New Hope, such as the house Mary worked in, but, as a lower middle-class Negro, unless he found housing in the servants' quarters of the big house, he was forced to live in "Darkeytown," the poorest, worst section of town. And, because of the disparate mix of people found there, as long as he was in New Hope, he was constantly on guard, on edge. He stayed chiefly for Mary's sake; he thought she wanted them both to be working and saving money, and it was doubtful she could find much work in the country.

But, it wouldn't hurt to ask. "Do you think it's possible we can find a place to rent in Buckingham?" he asked Joseph. "Mary is so unhappy in New Hope and, to be honest, I'm not truly comfortable there myself." He told Joseph about the drunken Irishmen and other incidents.

Joseph thought for a second and nodded. "I am sure there is something. I am thinking right now of one of the houses at Lahaska. A few rooms, a place to keep thy horse and wagon. That should suit thee well. I'll see what I can do."

Two weeks later, when he stopped back to see Joseph at the school, Lang was delighted to learn about the results of Joseph's inquiries.

"Brother Lang, would thee consider living with an elderly widow and helping to take care of her in return for room and board? She is childless and has a big house she does not wish to leave."

Lang nodded. "That sounds good. I'm sure Mary would agree to it in a minute." Then his face frowned with worry. "But, would she have us...I mean, does she know?"

"Oh, yes, I was sure to tell her, and she is not at all offended or concerned. She is a true Friend, Lang, a good Christian lady. Life has been very cruel to her, yet she is not bitter or angry. She has a soft, sweet nature. Thee must promise me thee will care for her as thee would thy own mother—no, *better* than thee would have thy own mother."

"We will. I promise." Lang understood very well that Joseph and the other Friends would be watching them carefully. In return, Langhorn and Mary could depend on the friendship and protection of the Quakers for as long as they lived in their midst.

And so it came to be, in the spring of 1836, that Langhorn and Mary went to live at the village of Lahaska with seventy-eight-year-old Widow Tamar Lacy, and in exchange for caring for the widow and her home and property, received their room and board. According to the terms of her husband's will, while Widow Lacy would not inherit the property out-right, she was given full use and benefit of the homestead, according to the common practice of the day, for as long as she lived or until she remarried. Upon the widow's death or remarriage, the property would be sold and the proceeds distributed among the heirs after the payment of debts.

Becoming feeble in body and unable to keep up the normal house-keeping chores, yet desiring to remain in her home for as long as possi-ble—indeed, to lay down her body in her own bed for the final time—having Langhorn and Mary to look after her until that day was the best answer for everyone concerned.

Mary found that taking care of an elderly Quaker woman was infi-nitely easier than working for the pampered ladies and spoiled children of the mansions of New Hope. Mrs. Lacy's needs and desires were cer-tainly much simpler. There was less food to cook, less laundry and most definitely less brushing and primping.

Mrs. Lacy rented out the fields to a nearby farmer, giving herself a little extra income to use for upkeep and taxes. Lang took over responsi-bility for major repairs and maintenance on the house, keeping the barn clean and caring for the few animals that the widow raised to supply eggs, milk and meat. He and Mary both tended the vegetable garden, and Mrs. Lacy still enjoyed planting and weeding her lovely flower patches whenever her aching body would allow.

Widow Lacy was quickly reassured that this little German girl and her Negro husband were clean, hard-working, caring people. "Thee are like son and daughter to me," she said to Mary one day in the summer, and Mary began to think more about her own mother and missed her even more. Shortly after they settled in Lahaska, she wrote her mother a letter and sent it to Wormansville; she did not know that the family had moved to Doylestown.

"Did you never have children?" Mary asked the widow.

"Oh, yes, four, but they're all gone now. Three died very young, many years ago, in a cholera epidemic, and my surviving son was drowned while fishing in the Delaware."

Mary was aghast with shock and sorrow for the sweet old woman. Mary had never known that kind of loss in her own large family. "How awful for you! I am so very sorry."

Yet the widow was accepting of her fate and philosophical. "'Tis no matter. 'Twas God's will that none of my children was destined for long life in this world. They were a joy to me when they were here, and I know they await me with my husband in the next, and I am content with that."

She showed Mary the little silhouettes that were made of herself, her husband and children. Early Quakers did not approve of having portraits painted, although a cutout of the impression one's shadow made was acceptable. "I am so happy we had these pictures done to remind me of my family, and now that thee are here I will not be so lonely waiting to join them."

"On our part, Mrs. Lacy, we will try our best to show you how very grateful and happy we are that you have taken us in." Mary had told the widow some of their unfortunate experiences in New Hope. "I am so much more at ease here in the country."

"Now, thee must know that we Friends do not hold with honors and titles. Thee must not call me 'Mrs.' How would it be if thee calls me 'Mother Lacy'?"

Mary was visibly touched. "We would be honored."

Within months, Mary brought the house back to immaculate condition and eventually found enough time on her hands to take up needlework and other crafts and handiwork that she had not been able to do for years. And her health began to rebound in the clean, fresh air of the countryside.

Lang's mood improved considerably, as well. He didn't know it—and he would have scoffed at you if you had brought it to his attention—but he was in many ways like a chameleon whose "color" changed with those closest to him, and that was Mary. When Mary was happy, Lang was happy; conversely, when Mary was ill or "in a mood," Lang became depressed and tended to stay away from home more often and for longer periods of time.

For entertainment, in the evenings Mary, Mother Lacy and Lang, whenever he was home from his many jobs around the county, attended several meetings of the Buckingham Lyceum, a group of people who were interested in furthering their education by exposing themselves to great speakers, books, and new ideas. The meetings were held at first at Bill Johnson's home, then at the Buckingham Friends School.

On other occasions, Mother Lacy would entertain Mary and Lang with stories about her experiences when she was a young woman during the Revolution. She was married just a year before the Declaration of Independence was signed.

She told them about how President George Washington himself, when he was still a General during the war, stayed at the Summerseat House in Morrisville and at William Keith's house in Upper Makefield in December 1776 after being routed from Long Island and New Jersey. She described the English troops that marched back and forth and camped for a short while in the region, and told how the Continental Army massed on the banks of the Delaware—now known as Washington Crossing in honor of that occasion—for the boat ride across the river on Christmas Eve to surprise the English and Hessian troops in Trenton.

Even though few of the Friends became involved in the fighting during the Revolution, Mother Lacy explained, the Buckingham meetinghouse had been turned into a hospital for much of the time. As a young woman, she had helped to minister to injured soldiers of both sides of the conflict.

Living on York Road, the major highway in that day from Philadelphia to New York, Mother Lacy had seen many beautiful coaches filled with important people pass by over the years, the most memorable being Benjamin Franklin who stopped at her door one day and asked for a bit of refreshment. In payment, although she tried to refuse, he insisted on giving her a coin—a shiny, still new-looking copper penny—that she had kept to this day and showed to Lang and Mary.

She told them about the infamous Doan Gang that terrorized the countryside in the years during and following the Revolution. Originally called "cowboys," which meant "Tory marauders, adherents to the British cause in the American Revolution, who infested neutral ground and plundered their patriot opponents," the Doan brothers—also spelled with an "e" on the end—came from two Quaker families who lived near Plumsteadville. The leader, Moses, four of his five brothers and cousin Abraham, began their life of crime in the early 1770s stealing horses, which they sold in Philadelphia, Baltimore and North Carolina.

When the Declaration of Independence was signed in July 1776, the Doans turned their malice on Whigs and patriots, apparently because of the higher taxes imposed on the Colonials by the new government to finance the Revolution. It was reported that Moses Doan offered himself as a spy to British Commander-in-Chief General William Howe and was credited with finding an unguarded access to the Continental Army's camp on Long Island, thus leading to the defeat and flight of Generals Washington and Putnam to Pennsylvania.

Howe and his troops took over most of New Jersey, and it was the Hessian troops camped at Trenton who were overrun and defeated by Washington that fateful winter night. There is a story that the Doans had become apprised of Washington's intentions. They jumped on their horses and quickly crossed the river and rode to Trenton to warn Colonel Rahl, the commander of the Hessians. Either Rahl never looked at the note the Doans brought him, or if he did so gave little attention to the warning, and the story has it that his body was found next day and still in his pocket was a note that read, "Washington is coming on you down the river, he will be here before long. A. Doan."

After the British surrendered in 1781, the Doans continued their plundering and pillaging but changed their victims much more dramatically: On October 22, 1781, the gang, their ranks now augmented by a number of other villains, raided the Bucks County Treasurer's house and the Treasury at Newtown. The reports of the amount stolen vary, but it is believed that each of the thieves received about $140 when the loot was divvied up.

The gang eventually came to an end by 1787. Moses was killed in a shoot-out with a posse led by Revolutionary war hero Colonel William Hart in 1783. Abraham took over leadership of the gang that continued robbing tax collectors in Upper Makefield, Buckingham, New Britain, Tinicum, Wrightstown and Quakertown until he and cousin Levi were captured and hung in Chester in 1787. The rest of the gang were either executed or scattered to safe haven in Canada, and two of them served on the side of the British during the War of 1812.

"In fact," Mother Lacy was quick to point out, "many of the Doans who are still living in the neighborhood and whom I have known well since childhood are cousins of the outlaw 'cowboys.' For the most part, the Doan family members have remained respectful, law-abiding Quaker folks and had nothing to do with their notorious cousins."

Mary and Lang were greatly entertained by these stories.

To further add to her delight at living in the village, Mary found out there was a magnificent library at the Buckingham Friends school. Almost the entire second story was devoted to housing about two thousand volumes, many of them valuable books. It was opened for an hour on Fourth-day, and, even though Mary was not a member of the Meeting, Joseph knew of her love of reading and arranged for her to have full use of the many wonderful books. She enjoyed the library as long as she lived in Lahaska and was heartbroken to hear many years later in 1853 that it had been abandoned for lack of use, and all of the books were sold off at public sale.

One day Joseph told her about an incident that happened about twenty years before when it was determined by the "powers that be" that one of the books in the library supposedly contained heterodox views.

"Upon consultation," he told her, "they determined that the offensive book should be destroyed. Accordingly, the leaves were cut out and taken out to the back of the school. Someone went to the larger group and said there were men who desired to smoke in back, lest suspicion be aroused. And the leaves of the book were burnt."

Mary was appalled. "How could they do that? It's sacrilege to destroy any book, in my opinion."

"In mine, as well, Sister Mary. But, listen further. Apparently, the book back was left on the shelf and, although previous to its burning the book had generally lain dormant upon the shelf, someone noticed that the leaves were missing, several more copies of the book were procured, and it was circulated and read extensively by the people!"

"Oh, that's wonderful!" Mary laughed. "That will teach them to censor anything!"

It was also during this time in Lahaska that Mary became a faithful reader of the *Intelligencer*. Every Wednesday she obtained a copy in the village, and would read aloud for Lang and Mother Lacy—every page, every article, even the advertisements, which in those days almost all consisted of announcements and testimonials about the miraculous cures that could be performed using this or that medicine or tonic.

"Oh, look here," she would read as though it were the latest scientific achievement of the day. "Here is Marshall's sarsaparilla 'for the cure of rheumatism, ulcers, scrofula, tetter, white swellings, gout, pain in the bones, cutaneous eruptions, and other diseases arising from impurities of the blood' at only one dollar per bottle." There were dozens of medicines, lozenges and pulmonic syrup for coughs, and, if all else failed, cod liver oil for whatever else ailed you.

In 1837, the paper was published by James Kelly, who was probably the first to begin the feud that was to last for a full thirty years, until after the Civil War, with the rival *Doylestown Democrat* newspaper. He began by calling the Democrats "Locofocos" and lambasting the paper's publisher and its political stances. Mary did not quite understand all the political rhetoric between the Whigs and the Democrats, however, she knew that the *Intelligencer* stood foursquare in favor of abolition and that was enough. She would have nothing to do with the *Democrat*, indeed, would not even allow a copy of it in the house and so was spared most of the worst anti-Negro vitriol.

In March of 1838 Kelly sold the paper to William M. Large, who expanded and changed the format somewhat by publishing poetry, words to popular songs of the day, and excerpted stories and articles from *Blackwood's Magazine* and *Chambers' Journal.*

Another popular magazine that became a favorite of Mary's was *Godey's Lady's Book* published in Philadelphia by Louis A. Godey beginning in 1830. In 1837, Sarah Josepha Buell Hale became publisher. A self-educated widow and editor of a women's magazine in Massachusetts, Hale moved with her five children to Philadelphia to take over the magazine. She was one of the most outspoken, influential ladies of her time, a great proponent of education for all children, professions for women, and women's property rights, yet still she did not believe in female suffrage nor did she condone women speaking in public.

"Nor need we power or splendor, wide hall or lordly dome; the good, the true, the tender—these form the wealth of home," she wrote, and Mrs. Hale was determined to show the ladies how to make every house a home and "How to Live Well and Be Well While We Live."

As Mrs. Hale described in one of the issues in the 1850s the beginnings of the magazine by her predecessor, a "magazine of elegant literature was cast, doubtingly, upon the uncertain stream of public favor—its name the *Lady's Book* and Louis A. Godey the publisher. It was a novel enterprise at the time, and few thought it would outlive the first year of its nativity. It soon became apparent, however, that its management was in the hands of one who knew the want of the time, and had the tact and taste required for its supply."

Without doubt its popularity was also due, in no small measure, to the support from local newspapers such as the *Intelligencer* in the

1840s, with its reprinting and serializing portions of the magazine. There were articles and illustrations on fashions, cooking, gardening, architecture, etiquette, art and literature, and many pieces of fiction and poetry.

Mary took a subscription to the magazine and became a faithful reader from then on. She and Mother Lacy spent many happy hours, especially during the cold winter months, reading to each other and to Lang.

"Unless it's one of them fee-male love stories," Lang would screw up his face and protest. "Don't want to hear 'bout that silly nonsense." The ladies would laugh delightedly at this.

In the winter of 1836, a note in the *Intelligencer* gave Mary the idea that the widow could earn extra money by opening her home as a guest-house during the summer. Many people in Philadelphia, especially upper middle class who could not afford to own or rent a country home for the season, went to stay on farms in the country for the summer to escape the oppressive heat and humidity of the city. Also, many of them suffered from persistent coughs, fevers and agues, which, if one could afford it, were often relieved with a rest in the country.

"We have all these rooms that are not being used," Mary said. "I'm accustomed to cooking and cleaning for a great crowd, so it will be no trouble for me. And we will get to meet people from Philadelphia and other far-away places."

The widow eventually agreed to try it out. Although she did not particularly relish having strangers in her home, Mary convinced her their guests would undoubtedly be quality folks.

"I will only agree to this if thee will take a portion of the profits for thy work," she insisted.

Mary figured they would be able to accommodate up to six guests at one time, depending on whether they would occupy the three extra bedrooms singly or doubly. At the rate of a dollar per week per guest, they would be able to make almost a hundred dollars for the summer minus expenses, which were minimal.

"This certainly seems to be a better proposition than the hare-brained idea of raising Chinese silk worms that's so popular now," Mother Lacy conceded. She was referring to the latest money-making scheme making its way through the county, whereby silk worms were imported from China and thousands of mulberry trees had been planted to provide food for the worms.

"It might come to something some day, but I just can't see it," she said shaking her head in bewilderment. (She was right. It eventually failed; in the meantime, many people made and others lost fortunes.)

Mary worked through the spring to prepare the house. In April, she wrote to the Philadelphia paper to place an ad for four consecutive weeks offering

> Rooms—Bucks Co. Farm
> Clean, Well-App'nted, Meals Incl.
> T. Lacy, Lahaska, Penn

Mary was right. A few inquiries came in immediately, and reservations were eventually made for the summer. The guests began arriving in the first week in June.

Although it was certainly more work for Mary, and from sunup to late at night she was busy cooking and cleaning, for the most part the guests were as she had expected, upper middle class, educated people. The majority were government clerks, and the families of small business owners who, while they themselves could not leave their business establishments, made sure to send their families to the cool tranquility of the countryside for a few weeks in the summer.

When Lang did not have a job away from home working at the limestone quarries or helping out on a nearby farm, he would entertain the children with games—that is, more often, he would keep the children out of mischief in the barn or prevent them from drowning in the pond. Since the children were determined to play in the barn, Lang made it as safe as possible. On one end, he dumped a huge pile of hay under the upper-story window, and the children would spend hours delightedly jumping out of the window into the hay pile below, then running back up to do it all over again.

He let them help out with the animals, gathering eggs, milking the cow. "Silly kids," he laughingly told Mary, "they even enjoy mucking the stalls!" One time she looked out and saw that he had put three children up on his horse and was leading them slowly around the yard. She loved to see Lang playing with the children, and she longed for babies of her own some day soon.

Lang found a large, old passenger carriage in the barn that was still in surprisingly good condition and just needed cleaning and minor repairs. To make a team, along with his horse, he borrowed a horse from a neighbor and took the guests on day trips to New Hope to see the canal and the Delaware River, to Newtown and to Doylestown to shop. Mary could not go, as she was unable to leave her household duties (not that she ever wanted to step foot in New Hope again).

Except one day, he arranged a picnic up on Wolf Rocks. Mary packed up the lunch in a big basket and everyone piled into Lang's work wagon on which he had placed barrels and boxes and hay for them to sit on. There was a dirt lane leading up the mountain now. To his joy, Lang found out when they got to the top, a little African Methodist Episcopal meetinghouse was being built there, called the Mt. Gilead church. It sure had changed since he was a young boy wandering the woods and mountains just fifteen years before.

The only negative counterpoint to this otherwise happy summer was that Lang had to sleep away from Mary, and they were forced to meet secretly in the barn (which actually turned out to give them a little thrill and intrigue in their otherwise dull daily routine). This was necessitated after one of the earliest guests came into the kitchen one morning and made a casual request to Mary to ask the hired man to do something.

"Oh, you mean Lang? He's not the hired man," Mary answered the lady innocently. "He's my husband."

The woman was so shocked and nonplussed she could barely breath. She immediately turned around without a word, went upstairs, packed her bag, and walked to the village to await the coach to Doylestown.

Mary could not take a chance that any more of her guests would be so offended. Lang and Mary had not made a practice of sitting at the dining table with Mother Lacy and the guests, instead taking their meals at the large table in the kitchen—usually with Mary constantly jumping up and down to serve the guests—so no eyebrows were raised in that regard.

One afternoon in mid-July Mary heard the door pull ringing and ran to the front entry thinking another one of their guests was arriving. She opened the door and instantly cried out with joy.

"Jonas!" It was her younger brother, Jonas, her dearest friend, born just two years after her. She had seen him only once or twice since he had left for Philadelphia several years before to begin his apprenticeship as a shoemaker.

"Jonas!" she cried out again and could not hold back her tears of joy. "How are you? Come in, come in!"

"Wait! I have something for you." Jonas ran back out to the wagon and brought a large trunk into the house, seeing which Mary could barely contain her excitement.

"My hope chest! Oh, Jonas, God bless you!" This time she sat down and openly wept. The chest was filled with many precious items she had made by hand from the time she was a young girl to prepare for her marriage—quilts and bed sheets, nightgowns, shirtwaists, petticoats, collars, tea towels and more. "I thought truly I would never see any of you again, let alone my hope chest!"

Jonas sat and hugged Mary while she cried. "Why, sister Mary, I made that chest for you, and I'll be darned if you will not have it as you were meant to."

She wiped her eyes. "How did you find me?"

"I was just home to see the family—you know they've moved to Doylestown."

"No, I didn't. Why? What happened?" Mary was mortified when Jonas told her what had transpired after she ran away, and she began crying again. "I had no idea my actions would result in this. I would not have hurt Mama—or even Papa—for the world."

"I know, Mary. I've seen love do many strange things to people. I sure hope you're not sorry for what you did, though."

"Oh, no, Jonas! While our marriage necessarily has a great many peculiar difficulties, we are very content now." She told Jonas briefly about their unfortunate experiences in New Hope and the move to Lahaska.

"He is a good man, Jonas, so strong and handsome, and with a gentleness and kindness that belie his size and appearance. He is so good with the summer children."

By this time, Mother Lacy and a couple of the summer guests had wandered in from sitting in the back yard and came to see what the commotion was about. Mary introduced her brother, and politely waited while he chatted amiably with Mother Lacy for a few moments. The guests quickly became bored and went off to continue their reading and napping.

"Thee will stay for the evening meal and sleep here for the night," Mother Lacy offered. "I think we have room, don't we, Mary?"

Mary nodded. "Yes, we can set up a bed on the kitchen porch. It'll be cooler for him out there."

"Thank you, ma'am, very kind of you," Jonas said to Mother Lacy. He went to sit in the kitchen with a cup of coffee and chat with Mary while she prepared supper.

"So, how *did* you find me?" Mary asked.

"Mother told me where you were. She got a letter from you just a month or so ago."

"Goodness! I wrote that letter to Wormansville over a year ago, I think."

"Well, from what we can determine, it was a new postal clerk who couldn't tell the difference from all the Stones there. It was put in Uncle Henry's box, but he didn't pick up the mail that day—thank goodness for that, for he surely would have intercepted it and given it to Papa. Aunt Sarah realized it was from you and didn't dare send it on to Doylestown for fear Papa would get it first. So she waited until Cousin Levi had an opportunity to go to Doylestown, which wasn't until this spring, so he could give it to Mama personal."

"And I practically could have walked back and forth five times in the meantime," Mary laughed. "If I had dared show my face, that is. What did she say? Is Mama mad at me still?"

"No, Mary, she never was angry with you. She's mighty worried about you, though. She said she would have written to you, but you know she doesn't know English too good, and she really doesn't write German that good, neither. She did want me to tell you that she loves you. You are her daughter forever."

Mary stopped cutting the biscuits she was making for supper and sat down to listen to Jonas, her eyes glistening with tears again.

"What else did she say?"

"Well, she said she was most upset that day, not only that she knew Papa would be furious that your husband is black, but because she saw that you were in love. 'And that's a dangerous thing,' she said, 'because when you're in love you only open yourself up to hurt.' She saw you as being vulnerable, I guess, and she didn't know what could become of you at this man's hands. Curious, she said she didn't love Papa when they married, but grew to love him over the years."

"Well, I should say so, after seventeen children!"

"Right, and that was her point, I think. She married him because she knew he would be a good provider. After Papa had shown his steadiness, I guess, and...fidelity—that's the word I'm looking for—Mama knew she could trust him and felt safer about giving her heart. Well, except for his temper, of course!" Jonas and Mary both nodded and grimaced.

"But his temper was never directed towards Mama, did you notice?" Mary observed. "Only us kids."

"Oh, boy, 'n then some!" Jonas laughed.

Mary resumed her biscuit-making. "What about Papa? Is he still mad at me?"

"I'm afraid so, Mary. He won't even allow your name to be mentioned. But, you're not alone. He's mad at all of us! We can't do nothin' right far's he's concerned. I've given up trying to please him, honest."

"Tell me, what are you doing now? Are you still living in Philadelphia? Tell me about the city. I would so love to see it."

"Well, for starters, I'm married, too. I got married shortly after you did."

"No! Oh, Jonas, that's wonderful news. Who is she?"

"Lydia Gaskill. She's from Jersey. She's sister-in-law to a friend of mine, Robert Love. I went home with him to visit one day, and she happened to be there, 'n there we are!"

Mary bent over and gave her brother a warm hug and a kiss on the cheek. "Oh, Jonas, I'm so happy for you. I'll bet she's a wonderful girl."

"Oh, yes, the sweetest disposition a man can ask for, just like Mama. Comes from an old Quaker family, as a matter of fact. She's a coupla years older than me, almost exactly your age. And we have a baby, Richard. He's over a year old already."

"Oh, my! More wonderful news!" Mary was delighted. "But, why would Papa be mad at you?"

"Well, I've quit shoemaking for one thing. Ah, Mary, I just couldn't stand it no more. You know me. I gotta be up movin' around. I can't be sittin' at a little bench all day long pounding leather!"

"So, what are you doing?"

"I've taken up boilermaking at the Baldwin Locomotive Works in North Philadelphia. It's the best thing, Mary. You wouldn't believe it! We build these huge boilers, like tanks, out of steel. Then they're fitted onto the train over a wood-burning firebox, and filled with water that's heated to boiling. The steam is controlled to turn the wheels of the train. Oh, it's a wonderful sight! And, I've heard some of the shipyards are going to steam engines, so there's certainly a future for it."

Mary had never seen a train or a ship, for that matter, except in pictures, and was appropriately impressed. "That's wonderful, Jonas! Now, how could Papa be upset with you about that?"

"Oh, I don't know. I suppose it's just that I haven't bowed to his commands—that I be a shoemaker, I mean. But, none of us has been able to please Papa, really. You know, Mahlon's taken off for parts unknown."

"No! What happened?"

"Who knows? He had it out with Papa one day and just took off. Aaron and Amos are doing their shoemaking apprenticeship, and he's expecting Chillian to go soon, too, but Chillian's none to happy about it. Actually, I think Aaron and Amos are the only two of us boys that Papa approves of."

"And the girls. I'm the only one of the girls who has gone against Papa's wishes."

"That's true, I s'pose. The others are prob'ly too timid." Mary and Jonas nodded acknowledgement of the truth of what they were saying.

"Oh, speaking of. I almost forgot. I do have a letter for you from Elizabeth." Jonas fished in his pocket and brought out the folded paper, and Mary read it aloud.

Dearest sister Mary,

We are so happy to hear you are safe and well in Lahaska. We miss you terribly. Our hearts long for news of you.

We are getting settled in our new home, which is really quite lovely. In fact, I wish to thank you in a way for helping us to get out of that provincial little village and into the city. Doylestown is full of so many wonderful activities, and it's only two miles from our door to the center of town. We've even heard there is a circus coming next summer! Camilla and John are in school. Reuben is helping

Papa with the farming. Rachel is preparing to marry her Mr. VanSant next summer.

Mama sends her love. She is always busy with the young children. We all have to work twice as hard to make up for your going away. You were always the hardest worker of all of us.

I hesitate to tell you, but you must know, Papa is still very upset with you. You must write to us in care of Mrs. Owen Swarts, New Britain Village. Lydia is our closest neighbor and has promised to relay your letters."

Your loving sister, Elizabeth

As she finished the letter, Mary suddenly remembered it was July 19th. "Jonas, it's your birthday! You're twenty-five years old today!"

Jonas blushed and laughed. "Aye, so it is, I s'pose, and yours, too, this month. And Sarah and Elizabeth in July, as well."

"I'll make a special cake for supper and we'll celebrate!"

When Lang came home, he was surprised and pleased to meet Jonas, yet reserved and even a little afraid until Jonas assured him as they sat on the kitchen porch waiting for supper that, unlike most of the others in the Stone family, he had no prejudices as far as race was concerned.

"I look to what's inside the man. But I am more than a little partial when it comes to my sister. I care for her very much. As she has chosen you for her husband, I will abide by her decision, and I expect you'll treat her right. I hope that's clear."

Lang nodded. Jonas had made it perfectly clear. "Absolutely. I appreciate you being up front with me, Jonas."

Jonas left the next morning with an armload of handmade gifts from Mary for Lydia and baby Richard. They both promised to write, but Mary knew it might be years before she would see him again, even though he lived less than fifty miles away in the West Kensington area north of Philadelphia.

Summer passed into fall, and by the middle of September everything was peaceful and quiet at the house once more, for which Mary was grateful, since in truth she was exhausted after the summer guests had finally left. Shortly after the last guest had departed, Mother Lacy came into the parlor one afternoon, where Mary sat mending the bed-clothes before putting them away for the winter.

"I want thee to have this," she said and handed Mary a little bag filled with twenty dollars in coin. "'Tis only fair since thee did most all of the work." Thereafter, every time she felt tired, Mary remembered the little bag jangling with coins, and she smiled. They were twenty dollars closer to having their own home.

And she clung to her dream, even though Lang couldn't help but disparage it. "Mary, you're crazy. There's no way in God's green earth we're gonna earn enough money in a lifetime to buy a place!"

"Hush now, Lang. Look at your friend Andrew. Why, he's already starting to buy up land, and he's just a little older than you."

And Lang could not contradict that truth. Andy Hartless and even Mahlon Gibbs, ten years younger than Lang, were both married now and beginning families, and each had already taken the first steps toward what would turn into considerable land ownership over the lifetimes of both men.

"It's different for them," Lang couldn't help but observe. "Mahlon at least started out with more opportunities and privileges than I had," he said, referring to Mahlon's *de facto* adoption by Mr. Reeder, "and Andy is advertising in the newspaper and getting more business than I am. Are you gonna spare me enough money to do that and fix up my wagon and buy another horse?"

One evening in September, Joseph and some of the other elders from the Buckingham Monthly Meeting, including Bill Johnson and Joseph Yardley, President and Secretary, respectively, of the Anti-Slavery Society of Bucks County, came to call on Lang.

"Friend Lang," Joseph said, " we are here to see you…I mean, thee on an important matter. 'Tis about thy rights as a citizen…"

"And responsibilities, Brother Fell," another of the men, a stern--faced elderly fellow, interjected solemnly.

"…yes, yes, responsibilities, as well, as a citizen of Bucks County and Pennsylvania. We have been researching the matter and can find nothing prohibiting thee and thy fellow Negroes from participating in the general election that is coming up this fall. We need thy help in gar-nering the votes."

In fact, Lang had been ready and waiting for this call. Because of conversations with Joseph, and since Mary had resumed reading the *Intelligencer* to him and Mother Lacy in the evenings, he was fully apprised of the political debates and Negro enfranchisement issues in Bucks County, so that he was able to impress the Friends with his knowledge of the candidates and ability to speak on the issues, despite the fact that he did not read or write. By the time the men left, they had Lang's promise to not only vote in the general election, but also to speak to all of his friends and fellow workers to encourage them to vote, as well.

The fact that he was able to participate in democratic society, along with what they were lulled into thinking were the pervasive sentiments in the county, if not in the state, that had led to Pennsylvania being among the first to abolish slavery, gave Lang and Mary a false sense of promise and optimism for the future of the Negro people in Pennsylvania, if not in the United States.

The aftermath of the ensuing local elections that fall came as a critical blow to the cause of Negro citizenship and suffrage in Pennsylvania. In October of 1837 the Democratic party of Bucks County attributed the defeat of its candidates, particularly Abraham Fretz, to the margin of forty Negro votes in Buckingham and Solebury, and raised public outrage against Pennsylvania legislator Thaddeus Stevens and other abolitionists for inciting the Negroes "to contend for the rights of a white man at the polls! by his zealous support of the accursed doctrines of ABOLITION."

And how the Democrats stirred up animosities and emotions with articles such as the one written by John Bryan claiming that a number of Negroes had shown up at the polls with guns, and one of them said he had his gun loaded and would have shot if he had been molested in voting.

"Is such conduct of negroes to be tolerated?" the article cried out in protest. "Tolerate such indulgence of the blacks for a few years longer, hold out inducements and protection to runaways and help them in the lower end of Bucks, and they will make the streets run with white man's blood!"

Bucks County's Judge John Fox agreed with the plaintiffs, and in December 1837 ruled that the Negro—"a degraded and inferior race"—"has not the right of suffrage" in Pennsylvania, noting that they had been deliberately excluded from the Constitution of the United States, since the framers of that document had been "a political community of white men exclusively."

"What white man," Judge Fox was quoted in the paper, "would not feel himself insulted by a serious imputation that he was a Negro, and who, having believed himself to be of the white race, if he should be found to be strongly tainted with black blood, would not feel and experience that he had fallen greatly in the social scale?"

Judge Fox correctly pointed out in his decision that the black man had never voted in Philadelphia, where, although they had the legal right for many years, they could not appear at the polls without being mistreated. "Just let them try!" was the not-so-veiled threat spoken vehemently to one European visitor to Philadelphia when he asked why the Negro men of that city did not vote.

Elsewhere in Pennsylvania, sentiments continued to run high against Negro balloting and socialization. One delegate to the constitutional convention in 1838, speaking from the floor noted that, even if the "rights of the people—of the commonwealth" were extended to the Negro, he would still not be received in white homes or at table, or allowed to marry with whites.

An end result of the constitutional convention was that the word "white" was inserted before "freedman" in the description of the qualified electorate of the Commonwealth of Pennsylvania.

Mary and Mother Lacy were appalled and deeply saddened as Mary read about these events in the *Intelligencer*, in which it was alleged that Judge Fox was controlled by the *Democrat* newspaper and party. Lang was downright hurt and angry. He got up, without a word, and went out to the yard to smoke and be alone.

Life sure is like the fickle wind, he mused sadly as he looked up at the stars. *Lift you up high one minute, throw you down just as fast the next. They say you got to pick yourself up and keep on goin'. Trouble is, it gets harder and harder to get up again.*

The only good thing to happen politically in the fall of 1837 was that Joseph was elected to the State Legislature as a representative of Bucks County and succeeded in helping to introduce and establish the Common School Law of Pennsylvania, which superseded the Free School Law of 1834 and gave access to education for all children, black and white.

DESTRUCTION OF THE PENNSYLVANIA HALL.

During most of the day, yesterday, large numbers of persons were standing round the Hall, and it was evident that there was a purpose of injury.

In the afternoon the Mayor went to some of the leading members of the society owning this building, and represented to them the great danger of continuing to hold their meetings, and he especially urged upon them the propriety of not assembling *that evening*, as he had every reason to believe that there was an organized band prepared to break up the meeting, and perhaps do injury to the building—and crowded as the walk must be by the company, this could not be done without personal injury and loss of life. It was agreed to forgo the evening meeting, and the mayor took the keys, and went out and addressed the persons then in the street, stating that there would be no meeting, and requested them as good citizens to retire. The people cheered the mayor, who returned to his office, placing persons to bring information of any attempt at injury, calling around him all his possible force, and having some volunteers.

Early in the evening notice was given that a crowd had come down the street & was attacking the North side of the Hall; the Mayor hastened up Fifth street with his force, and when he met the crowd, which was dense and numerous, he sprang his rattle, and his police called upon the people to sustain the Mayor, but not one person appeared to give aid. It was then seen that those who had assailed the building, and broke open the doors and lower windows—obtained enterence and were beating out the upper windows. By this time the Mayor and his police had attempted to arrest the course of destruction—but they were assailed with clubs, and almost every one severely wounded. Col. Watmough, the Sheriff, also made an attempt to restore peace and save the building, but he was attacked, severely bruised, and narrowly escaped.

We learn that the persons inside then gathered the benches, chairs and books in a heap, set fire to them and then left the Hall. The engines hastened to the conflagration, but the firemen were not allowed to play on the building, but directed to play upon those houses endangered by the flame, so that before 10 o'clock the whole wood work of the Hall was entirely destroyed, and shortly afterwards the crowd, which consisted of many thousands, began to disperse.

We give the above statement as we gathered it at a late hour. We have no time to indulge in any reflections upon the outrage against the laws and the city's character.

[*United States Gazette*, May 18, 1838]

Chapter VI

Philadelphia
May 1838

Early in March of 1838, a group of Friends, men and women, came to visit Mother Lacy. They sat in the parlor and quietly conversed. When Mary came in to serve tea, they stopped the point of their conversation to inquire politely as to her well-being, then resumed talking after she left.

It wasn't until the next day that Mary found out the nature of their business when Mother Lacy came into the kitchen where Mary was ironing. She worked with two heavy irons, one of which sat on a metal plate over the fire in the huge fireplace to heat up as she used the other to press the cloth, always with a folded-up towel covering the handle to protect her hand from burning. Every so often she would gently sprinkle water from a bottle to soften the cloth and make the ironing easier. Although she had heard of some women who could take a great mouthful of water and blow it out evenly over the cloth, she had never learned to do it that way.

"Sister Mary, it seems we are soon to have an important guest in our home," Mother Lacy said.

Mary set the iron on a wrought-iron trivet. "Who is it?"

"Sister Lucretia Mott is coming to visit. The Friends informed me last night she will be here to consult with them about a large anti-slavery meeting to be held in Philadelphia this May, and they asked if we would provide hospitality for her."

From reading the *Intelligencer* and the tracts that the Anti-Slavery Society of Bucks County distributed at the Buckingham Library, Mary was already aware of Mrs. Mott, who was becoming well known for her activities and speeches in the cause of abolition. Born Lucretia Coffin in 1793 in Nantucket, Massachusetts, the daughter of a sea captain, she was raised in the New England Quaker environment and was well educated from a young age. As early as the age of fifteen, she became interested in the rights of women, particularly the right of female teachers to earn as fair and equal a salary as their male counterparts were paid.

In 1811, she married James Mott, a fellow teacher at the Friends' boarding school in Poughkeepsie, New York. They moved to Philadelphia, and within a few years Mrs. Mott began speaking out eloquently at Quaker meetings about religion, social reform, peace and the abolition of slavery. They joined the liberal Hicksite movement in the late 1820s. Even in the Quaker community, however, there was some opposition to her speeches, and at one time there was a movement to remove her ministry and membership in the church.

Just recently, Mrs. Mott had organized and become the first president of the Philadelphia Female Anti-Slavery Society and was traveling around to the Quaker meeting houses in particular trying to boost interest in membership in the organization and attendance at the first convention to be held in Philadelphia, May 16th to 18th.

Mary was enthusiastic in her response. "Of course, we will do all we can to welcome Sister Mott," she said. She couldn't wait to share with Lang the news of the important houseguest.

They learned later that Mrs. Mott would be accompanied by Angelina Grimké. Miss Grimké and her sister, Sarah, were born in Charleston, South Carolina, in the late 1790s, the daughters of a prominent Southern judge, a slaveholder. These outspoken ladies formed an intense loathing of slavery, converted to the Quaker religion, moved north and began writing and speaking out in public.

In 1831 William Lloyd Garrison began publication of *The Liberator,* a journal dedicated to "the immediate and unconditional abolition of slavery" as the "right of the slave and the duty of the master." A letter Angelina wrote in 1835 was published that year in the *Liberator,* and people on both sides of the issue began to take notice of her.

It was a casual remark from Miss Grimké one afternoon as Mary served tea in her room that sparked the idea in Mary that she might be able to realize her dream of seeing Philadelphia. In the two days Miss Grimké and Mrs. Mott had been their guests, the two ladies had been busy in meetings, away at the Quaker meeting houses, and invited out to dinners, and Mary had not seen much of them.

"Come in," Miss Grimké called as Mary tapped lightly on the door.

"Tea for you, Miss."

"Come in, Mrs. Wellin's. Thank you so very much." Mary thought Miss Grimké's soft Southern drawl to be a delightfully different sound on her ears. Miss Grimké sat at a little table next to the window. Books and papers were laid out in front of her. The afternoon was mild, not too cold, and she had opened the window a bit so that the March breeze made the white curtains flutter. Even so, she was bundled in a shawl.

"Ah do so miss the wahm weather of the South where we could open our windows nearly year 'round." She gazed out of the window. "It's one of the things ah miss the most about home. Ah just can't seem to get used to cold weather."

"I've never been anywhere but Bucks County," Mary said, and Miss Grimké smiled as she detected the slight German accent in Mary's voice.

"Well, then, you must plan to go somewhere some day. Ah'm all for women takin' chahge of their lives."

"I know. I've read some of your letters."

"You have? Please, sit down. Do you have time to talk with me a few moments?" Mary was honored and felt humbled in Miss Grimké's presence. She sat demurely on the edge of the bed.

"Oh, yes. I know all about you and Mrs. Mott and the work of your abolition groups. I am so honored to serve you." Mary looked down shyly at her folded hands.

"But, mah dear Mrs. Wellin's, it is we who should be honorin' you. Ah understand from our gracious hostess that you have gone far beyond the mere rhetoric of anti-slavery and Negro freedom. You have actually given yourself in matrimony to a man of the ebony race, to serve him as wife and helpmate and mother of any children God may bless you with. Why, ah dare say there is not another woman in my acquaintance, north or south, who is brave enough to take that audacious action."

Mary was a little embarrassed with this profuse attention. She did not tell Miss Grimké what she was thinking, that it was out of ignorance, not bravery, when she first fell in love with her husband as to the reaction their marriage would induce from nearly everyone except Quakers and other blacks, and even then she couldn't be sure.

"Indeed, Mrs. Wellin's, ah wish we could bring you to the forefront of the movement and hold you up as a paradigm for people who truly aspire that their deeds speak more mightily than their words. Alas, however, ah fear to do so would gravely endanger you and your husband."

"As we have found out," said Mary. She told Miss Grimké a little about her family and some of their experiences in the first year of their marriage.

"That is truly a shame, but certainly not unexpected according to my experience. Why, ah dare say, ah don't believe your marriage would even be legal, let alone accepted, in any other quarter of the country—if not the civilized world."

Mary was surprised. She knew that she and Lang were unique in Bucks County; she had no idea their uniqueness extended that far.

"I think we truly are fortunate," she said, "to have the protection of the Quaker Friends. Even so, we must be careful." She told Miss Grimké about the guest last summer, the first and only outsider to find out about their relationship.

Miss Grimké lowered her head. "That is most definitely a shame. You are forced to hide in your own home. Ah still wish there was a way for you to come to Philadelphia to tell your story, at least to the governing board of the Society, if not publicly. Ah believe these are good people whom you can trust."

Mary's spirit was momentarily lifted. "Do you really think that's possible?" Then she thought about it for a second. "I don't know. I don't think we could afford the expenses. And where would we stay? Do you think we could take a chance that a hotel or boarding house would accept us? I certainly could not go alone."

Miss Grimké reluctantly nodded agreement. "Ah suppose you're right. Ah'm sorry ah mentioned it and unduly raised your hopes." She leaned over and gently took Mary's hand in hers. "But know that our thoughts and good wishes will follow you forever. Please do not hesitate to contact me and mah sister if we can ever be of service."

A few weeks after the ladies left, Mother Lacy and Mary were sitting in the parlor sewing, when a casual remark by Mother Lacy that she had received a thank-you note from Mrs. Mott and Miss Grimké raised Mary's hopes once again that she might be able to go to Philadelphia.

"Miss Grimké says she hopes a way will be found for thee to come to Philadelphia, Mary. Were thee seriously planning to go?"

"Oh, we had talked about it, that's all, but it's not possible, really."

"I had thought myself about going. I'm really feeling quite well—thanks to thy wonderful care, my dear—and, if I don't go now, it's doubtful I will be able to in the future. Philadelphia is so beautiful in the spring. The apple and cherry trees are blooming. The lilacs...." She smiled with the memories of previous visits that she and her husband had taken to yearly Quaker meetings.

Mary put down her sewing and looked at Mother Lacy. "Are you sure?"

"Oh, yes. I think we could easily make the trip in four or five hours. The coach is quite comfortable."

"But what about Lang? I couldn't possibly go without him."

"Oh, thou art right. I did not consider whether he would be given passage on the coach. I really don't know."

"Not to mention the fare. Or the hotel and other expenses."

"Oh, my! That does it, then. I cannot possibly go without thee, and thee will not leave thy husband, and rightfully so."

Later that night, Mary brought up the subject with Lang. She had told him weeks before of her heartening conversation with Miss Grimké, but he was skeptical then and remained so. "I just don't see how we can do it, Mary."

However, in the morning at breakfast with Mother Lacy, he broached the subject. "Mary tells me you're wantin' to go to Philadelphia. I think there's a way we can do it, if you're willing."

"How?" Mary and Mother Lacy both said at once.

"Well, we've got the big carriage. I can borrow another horse to make a team and we can rent fresh horses about halfway in Jenkintown and exchange them on the return trip. If I sit up front and drive you ladies, no one'd need know I'm not just your servant. You ladies can stay together at a hotel near the convention hall, and I'll find a colored hotel nearby. That way, we can all go see the big city at the least expense."

Mary jumped up and hugged and kissed her husband. "Oh, Lang! You are so sweet. You would do that for us—for me?"

Lang made a pretense of being embarrassed. "Now, we got a lot of details to work out. And only if you're sure you want to do this. It's a long, tiring trip, and there could be risks."

"I'm sure!" Mary's voice rang out. She looked at Mother Lacy.

"And I, too, my dear. Let us go to Philadelphia!"

Mary could barely contain her excitement. She began at once to sew a new dress and mantle for the trip. For the dress she found a bolt of lovely blue-flower on white background print calico cotton at the general store in Lahaska and a light-weight wool in dark blue for the mantle and a matching draw-string purse. She purchased enough of the blue wool to also make a jacket for Lang, and there was dress material left over to make a bonnet. All of this had to be cut, measured and sewn by hand, and each item of clothing took many hours to complete.

The pattern for the dress came from Godey's Lady's Magazine and was the latest style. It had a very large collar in plain white cotton that lay almost like a cape around her shoulders, a V-front that came to a point just below the waist, sleeves puffed from the shoulder to the elbow then tapered to fit the wrist, and a full skirt that whisked the floor lightly, under which she would wear three stiffened cotton petticoats.

She found an advertisement for the hat in the *Intelligencer* announcing a new millinery shop in Lahaska being started by Sarah Betts in her husband's store. She went to see Mrs. Betts and bartered some cloth in exchange for instructions on how to shape and sew the bonnet. Mary became a frequent visitor and assistant to Mrs. Betts thereafter, and the ladies formed a friendship that lasted many years until Sarah's death in 1856.

Sarah's husband, Tom, and their son, Cyrus, ran the general store in Lahaska for many years. He had a big sign in the window offering "Free Sugar," which meant that it was sugar that was not grown or produced using slave labor. It was more expensive, but made an important statement of their sentiments. For years afterward, Mary remembered fondly how Tom would always escort his female customers to the door. What a gentleman he was, to high and low-born alike, holding the door open, untying the horses and helping the ladies up into their wagons or carriages.

Mother Lacy's wardrobe for the trip was much simpler. For her entire life she had worn plain cotton dresses and white aprons around the house, and to Quaker meetings she wore black or dark blue wool dresses, with little or no embellishment, except a bunch of keys at her waist that were used to lock up everything in the house from spices and tea to silverware and bedsheets. Her outerwear consisted of a full-length woolen cape and a simple hat, white in summer or blue in winter, with a short eyeshade and a tie under her chin beneath which was worn another, small white cotton or lace cap surrounding her hair bun.

Mother Lacy did manage to find in her sewing basket some old dark blue satin ribbon that Mary folded and sewed ingeniously into tiny little rosebuds to decorate the collar of her new dress, and there was enough ribbon left over to make ties for the mantle, the purse and the bonnet.

Lang found a neighbor who promised to see to the animals every day, and borrowed a traveling map from a farmer who went to the markets in Philadelphia at least once a year. With Mary's help, he memorized the names of villages and other important milestones along the way. There were two ways he could go: Durham Road to the Second Street Pike, or York Road down to where it intersected with the Easton Road and on into Philadelphia.

May 14, 1838—traveling day dawned mild and cloudless, but because it had rained for a couple of days previously, at the last moment Lang decided to go all the way to Philadelphia by way of the York Road turnpike, instead of down the Durham Road, since York Road and Easton Road were kept in better condition and would have fewer mudholes to circumnavigate. Although that meant they would have to pay more tolls at several points along the route, it was definitely a safer route and with more traffic. In case there was any problem, there would be people around to assist.

Lang looked so handsome sitting tall in the driver's seat of the carriage in his new jacket and top hat. Mary was glad she had made the jacket in the old style—with a wide lapel, high waist, two rows of buttons in the double-breasted fashion, and long "swallow-tails" that hung neatly through the opening between the back of the bench and seat-back. His shirt was pure white cotton with a high collar and ties that formed a large, floppy bow. The hat, a black silk with a flaring brim turned down in the front and back, Mary had cleverly found for a very good price at an estate sale in the neighborhood that she read about in the *Intelligencer*.

The weather was warm enough to have the carriage top down, and Mary and Mother Lacy immensely enjoyed the view as the horses trotted easily along. The load was light, as Mary and Mother Lacy needed only enough clothing for five days, and they were able to share one trunk, which Lang strapped onto a ledge at the back of the carriage. Lang had a smaller, separate valise.

Leaving Lahaska, they passed down through Greenville, then Centreville, where the road went off to the right to Doylestown. Lang kept on the Old York Road, veering to the left, through Bushington and Bridge Valley where he pointed out the road leading to the Alms House where, he had been told, he was born twenty-seven years ago. He had gone there once a couple of years ago, he told the ladies, to see if there was anything he could find out about his father, but was told they had no records.

It took almost all morning to reach Willow Grove, just above where the Easton Road intersected in a "Y" with the York Road. Lang let the horses walk at an easy pace. He did not want to unduly work them. They had all day to get to Philadelphia in a leisurely manner, and there was no reason to race down the pike as did the commercial coaches that made the run from Doylestown to Philly in three and a half hours, stopping at several towns along the way.

As it turned out, when they got to Jenkintown, where he had initially thought he would exchange the horses for rented ones, after watering and grooming the animals and allowing them to eat and rest while he and the ladies relaxed and enjoyed a picnic lunch that Mary had packed, Lang decided they were doing fine and could easily make the remainder of the trip to Philadelphia. And he was right in his estimation that everyone would think he was the ladies' servant. No one even once glanced askance in their direction.

By two o'clock in the afternoon, Mary began to notice the farms gradually give way to huge mansions with gated drives and immense formal gardens, and a few private schools and colleges that lined both sides of the road just north of the city. She had never in her life seen such big buildings and beautiful gardens and could scarcely believe it when Mother Lacy told her that each one was a private home for only one family, and servants, of course.

"Why I've heard sometimes there are more servants than members of the family," she said.

As they drew closer to the center of the city, they came to the row houses, some wooden and others made of brick or brownstone, then eventually very tall buildings, a few six and seven stories high, interspersed with tall church steeples. Mary was truly amazed, and Mother Lacy herself admitted it had been a long time since she had been to the city and there had been many changes in the meantime.

Lang was also in awe of these surroundings. He had never been to Philadelphia—indeed, except for an excursion or two to Lambertville, New Jersey, he, too, had never been out of Bucks County. He became a little concerned as they ventured further into the city, as he had not before driven with so many other carriages on the same road at the same time, but he quickly picked up the rules of the road and managed to keep his team in the flow of traffic.

Even with the persistent instructions from Mary in the back seat, for example, one time when he was unable to avoid a gaping pothole in the road because there was another carriage to his left.

"Oh, do be careful, Lang!"

"I'm doing the best I can."

He looked to his left and saw the other driver, also Negro, touch his hat lightly with his horsewhip and smile in his direction with a shrug of his eyebrows that so much as said, "Brother, I know what you're dealing with." Lang couldn't help but wonder what the man would think if he knew Lang's back-seat driver was his wife!

When they passed an intersection with a little sign reading "Kensington" pointing to the left, Mary called out, "That's where Jonas and Lydia live." She noted to Mother Lacy that she had written to Jonas telling him of their journey to Philadelphia and her hope to see him and his family. It would not be until they returned to Lahaska that she would find his return letter sent hastily, but too late, warning them against coming.

> *Dearest sister, I pray you, do not come to Phila. to this anti-slavery convention. I have heard the men being agitated. The opposing sentiment runs so hot here that I fear for your safety at such a gathering. I shall write more later, but hasten to post this message.*
>
> *Your loving brother, Jonas*

When Lang, Mary and Mother Lacy traveled to Philadelphia in May 1838, it was already a big city—by some accounts the third largest city in the world, after London and Paris.

In 1842, a soon-to-become-famous visitor, Mr. Charles Dickens of London, England, described his impressions of the city with its broad, flagged streets. It was "a handsome city, but distractingly regular," he wrote, referring to the "checkerboard" layout of the streets, "that is most bountifully provided with fresh water, which is showered and jerked about, and turned on, and poured off, everywhere. The Waterworks, which are on a height near the city, are no less ornamental than useful, being tastefully laid out as a public garden, and kept in the best and neatest order. The river is dammed at this point, and forced by its own power into certain high tanks or reservoirs, whence the whole city, to the top stories of the houses, is supplied at a very trifling expense.

    * * *

"The Waterworks had been built before 1824. From the great reservoir the water runs through pipes and conduits to every quarter of the city, indeed, almost every house, where any desired quantity may be had merely by turning a faucet. There are stand-pipes in every street which can be used as long as need be in case of fire. When the hose from a fire engine is connected to one of these, the water gushes out with double the force provided by an ordinary fire pump."

Mr. Dickens also described "various public institutions, among them is a most excellent Hospital—a Quaker establishment, but not sectarian in the great benefits it confers; a quiet, quaint old Library, named after Franklin; a handsome Exchange and Post Office; and so forth."

In 1835 gas lines were beginning to be laid out. At first only streetlights were lighted by gas, then gradually the inner-city offices, hotels, theaters and businesses were fitted for the convenient new lighting system.

When Mother Lacy asked Bucks County Friend Marmaduke Watson, who owned the Barley Sheaf Hotel at Second Street between Vine and Race, about accommodations, he replied that he was completely booked with conventioneers and referred her to the Mount Vernon House, operated by Ferdinand Roberts and Daniel Mixer, located on at No. 95 North Second Street, nearby the just-opened Pennsylvania Hall, at Sixth and Haines Streets, where the meetings of the convention were to be held.

Pennsylvania Hall had just been dedicated the preceding Monday evening. The imposing Georgian-style structure, framed with wood and with marble and granite façade, built by a consortium of abolition groups with donations from around the country, had cost an incredible forty thousand dollars to build.

As they checked into the hotel, they were pleased to find out there was separate, but affiliated, housing close by for Lang—the "servants' quarters"—through the courtyard in the back near the stables where the horses would be sheltered during their stay.

Mary's heart ached with gratitude for her husband's sacrifice as she watched him unload their trunk and lead the carriage and horses around to the stable. The hotel's porters and hostlers did not assist, since they assumed he was a servant as they were. Mary learned to her further profound disappointment that Lang was not allowed to sit at table with them in the dining room, but she felt better when she heard they could take their meals in their room, and he was allowed upstairs until the hour of ten o'clock to wait on the ladies.

As they stood waiting for Lang to return, their attention was quickly diverted by a commotion in the small parlor off the lobby. Several of the other people attending the convention were there, and all were abuzz about the mob of men who had apparently marched on the hall earlier in the day protesting the meeting. Several of the people held printed leaflets warning the abolitionists of "dire consequences should you fail to cease and desist this folly." Mary and Mother Lacy became somewhat concerned, but were reassured by one of the men who spoke out with an air of authority.

"Now, there's nothing to fear, ladies. You must not allow these bullies to alarm you. We have found for the most part they are just ignorant laborers whose passions have been inflamed by the minions of slavers to wrongfully believe that, if we are successful in abolishing slavery, their jobs will be taken away and given to the freed Negro class. These poor souls are merely the hapless pawns—indeed, no better than slaves themselves—to the interests of those who seek, at all costs, to protect and preserve their own financial status without the slightest care of the consequences to their fellow man."

He answered a question from a woman in the crowd that Mary could not quite hear by holding up his hands and pushing them down in a calming motion. "Please, ladies, be assured, we have procured security men and police who are posted everywhere for your protection. Do not think for a moment we would allow our dear wives, mothers, sisters and daughters to be endangered in any manner."

The crowd broke up into smaller groups, and all were chatting at once. By this time, Lang had come back from the stables and was ready to carry the ladies' trunk up to their room—three flights of stairs—until Mother Lacy inquired and was told there was a "dumb waiter" that could be used to lift the trunk up to the third floor.

The room, compact and tidy, contained a double bed with wooden headboard, a wooden chiffrobe with mirror, chaise longue, and small table with washbasin. The wooden floors were painted brown, and there was a large, rough-stitched, and painted carpet made out of hemp in the center of the room.

When Mary first entered the room, however, she took no notice of the furnishings because all she could see was the window facing the street and looking toward the east out to the great Delaware River and harbor.

"Look Lang!" she cried out rushing to the window. "We can see all the way to the river!" Then she looked down to the street below and became slightly dizzy.

"Oh, my, I've never been up so high in my life!" She had to sit on the chaise longue for a moment, but soon the lure of the vista overcame her vertigo and fear. Even though the window was open but a foot or so, she held onto Lang, just in case, as she gazed out at the stunning view.

The river and harbor were filled as far as the eye could see with ships and boats of all sizes—tall-masted ships at anchor, large and small boats coming and going, sails tied up and unfurled. There seemed to be, even from a distance, a great bustle of activity.

"Can we go to the wharf? Lang, what do you think?"

"Oh, I don't think the wharf is any place for a lady, my dear," Mother Lacy interjected. "I have heard 'tis filled with ruffians and vermin and filth. There is so much else to see in the city, and perhaps we can take a ride past the wharfs on the way home. Would that suit thee?"

Lang nodded agreement. "Perhaps we will even find a train."

"All right, that settles it, with two of you against me." She laughed merrily. "Have you seen a chamber pot? I must relieve myself before we go."

Mother Lacy looked under the bed, and found nothing there. Then she noticed a hand-printed sign on the door that announced, "Conveniences are located on each floor at the far end of the hall."

Mary was incredulous. "You mean they have a whole room for noth-ing but chamber pots!? Whatever will we find next?" To her delight, the next amazing thing she discovered was that running water was piped to a faucet in the "convenience room" on each floor.

They spent the rest of that afternoon and the next day exploring Philadelphia, and they found overall a very lovely city, if one was able to keep one's eyes above the streets, which, in many cases, were filled with running drainage. Mary and Mother Lacy had to be extra mindful of lift-ing their skirts when crossing the oyster shell and cobblestone paved streets. The roads back home were dusty, for sure, but it was good, clean dirt there, not raw sewage as was found here.

They saw beautiful public gardens and the Philadelphia Mint and the graveyard, in the corner of Christ Church yard, where Benjamin Franklin, his wife, and several other famous people were buried. Mother Lacy tossed a penny on the small marble slab that marked Franklin's grave. "For good luck," she said. (Of course, as soon as they were out of sight, one of the ubiquitous street urchins raced in to claim the prize. It was certainly good luck for him—it meant a filling supper that evening consisting of soft pretzel and beer.)

They saw the new Washington Monument, which was in the pro-cess of being built, and Independence Hall, with its stately bell and clock tower, that they learned had just a few years before been turned from its original Georgian style, designed by Alexander Hamilton and Edmund Wooley, into a Greek revival building by architect John Haviland. It was in use at the time as a courthouse, and they could not enter the room where the Declaration of Independence was reportedly signed.

They heard an unusual amount of barking coming through the grates to the basement of the building and were told, to Lang's revulsion, that the city's stray dogs were brought there and housed until they were claimed or euthanized. "At least they're kept off the streets, Lang," Mary comforted him, knowing of his extraordinary fear of the animal since he was a child.

While they were walking from Independence Hall in the adjacent park back toward the hotel, the tower's bell began pealing. All three commented that it produced a distinctly odd, almost off-key sound.

They came to a house on Arch Street that purportedly had belonged to Betsy Ross before and during the Revolution and, it was said, where she had sewn the famous flag. Mrs. Ross had just passed away two years before at the age of eighty-four, and, in fact, had moved from this place long ago, in 1786.

The present owner of the home made it distinctly clear he did not suffer these meddlesome fools kindly. "Fuss and bother!" he fumed, when one bold lady ignored the "Private—Keep Out" signs and a smaller sign that read, "NOT Mrs. Ross's home," and knocked on the door anyway.

Above all, Mary was most impressed with the library. When she saw all the books, she nearly cried with joy. She caressed the spines of several of them, and said dreamily, "Oh, how I long to be close to such an inexhaustible supply of reading matter! Why, Mother Lacy, I could begin reading this minute and never finish in a lifetime." She thought for a second of Papa and how he would have loved to see this, as well.

During their walks, Lang kept discretely behind the ladies a few steps, yet noticeably "with" them, as he had observed servants, both colored and white, behaving. He would walk in time with them; if they stopped to look in a shop window or admire the scenery, he would stand still and wait until they were ready to move on.

Mary learned how to move her parasol just slightly on her shoulder, turn as if speaking to Mother Lacy and make a comment within easy hearing volume of Lang in order to keep him in the conversation as much as possible.

One of their lunches was purchased from a street vendor and enjoyed sitting on park benches—separate park benches. Otherwise, whenever they stopped for lunch or tea at a restaurant, Lang sat alone or with other "servants" in the adjacent bar or at a separate table in the back toward the kitchen. Mary was personally grieved with having to be separated from her husband, but Lang laughed it off.

"It's no matter," he said. "Besides, I really do enjoy meeting and talking to the other men. I'm learning a great deal from them about conditions in Philadelphia." He didn't say it, but she knew he meant conditions for the Negroes.

A couple of times, Mary forgot the "arrangement" when she became particularly excited by something. "Oh, look, Lang!" she cried out one time and grabbed his arm to show him whatever it was that had engaged her attention. Lang quickly looked around; thankfully, no one had noticed.

One time her attention was drawn to a playbill posted on the side of a building announcing a play by Shakespeare starring Edwin Forrest at the Walnut Street Theater. Mary became excited about the prospect of actually seeing a production of one of Shakespeare's plays until Mother Lacy innocently said, "I'm not familiar with his plays. How docs thee pronounce the title—is it O-tello or O-thello?"

"Oh, no! I guess we'll not be seeing that!" Mary said.

"What's wrong with it?" Mother Lacy asked, and Mary replied, "Oh, nothing. Just not one of his best plays." She was not about to tell them the true reason and was grateful the playbill had no depiction of Forrest in blackface make-up.

They settled instead for a performance of concertos, written for the pianoforte by Felix Mendelssohn-Bartholdy, performed in a little theater where they were able to procure a ticket for Lang to sit in the balcony. Mary was enchanted with the music and remarked that she couldn't wait to have a piano once again, not that she could ever hope to play that well, of course. Lang thought it very nice, but still couldn't help nodding off a couple of times. He was actually grateful he was not sitting next to Mary as undoubtedly she would have indignantly rapped him on the head with her fan to wake him up.

All day on May 16 and into the evening was spent in meetings at Pennsylvania Hall. That morning, as they came around the corner on Haines Street, they were alarmed to see a large crowd of men gathered in front of the hall. Most of the men stood murmuring among themselves in small groups. Others were quietly handing out leaflets, and still others were hurling insults at the women and men who walked to the front door, saving their worst invectives for the Negroes, who walked straight ahead with a dignified poise seemingly deaf and blind to what was going on around them and refusing to allow the hooligans the satisfaction of a reaction.

Mary and Mother Lacy stiffened and slowed their pace for a second.

Lang urged them on in a whisper. "Go ahead. Look at the guards standing against the building."

Mary looked up to her right and saw, indeed, there were several men, some with guns openly displayed, standing along the front of the hall. There were also several mounted officers posted across the street. She continued and tried to keep her eyes focused straight ahead, not at the mob.

Once inside the building, Lang felt welcomed by everyone around him and was invited to sit in the hall right alongside Mary and Mother Lacy. It was the only place in the city they dared to let down their guard, although they still did not allow anyone but the directors of the Society to know their true relationship, especially after a private meeting with the Executive Committee after lunch that afternoon.

It was Miss Grimké who invited them to address the Committee. She had caught sight of Lang, Mary and Mother Lacy that morning in the main saloon of the hall and come rushing over to welcome them profusely.

"Oh, mah dears! Ah'm so happy you were able to come after all. Please, allow me introduce you to mah sister, Sarah"—with her Southern drawl, she said it as "Say-rah" and Mary found it so sweet to hear—"and mah fiancé, Mr. Weld."

She invited Mary and Lang to appear that afternoon before the Executive Committee of the Philadelphia Female Anti-Slavery Society, who turned out to be all Caucasians. Mary found out later than the only Negro members, Mrs. Charlotte Vandine Forten and her daughters, Harriet Forten Purvis and Sarah and Margaretta Forten, were unable to attend that afternoon due to a family commitment.

The ladies warmly welcomed the couple and listened politely as Mary told their story. Lang was too shy and reticent to speak before these famous and formidable-looking women.

When she was finished, Mary got the distinct impression that a couple of the women were somewhat offended, if not downright hostile. One of them spoke up. Mary could not remember to tell Mother Lacy later if it was Mary Grew, Mary Ann McClintock, Sarah Pugh or Abby Kimber, who, in addition to the Misses Grimké and Mrs. Mott, were present. "May we ask you a few questions?" she inquired.

"Of course," Mary replied.

"I am wondering how it was that you were able to, ah, lawfully marry. I was under the impression that it was not legal in any state in the Union."

Mary explained what Reverend Miller had told her—that the law simply stated whatever was acceptable to the church was legal in the Commonwealth.

"Very interesting," the lady responded. "I'm not at all sure we want to call attention to that."

One of the other ladies agreed and asked if Mary and Lang were aware of any other interracial marriage.

Mary shook her head "no" and looked at Lang. He shrugged and whispered something in Mary's ear that caused her to become momentarily flustered.

"What is it?" Mrs. Mott asked.

Mary blushed. "Oh, nothing. I mean, my husband was simply pointing out the evidence all around us, ah, that is…of the races mixing in, ah…well, I mean, in the procreation of children. But, I don't suppose that would be considered a 'legal marriage'."

Several of the ladies cleared their throats and looked at the floor in obvious embarrassment.

After a little more discussion, Mary and Lang were excused to wait outside in the hallway while the Committee deliberated. Lang leaned against the window frame and looked out the window at the mob of protestors in the street below that seemed to be growing in number and clamor.

"Just what is it you expect from these people?" Lang asked Mary when they were alone in the hallway.

"I don't know," she replied honestly.

"Were you thinking about getting more involved in this?"

"I will admit the thought had crossed my mind that I might have something to contribute to the movement, but I hadn't thought about it enough to make a decision."

Lang resumed looking out the window. Then he turned back to Mary and said, "I don't know, Mary. It's not such a good idea, in my opinion."

"But, I'm amazed, Lang. Don't you want to help your fellow people who are still struggling under the yoke of oppression?"

"Absolutely," he said and turned back to look at the menacing crowd below, "but there are probably less obvious and dangerous ways to do it than openly attending meetings, giving speeches and such, like these ladies do."

When they were called back into the room, Mrs. Mott assumed the role of spokesperson for the group.

"Mr. and Mrs. Wellings, first of all, the Committee would like to extend to you our warmest greetings and deepest appreciation for your willingness to come here and attend our Convention. You are both to be commended and honored in your genuine bravery and perseverance in the face of the most extreme resistance to the level of unity of the races that your marriage so enormously signifies.

"That being said, however, the Committee feels it would neither do your well-being nor our movement any good to call attention to yourselves and your true relationship. In fact, we are firmly convinced, so great is the opposition to our cause of merely freeing the slaves, let alone granting the Negro the basic human rights accorded to all men by the Constitution, that to do so would be to bring our movement to ruin and would place yourselves in serious personal danger. Unfortunately, there are still a great many people who, while professing sympathy for the cause of abolition, and even attending our meetings, would have nothing to do with an organization that promoted open intermingling of the races to that degree.

"I believe Miss Grimké has shared some of these thoughts with you previously. I do hope you understand that we value your friendship and support. At the same time, we would hope that you continue to keep your secret as much as you possibly can. Mrs. Wellings, I understand you have been telling people here in Philadelphia that your name is Mary Stone. We would appreciate it if you would continue to do so, at least in front of our general membership.

"We do wish you the best of health and happiness and fervently pray for the day that conditions will improve to the point that you will be openly welcomed, not only here in our midst, but in society in general."

Mrs. Mott smiled kindly and nodded at the other ladies signifying she was finished. They all rose at once and came around the table to shake hands with Mary and Langhorn, some stiffly, yet politely, and others with genuine warmth and friendship. Angelina, in particular, gave Mary an affectionate hug and whispered, "God bless you and keep you, my dear."

Although intellectually, she perfectly understood their reasoning, still Mary felt a profound hurt and rejection by these women who, of all the people on the earth, she would have expected to embrace and champion their union.

She covered it well by smiling sweetly and thanking them all for their time and friendship.

That evening, Angelina was scheduled as the keynote speaker. Lang, Mary and Mother Lacy took a light supper in their room and walked back to the hall for the meeting.

The crowd outside seemed to have grown even larger. Mary noticed a man, obviously an authority—she learned later it was the Mayor of Philadelphia—entreating the mob to give up the protest and go home.

As they walked closer to the front entrance, they saw a carriage inch its way through the crowd and come to a stop. A white man opened the door from the inside and alighted. He was quite distinguished-looking, tall and lean, with a thin face and nose, a mass of tangled dark brown hair, and long "mutton-chop" sideburns.

Mary would remember the rest of what happened that night for the remainder of her life. She would play it over and over in her mind through the years, almost in slow motion, and every detail would be as clear as—indeed, clearer than—the moment it actually happened.

In fact, she didn't take much notice of the man until he turned around and extended his hand toward someone inside the vehicle. One gloved hand took his; the other hand momentarily clutched the bearer's voluminous skirts—made from a lovely, shimmering purple taffeta—until her toe could touch the carriage step, then went to the hand-grasp on the door frame to steady herself as she got out of the carriage.

She was a Negro. The thing that impressed Mary immediately was that the lady was particularly beautiful—and very rich, by the looks of her toilette, jewelry and clothing.

Then the man did an extraordinary thing. He took the woman's hand, hooked it through his crooked arm, at the same time pulling the lady close to him and smiling at her lovingly. He patted her hand gently, probably unconscious that he was doing so, as they proceeded into the hall just ahead of Mary and Mother Lacy, then Lang, who was followed by an important-looking black gentleman who got out of the carriage right after the lady but stopped briefly to speak with the driver.

The crowd immediately reacted. "Did you see that?" "…Easy familiarity…." "…fraternizing with the coloreds."

Mary was at first hurt and confused. *How dare they tell Lang and me to keep our marriage a secret, then let this couple openly touch and flaunt their affections?*

She watched as the two and the other man were warmly greeted by everyone inside the hall. *They're obviously very highly placed in the organization and rich, too.*

Lang himself was puzzled. "I guess that's all that really talks around here, Mary—money," he whispered to her. Mother Lacy patted Mary's hand, "Never mind, my dear. Don't be too disappointed. Trust there is a reason in God's plan for everything."

Their attention was immediately diverted by Mrs. Mott who pounded the gavel on the podium to begin the meeting. There appeared to be an immense crowd, at least a thousand people, if not more, in the audience. As part of her summation of the convention Mrs. Mott mentioned the protestors outside.

"Ladies and gentlemen, we must pay no mind to these poor, misguided creatures. We have never before been cowered by opposition, and we will not become feint of heart now—nor ever!"

The audience clapped enthusiastically, and a couple of the men yelled, "Hear! Hear!" and banged their canes on the wooden floor.

Mrs. Mott then acknowledged the presence of several, obviously well-placed individuals in the Society who were sitting in the front of the hall, including the couple Mary had been so confused and hurt about.

"…Mr. and Mrs. Purvis" she bowed, and the audience clapped. "Mr. Forten"—more clapping. *They're married!* Now she was even more puzzled and angry. *My husband is just a poor workingman, so we're not acceptable. I suppose that's it, then. It's different if it's a white man and a colored woman.* Her eyes misted with pained tears.

The chairlady then gave a heartfelt tribute to Angelina in introduction, who stood up to great applause and began to speak. And what a powerful speaker she was! Mary was immediately caught up in her eloquence and fervor.

As she was talking, the audience couldn't help but hear outside the mob of angry protestors shouting and brandishing their torches. One in particular had jumped on a box and was inciting the crowd.

"This is what these women have in mind for you and your wives and your daughters! They intend to give away your jobs, your homes AND YOUR WOMEN to these niggers!"

The crowd noise swelled along with the speaker's voice. Miss Grimké couldn't fail to notice either.

"Men, brethren and fathers—mothers, daughters and sisters, what came ye out for to see? A reed shaken with the wind? Is it curiosity merely, or a deep sympathy with the perishing slave, that has brought this large audience together? Those voices without ought to awaken and call out our warmest sympathies. Deluded beings! 'They know not what they do.' They know not that they are undermining their own rights and their own happiness, temporal and eternal. Do you ask, 'What has the North to do with slavery?' Hear it—hear it. Those voices without tell us that the spirit of slavery is *here*, and has been roused to wrath by our abolition speeches and conventions: for surely liberty would not foam and tear herself with rage, because her friends are multiplied daily, and meetings are held in quick succession to set forth her virtues and extend her peaceful kingdom. This opposition shows that slavery has done its deadliest work in the hearts of our citizens.

"Do you ask, then, 'What has the North to do?' I answer, cast out first the spirit of slavery from your own hearts, and then lend your aid to convert the South. Each one present has a work to do, be his or her situation what it may, however limited their means, or insignificant their supposed influence. The great men of this country will not do this work; the church will never do it. A desire to please the world, to keep the favor of all parties and of all conditions, makes them dumb on this and every other unpopular subject. They have become worldly-wise, and therefore God, in his wisdom, employs them not to carry on his plans of reformation and salvation. He hath chosen the foolish things of the world to confound the wise, and the weak to overcome the mighty."

She then began to talk about her experiences with slavery in the South and as she was talking, bric-a-brac and cobblestones that had been pried up from the street outside were thrown against the windows and doors.

Angelina drew herself up taller and spoke louder, "What is a mob? What would the breaking of every window be? What would the leveling of this Hall be? Any evidence that we are wrong, or that slavery is a good and wholesome institution? What if the mob should now burst in upon us, break up our meeting and commit violence upon our persons— would this be anything compared with what the slaves endure? No, no, and we do not remember them 'as bound with them,' if we shrink in the time of peril, or feel unwilling to sacrifice ourselves, if need be, for their sake...."

More shouting and noise from the front door of the hall, interspersed with appreciative clapping for Angelina's points.

"...I thank the Lord that there is yet life left enough to feel the truth, even though it rages at it—that conscience is not so completely seared as to be unmoved by the truth of the living God."

She went on to say that many Northern apologists of slavery who speak about the gentility and graciousness of the Southern slaveholder have never witnessed the perniciousness of slavery first-hand, but have spent their time in the big houses and mansions and never stepped foot into the slave hovels or seen how the slaves are beaten down and worked to death.

The mob outside shouted, unintelligible to the audience inside, but almost as if in rebuttal to Miss Grimké's speech.

She described how she grew to detest the institution of slavery, but felt herself "alone, crying out in the wilderness, with no one to respond, 'I, too, sister.'" She came to the North.

"I fled to the land of Penn; for here, thought I, sympathy for the slave will surely be found. But I found it not. The people were kind and hospitable, but the slave had no place in their thoughts. Whenever questions were put to me as to his condition, I felt that they were dictated by an idle curiosity, rather than by that deep feeling which would lead to effort for his rescue. I therefore shut up my grief in my own heart. I remembered that I was a Carolinian, from a state which framed this iniquity by law. I knew that throughout her territory was continual suffering, on the one part, and continual brutality and sin on the other. Every Southern breeze wafted to me the discordant tones of weeping and wailing, shrieks and groans, mingled with prayers and blasphemous curses. I thought there was no hope; that the wicked would go on in his wickedness, until he had destroyed both himself and his country. My heart sunk within me at the abominations in the midst of which I had been born and educated. What will it avail, cried I in bitterness of spirit, to expose to the gaze of strangers the horrors and pollutions of slavery, when there is no ear to hear nor heart to feel and pray for the slave."

She reminded the audience of how Egypt was punished by God, and Judea was torn down, as well, because of slavery. Then she turned her attention in particular to the ladies in the room by answering their unasked question, yet apparent on their faces, of "What can I do, a mere woman?"

First, she answered, they could start by educating themselves as to what slavery is, by buying books and lending them to their neighbors. Next by donating money: "Give your money no longer for things which pander to pride and lust, but aid in scattering 'the living coals of truth' upon the naked heart of this nation—in circulating appeals to the sympathies of Christians in behalf of the outraged and suffering slave."

"Women of Philadelphia! allow me as a Southern woman, with much attachment to the land of my birth, to entreat you to come up to this work. Especially let me urge you to petition. *Men* may settle this and other questions at the ballot-box, but you have no such right; it is only through petitions that you can reach the Legislature. It is therefore peculiarly *your* duty to petition. Do not say, 'It does no good.' The South already turns pale at the number sent. They have read the reports of the proceedings of Congress, and they have seen that among other petitions were very many from the women of the North on the subject of slavery. This fact has called the attention of the South to the subject. How could we expect to have done more as yet? Men who hold the rod over slaves, rule in the councils of the nation: and they deny our right to petition and to remonstrate against abuses of our sex and of our kind. We have these rights, however, from our God. Only let us exercise them: and though often turned away unanswered, let us remember the influence of importunity upon the unjust judge, and act accordingly. The fact that the South looks with jealousy upon our measures shows that they are effectual. There is, therefore, no cause for doubting or despair, but rather for rejoicing."

She then compared the potential work of the women of America to the successes of their English sisters. "It was remarked in England that women did much to abolish Slavery in her colonies. Nor are they now idle. Numerous petitions from them have recently been presented to the

Queen, to abolish the apprenticeship with its cruelties nearly equal to those of the system whose place it supplies. One petition two miles and a quarter long has been presented. And do you think these labors will be in vain? Let the history of the past answer. When the women of these States send up to Congress such a petition, our legislators will arise as did those of England, and say, 'When all the maids and matrons of the land are knocking at our doors we must legislate.' Let the zeal and love, the faith and works of our English sisters quicken ours—that while the slaves continue to suffer, and when they shout deliverance, we may feel the satisfaction of *having done what we could!"*

Angelina sat down, nearly exhausted from the emotional intensity and labor of her speech, to thunderous applause and rapping of canes and parasols.

Mary's previous hurt and dishonor were immediately overcome with the passions aroused by Miss Grimké for the great work to be done.

Suddenly, the sound of breaking glass and a shout from the back of the room brought everyone to their feet as they turned around to see what had happened. One of the torches had been tossed through the broken window. A security guard saw it and grabbed it before anything caught on fire, but the audience was alarmed.

Mrs. Mott came back to the podium. "Please, dear friends. You see that everything is under control. Let us now end this day's program and exit this meeting on a positive note. Reinforced with the power of God, let us go forth from this great gathering calmly, with our heads held high, secure in the knowledge that our cause is a God-given charge, and that He will be with us in everything we do."

As the guards formed a phalanx along the sidewalk from the front door out to Sixth Street, the conventioneers walked quietly out of the building, subdued yet seemingly armed, as well as by the guards, with an invisible shield that protected them from the epithets and wild shouting and menacing gestures of the mob without.

Mary, Lang and Mother Lacy went with a large group of people back to the hotel, picking up the pace of their walk as soon as they were out of sight of the mob. From behind they heard the yelling of the men swell into a crescendo, followed by the sound of breaking glass. The guards, unable to control the mob any longer, retreated from the hall behind the conventioneers.

At the hotel, the people fell into small groups, some in the lounge, others in the dining room. Mary, Lang and Mother Lacy stood for a moment in the lobby, not speaking about what they had experienced and were feeling, but instead conversing in an almost distracted manner about mundane things—as if in shock and unable yet to voice their true emotions.

The next day being devoted to business meetings of members of the Society, Mary, Lang and Mother Lacy resumed touring Philadelphia. And Mary was thrilled almost beside herself when they found a train station and she could actually see for herself up close this magnificent machine, seemingly alive with puffing smoke and steam, as it sat on the rails alongside a platform waiting for the next load of passengers and freight.

She and Mother Lacy, and even Lang, stood respectfully back from the imposing creature, which reminded Mary of the dragons she had read about in fairy tales. "I think I understand the lure this great beast has for Jonas. To actually have a part in building something like this."

When they returned to the hotel, they learned that the evening meeting had been cancelled. The Mayor had apparently succeeded in convincing the leaders of the Society to forego any more gatherings. He could not assure them of their safety any longer, he told them.

Mary and Mother Lacy had dinner in the dining room. Lang said he would eat a little something in his room; he wanted to rest anyway. He joined them later in the lobby where they sat for a while talking with other guests, while someone played the piano and others sat reading.

A white man began a conversation with Lang. "Were you a slave before?"

"No, sir."

"Oh. Where were you born?"

"Doylestown, Bucks County."

"And you've worked as a servant your whole life?"

"No, sir. I'm a limeburner."

The man seemed confused; he looked away and pretended to watch the piano player. He gradually drifted off to another conversation.

Lang watched him walk away and mused, *I wonder if he was only interested in talking to me if I had some horrible tale about slavery to tell? Is it possible we would have nothing else to talk about?*

Mother Lacy then remarked that it was getting late. "If we want to get an early start in the morning, we had best get some sleep now."

Mary and Lang agreed. "Alas, our trip is almost over and it's time to start for home already," Mary remarked sadly.

Then she turned her head toward a sound coming from outside. Through the closed doors, they could hear a tremendous noise of bells clanging, the wheels of the fire wagon rattling and the hooves of six great horses clopping upon the cobble-stoned streets.

Mary gave Lang a look of alarm and started to grab his arm seeking comfort and strength, but Lang said in a calming voice, "Yes, you are right, Mother Lacy. We must get our rest. I'll go check on the horses now. You ladies go on to your room."

As soon as Mary and Mother Lacy came up the landing to the third floor, they could see out the window looking west at the end of the hallway the red clouds of fire and smoke billowing from the direction of Sixth and Haines Streets. They knew instantly: Pennsylvania Hall was on fire.

They sat on the floor in front of the window and watched the fire. They could hear clanging and commotion all around and saw glimpses through the buildings of several fire wagons that came down the street to the side of the hotel.

Mother Lacy reminded Mary that Philadelphia had the most modern fire department in the country. "Remember the standpipes that we noticed on the streets. Those are for the fire hoses."

Suddenly, they heard urgent footsteps on the stairs and looked up to see Lang running down the hallway.

"Lang! What...?" Mary rose to meet him.

He was breathless from running up the stairs. "There's no time now, Mary! I've heard in the servants' quarters that the mob is marching on Mrs. Mott's home and is coming to this hotel, too. They know that many of the people attending the convention are staying here!"

Mother Lacy got up from the window. "Oh, my! What should we do?"

"You pack your trunk. I'll go hitch up the horses. We must leave at once. We can start back to home and sleep in the carriage, if necessary, once we are out of the city."

He looked at Mary. "Can you manage the trunk to the dumb waiter?"

"Yes, yes! Go now," she said, then cried, "Lang! I'm frightened!" and reached out to him. He hugged her close to him, kissed her quickly on the mouth and was gone.

By the time they got down to the lobby, the hotel staff were pulling the heavy wooden outer shutters closed to cover the windows and the two expensive glass doors that had "Mount Vernon Hotel" etched on each in an arch.

"You'll have to go out the back way, Miss," one of the clerks said. "It's not safe in the front, and we've shut the outer doors."

Just as well, Mary thought, *since Lang and the carriage should be waiting in the courtyard by now.* As Mother Lacy quickly settled up the lodging bill, Mary half-carried, half-dragged the trunk down the back hallway. She was happy she had packed lightly.

She found Lang and several other people in the courtyard also preparing their vehicles to depart. Mary and Mother Lacy hurried into the carriage and Lang, hoping to avoid the mob he presumed was gathering in front of the hotel, backed the horses around and went slowly out a narrow alley in back. He did not light the wicks in the carriage lamps, but was able to see well enough by the lights from building windows and the gas streetlamps on the major streets.

His next concern was how to avoid the traffic and commotion associated with the fire raging just three blocks to the northwest. He decided to keep to the alleys as much as possible while making his way steadily in a northerly direction.

He succeeded in doing so for several blocks, then came to Callowhill Road and, knowing that Callowhill intersected with the Easton Road, started toward that direction. It was quiet enough as they pulled out, but as they proceeded slowly down Callowhill, he could hear some commotion off to a side street on the left.

Suddenly, a group of about half a dozen men burst running onto Callowhill, some with torches, obviously part of the rabblerousers who had set the Hall on fire. They spotted the carriage.

"C'mon, boys, let's take the carriage!" one shouted. Lang stood up and tried to beat them off with his whip. "Go away! This is a private carriage!" he shouted. "There are ladies inside!"

The horses became jittery, then frightened and began rearing. Mary and Mother Lacy huddled together in the carriage, which was being jerked about by the horses' unsteady movements.

One of the men grabbed the reins and handed them to a youngish-looking boy about eleven or twelve and ordered, "Here, hold the horses!" Then he and the rest jumped up on the carriage, grabbed Lang, pulled him to the ground and began beating him with their fists.

Mary screamed and tried to get out of the carriage, and the horses reared again, this time with enough force to free themselves from the boy's grip, and Mary was thrown roughly back into the seat. Once freed, the horses began running off wildly down Callowhill.

The men looked away from beating Lang to see the horses and carriage getting away. "You little fool!" the older man shouted at the boy. "I told you to hold the horses."

"I couldn't help it, Pa! They was too strong for me!"

"Let's get out of here!" someone shouted, and the men ran.

Lang, beaten and bloody about the face and upper body, tried to get up. It was difficult for him to focus with blood streaming in his eyes, and it was impossible for him to reach the horses and carriage, which were already a block away, careering wildly from side to side.

Mary and Mother Lacy hung on to each other and the carriage as best they could. Mary tried calling out "Whoa!" but it was no use. She had the presence of mind to put her leg over Mother Lacy, wedge her against the seat with her body and hold on for dear life to the metal skeleton of the carriage top.

All at once, another carriage came at an angle through an intersection. The horses, seeing in their peripheral vision the other vehicle and its horses startled and rearing up, veered at once to the right. The carriage whipped about wildly, tipped up on two side wheels and then crashed to the ground with a terrible force. The horses, by now wild with fright, tried to keep running, but were brought up short by the tongue of the carriage having twisted suddenly between them as the carriage went over. Lang's horse lost his footing first and slid on his side on the cobblestones. The other horse fell on top of him and the carriage crashed into them both, all with the wrenching, sickening sounds of falling horseflesh, grating metal on cobblestones, and human and equine screams.

People began rushing out of houses and by this time a couple of the policemen who had been chasing the demonstrators came upon the scene. When they opened the carriage door, they found Mother Lacy, dazed and bruised but otherwise unhurt, laying on top of Mary who had received the full force of the fall. It was apparent that she was very badly injured. Blood covered her face and matted in her hair and stained her clothing.

The men lifted first Mother Lacy, then Mary out of the carriage as carefully as they could and laid her on a little grass plot in front of a row house nearby. Mother Lacy sat next to her. "Mary, Mary, please speak to me, dear." She ripped her petticoat and, with some water from a neighbor, began to clean Mary's face.

Someone looked down Callowhill and seeing Lang limping toward the accident scene went to help him over.

The horses, gravely injured, lay in a heap writhing and snorting with heavy breaths. One of the officers shook his head. "I'm afraid they're goners, by my reckoning." And at that moment, Lang's horse shuddered and died.

"Mary! How's Mary?" Lang pleaded when he saw Mother Lacy and Mary on the ground.

"I don't know, Lang," she answered in a worried tone. "She's breathing, but she's not coming around."

One of the deputies came up. "Excuse me, can you tell me who is responsible for these horses?"

"I am," replied Lang.

"Well, one of 'em's already dead. We'll have to shoot the other one. We need your permission."

Lang hung his head sadly. "Yes, yes, of course. Don't let the beast suffer, please." He turned away and a few seconds later heard the shot ring out.

One of the homeowners brought Lang and Mother Lacy into his house and his wife began washing Lang's face and examining him and Mother Lacy for injuries. Some men rigged a stretcher to carry Mary, and others rode quickly to the hospital to get the ambulance wagon.

When Mary woke in the hospital early in the morning of May 18, Mother Lacy was sitting by her bedside in the darkened room, the only light coming from a gaslight in the hallway. She was alone in a room with four beds that consisted of simple, low wooden frames, with a wooden plank over which was placed a thick down comforter encased in a heavy, rough cotton fabric that served as a mattress.

"Mother…." she cried out weakly.

"Oh, Mary, dear. Hush, my sweet. Thou art going to be fine."

"…You?"

"Just bruised a bit. Nothing serious."

"Lang?"

"He's all right, as well. A little the worse for the beating and roughing up he received." She told Mary about the horses having been killed and the carriage being completely destroyed.

"Oh, God," Mary sighed. "Whatever…to do?"

"Don't fret about it, my dear. Thee must rest and get well."

"I want Lang. Can I see him?"

Mother Lacy wagged her head. "I'm afraid not. They refused to believe he is thy husband. They insisted it was not possible." She smiled and caressed Mary's hand.

"What's wrong with me? I can't breath." She put her hand on her stomach and realized her upper abdomen was bound tightly. Then she reached her hand up to her head and found there, too, she was completely bandaged in cotton.

"Thee has apparently broken some ribs and there are other wounds, the worst being a deep gash on the side of thy head. I'm afraid it was me who caused thy injuries when I fell on thee. Thee saved my life, Mary."

"…praise God…you are safe. Could not live with myself…"

"Go back to sleep now. They have given thee medicines to sleep."

Mary slept all day, and the next time she awoke it was in the evening of the 18th, although she did not know it; she had no concept of time. She opened her eyes to see a man standing beside her bed. Her head was throbbing and she had trouble focusing.

"Who's there? Doctor?"

"No, I am not a doctor, Mrs. Wellings. My name is Robert Purvis." As he spoke, he leaned further into the faint shaft of light coming from the hallway. "We heard about your unfortunate accident, and I came from the Anti-Slavery Society to inquire as to your well-being."

Upon hearing the name, Mary blinked several times to focus. It was true—it was the man she had seen walking so closely with the Negro woman, apparently his wife, at the Hall the night before the fire.

"...don't need your help," she said and closed her eyes to avoid looking at him.

"I beg your pardon, Madam. Have I done something to offend you? I am sincerely regretful if I have."

Mary's mouth was so dry it was difficult to talk. "May I have some water?"

"Yes, of course, here is a carafe and cup." He poured a cup and gave it to Mary. "Pray, tell me now why you are obviously upset with me so that I may make amends?"

"You know that my husband is colored?"

"Yes."

"They tell me and Langhorn to keep our marriage a secret, yet you and your wife flaunt yourselves in public."

He looked puzzled for a second, then suddenly realized. "You mean...you think I am white? Oh, Mrs. Wellings! I thought everyone in the abolition movement knew. I am descended from slaves and have more than one-quarter African blood, which, in the definition of every racial law in this country, classifies me as one-hundred percent Negro."

"Oh!" Mary blinked in an attempt to clear her eyes and looked more closely at him.

"May I sit down for a few moments, Mrs. Wellings, and tell you my story?" Mary nodded, tried to change position and grimaced in pain. Mr. Purvis brought a chair closer to her side. "Oh, my. I won't stay for long," he said. "I see you are in discomfort."

He began: "I was born in Charleston, South Carolina, on August 4, eighteen ten."

"One month, two days after me," Mary remarked.

"For certain your parentage was...ah, shall I say, more conventional and *acceptable* to polite society. You see, Mrs. Wellings, my grandmother—my mother's mother—was a slave captured in North Africa. My grandfather was a German-Jewish merchant. My mother was unusually beautiful. She was freed by her father and became the common-law wife of my father, William Purvis.

"Father came to South Carolina from England and had made a small fortune by brokering cotton. However, he despised the fact that his wealth had been gained by the slave work of others, as well as the fact that he could not legally marry my mother there in the South, nor were they accepted into society. So he brought us north when I was just nine—mother, me, and my two brothers. We lived in Philadelphia and New England for a while.

"About two years ago I married Mrs. Purvis—Harriet Forten. I guess you saw us at the Convention Hall."

Mary nodded.

"And her father was with us—he is James Forten, a sailmaker here in Philadelphia, who has used his influence and financial resources all his life to fight slavery and injustice."

"You could easily have married a white girl, Mr. Purvis. Why a dark-skinned Negro?"

"And I can easily answer that by asking you the same question, Mrs. Wellings." Mr. Purvis smiled.

Mary nodded her head slightly in understanding.

"I cannot answer to God for any other man, Mrs. Wellings. I must answer for myself, and, for me, it was imperative that I not deny my heritage—indeed, it was critical that I embrace it and struggle to do whatever I could to improve the condition of its descendants. There have been many times that people, such as yourselves, have assumed I am white, and I will admit it has its advantages, especially when I am ferrying slaves to freedom. Oh, there was one particular occasion, if you would like to hear about it, when I deliberately 'passed' for white in order to exact revenge that proved to be quite entertaining indeed."

Mary's eyes opened in question; she obviously wanted to hear. So he told her of the time four years ago when he was denied passage on a ship to Europe because of the objections of a Southern white bigot, a wealthy Virginia slaveholder.

"So I took another ship to Europe. On the return trip, I found out on which ship this other *gentleman*—I use the term loosely—had booked passage and arranged passage for myself under an assumed name. I put on my finest Southern manners and speech and purposefully made acquaintance with this man and his friends. I was invited to dine with them and enjoyed many after-dinner conversations over cigars and brandy. I danced with their wives and daughters. I was really quite the dapper Southern gentlemen, if you will." Mr. Purvis raised his eyebrows and contorted his face to appear like a snob.

Mary smiled and chuckled. "Ouch!" She didn't know whether to hold her throbbing head or painful side.

"Oh, I am so sorry, Mrs. Wellings. Do you wish me to leave?"

"No, please. What happened?"

"On the last day, we arrived at the wharf and as our baggage was being taken onto the dock, and we were all standing around waiting to walk down the gangplank, as soon as I saw my trunks safely installed in my carriage, I swept my hat off and bowed in an overly-grand gesture to this gentleman, and in front of his family and entire entourage I said, 'I wish to thank you, sir, for your bountiful kindness and hospitality to one so humbly born. That you should offer your right hand so graciously in friendship to the grandson of slaves deeply touches my heart.' The man turned red and looked as if he was going to have apoplexy. And without another word I was gone to my waiting carriage."

Mary was enthralled. "That's a wonderful story!"

"It's one of the best experiences I have ever had." Mr. Purvis stood and pushed the chair back. "Well, I don't want to intrude and tire you any further. I just wanted to come and say that you mustn't worry about anything. The Society will see to it that your hospital bills are paid. I am sending your husband and Mrs. Lacy home in my carriage tomorrow. And, as soon as you are able to leave here, Mrs. Purvis and I want you to come to our home at Byberry to recuperate, and we will see that you get home in all possible haste."

"Thank you. I am very grateful…your generous friendship and kindness."

"Pas de quas," he said in French, "Not to mention it, Mrs. Wellings. But I must be going." He started to walk away, then came back. "I hesitate to risk adding to your injuries by telling you, but I think you should know. The mob turned their wrath today on a Negro orphanage. Thank God, most of the children escaped, but a couple of them were injured, and they are here in the hospital. I must see to them."

"Dear God, no! Innocent children!"

"Yes. Unfortunately true. I'm sorry to be the one to tell you, but you undoubtedly would have found out eventually, being here in the hospital, especially. Now, I definitely don't want to tire you because I see Mr. Wellings in the hallway. I hope you will forgive me, but I have used my influence to secure his admittance to your room. I'll go bring him in."

"Thank you, thank you, again."

Mr. Purvis bowed and left. A few seconds later, Lang came quietly into the room and knelt on the floor next to Mary's bed.

"Lang!" Tears came to Mary's eyes as soon as she saw him. His face was bruised and swollen, one eye almost completely shut.

"I'm afraid to touch you, Mary. You look like a little wounded bird."

"And you!" She gently touched his face.

"I guess I ain't so pretty any more," he said and raised his swollen lip to reveal a blank spot where a tooth once dwelt. "You still love me?"

"If you'll forgive me for wanting to come to Philadelphia."

"No, no, it was my idea in the end. There's none of us to blame."

"I'm so sorry about the horses, Lang. What are we to do?"

Lang hung his head and sighed deeply. "Well, I have to get another horse, and I'm bound to replace the one we borrowed. Then there's the carriage. I've got a little money put aside, and I guess I can work off what remains."

"And I've still got most of the twenty dollars that we earned last summer. We can take more summer guests this year." She tried to move and winced in pain.

"Oh, no! You're not going to be in any condition to be working so hard. If Mother Lacy wants to do that, we'll have to hire someone from the village to help out."

"And there goes my profit," Mary sighed "and my house." All her dreams were crashing in a heap almost as tragic as the carriage accident.

Lang hugged her gently. "It's all right, Mary. Everything will work out."

"Where's Mother Lacy?" Mary asked.

"She's very tired. The crash 'bout done her in. She's been sitting with you as long as she could, but she just had to get some rest."

Lang told her about the hotel run by Quakers they had located very near the hospital. "And as soon as Mr. Purvis and his father-in-law, Mr. Forten, and the rest heard about our accident, Mr. Purvis come to see us. He really is a fine gentleman, Mary."

"So I've found out. I guess I was hasty in my judgment of him."

Lang and Mary chatted for a few more moments. Lang told her more about the children's home that was burned. They both agreed they would like to get back to Bucks County as soon as possible, away from this frightening mass of malicious criminals who were allowed to roam and vent their rage at will. Philadelphia—ironically, the "City of Brotherly Love"—was not safe for anyone, and especially not for people of color.

Finally, it was time for Lang to go, but Mary clung to him.

"I have to go, Mary. The day people wouldn't believe me that I am your husband, and Mr. Purvis had to bribe the night watchman to let me in for a few moments. He told them I was here to visit the children from the Negro orphanage. They're just down the hall from you."

"Oh, Lang, I'm so frightened. We've never been separated by this great a time or distance."

Lang lifted her gently and cradled her in his arms. "You'll be fine. It's all right, dear girl. You'll be home safe 'fore you know it." He kissed her and laid her carefully back in the bed and was gone.

It would be two more weeks before she would see him again and, oh! how she missed him. Sometimes, in the wee hours, when a stray pain would strike her mending ribs, she thought it must be her heart busting from loneliness.

But, for tonight, other problems presented themselves. Mary had to relieve herself, badly. She gradually took the covers off and tried to lift her legs. She realized there was a sort of cotton diaper wrapped around her pelvic area encased in something that felt like sheep's bladder and tied around her waist. She didn't know it at the time, but it had been placed on her when she was first brought to the hospital and had not been changed since the initial examination.

She tried calling out, but it hurt to exert her lungs. There was no one there but the night watchman and a few people who were visiting or tending to family members. The matrons and maids had gone home for the night.

Mary knew she had to get out of this diaper and managed, after several tries, to untie the cord, then lifted her lower body, taking the strain against her shoulders, and pulled the swaddling out from under her in one, painful movement.

She relaxed back into the comforter carefully. There, that felt better.

Now, what? She still had to use the convenience wherever it was.

I've got to get out of bed. That's all there is to it.

Gradually, she moved first her feet and legs over to the side of the bed. Then, using her arms crossed over her chest, she slowly rolled over so that her knees touched the floor. Then she straightened up—oh! ow! After each effort, she had to rest.

Suddenly a man, a watchman on his rounds, appeared at the doorway with a lamp.

"What're you doin', miss!? You musn't be movin'. We'll have to tie you down."

"No, I'm fine. Really. I…" she struggled to overcome her propriety with talking to a strange man about personal things. "I have to use the convenience."

"Oh! Here, then. Let me help you." He came over and placed the lamp on the little side table that held the carafe and water cup. Then he lifted the seat of the chair and Mary was surprised to see that a chamber pot had been fitted into the body of the chair under the seat. *I never would have found that on my own!*

"Here you go, miss. Let me help you up."

As soon as she stood, Mary swayed and leaned against the man. Her need for support overcame her embarrassment and nervousness. She steadied herself with the arms of the chair.

"Thank you. I think I'll be all right now."

The watchman took the lamp and left, and Mary sat on the chair for a long time mostly resting. Then she used a corner of the diaper to clean herself with some of the water from the carafe and slowly got back into bed.

The next day, when the maid came who had been hired by Mr. Purvis to bring Mary's food once a day, clean her room and tend to her personal needs, Mary learned more about the hospital facility she was in.

"There are actually several hospitals in Philadelphia, ma'am," the girl told her. "There is one just for diseases." It had been established in 1810 in response to the numerous, recurring plagues of yellow fever, cholera, and malaria that swept over the city every few years. In 1793, for example, a great many people were stricken with yellow fever, and ten percent of the population eventually died from it.

"Then there's a hospital just for eyes." That was the Wills Eye Hospital, started in 1832 with a bequest from Quaker merchant James Wills. "I like working there the best. And then this hospital, the Pennsylvania Hospital, founded by Mr. Benjamin Franklin hisself almost a hundred years ago. You're lucky to have been brought here, ma'am, even though it is mostly for insane people. The other hospital is full of terrible diseases. No one I know wants to work over there. Myself, I'll take the crazy people any day!" She resumed changing Mary's bedding as Mary sat on the chamber-pot chair and waited.

She turned with an afterthought that gave Mary chills. "Oh, and be grateful you're not down in the charity ward, ma'am. Oh, that's a terrible place to be. I surely wouldn't want to be sick in a place like that. Why, it's no better than the streets, in my opinion.

"That's it, then," she called out as she rolled up the soiled bedding. "I'll be back tomorrow, ma'am, if there's nothin' else you'll be needing from me."

The next night, Mary could not sleep. As she lay awake, still alone in the ward, she listened to the sounds drifting faintly through the great building. Eerie shrieks, groans and wails wafted in and out of her hearing. It was very frightening, made even more so when she learned next day that the sounds were coming from the wards for the insane, which consisted of long rows of barred cells with men on one side of the building and women on the other end.

The cells contained nothing but bare cots and a large drainage pipe in the middle of the floor for the patients to relieve themselves. The cells, including the inhabitants, were hosed down once or twice a week.

All around the outside of the building there was a large, moat-like walkway. This was where the inmates were exercised. In the early years of the hospital, it was quite an entertainment for the people of Philadelphia—to come and watch the "loonies"—lunatics—parade around and around. The hospital at one point even charged admission of a few pence to raise funds for building projects.

And this was the first and most advanced psychiatric care facility in the country. Mary was truly grateful that Mr. Purvis' money and influence had saved her from being housed with those inmates.

She later learned from one of the doctors who came around each day to examine her that there was yet another hospital for the insane, the Friends Hospital started in 1813. "You know, Mrs. Wellings, it's estimated that one in five hundred people—especially women, for some reason—is afflicted with some degree of mental disorder. With the population of Philadelphia and its surrounding areas upwards of two hundred thousand, that makes…well, as you can imagine, there are hundreds of insane we must care for. Not to mention all the diseases, surgeries, accidents and injuries such as yours. It's overwhelming, absolutely overwhelming.

"As a matter of fact," he added as an afterthought, "we are in the process of converting these wards to house the insane. That's why they're empty, in case you were wondering."

The doctor had removed Mary's head bandage and pronounced her healing well. Mary had not seen herself in a mirror for days—it seemed like weeks. When the doctor looked away for a moment, she reached up unconsciously to touch the side of her head and felt stubble and a large scab where her hair used to be. *Oh dear, I must look like a sight!*

"Mustn't touch, Mrs. Wellings!" The doctor turned around to roll a new, smaller bandage over her wound. Then, sensing her distress, he said, "The hair will grow out in no time. I must say it was quite clever of them to shave only the hair around the wound. Usually, they just lop everything off and be done with it." He laughed and wagged his head. "This way, you will be able to brush your hair to cover the bald spot until it grows out. The ribs will eventually knit by themselves. Just take it easy and certainly nothing strenuous. I think you're well enough to go home and continue your recuperation."

Later that day, Mary was startled from a nap by the sound of almost hysterically loud talking close by. She looked around. Still no one in the room with her and in this she was of mixed emotions—she was lonely and fearful being by herself, yet was even more frightened by the horror stories she had heard about the diseases and mental illnesses that could possibly be manifested in a ward-mate.

She got up slowly and walked carefully to the hallway. This was the first time she had ventured so far from her bed. She looked up and down the hall and saw, a few doors away, two women, one of whom was the matron scolding another, younger woman who was crying and had her face buried in her hands.

"I'm tired, can't you see!" the woman cried. "I've been here for two nights and two days with no rest—no sleep!"

The matron appeared unmoved. "Until they send a relief for you, you will stay at your post. You'll just have to nap when you can."

"I just can't, ma'am. I can't. And it's cruel of you to expect me. I've got children of my own at home and my husband has to be off to work, as well. My babies are left on their own!"

Mary's compassion for the obviously distraught woman drew her further down the hall. She walked slowly toward them, bracing herself by sliding one hand against the wall as she walked. Matron looked up and saw her.

"Mrs. Wellings! You mustn't be out of bed! I'll have the devil to pay Mr. Purvis if anything happens to you."

"And what about me!" the other woman cried. "Why can't Mr. Purvis help me with all his concern for the colored children!"

Mary reassured the matron. "I'm fine, really. I'm not in as much pain anymore. Is there something I can do to help? I'm going mad...I mean, I'm bored and lonely in there by myself." Not to mention that she had no work or activity to do—not even a book to read—for the first time in her life that she could recall.

"You mustn't concern yourself, Mrs. Wellings. We'll handle this."

"Please, let me help. What is it this lady does? Is it possible I may relieve her and allow her to go home at least to see to her children?"

The matron continued to protest, but the other woman grasped at Mary as a savior. "Oh, would you, miss? It's not much I have to do. Just watch these poor little colored children who was injured in the fire. There's no lifting or anything like that," she added, noticing Mary's obvious injuries.

"Oh." Mary was taken aback for a second. She had never been around injured children, except for minor scrapes and bruises that her little brothers and sisters were constantly receiving. Still, she had made the offer.

"Well, I suppose that won't be too demanding, Matron."

"I'll just go home quickly and check on my babies and freshen up. Thank you, ma'am. Thank you so much." The woman was gone down the hall before Matron had a chance to protest or Mary to change her mind.

"Well, then, that's it. Here, let me show you the ward, Mrs. Wellings. If you insist you want to do this."

Mary followed as best she could as Matron walked briskly down the hall and turned into the room.

"There are two children here," she said matter-of-factly. "The little girl here is very severely injured and is sedated to keep her from moving. The other little fellow is much luckier. He'll be going to a new home today, won't you, dear."

A little face looked up at Matron with almost fear in his wide eyes. Mary guessed he was seven or eight years old, just about the same age Lang was when he was orphaned. Her heart did a little ping when she thought about Lang.

"There's an extra cot for you in case you need to lay down. They should be here for the boy—what's your name, boy?"

"Thomas, ma'am."

"They'll be here for Thomas sometime soon." And Matron was gone, just as briskly as she had arrived.

Mary smiled at the boy. "Hello, Thomas. My name is Mrs. Wellings. May I sit here on your bed?"

"Sure."

Mary looked around the ward. It was larger than hers and empty except for a couple of cots, a chair and a large table in the center of the room.

"How old are you, Thomas?"

"Eight, ma'am."

"How long have you been an orphan?"

Thomas frowned and shrugged. He looked down at the bed and started picking at the tightly-woven woolen blanket.

Well, that's that, I guess. He doesn't want to talk to me. Now what?

"Shall I tell you a story, Thomas?"

"Sure. I mean, yes, please, ma'am."

"Once upon a time there was a little boy named Langhorn. He was born in the Alms House in Doylestown, Pennsylvania…."

"Was he a black boy?" Thomas perked up a bit.

"Yes. Yes, he was. Anyway, his mother was very poor. And his father was either gone away or dead. He never found out…"

By the time Mary was finished telling the story of Langhorn Wellings of Bucks County to Thomas, the little guy had wiggled his way into her arms.

"Is that a real person, ma'am?" he asked.

"Why, yes, Thomas. He's my husband."

Thomas sat up and looked at her in awe. "You married to a black man?"

"Yes. Yes, I am. And I hope some day to have little children just like you."

"You do!?" Thomas could barely contain his surprise and confusion. "I wish you could be my mommy now. I ain't seen my mama for I don't know how long."

"Tell me about her."

Thomas shrugged and began picking at the blanket again. "I don't know. I never seen much of her."

"And your father?"

Thomas shrugged again. "He went to work on the docks is all I know'd. Didn't come home after a while."

Mary learned later from Mr. Purvis that little Thomas had been found begging on the streets of Philadelphia. He was taken to the orphanage and no one came to claim him for more than a year. Just before the fire, the orphanage had found a home for him as an indentured servant in a house in Chester County where he would learn to be a bootblack, footman and, eventually, butler. He didn't know his last name; therefore, his parentage and the history of his family could never be known.

"Mrs. Wellings, we are more fortunate than ninety percent of the people of this world in that we even know who our grandparents were."

Mary nodded in agreement and then paused to wonder for a few moments that she did not really know anything about her grandfather Stone, her father's father. All she had ever heard was, "We're from Germany, and you should be proud of it."

Mary and little Thomas talked for a while longer until the people arrived to take him to Chester County.

"May I have a hug, Thomas?" Mary asked as he stood before her to say goodbye. He hugged her gently.

"Good luck to you, Thomas."

"Thank you, ma'am." The boy smiled a big smile revealing spaces waiting for permanent front teeth. "And I hopes you have lots of li'l childrens just like me, just like you wants!"

The people waiting to take Thomas looked at each other in bewilderment.

All the time Mary had been there, the little girl had not moved or uttered a sound. After Thomas left, Mary got up and went to the child's bedside, which was under a window on the opposite side of the room. The instant she saw the girl, she was mother-love struck by her compelling beauty, her medium-brown, unblemished face with long black eyelashes lying softly against cherubic cheeks. *What an astonishingly sweet face. Like an angel!*

She appeared to be about two, or maybe as much as four years old. And she was deathly ill. Mary pulled back the sheet. The baby was naked, and her entire torso was swathed in salves and bandages. Mary could see open, unbandaged wounds on the girl's legs and arms.

"Oh, God!" Mary unconsciously brought her hand up to her mouth, and she gasped with a catch in her throat as she realized the extent of the child's injuries. She felt faint.

She covered the child again and went to the chair to sit and recover her composure.

The sight of this little child's injuries would haunt Mary for the rest of her life not to mention what happened later that night.

She went back to the bedside, torn by compassion and fear, the need to do something to alleviate the baby's pain and suffering, and yet the desire to flee as far away from this scene as she could. Finally, she decided to concentrate on the beautiful little face.

She remembered how much she enjoyed having her mother and grandmother stroke her forehead and hair when she was little. She reached out tentatively and touched the baby's forehead. The girl did not move.

Mary went to get the chair and brought it back to the bedside. She sat for it seemed hours looking at the child, stroking her forehead and hair. She reached under the covers and found the girl's little hand that was not injured and held the tiny fingers in her hand. *If only I could come up with some magical medicine to make her well.*

Finally, as it was growing dark outside and the night watchman came around to light the gaslights in the hallway, the caregiver came back.

"Oh, thank you, ma'am! I was so worried about my children, running about with no supervision. I've given them a good supper and my neighbor says she'll check on them every now and then. I see Thomas is gone. I can take my rest now since there's only the little girl to take care of. Poor little thing. It don't look good for her."

Mary closed her eyes and shook her head sadly. When she went back to her room, she found that the maid had been there and left her dinner on the table covered with a tea towel—a bowl of potato and cabbage soup with two pieces of bread. Mary was too disturbed to eat or to sleep well.

She lay on her bed for what seemed like hours. She must have drifted off to sleep because she was awakened with a start by a child's faint cry. "Mama…. Mama."

She got up and walked toward the little girl's room. The dark hallway was lighted only by the gaslights turned very low that were placed every twenty feet or so. She entered the ward and looked for the caretaker but did not see her anywhere.

The little girl was awake and whimpering, obviously in pain.

Mary sat in the chair next to her bed and began stroking her forehead. "I'm here, dear. I'm here."

"Mama," the child cried. Mary was astonished that the child could speak.

"Hush, dear. I'm here. What's your name?"

"Woo…. Wooth A…," the baby whispered in a barely audible voice. Mary struggled to understand.

"Ruth Ann. Is that it? Oh, what a sweet name for a sweet baby." The tears came coursing down Mary's cheeks as she felt more than saw in the dimly-lighted room the child's labored breathing and distress.

"I… Mama…"

"It's all right, Ruth Ann. I'm here. Jesus will come for you…" Mary tried to stop crying but her sobs began coming in gulps. She didn't know what to say or do to relieve the child's suffering. She wanted to scream out for help. Where is everyone?! *Dear God, where are you? Jesus! Help me!*

Ruth Ann began breathing in heavy sighs that came slower and slower, fainter and fainter, with a small, rattle-like sound deep in her throat. One more time she said, "Mama" very quietly, and sighed a final deep, soft moan.

Mary was heart-stricken. She hardly knew this angelic little creature, yet felt to the depths of her soul a kinship unknown to her before in her life—even beyond the love she felt for her husband, her mother, her little brothers and sisters.

At twenty-seven years of age, this was Mary's first direct association with death. She knew it had been important that she was there for Ruth Ann, almost as if she had delivered her spirit to heaven, just as the girl's physical mother had delivered her body to this existence. She was completely exhausted emotionally by the experience and physically drained, as well. Her ribs hurt and her head throbbed from crying, yet she could not stop sobbing. She laid her head on the baby's bed.

She woke in the morning in her own hospital bed. She did not remember having walked back to her room. She did not remember anything beyond the moment little Ruth Ann had died the night before. It was almost as if it had been a dream.

She stood up quickly and went down the hall. Ruth Ann's room was empty, no one there, not even the caretaker. She walked back to her own room and sat on the chair for it must have been hours until Matron arrived with the news that Mr. Purvis would be coming to take her to his home this day.

Mary sat with her head resting on her hand. "The baby died," she said.

"Yes, yes. So I found out when I came in this morning." Matron bustled about the room officiously. "Such a pity. I've seen so many over the years. And no one cares. Just another little nigger…."

"Don't call Ruth Ann that name!" Mary half came out of her chair. She was startled by the depth of her indignation.

Matron stiffened. "Well!" She turned around and marched out the door.

A few hours later when Mr. Purvis arrived, he found Mary sitting in the chair wrapped in her blanket, red-eyed from crying and twisting a corner of the blanket absent-mindedly. She told him what had happened.

"Mrs. Wellings, I'm stunned. I don't know what to say. Surely you must have been dreaming. The caretaker didn't mention anything about you being there, and she said she was with the little girl when she died."

"But I was there, and the caretaker was not, I tell you. I didn't imagine it." She told him about sitting in for the caretaker in the afternoon and evening and being with Thomas when the people came to take him to Chester County. "And how did I know her name was Ruth Ann? Perhaps the caretaker is afraid she will lose her job if you knew she had left the child alone."

"Perhaps, perhaps," Mr. Purvis agreed it was possible. Still it made Mary begin to question her own sanity and she would wonder for the rest of her life.

"I *was* there. I *didn't* dream it. It was too real," she said, half to convince herself.

Mr. Purvis sat on the edge of the bed and pleaded with her. "Please, Mrs. Wellings. Don't upset yourself. If it was so, I wish you had not gone there. There's nothing we can do to save a great many of these poor children. I can't say I will ever get used to seeing a child suffer and die, or even an adult, for that matter. And, of course, we must console ourselves with the knowledge that God has something so much better in store for them—especially these innocent little babes who have offended no one, 'original sin' or no 'original sin'."

They sat for a few moments not speaking until Mr. Purvis felt it was time. "Do you think you are well enough to leave now?"

Mary nodded. "I guess so. I do want to go home very much."

Mr. Purvis stood up. "Very well, then. I'll step outside in the hallway and wait for you to dress. Look. I've brought your trunk with a very pretty white dress with blue flowers, I see. They saved it from the carriage accident. I'm afraid we couldn't save your mantle and bonnet, but I think there are some additional things that Mrs. Lacy sent back with the carriage from Lahaska."

Mary brightened up. "Do you have news of Langhorn and Mother Lacy?"

"Oh, yes, everyone is fine. They are anxiously awaiting your arrival at home, so you must hurry and get well. You will rest at our home for another week or so until we are assured that you are completely mended."

After she had dressed and packed her few things in the trunk, Mary joined Mr. Purvis in the hall, who sent his driver in to carry the trunk.

He escorted her down the hallway to the large staircase. "Before you go, Mrs. Wellings, I want you to see the famous painting, 'Christ Healing the Sick in the Temple.' It was done by American artist Benjamin West and donated to the hospital in eighteen seventeen."

Once she could see the whole structure, Mary was impressed with the beautiful buildings, especially the main entrance, called the "Great Court" with its wide-planked, polished pine floor, imposing columns and grand staircases. She learned there were an apothecary and a library that housed the largest collection of medical books in Pennsylvania, if not the whole country. In fact, the library had just recently been turned back to house books, having been used from 1824 to 1835 as a lying-in facility for women to give birth.

And, wonder of wonders, an amazing, delightful contraption called a "musical planetarium clock," built by David Rittenhouse in 1780. It had been donated to the hospital by Sarah Zane and installed in the lobby since 1819.

As she looked back at the building before stepping into the carriage, it struck Mary as rather incongruous that this magnificent structure and its decorations should serve as a frontispiece for the madness and misery that lay just beyond the hallway doors.

Mary did not question the fact that, in addition to the driver, there were two young footmen in matching costumes, an older black man sitting up front, and a woman inside the carriage with them who smiled shyly but did not speak during the trip to Byberry. Mary found out, much later, they were "travelers"—escaping slaves—posing as Mr. Purvis' servants, and that this was another of the many artifices he used to ferry people to freedom.

"No one ever questions me," he would tell her, "because, once I get the costumes on them, one Negro servant looks just like another. The bounty hunters and patter rollers never notice the difference." He chuckled derisively as he said it. "Stupid slavers."

THIS INDENTURE, made the twenty fifth day of March in the year of our Lord One thousand eight hundred and forty five, between Thomas Betts of Buckingham Township in the County of Bucks and state of Pennsylvania, and Sarah, his wife, and Cyrus Betts of the Township of Solebury, County aforesaid, and Elizabeth, his wife, party of the first part, and Andrew Hartless, of Buckingham Township aforesaid, party of the second party, Witnesseth that the said party of the first part, for and in consideration of the sum of two hundred dollars lawful money of the United States of America to them in hand paid and secured to be paid by the said party of the second part, the receipt whereof is hereby acknowledged, have and each and every of them hath granted, bargained, sold, released, and confirmed, and by these presents do, and each and every of them doth, grant, bargain, sell, release and confirm unto the said party of the second part and to his heirs and assigns, a certain messuage and lot of land situate in the aforesaid Township of Solebury, meted and bounded as follows:

Beginning at a stone in the public road and in the line of Mordicai Pearson's land, thence along said road north forty degrees and a quarter East nine perches and three tenths to a stake, thence by Thomas Bye's lot South forty three degrees and a half East ten perches and two tenths to a stone, thence by Dixon Naylor's lot South fifty four degrees and a half West eight perches, and forty five hundredths to a corner in Isaac Scarborough's line, thence along said line North forty nine degrees and a quarter West eight perches to the place of Beginning, containing half an acre, more or less,

Together also with all and singular the other buildings and improvements…

To have and to hold the said messuage and lot of land above described, hereditaments and premises hereby granted and mentioned and intended so to be with the appurtenances unto the said Andrew Hartless, his heirs and assigns… in trust nevertheless to hold for the uses, intents and purposes following, that is to say, in trust for the sole and only proper use, benefit and behoof of Mary Wellings, the wife of Langhorn Wellings, her heirs and assigns forever, and also upon special trust that the said Andrew Hartless, his heirs and assigns, shall and will either receive and pay to or permit and suffer the said Mary Wellings, her heirs and assigns, to receive all the clear yearly rents, issues and profits of the lot hereby granted, the same to go to and be to and for the sole, separate and peculiar use, benefit and disposal of the said Mary Wellings, her heirs and assigns, and that the same or any part thereof shall not in any wise be subject or liable to the disposal, intermeddling, control, engagements, debts or encumbrances of him, the said Langhorn Wellings, her husband, or any future husband, their creditors or any of them.

And it is the true intent and meaning of these presents that nothing herein contained shall be taken and construed, either at law or in equity, to vest any title, claim or challenge whatsoever in the said Langhorn Wellings, or any future husband or any person or persons claiming or to claim by, through, from or under them, or either of them, in or to the said described premises or any part thereof.

Sealed and delivered in
the presence of us . . .

Merrick Reeder   Thomas Betts   Sarah Betts

William C. Ely   Cyrus Betts   Eliza Betts

Received on the execution and delivery of the above written indenture of the above named Andrew Hartless the sum of One hundred dollars and a Mortgage for One hundred dollars, being the full consideration money above mentioned.

Witness: M. Reeder   Cyrus Betts

                                      Thomas Betts

Chapter VII

Lahaska
1838-1845

By the time Mary finally returned to the Lacy home in Lahaska in June of 1838, she had been away for three weeks. She had originally intended to be gone for only five days. In that three weeks, she had noticeably changed so much it was almost as if she was a different person, and it was not just physical changes that Lang and Mother Lacy noticed.

Lang was away working when Mr. Purvis' carriage arrived, carrying Mary and her few belongings, supplemented with several gifts from Mrs. Purvis. Mother Lacy and a young girl from a neighboring family whom she had hired to help out, cook meals and such, were at home, and a few of the summer people had already arrived.

"I suppose I was more exhausted from the trip than anything else," was Mother Lacy's response when Mary asked urgently if she was truly all right. Mary was not reassured and always felt a pang of conscience whenever she thought about it thereafter that she had dragged everyone off to Philadelphia against their will and with disastrous outcome.

It didn't help when Lang returned home. Mother Lacy came into the kitchen, and they talked after dinner, when he said, "We had the devil to pay Joseph, you know."

"How so?" Mary asked.

"He come over with a delegation of Friends and says in this serious voice, 'Brother Langhorn, we are not pleased that thee took Friend Tamar to Philadelphia without consulting with us and that thee placed her in extreme danger,' and things like that."

Mother Lacy smiled. "And I heard them talking to Lang and went into the parlor and said to them it was none of their business, and besides it was I who had insisted we go, that I'm a grown-up and I'll darn well do as I please!"

"Oh, Mother Lacy, you didn't!"

"Oh, yes, I did! They'll probably bring it up at monthly meeting, old prigs…"

"Mother!"

"I don't care. I'm eighty years old, by golly, and if I want to go traveling to Timbuktu…"

"You'll have to find someone else to go with. I'm finished!" Mary insisted, and Lang and Mother Lacy smiled sheepishly and nodded understanding. At the same time, Lang couldn't help but have his own guilt pangs that he was the reason she was now afraid to travel, that if it weren't for him, she could go practically anywhere she wanted. He should have known that wasn't completely true. Traveling held a myriad of risks for everyone, though admittedly much more complicated for people of color.

From that time on, the farthest Mary would ever travel for the rest of her life would be to Doylestown. She tended to keep her forays out of the house and immediate neighborhood limited to places where she knew everyone and they knew her and Lang and the children. This was especially true after going to a new shop in Doylestown one day in the mid-1840s.

She was standing at the counter buying something for little Elizzie, four or five years old at the time, who was by her side, when a strange woman smiled benevolently and said, "So kind of you to take care of one of these little darkies. Do you have an orphanage?"

Mary felt as if the lady had struck her physically. Her shoulders slumped, and her immediate reaction was to strike back, but she restrained herself and said, "This is my daughter, and I'll appreciate it if you not speak about her in those terms." She took Elizzie by the hand and left the store.

"Well, I never… Did you ever?" she heard the lady say haughtily to the shopkeeper.

In the end, Lang was much freer to travel about the countryside with the children than Mary was, since she was subjected to a particular form of discrimination reserved for whites who intermarried with blacks.

It was not physical, except for the shunning, but more of a subtle form of psychological hurt that was inflicted upon her even by some of the well-meaning Quakers. It consisted of remarks and questions that, while most of the bearers would have vehemently denied it, were mean-spirited and prejudiced. The physical injuries would become Lang's "croix de vivre"; the emotional consequences would become Mary's.

Mother Lacy and Lang were eager to hear about Mary's experiences in Philadelphia, starting with the hospital, and Mary described her days there, the buildings and the history she had learned. She told them about Thomas, but did not say anything about Ruth Ann, just that another child had been in the room who died the night before she left. She was still too unsure of her own feelings to talk about the experience.

"Now I want to hear all about thy visit with the Purvises. Do tell."

"Oh, let me tell you, they are such wonderful people! So gracious and hospitable to me."

Mr. Purvis had arranged a quilt and pillows in the carriage to make Mary's ride as comfortable as possible. As they drove to Byberry, the farther she got away from Philadelphia, the better she felt physically, although the painful memories of the accident and Ruth Ann's death would never leave.

"Byberry is in northeast Philadelphia County and is on the way to Bucks County," Mr. Purvis explained, "so you'll be that much closer to home." The township was established in 1675 by the Walton brothers—Nathaniel, Thomas, Daniel, and William—and named in honor of their home near Bristol in England.

"I bought this farm before Mrs. Purvis and I married. Now that we have our son William, who is five years old, we spend most of our time here. I want him to be out of the city as much as possible. We really are very fortunate, Mrs. Wellings, to be able to live in the country."

"Yes, I am beginning to appreciate that,'" Mary agreed. "I've never lived anywhere but Bucks County."

"I daresay you and your husband would not be able to find peace and comfort anywhere else in the country—or the world, for that matter. My parents had a very bad time of it. We lived in Connecticut for a while, and I went to Amherst College. In the process we have had a most bitter taste of the unfathomable hatred and vitriol that it seems most of white America has for the sons and daughters of its African immigrants."

He gave her some examples of incidents he had experienced, including just recently when he had been refused the right to show some of his stock at an Agricultural Fair in Byberry, as well as that year's debates in the Pennsylvania legislature and constitutional amendment disenfranchising the Negro voters.

"I am in the process now of writing a treatise in response. I think I am going to call it 'Response of Forty Thousand Citizens.' I haven't quite decided yet."

"Langhorn was one of those voters," Mary said, and she told him about Lang's personal feelings of disappointment and setback.

Once they got to the farm in Byberry, except for occasional dinners, Mary did not see much more of Mr. Purvis, who was busy for the rest of her stay going back and forth to the city. Mary knew he was constantly involved in anti-slavery and Underground Railroad activities, as well as keeping up with his business interests and properties. And there was an almost constant stream of visitors to the house.

"And, oh, what a lovely woman is Mrs. Purvis," Mary told Lang and Mother Lacy. "So talented, so beautiful. She is a poet and writer, as well as her sister, Sarah, who was visiting at the time. Sarah is engaged to be married to Mr. Purvis' brother, Joseph. Isn't that darling? Sisters marrying brothers."

Mary was almost overwhelmed by the graciousness and warmth of the welcome she received from Robert and Harriet Purvis, not to mention the beauty of the surroundings of the Byberry farm.

"It is the most tastefully and grandly decorated home I have ever seen in my life. Everything is of the finest quality—the furniture and furnishings, the décor, food—a piano! And a library! I was waited on hand and foot. I have never been so pampered in my life. Mrs. Purvis would not hear of me lifting a finger, and they insisted that I remain with them until their personal physician pronounced me well enough to come home.

"The maid helped me with my bath and with washing my hair—we had to be careful of the wound." Mary showed the bandage around which the maid had deftly brushed and wound her long hair so that the bandage looked somewhat like a headband.

"Mrs. Purvis insisted I use her perfume—from Paris! Here, maybe you can still smell it…" She extended her neck toward Lang who wrinkled his nose and looked somewhat embarrassed.

"She even gave me two of her dresses—she's just a little larger than me, and I can easily fix them to fit.

"Oh, what would I give to have such wonderful things," she said dreamily.

"Uh oh," Lang muttered under his breath and rolled his eyes.

"What's the matter?" Mary asked. "Is there anything wrong with wishing for nice things?"

"Oh…no, I suppose not. Just don't go wishin' beyond our means and station in life, is all."

Later, when they were going to bed, Lang said, "Tell me what else happened, Mary."

"I've told you everything. Why do you ask?"

"I don't know. You've changed. Not my sweet, innocent old girl any more, I guess. Seen enough of the world?"

She rolled over into his arms. "Seen enough to know that you and Bucks County are all I ever want…and my own house ..."

"You're not still dreaming of that!? Why, at the rate we're going we'll never have any money." He told her what steps he had taken, including getting extra jobs working day and night for the whole summer, in order to buy a new horse for himself, as well as replace the one he had borrowed and the carriage.

"I went over to George Watson and John Mathews in Centreville and made a deal for a replacement carriage. Thank God the Society took care of the hospital and doctor. I would have had to borrow for the rest of my life and then some! And now I won't be able to help you with the summer people."

"It's all right, Lang. You can have what I've got left from my savings. That should help some. We'll get the money together, maybe not this year, maybe not in five years."

Indeed, Mary was not quite well enough to resume her full schedule with the summer guests, and she had to share her portion of the earnings with the hired girl.

When she was visiting the Purvises, Mary asked Mr. and Mrs. Purvis at dinner one evening what she and Lang could do to help in the anti-slavery work.

"Mrs. Wellings, may I be honest with you?"

Mary nodded. "Please."

"I agree with Mrs. Mott, Miss Grimké and the other ladies of the Society. It's much too dangerous for you and your husband. My father-in-law, Mr. Forten, and I are another story entirely. We have the financial means to protect our families. Whenever my family and I travel, there are armed guards accompanying us. Did you know that?"

Mary shook her head.

"You've seen what the mob can do when their passions are whipped to a frenzy. I'm not afraid for myself personally, but there have been many threats against my wife and son. I don't want to take any chances with their safety and welfare. I feel the same about you and your husband. In fact, Mrs. Wellings, this is a white man's problem. Let them take the lead. It was they who caused it. It is they who must resolve it. The only things I can do are write, speak out, give financially…"

"And ferry runaways by the hundreds!" his wife reminded him teasingly.

"…Well, of course, I do what I can in that regard, as well." Mr. Purvis smiled.

"Mrs. Wellings, did you know that it was only two years ago that the Pennsylvania Anti-Slavery Society even gave Negroes admittance to their membership?" Mary shook her head no. Her host continued, "The thing I am trying to say, Mrs. Wellings, is that you have accepted a very grave responsibility by joining your hand in marriage to a black man. It's understandable that your view of the world and your desire to alleviate its ills expand as you become more enlightened as to the plight of his people, and it is commendable that you should want to help in some way. However, if…do you want children?"

Mary said, "Oh, yes, ardently so, especially if they will be as sweet and charming as your dear William." *And Thomas and Ruth Ann.*

"…when you have children, I have no doubt you will have to come to terms with your altruism for the entire race versus your mother's love and protection for your own. It's up to you, but I'm not even sure you should join the Anti-Slavery Society. If someone whose interests run counter to the Society's gets hold of the list of members, well, the potential… I don't have to say any more. You decide what's right for you."

It turned out Mary did not have to make a decision. The Society made it for her. They held a large annual meeting at Marmaduke

Watson's schoolhouse in Lower Makefield on June 9, 1838, just days after she returned home, and she was unable to attend.

At the meeting, the officers elected were Richard Janney, President; Dr. Ralph Lee, Vice President; Bill Johnson, Corresponding Secretary; Joseph Yardley, Recording Secretary; Stephen T. Janney, Treasurer. Other members of the board included Joshua Dungan, Jonathan P. Magill, Mahlon B. Linton, Joseph Janney, and Charles W. Swain.

A ladies' committee "to cooperate with and assist the Executive Committee in the performance of their duty" was composed of Martha Smith, Mary W. Magill, Achsah Janney, Sarah Beans, and Hannah Lloyd.

Out of the meeting came a long and remarkable document for its time, containing the resolutions of the Society, which was published in the *Intelligencer* in July of that year. It started out by talking about the efforts that had been undertaken over the past year including speeches around the county by Charles C. Burleigh, and that he and other lecturers had presented many citizens "with an opportunity of knowing their duty in reference to that system of slavery which we have all been instrumental in extending and perpetuating to the disgrace and, perhaps, ultimate ruin of our country."

It pledged the sum of four hundred forty-six dollars to be donated by its members and used to propagate materials for the purpose of "awakening the people of this nation from their insensibility and indifference to their national iniquity in sanctioning…a system which deprives one-sixth of our countrymen of all their rights, and is constantly inflicting upon thousands the utmost wretchedness and wo [*sic*]."

The document acknowledged the many works being carried on "to the moral and intellectual improvement of the colored people, a race amongst us whose moral character has been very much neglected, and who have been presented with but few motives or opportunities to improve their condition."

It talked about the vicious and pernicious propensities of those who had participated in and condoned slavery and noted that any danger of foreign hostility "sinks into insignificance in comparison with their evil influence. They are the deadly foes of that public and private virtue on which depends the continuance and efficacy of our inestimable form of Government, and on which depends our peace and prosperity. They are preying on the very vitals of society, on the very life blood of our republican institutions."

The Society apologized to the members of the Negro race in that it appeared the abolitionists' efforts had entrenched and hardened those who had "been so long reveling and rioting in the blood and sweat of the colored man, continued so long in the habit of violating and monopolizing his rights, that they have become inured to the practice of oppression, hardened in iniquitous prosperity, and unwilling to relinquish any fancied advantage they may enjoy from their encroachments upon the rights of others. The evils which arise from the practice of injustice and the spirit which it evinces and inculcates, must in accordance with the immutable laws of the human mind ultimately fall upon our own heads, and the longer the spirit is nourished and the practice continued, the more desolating will be the consequences."

The members of the Society pledged fully "our property, reputation and even our lives, rather than our principles and privileges," "under the guidance of a superintending Providence, to exercise the rights of conscience, the liberty of speech and the press for the general good."

In practical measures, the Society vowed that they would not support any candidate for public office who was not firmly in favor of the abolition of slavery. They condemned the American Colonization Society, which had been actively working to remove American Negroes and send them to Africa, even though most had been here for several generations, as being partially responsible for the recent outrage in Philadelphia, including the burning of Pennsylvania Hall.

The Anti-Slavery Society called for no less than the "complete eradication of prejudice against the colored man" hand in hand with "universal emancipation" of all slaves.

Finally, they pledged support for "our friend and co-laborer" William Lloyd Garrison and recommended that the citizens of Bucks County peruse the "Appeal of Forty Thousand Citizens Threatened With Disfranchisement," by Robert Purvis.

When Mary approached Bill Johnson, at whose limekilns Lang often worked, about what she could do to assist, she was given the same answer as she had received in Philadelphia and from Mr. Purvis.

"It's much too dangerous, Mrs. Wellings. You know the slavers and bounty hunters are constantly about the area. They have particularly chosen us for their scrutiny because of our open defiance of their evil practices. I fear if you were to become more involved, they would turn their venom on Langhorn and other Negroes to whom we have sought to bring some measure of peace and safety."

He frowned and purposely made eye contact before continuing his thoughts to underscore the gravity of what he was saying. "In fact, Mrs. Wellings, I tremble at the thought of what the slavers would do if they learned Langhorn is married to a white woman. Do I make myself clear?"

"I understand, really, I do," Mary said. "It's just that I have a need to do something."

"I think I have something. How about if you assist us with the library. It's being housed at Martha Hampton's School here in Buckingham. She would undoubtedly appreciate the help and that way you would feel you are doing something beneficial for the cause."

Martha Hampton and Hannah Lloyd ran a successful boarding school for girls in Hannah's home in Buckingham. Hannah was a widow with four children. She took care of the housekeeping, and Martha served as administrator and teacher. At the height of its operation, the school housed about fifteen girls from Bucks and Northampton Counties and Burlington County, New Jersey, in addition to a few day scholars. The concept of education for girls was revolutionary for its time and sprang directly from the Quaker concept of education being the key to developing the "inner light" inherent in all people.

Mary agreed immediately, although it was difficult for her to get to the school. She had to wait until Lang was home from work to drive her in the wagon or she could try to walk the several miles round trip. She was still recuperating from the accident and tired quickly, so walking was not a good idea. And, as a result, throughout that summer and fall she began to gain weight, just a little at first.

Mary and Lang were also invited by Joseph Fell to attend monthly meetings of the Hughesian Society, of which he was administrator. The group had been started by Amos Austin Hughes, a Friend who left ninety-one acres and eight thousand dollars in 1811 to establish a school to educate the poor children of the township. It lay dormant for many years, after a few starts, for lack of a teacher and effective administration, until Joseph took over in 1837. In addition to providing educational scholarships, the group formed the Hughesian Society, which invited guest speakers to discuss the important issues of the day—scientific, political and social.

Whenever she was able to go, Mary enjoyed working at the library and reading the materials, including the works of Thomas Clarkson, E.M. Chandler, Mrs. Lydia M. Child, William Lloyd Garrison, E.P. Lovejoy, James Williams, and Moses Roper (the latter two being recollections of former slaves). She especially enjoyed the letters and pamphlets of her friend Angelina Grimké (now Weld) and the writings of Angelina's husband, Theodore Weld, on *Bible Arguments against Slavery*.

Angelina had written to her personally, as well, a letter that Mary cherished for years in which she apologized for not coming to see Mary in the hospital in Philadelphia, and informing her that she had left for Illinois almost immediately after the disastrous events of May and did not know of the accident until just recently.

Still, whenever she went to the library or meetings, Mary felt something vague that she never expressed to Lang, or anyone else for that matter, and that was a slight coldness on the part of some of the committee members that made her feel unwanted. It was a small thing after all, nothing to get upset about and so intangible that it was hardly worth bringing up. But, the cumulative effect on her was that it added another little "brick," fashioned from hurt and mortared with anger, to the invisible, protective wall that she would gradually build around herself over the years.

In the early spring of 1839, Mary learned in a letter from Jonas that Lydia had delivered another child, Jacob, and in a letter from her mother and older sister Elizabeth, she found out that Eliza, who had married John German, had given birth just months ago to a son, Tobias. They were living a few miles northwest from Mary in Plumstead.[3]

A few weeks later, Mary learned that the months of enforced quiet, rest and recuperation had produced an additional benefit—she was pregnant, too! She was immediately exhilarated, scared, anxious, joyful, and sick—oh! so sick. In fact, she had never been so sick in her life. Her

---

3   These were the first grandchildren for Jacob and Mary Stone, who would
     eventually have seventy-two that we know about, most of whom they
     never saw, since the families moved from Pennsylvania all over the
     country—to New Jersey, Maryland, Missouri, Kansas, Illinois, and
     California—far out of the range of Jacob's and Mary's traveling ability.

morning sickness extended well into the afternoon and evening. She could barely get out of bed some days.

Before the sickness passed, the summer visitors began arriving, and she had to hire another helper, but this time there was difficulty finding a girl close by in the village, and Mary was forced to look as far away as New Hope and Doylestown.

She mentioned in a letter to her mother that she was with child and ill and having difficulty finding help, and received one day in June a note:

> Sister,
>
> Arriving on Friday by the 2 o'clock stage.
>
>   E.

Lizzie was coming! Mary immediately felt a sense of relief just knowing that her closest sister, her dearest lifelong companion, was coming. They had not seen each other in almost four years.

"However did you do it!? How did you get Papa's permission?" Mary exclaimed when she and Elizabeth hugged and greeted each other in the village.

"Mama told Papa I was going to visit Eliza to help her with the baby. Well, she didn't exactly say it that way. What she said was, 'Elizabeth's going to help *her sister* with the new baby.' She just didn't say *which* sister."

The women clutched hands and laughed.

"Oh, Lizzie, I'm so happy to have you here! I don't care how you did it," Mary said.

"Old Papa doesn't care anyway. I think he was just as happy to be rid of me."

"Oh, Elizabeth! Don't say that. I'm sure that's not true."

In fact, Elizabeth was being quite honest. Jacob had been almost relieved when she announced she was going visiting.

"The girl's been acting plenty odd lately, Mütter. What's wrong with her?" he asked his wife after Elizabeth had left the room to go pack her things.

Mother Mary looked thoughtfully at her husband. "Well, Jacob, I suppose it's because she's almost thirty years old. She's beginning to think there is something wrong with her. Three of her younger sisters have found husbands—four if you count Mary—and her time ..."

"I told you not to say that name in this house." Jacob put his pipe back in his mouth, rustled the pages of the *German Demokrat* paper and started to read again, his ears closed to further discussion about the matter.

Elizabeth was all-too-well aware that life for a spinster held very little promise of romance, fulfillment or happiness. She had nothing to look forward to but caring for her younger siblings, and then for her parents as they grew older, became ill and weak, and died. Or traveling around from one sibling to another, imposing on their families and hospitality, while trying to make herself useful and not be a burden. Or working as a housekeeper for the remainder of her life, like her aunt Elizabeth Trullinger, her mother's sister, and having to scrimp and save every penny toward the day she would no longer be able to work and would not be welcomed anywhere but as a paying guest in a boarding house.

One could count on one's fingers the number of uneducated women who were able to work in a profession. And, even if a woman had the money and the parental permission to attend college—and was able to find a university or college that would accept her—about the most she could ever hope for was to become a teacher at fifteen or twenty dollars a month. Unless she had some other income, she would have to board with a family.

Elizabeth was indeed beginning to act very oddly, as Mary was to notice within days. She was developing a serious tendency toward melancholy. She would spend hours sitting alone on the porch swing reading novels or curled in her bed, unable to get up, saying she was ill. A couple of times, Mary could swear Lizzie was talking to herself.

Another one of her unusual behaviors was an unreasonable, almost extreme fear of Langhorn. She would not look at him when they talked. She shied away from him if he passed too closely to her.

"What'd I do to the girl?" Lang asked in bewilderment.

"Nothing, Lang, absolutely nothing. I don't understand it."

And Elizabeth herself could not explain it. "He just frightens me, Mary. He's so *large* and *black*."

"But he's the most gentle, kindest man in the world, Lizzie. Really, you must try to get to know him better. You'll see."

Elizabeth did try, but continued to maintain a respectful distance. In truth, she would have completely gone over the edge if anyone had guessed at the actual nature of her fear—it was her *attraction* to Langhorn, not her repellence from him that formed the basis of her aberration. She was falling in love with him and beginning to have fantasies about him and loathed herself in the process.

One somewhat funny incident occurred in late July. Mary was already getting big with the baby, but still managed to do most of her housekeeping duties and chores. She was out in the back yard heating the water for the laundry in two large tubs. She would rub the clothing on scrub boards in one tub, with homemade lye soap, then switch the clothes with a large paddle into the other tub for rinsing. Wringing the wash out and hanging it on the clothesline was much too difficult for one person, even one not pregnant, as the clothing and bed linen became very heavy and impossible to lift. She went to look for Lizzie to help.

As she walked around the front of the house she saw Lizzie's back. She was leaning against a large oak tree talking rather animatedly. Mary could not see anyone else.

Good grief! Now she's having regular conversations with herself! Mary thought, rather petulantly.

"Lizzie?"

Lizzie stopped talking and looked over her shoulder at Mary.

"Who *are* you talking to?" Mary asked in a loud, almost exasperated voice.

And suddenly a man popped out from behind the tree and nearly started Mary on her way to the next world. She truly thought she had caught Lizzie talking to herself and had not expected anyone else to be there.

"Oh!" she screamed.

"Oh, Mary, don't frighten us like that!" Lizzie said, then seeing her sister in distress, "Do sit down here."

Mary sat holding her swollen belly and fanning herself with her apron. In a few seconds, once she had recovered, she began to laugh at herself, though she did not tell them the nature of her self-directed humor. Lizzie introduced the young man.

"Mary, may I present a friend of mine, Aaron Hite. Aaron, meet my sister, Mrs. Wellings."

Aaron took his hat off. "Pleased to meet you, ma'am," he said sheepishly. "Hope I didn't scare you too bad." He behaved rather shyly, almost backward.

They chatted for a few moments more, and Mary learned that Aaron worked as a wagon driver and farrier—one who took care of horses in addition to blacksmithing. He lived in Warwick and traveled all over the county with his work.

After Aaron left, Mary and Lizzie talked as they wrung out the laundry together and pinned it to the line.

"I met him at the stage station in Doylestown on the day I traveled here to Lahaska," Lizzie explained in answer to Mary's casual probing. She told Aaron that day where she was going and was extremely flattered that he had come looking for her.

"That's not too smart, is it, Lizzie? Talking to a strange man and telling him your personal business." Lizzie was behaving like a foolish young girl. Mary could see the signs, and it wasn't that many years since she had initially fallen in love herself.

"Oh, I knew instantly that he is a kindred spirit, that I could trust him with my life if need be," Lizzie said with a romantic sigh in her voice.

"He's quite a bit younger than you," Mary said cautiously.

"A few years maybe."

More like eight or ten years maybe! Mary thought but did not voice. *He's practically still a boy.*

She did not say any more to Lizzie about Aaron, but talked at length with Lang later that night about the happenings of the day and her concerns for her sister. She sat on the edge of the bed and talked as he was getting undressed for bed.

When she was finished, she looked at Lang for a reaction. He shrugged. "She's a big girl, Mary. She's almost thirty, old enough to know what her choices are, and you know there aren't many."

"Of course, I would not deny my sister happiness. But this Aaron is so young, Lang, and seems rather shiftless. He's obviously not educated, not nearly so refined as Lizzie. It's just not a good match for her."

"You're already becoming a mother hen," he teased. "Have you forgotten so quickly our own elopement?" He lifted her chin and smiled at her. "Your father said the same things about me, and worse!"

"I know, I know. 'He that is without sin among you, let him first cast a stone at her…' Is that what you're saying?"

"Well, yes and no. I wouldn't say there is anything sinful about you. But, you, of all people, should probably not say anything to her. It will jeopardize your friendship if you criticize your sister's beau. And I don't want her getting mad and leaving you."

He sat on the bed next to Mary and caressed his wife's ever-expanding stomach. "The baby is obviously wearing you down, Mary. I can't be here with you all the time, and Mother Lacy won't be able to help you."

Mary nodded, and looked out the window. "I'm just so worried about Lizzie. There's something terribly wrong."

Within a few months, Mary had much more to be concerned about than her sister's boyfriend. The pregnancy was tremendously difficult for her. She gained a great deal of weight very quickly in the last trimester and carried the child so high she could barely breath. In the last weeks, walking was even curtailed. Mary was confined to her bedroom for the better part of October.

Deep in her heart she knew she had good reason to be concerned. Childbirth, with its related illnesses and traumas, was the number one cause of death of women. There was an ever-present threat, not only of contracting the commonplacc diseases, such as German measles, but also, as in Mary's case, of quick weight gain triggering hypertension, and kidney and liver malfunction resulting in toxemia, later known as eclampsia.

There were "breech babies," fetuses turned around presenting feet or buttocks first. There was always the threat of ruptures, hemorrhaging and infections. If a woman was lucky, she could deliver the child at home with a midwife or her mother or other women of the family present who were highly conscious of cleanliness. A hospital was the worst place to be. In fact, if Mary had seen the operating room of the Pennsylvania Hospital, she would have fainted dead from fright. It looked very much like a torture chamber might appear after a hundred prisoners had been through it. Until well into the 1800s, the physicians never washed their hands or instruments and simply donned heavy aprons over their street clothes that became filthy with blood and were never washed. They were hung upon pegs and used over and over again.

On the other hand, Mary felt reassured whenever she thought about her own mother Mary, who had delivered seventeen babies one after another with little or no trouble. It was said in awe for generations that mother Mary could deliver a baby, strap the infant in a sling at her breast and go out to pick vegetables and haul water for dinner. Daughter Mary had no reason to suspect her body and her experience with childbirth would be any different.

As the time for delivery grew closer, Lang became more concerned. Mary was getting heavier and heavier. She lay in bed or on the chaise longue all day and ate whatever Elizabeth prepared, and Elizabeth, in her kind-hearted ignorance, prepared all the goodies Mary loved to eat—apple cobbler, peach pies, biscuits and bread, meat and gravy. It looked to Lang like his wife's little body was about to burst. This was not good.

He consulted privately with Mother Lacy and Joseph about his fears, and Joseph suggested they consult Dr. Arthur D. Cernea, a Frenchman who had come to the county as a young orphan, gone to medical school and opened his practice in Centreville a few years ago. Now they were going to have the extra expense of a physician, but Lang was willing to do anything to keep Mary and the baby alive and well.

Next to overcome was Mary's squeamishness and reluctance to allow any man other than her husband within five feet of her body. She was quite discomfited when Dr. Cernea began to examine her, but her embarrassment was quickly overshadowed by her understanding of the life-threatening situation toward which she was heading.

In those days, the uneasiness ran both ways. "Did you know that the stethoscope was invented just twenty years ago by a French doctor who was too embarrassed to put his ear directly upon a female body?" Dr. Cernea asked her in an effort to reassure her as to his propriety.

On the other hand, Dr. Cernea was appalled when he did see Mary's bloated body and could not contain his displeasure. "Mrs. Wellings, how could you let yourself get this big? This is not good for you and is going to make the birth that much more difficult."

Mary began to cry. "I didn't know. I've always been able to eat anything I wanted…"

"Because you were active. You burned up the food as you worked and moved about. Now that you are sedentary, the food turns to fat.

Undoubtedly, the baby is becoming large, as well, and will be difficult for you to deliver. I'm going to ask your sister to limit your intake of food from now on, and I want you to walk about the upstairs rooms as much as possible. But, don't try to go downstairs."

Dr. Cernea had been battling for years the ingrained misperceptions of these country folk, especially the Germans, that heftiness equaled good health and signified wealth. He also realized he was frightening Mary with his harsh voice and pronouncements of danger. He smiled kindly. "It's all right, Mrs. Wellings. You do what I tell you, and we will have a healthy, lovely baby. Are you with me?" Mary sniffled and nodded.

As he left the home, he gave instructions for Lizzie to give Mary a strict diet of vegetables and fruit, which fortunately were abundant in the harvest season, and milk products—lots of fresh milk. Dr. Cernea calculated that he had only a few weeks to get Mrs. Wellings back into good health for the delivery. He did not share with anyone his concerns that, with Langhorn's large size, it was probable their child would be big, even without the added fatty nourishment.

He was correct. When the time came for delivering the baby, Mary was in labor for days, not just hours. She honestly thought she was going to die. The pain was excruciating. She wafted in and out of consciousness. Several times Dr. Cernea weighed the possibility of a Caesarian section, which he had seen done only once in medical school, and that was on a dead mother.

Finally, the infant presented itself! October 20, 1839. First a head of thick, black matted hair. Dr. Cernea had never seen so much hair on a newborn. Then quickly after that a chubby body and well-formed legs. It's a girl!

Mary smiled, thanked God and fainted.

And what a beautiful little girl! Being completely formed out, the baby had none of the scrawny look of most Caucasian newborns. Once the uterine fluids were cleansed from her body, the skin color settled into a lovely milk chocolate with pink and golden tones or, as Mary would say often in the years to come, "My sweet, golden honey babe."

"What are thee going to name her?" Mother Lacy asked a few hours later after Mary had rested and was able to see her and Lang.

"Ruth Ann," Mary said unhesitatingly. Lang looked at her questioningly and later asked, "Where did you come up with that name?"

She had qualms about telling him, but decided to be honest and immediately regretted it.

"Good God, Mary! That's downright superstitious, talkin' about angels and such. I've never heard of naming a baby for a dead child."

"Nonsense. It's done all the time. I know for a fact that the Dutch do it. And I read one time where Jewish people are not allowed to name a child for a living person. It's bad luck."

Lang was still not convinced. "I thought Germans were supposed to name the babies after the grandparents."

This was generally true. The first boy was to be named for the father's father, the second boy for the mother's, the first girl for the father's mother, and so on. This was the Dutch practice, as well, although the tradition had been dropping in use in America. Also, the Quakers followed this procedure, although the girls were reversed, mother's mother first.

If Mary followed the German practice, the first girl should be named after Langhorn's mother. To be honest, she didn't want to embarrass him; he did not know his mother's first name. He had called her simply "Mama" the few years he had to spend with her, and everyone else had called her "Mrs. Wellings" or "Sister Wellings."

Mary took his hand. "This is important to me, Lang. I know it sounds crazy, but I just feel that God has given Ruth Ann another chance, that He would not take both Ruth Anns so young. Almost like she was destined to come back to be with me…."

"Oh, now, don't go talkin' that weird nonsense on me!" Lang didn't want to listen to any metaphysical philosophy, that's for sure, even if he had known what it was or could pronounce it. In the end he just shook his head and let Mary have her way. The child's name would be formally Ruth Anna, and she would be called Ruth Ann.

Baptism—where, when and how—was another predicament. Mary had not been back to her church in Tinicum since their marriage by Reverend Miller four years ago. Lang attended the little African Methodist Episcopal churches once in a while with his friends Mahlon and Andy, but the membership was all Negro, and Mary was not completely comfortable there. They brought Mother Lacy to the Quaker meetinghouse whenever she wanted to go, but neither Lang nor Mary enjoyed those services. It was very awkward having to sit sectioned off from Mother Lacy and the other whites and Mary never could get accustomed to the hard benches and lack of structure or music.

In the end, they did nothing, and Mary was torn for years by fear that something would happen to Ruth Ann, and she would go to hell because she was not baptized—at least that's what she had been told all her life—and the immediate opposite feeling that this was nonsense, that God would not take Ruth Ann and, besides, He would not be so cruel as to consign this perfect little creature for eternity to the nethermost realms of "fire and brimstone" just because she didn't have some water sprinkled on her and a blessing said over her.

Ruth Ann Wellings, my beautiful baby girl. Truly sent from heaven just for me. I will pray for you and teach you and dedicate you to God.

Mary was consumed with Ruth Ann. She was a delightful and beautiful baby, with thick, curly, dark brown hair, brown eyes, chubby cheeks, and a "cupid's bow" mouth. Mary adored her. Sometimes she would bury her nose in Ruth Ann's soft belly and just inhale the sweet essence of newborn.

Being a mother was everything Mary had ever hoped for. The rest of the world melted away, unfortunately including Lang who soon came to feel somewhat excluded but did not think about it enough to give voice to his feelings.

All that winter, Lizzie began to act even more oddly than before. She became jumpy and testy and began snapping at Mary for no apparent reason. "She's acting awful skittery," Lang remarked one day.

Finally, Lizzie announced one morning in February, "I'm leaving, Mary. I'm going mad here, and you don't need me anymore."

Mary suddenly understood. She had not realized how serious was Lizzie's jealousy. Mary was broken-hearted that their relationship seemed to be quickly souring, and at the same time hurt and angered by her beloved sister's behavior.

"Why can't you be happy here with us? Where are you going, home to Papa? That's not much better, is it?"

"No, I'm not going home. I have a surprise for you. Mr. Hite has asked me to be his wife, and I've decided to accept."

Mary was stunned. "Oh, Lizzie, no! He's not right for you, don't you see…"

"You just don't want me to be happy, that's it!" Lizzie screamed suddenly. "You want me to stay here for the rest of my life and wait on you and your big, black husband and little black baby hand and foot!"

"Lizzie!" Oh, this was terrible! The mean things that were said by both women that could never be retrieved. An arrow straight through the heart would have been more merciful.

"Can't you see, Lizzie? This man—this boy—is much too young for you. He's lazy and shiftless…"

"And who's calling the kettle black?" Lizzie shot back.

"My husband is neither lazy nor shiftless, dear sister. He works very hard."

And on it went like this far too long until finally Mary heard Ruth Ann crying and ran to see what was wrong. Lizzie went upstairs and packed her things and was gone without a word of goodbye to anyone except Mother Lacy.

Mary cried for hours. She was inconsolable. Lang was away on a two-day job and when he came home, she poured her heart out to him, omitting the mean things Lizzie had said about him.

He shook his head in disdain. "There's nothing you can do, old girl. Your sister is a silly, stupid old maid and she's mighty determined that this fella is what she wants. You got to let her go and find out for herself. You just take care of yourself and me 'n Ruth Ann. I won't have my wife gettin' all worked up over something we can't do nuthin' about."

"Don't talk about my sister like that!" Mary sobbed. "You just don't understand or care! You've never had family." Lang just shook his head again. *Women!*

Mary quickly wrote to her mother to warn her about what Elizabeth had done, but Lang was right, darn it. There was nothing to be done, especially not by Mary who had herself run off with someone unacceptable to the family. Mary read in the paper in March that Aaron Hite (they spelled it "Fite," probably misreading the flourished handwriting) and Elizabeth Stone had been married in Warwick by Justice of the Peace J.H. Rogers, Esq. on March 2, 1840.

Not even a church blessing.

Predictably, Jacob became incensed with his eldest daughter's choice of husband and disowned her, along with Mary. Mother Mary's hands were tied. She was afraid to go against her husband's decree, yet her heart was torn to pieces worrying over the fate of her firstborn.

It was not until several years later when Mary heard from her mother that Lizzie was having a bad time of it that they would see each other again. Mary took the stage over to Warwick. She found Lizzie in a terrible condition, living in a small, cold, dirty house, with two malnourished little children—a girl Elizabeth and a boy Edward—and a helpless husband who couldn't seem to hold onto a job or provide support. Lizzie was much too old and frail to be having children, but she had been so determined to be a wife and mother.

Mary stayed with Lizzie for a few days, as long as she could spare away from her own family and Mother Lacy, who was herself becoming gradually weaker and slowing down considerably. She cleaned Lizzie's house as best she could, and prepared some meals for the family. Lizzie was so thin, so pale and weak. She was as dangerously thin as Mary was heavy during her pregnancies and had a constant cough that Dr. Cernea said, when Mary asked him about it later, sounded to him like consumption or perhaps heart trouble.

The next time she heard about her sister, it was the heartbreaking news that Elizabeth Stone Height (the spelling changed over the years from Hite to Height to Heite) had died in childbirth with her fourth baby, which also died, when she was almost forty and sickly and had no business getting pregnant. She simply could not turn down her husband's demands for sexual relations out of fear of his anger. She was doomed if she gave in and doomed if she didn't. By that time, Mary was becoming far too wrapped up in her own problems to do anything to help Elizabeth's children, and she eventually lost track of them.

Motherhood rekindled Mary's happiness with life. She lost some of the weight she had gained during the pregnancy with Ruth Ann and resumed her life with renewed vigor.

Unfortunately, having Ruth Ann in the Lacy home precluded any more summer guests, the child being obviously mixed race and immediate evidence to strangers of the true nature of the relationship of Lang and Mary.

"'Tis not important, Sister Mary," Mother Lacy reassured her. "In truth, I was becoming a bit weary of the bustle and noise of so many people in the house. I'm getting too old and just want peace and quiet for the rest of my days, whatever God wills me."

Mary still needed to earn some extra money, so she went to see her friend Sarah Betts, the hatmaker. Sarah wanted to concentrate on millinery work and had enough jobs to keep herself busy from now until forever and was happy to refer to Mary all of the dressmaking requests from her customers. In addition, Mary made pies and pastries and canned the abundant pears, peaches and apples on the Lacy property, which Joseph Shaw, who operated the little inn in the village of Lahaska, was delighted to buy for his dinner tables. She scrupulously shared her earnings with Mother Lacy in payment for the fruit, although Mother Lacy tried to demur.

"Thee works so hard, my dear, thee deserves to keep what thee earns. Alas, most of the fruit would simply rot on the ground if thee did not use and preserve it."

But Mary was insistent. "I don't want anyone ever thinking we are taking advantage of your kindness and hospitality," she said firmly.

Her health had so much improved and, it seems, the mothering instincts within her had been so enkindled that by the early fall of 1840 she found herself pregnant again. The same conflicting emotions came rushing over her—exhilaration, anxiety, happiness, trepidation—and this time with a new worry: *How can I possibly love another child as much as I love Ruth Ann?* She never spoke to another soul about it, though, and tried to push away these thoughts with happy ones.

She was better prepared for the second delivery, as well, with Dr. Cernea's guidance and support from the beginning. In fact, she became so quickly and completely grateful to and dependent on him that he was to become the family physician for the rest of Mary's life. Even though they moved farther away from him within a few years, she would never listen to Lang's suggestions over the years that they find another doctor closer by.

Mary did not gain as much weight with this pregnancy, and her confinement over the winter of 1840-1841 was quieter and easier on her physically. Toddler Ruth Ann was just learning to walk, and chasing her around probably kept Mary fit, too.

For the first time in her adult life, Mary actually enjoyed Christmas. With Ruth Ann, so many things that had been chores in the past took on new vibrancy and meaning. The world was a wondrous place once more, and she wanted to show all the wonder of it to her baby. She made small gifts—scarves, gloves, socks and such—that she presented to Lang, Mother Lacy, her parents and her brothers and sisters, at least those she knew where they were. Sadly, she realized she had been gone from them so long that some of the younger siblings would not even remember her. She learned later that Jacob had forbidden her gifts from the house. Her mother brought the box to their neighbor Mrs. Swarts and then brought the gifts back one or two at a time so Jacob wouldn't notice.

Lang made little wooden toys for Ruth Ann—blocks, a miniature wagon, a puppet made of many small parts strung together with a silly face painted on the head. One day he came home with a special treat he had found in the market at New Hope: Oranges from the first load ever brought to Bucks County, just off the boat from South America. Mary and Mother Lacy had never tasted one before and were delighted with the sweet, juicy fruit.

On March 21, 1841—the first day of spring—the family received a special present: another baby girl. Not quite as pretty as Ruth Ann and one physical problem—a minor malformation of the hip that made one leg slightly shorter than the other. It was a very common problem, and Dr. Cernea showed Mary some stretching exercises she could perform on the baby, and told her there were special shoes she could buy later on, but the child would walk with a limp for the rest of her life.

"No matter," he reassured her. "Otherwise a lovely, healthy girl and nothing that will interfere significantly with her life."

Mary instantly bonded with the baby; she had no cause for concern after all. There was certainly enough love for both. This time she went for conventional naming practices—Mary Elizabeth Wellings—and Langhorn was pleased. She would be called "Elizzie" for short.

About a week after the delivery, Dr. Cernea came to visit and check on the newborn. After he had examined both Mary and Elizzie, he stood up and began putting his instruments into his bag seemingly engrossed in thought.

"Mrs. Wellings, I have to ask you this. I know it's a delicate thing to talk about, but…"

"What is it, Doctor?" Mary became alarmed at the somber tone of Dr. Cernea's voice. "Is there something else wrong with the baby?"

"No, no. Other than the slight malformation of the hip, which I don't expect will interfere with her life. It's not the baby, Mrs. Wellings. It's you. Is it possible...I mean, would your husband agree? What I am trying to say, Mrs. Wellings, is that, if possible, I don't believe you should have any more children."

"Oh, Dr. Cernea, is there something wrong with me?"

"No, no. At least not yet. The reason I am asking is that I detect in you a tendency to apoplexy, which is a condition of the blood circulation system. There is nothing that can be done about it except some herbs, medicine to thin the blood—actually barely effective. We have noticed that the condition is exacerbated in women by pregnancy and weight gain associated with it. So, if it's at all possible, I would like you to avoid pregnancy."

He smiled at wriggling toddler Ruth Ann and infant Elizzie and turned back to look at Mary. "You have two lovely little girls now, Mrs. Wellings, and I want their mother to be around to take care of them. If you take care of yourself, I think we can eliminate or at least forestall the effects of the disease for some time."

Mary was silent for a few seconds thinking about what Dr. Cernea had just said. Cernea pressed his case. "Would your husband agree? I mean, there are certainly some methods that I can teach you about to avoid..." He seemed almost as embarrassed as Mary to discuss this intensely personal subject.

Mary sighed and frowned and wagged her head in bewilderment. "I really don't know how he will react. I know he cares about me and certainly would not wish any harm to come to me, but..."

"Well, as I said, there are some things you can do, but some of them are costly and none of them foolproof by any means. Abstinence is still the only guarantee. You talk it over with your husband and let me know if you think it would help if I spoke to him."

When Lang came home and heard the news, he most definitely did not take it well.

"That's a bunch of nonsense! I never heard of such a thing. Interferin' with a man's rights to the comfort of his wife and home."

Mary was shocked by his reaction and mortified that Mother Lacy and the children would hear him yelling. "Please, Lang! Don't you believe Dr. Cernea? He feels it's important that I not have any more children."

"There's nothin' wrong with you. You're perfectly healthy. Not as if you're like an old lady all bent over with consumption 'n such. I don't want to hear no more of it. And I don't want that doctor comin' around here. It ain't right!"

"No! He saved my life, and Ruth Ann's, and I'll pay him with my own earnings if I have to before I'll give him up."

"Listen to yerself! That's not natural, I say. My wife choosin' this other man over me. Ain't right, I tell you."

Truly, it was almost as if Lang was exhibiting jealous rage. And pent-up jealousy had a great deal to do with it. He was jealous of Ruth Ann and Elizzie now that Mary had turned almost all of her time and attention away from him and to them. He was jealous of Dr. Cernea who seemed to have some sort of intimacy in his family that just wasn't proper in Lang's mind. He was even jealous of Mother Lacy who demanded her share of Mary's care, as well. Not to mention the dress-making clients. The list of his rivals for Mary's affection and attention was endless.

Lang couldn't voice any of these inner feelings he had been think-ing, and he certainly could not directly confront the sources of his hurt, so his rage exploded, like a volcano, in another corner of his world. Like most humans will do, he took his frustrations out on his spouse.

Mary was stunned and hurt beyond tears. *He doesn't care about me after all,* was all she could think over and over. From then on, she poured her heart into motherhood and housekeeping and avoided Lang when-ever possible, thus widening the chasm gradually but inexorably grow-ing between them. She spurned his sexual advances whenever and by whatever means possible by claiming it was her menses time, that she was not feeling well or was exhausted from a hard day's work, or "Lang, no, you'll wake the children," or "I have to sit with Mother Lacy; she's not breathing well." She even shied away from his casual embraces and kisses for fear it might lead to something more.

With few exceptions, the only happy family times from the spring of 1840 forward were holidays and after dinner in the evenings when Mary would read aloud to Lang and the children and Mother Lacy.

And, within three years, Lang's comfortable world would collapse a great deal more by his own foolhardiness that sprang out of a myriad of pent-up frustrations juxtaposed with the tedium of a quiet country life.

In the early spring of 1844, very late one night there was an urgent knock on the door and some commotion outside the house. Lang awoke and, without lighting a lamp or candle, proceeded down the stairs. Sleepy and confused, he went to the front door first, then realizing the knocking was coming from the kitchen door to the back yard, went there.

"Who's there? What do you want?"

"Lang, it's me, Joseph!" came the urgently whispered response.

Lang opened the door instantly. Although the doors were not locked, Joseph would never have entered without permission. Lang could barely make out anything in the moonlit darkness but, as his eyes adjusted, he recognized Joseph and another man standing behind him who was active in the Quaker church and anti-slavery group.

"What are you doing here this time of night?"

"May we come in, Lang?"

"Of course. What is it? Is someone ill?"

"Lang, we need your help. We need to ask the use of your horse and wagon and some hay for a very special purpose." Since the Hicksite reformation and the split in the meetinghouses, many of the Quakers had gradually begun dropping the "thee," "thou," and "thy" from their speech. Joseph was becoming more involved the public eye as a prominent teacher and school administrator as well as politician and community leader.

"What is it?"

"I wish you would not ask. 'Tis better if you not know."

Lang understood immediately. They were up to their Underground Railroad activities.

"What's wrong with your wagon?" he asked Joseph.

"Our eminent ex-Constable Hubbard and some of the…ah, emissaries of the South, shall I say, have been snooping about my place. Brother John here has kindly agreed to take the shipment, but we need a wagon.

Lang immediately became exhilarated with the prospect of an adventure. "All right, but only if I drive."

"No, Lang! I'll not be responsible if anything happens to you," Joseph protested.

"Nothing will happen. I'm not concerned. Even if Hubbard catches me, which I doubt will happen, he knows me. Besides, everyone *definitely* knows you both and the only thing you could possibly be up to in the middle of the night."

After a little more persuasion, Joseph was convinced, reluctantly. "All right, you win. Perhaps Brother John and I can help by leading them in another direction in my buggy."

Lang ran upstairs to get dressed while Joseph and John plotted the course of action. Mary was awakened and expressed vehement opposition to the scheme as soon as she realized what was going on.

"Please, Lang, don't do this! I see nothing good." In fact, Mary had been reading in the *Intelligencer* the distressing stories about continuing anti-Negro riots in Philadelphia and elsewhere throughout the past year. "You mustn't go out. It's not safe…"

"You hush now, woman. Don't be tellin' me what to do." Three-year-old Elizzie woke and sat up on the cot she shared with sister Ruth Ann in their parents' room. "Mommy…"

"Look what you've done now. You've wakened the children. Please don't disturb Mother Lacy. Lang…?"

Lang left the room to rejoin Joseph and John without another word.

The plan was hatched. Lang would proceed with the "baggage" to a spot that he knew only as a small cave in the woods near "the House on the Hill," the home of John Kenderdine on the Cuttalossa Creek in Lumberton. Someone would join him there between then and dawn. Joseph and John would drive around in a suspicious manner and, if seen, they would deliberately pick up as much speed as possible in the dark night, thereby enticing the slavers to follow and eventually overtake them.

It seemed a simple plan that could be handled quickly. The baggage was one Henry Miller, a fellow who had recently liberated himself from a particularly horrible place in South Carolina. He was a big man, like Lang, and just about the same age. Other than size and skin color, however, the two men were as different as if they had grown up on opposite ends of the earth—Henry's world was far removed from anything Lang had ever known, and vice versa.

Henry had distinguished himself a few years ago by "gettin' religion" from one of the Baptist missionaries who were beginning to go out to teach the word of God in the fields and baptize converts by the riversides of the South. Henry was a natural-born preacher. He could not read, but was able to memorize and expound on long passages of the Bible. The instant he was enlightened with the love of Jesus, he became a well-known preacher among the blacks in his neighborhood, after which he was singled out for additional abuse by his master who was adamantly opposed to either education or religion for his slaves.

"Gettin' too uppity ideas for yerself, ain't ya, boy? Ever'body knows a nigger can't read nor write and they's no way you can even begin to understand gawd. Now, you stop this here nonsense, you hear me, or I jes' have to whoop you to understandin'."

But Henry would not stop learning about and sharing his faith. He ran. It took two weeks before he was able to reach Philadelphia where he had heard the A.M.E. Church would help, and then another three days to Bucks County. He was being sent to a safe home in Massachusetts where he could continue his religious endeavors unhindered.

Lang hid Henry under the hay in the back of the wagon, and they proceeded toward Lumberton. It was raining steadily. Lang wore a slicker and held an umbrella above him, and threw an oilcloth over the hay to protect Henry. As they rumbled along slowly in the wagon, Henry raised his head up a little through the covering and talked with Lang

"God bless you, brother, for what you doin' for me. Yes, sir, praise Jesus. It's a wonderful undertaking for your people." He told Lang a little about his life in South Carolina, then said, "Tell me 'bout yo'self. You ever been a slave?"

Lang shook his head. "No, always been free." He talked about his early life, his mother, and his life as a limeburner, his wife and daughters. And he thought he would roll over laughing at Henry's reaction when he told him that his wife was white.

"You what?! You pullin' my leg, brother! She light-skinned you mean."

"No, sir. She's white. German."

"Lawdy, lawdy, praise Jesus. Things sho' is diff'rent up here. Never in all my born'd days did I ever think I'd see a black boy married—you say you married right 'n proper now?"

Lang nodded. "Yup, right 'n proper by a preacher."

"My goodness. I jes' haff to think 'bout dis fo' a while." He settled back in the hay murmuring to himself, and in a few minutes raised his head again.

"I been saying some extra-special prayers for you, brother. Way I figger it, you gonna need all the prayin' you can get. Life ain't gonna get better much soon, ways I sees it. For some reason, God has chosen us Africans for a lot of sufferin', and I shor prays Lord Jesus sees you and yo' precious little family through."

Within an hour, they had arrived at the appointed spot. Lang secured the horse and wagon by the side of the road about a quarter mile from the entrance to the woods. It was difficult getting through in the rain with only a small carriage-candle lamp, but they didn't dare risk a brighter light or a more direct route.

When they got to the small cave, they found some food for Henry and blankets. They settled down to wait for the next "conductor," whoever that may be. They chatted for a while, and Henry slept for a half hour or so. Finally, a man arrived at the cave—through the back! To his amazement, Lang learned there was a secret entrance that connected by way of a tunnel to the basement of John Kenderdine's home, and it was Kenderdine himself who came to fetch Henry.

He held up the lamp and looked at the two black men. "Which of you is Henry?"

"I am, sir," said Henry.

Kenderdine turned to Lang. "Are you an additional traveler?"

"No, sir, I'm Lang, sir. Langhorn Wellings. You know me." Kenderdine ran a lumber and construction supply business in Lumberton, and Lang had worked liming his farm a couple of times over the years. Kenderdine was active in politics, too, and was just defeated last year for a seat in the State Senate by only two votes.

"Brother Wellings! I didn't recognize you." Kenderdine extended his hand in a warm handshake. Lang felt awed to have this important man address him so respectfully. Kenderdine continued, "But, I'm surprised you're here. You really shouldn't jeopardize yourself. Where is Brother Joseph?"

"Constable Hubbard's been snooping around the neighborhood. I convinced Joseph that I could bring Henry this short distance to your place while he tries to lead Hubbard on a wild goose chase."

Kenderdine was not pleased. "Joseph never should have agreed to place you in harms way."

He turned to Henry and said, "Come inside. We have a warm meal and a cot waiting for you before the next leg of your journey to Massachusetts."

Then he put his hand on Lang's arm said in a serious tone, "Please be careful. I don't think you truly have any idea how vicious these animals are to colored people. We choose to do it knowing they would not dare to attack any of us. If they did, the entire country would be up in arms. But they know you have no one but the abolitionists to protect you or care if anything happens to you. We can protest until the cows come home, but they will not heed us and we cannot get relief or justice for you in the courts."

Lang began to get concerned for the first time the whole night of this adventure. "I…I didn't look at it that way. I wanted to help."

"We know you are good-hearted and wishing to help. Perhaps we can find less dangerous things for you to do." He smiled kindly. "God keep you, Friend Langhorn." Kenderdine and Henry disappeared into the back of the cave.

It was not yet dawn when Lang left the cave. He contemplated waiting until daylight, but then changed his mind. He didn't want his horse and wagon to be left for that long. *Besides, I'll be all right. Everyone around here knows me.*

As promised, he was careful. He stopped and waited at the entrance of the cave and listened for any unusual noises before leaving. Then he deliberately walked slowly in the opposite direction that they had come for several hundred yards before turning in a wide arc back to the road where he had left the horse and wagon.

It had stopped raining, but still the wet leaves and branches on the ground made movement slippery. On the other hand, it made the ground soft, and there was no crackle of leaves or snapping of branches to worry about.

When he got to the road, he crouched and waited for a few minutes before coming out of the woods. By now the dawn glow was beginning to light the horizon across the Delaware and he could see a fair distance. A slight mist hung in the air.

He was between a quarter to a half-mile south of his wagon now. Still not hearing anything, he crossed the road, jumped the fence and began walking back to the wagon by way of the newly-plowed field, figuring if anyone saw him he could say he was looking over the field in preparation for liming.

Just as he was almost to the wagon, he heard a buggy and two men on horseback coming up the road behind him. He couldn't see well enough to know if he recognized them, so he ducked into a ditch, but they had spotted him and the wagon first. The two men on horseback came galloping over.

"Hey, there!" one of them hollered. "Com'on out, now. We seen you!"

Lang stood up slowly.

"Well, lookee what we got here. Looks to me like that drawin' likeness of Henry Miller we got, don't it to you, Jed?"

The other man cocked his head and smiled. "Sure do look like it to me. Com'on out, now, boy. Give yerself up peaceful-like and you won't git hurt. You cain't run from us now."

"My name is Langhorn Wellings. I am a limeburner, and I have lived in Bucks County my whole life. I have a wife and two children here."

"Whoo-whee! Listen to that colored boy recitin' what he been told! Somebody said he learnt to memorize real good."

"I'm telling you…." Lang continued to protest. "Listen to me, please. I don't talk like a slave. I've never been in the South."

"You shut your mouth, boy! You don't be tellin' me nothing! Come on out now 'fore I have to come in there and git you."

Lang sighed and walked out to the road. Surely this would be cleared up soon. The third man had gotten down from the buggy and was waiting with his hands on his hips.

"What you got there, boys?" he asked with a smile on his face. "Look like our night's huntin' expedition been successful?"

Lang approached him. "I've been trying to tell these men that my name is Langhorn Wellings. I…." Suddenly he felt a sharp pain in the back of his head. His knees buckled from under him and he crumpled to the road. He rolled up and put his hand up to his head and felt the warm, sticky moisture of fresh blood.

"I done tol' you to shut up!" an angry voice came from above and behind him.

Lang tried to get up on his knees. "My name is…"

A boot caught him in the stomach and ribs and the blunt end of some sort of weapon came down on the right side of his head just above his ear.

"You got no name, nigger!"

Oh God! I'm going to lose consciousness. Stay awake! Stay awake! He stopped trying to get up and held his arm up in a gesture of defeat and to ward off further blows, but another came down on his shoulder nearly bending his arm back double, then another to his upper chest. *Please, God, make it stop.* He lay still. The pain permeated his body. His breathing came in short gasps, it hurt so much to even draw air.

He heard the man who was in the buggy. "You sure this is Henry Miller?"

"'Course ah'm sure. Looks jes' like him."

"I don't know. Could he have learnt to talk like that in so short a time? And what's he doin' out here all by hisself? I don't know, boys."

The men were frustrated and angry after a night out in the rain hunting for this man and were not about to give up their prey easily. "Well, so what if it ain't? What're we gonna do now?"

The other man interjected, "If it ain't Henry, and ah still says it is, it'll be a damn good substitute."

The man in the buggy stroked his beard stubble. "I s'pose you're right. But we better high-tail it outa here. Here, throw him in the wagon. Let's head down toward Bristol, get him on a boat to Virginny or South Carolina. He'll be long gone 'fore anyone knows."

The men picked Lang up and put him roughly in the back of the wagon.

"Here, cover him over with that straw and tarp. You know what, boys? I just thought. After we dump him, we can take the horse and wagon on over to Trenton or Philly and sell 'em. A little extra compensation at the expense of these stupid abolitionists."

The men laughed. They talked in hushed tones, and Lang could not hear what they were saying. It seemed to him that he was drifting in and out of consciousness because the next thing he knew they were on the move. They had turned the wagon around and were heading south on Sugan Road toward the York Pike. *Got to stay awake so I can figure out where we're going.* He could not see from under the covering how light it was getting or from which direction the sunlight was coming.

Lang didn't know it, but the man in the buggy had gone off toward New Hope after giving instructions to the other two men, one of whom had tied his horse to the wagon and was driving, the other trotting alongside watching to make sure Lang didn't escape.

Now he could hear the men talking. "Hey, Jed, what happens if somebody asks us? What're we gonna say 'bout the wagon?"

"We'll tell 'em we just bought it."

Oh, God! Lang thought. *Why didn't I paint my name on my wagon like everybody's been telling me to!* He tried desperately to figure out in what direction they were going. Next he tried moving his limbs, and realized his left arm was broken at the shoulder or out of the socket. The pain was horrendous, and he cried out uncontrollably as he moved.

A blunt instrument came at him and poked him in the back. "You better lie still and be quiet 'fore I have to gag you or worse!"

"Hey, Jed. Are there any tolls on this road?"

"Oh, you're right. I forgot 'bout that."

York Road! They wouldn't take me to Doylestown. Perhaps New Hope. Lang had no way of knowing they were passing through Lahaska at that very moment. It was too early for the tollgate keeper, Levi Hartley, who knew Lang and his wagon, to be on duty.

Then he realized when they made a left turn. *Durham Road! Of course, it's mostly woods. Not too many farms.*

Mary could not get back to sleep all night. She went downstairs and waited and watched. No sign. *Perhaps he's decided to wait until daylight to come home. That would be smarter.* The babies woke up and wanted breakfast. Still no sign. She brought breakfast to Mother Lacy in her room. She didn't say anything to her about Lang being gone or what he had done.

Finally, at eight o'clock she could stand it no more. *He should have been home by now.* She panicked and picked up Ruth Ann and Elizzie in her arms and ran as fast as she could to the neighbor and raised the alarm. By this time she was nearly hysterical with worry and fear.

Within half an hour, the neighbor's sons had raced by foot and horseback all over Lahaska, the Centreville area of Buckingham and Western Solebury Township. "Get to Lacy's right away! We need your help!" They rang the alarm bell at the schoolhouse. Farmers left their mules and plows standing in fields. Blacksmiths left their forges. Shopkeepers shut their doors. Teachers left their classrooms. It was astonishing the number of people who came immediately and unquestioningly to Mary's aid.

Joseph was among the first to arrive from the Buckingham school, beside himself with remorse. "Mrs. Wellings, I can't express how sorry I am that I let Lang go off on this crazy scheme! I won't live with myself if something happens to my brother because of me."

He immediately mobilized the men into groups that fanned out all over Buckingham and Solebury Townships. One group he sent to the Kenderdine home on Sugan Road in Lumberton, another toward New Hope, another group down the York Road and finally several men to Newtown on the Durham Pike. He tried to calculate, if Lang had been kidnapped, in what direction they would be going and how far they could have gotten. Like Lang, Joseph figured they would not take him toward Doylestown and, thankfully, he was correct.

All along the way, the posses roused more men to join them, and they broke off into more groups going in different directions. The Durham Road group learned at the tollgate that, indeed, two men with a horse and wagon matching the description of Langhorn's had passed about an hour earlier. The tollgate keeper, an elderly woman who was hard of hearing and all by herself, reported hearing a noise coming from under the hay and oilcloth and the men acting strange and taking off quickly. The posse sent a rider back to Lahaska with the news that they were giving chase.

The Sugan Road group came back and reported they had found blood and other signs of struggle on the road and could see where the wagon had been turned around with several more hoof prints alongside. "All right, that means he's probably still alive," reasoned Joseph. "Thank God for that."

Meanwhile, Lang had tried to figure out where they were on the Durham Road. *If only I can wiggle out somehow. Maybe I can hide in the woods. No, I can't get away fast enough.* When the wagon slowed down and he heard one of the men ask, "You got a penny?" He realized. *The tollgate! If I yell out, I may be able to alert someone.*

He tried crying, "Help! Help me!" several times, but there was mucous in his throat, his voice was weak and muffled further by the hay and oilcloth covering. Then he heard one of the men coughing and the other saying in a very loud voice, "I say, thankee, ma'am. We'll be on our way now." He realized it was the old, deaf lady on duty. *There goes that chance!* He tried to think and plot but oh! he hurt so bad, it was hard to think straight. This was far worse than the beating he had taken in Philadelphia. This was with weapons more than just fists.

As soon as they were out of sight of the toll booth, the man driving turned around and yelled, "Ah'm tellin' you, you better be still. I'll knock you silly, if you don't."

"Let me at 'im, Jed," the other man said.

"No, we won't be able to get a good price for him if you bust him up too bad!"

When the rider from Durham Road showed up, Joseph was confirmed in his fears. They were on their way to Bristol. "If we don't get there soon, we'll lose him at the docks," he told the men out of Mary's hearing. He and some of the others galloped south to catch up.

In Newtown, several of the farmers and others along the road who had been alerted to the chase confirmed that the wagon had passed and was on the way to Bristol. The time span and distance were growing shorter and shorter. *Please let them stay on the main road,* Joseph pleaded. *It's our only chance. And, please, let it be Lang's wagon.*

The lead group of men caught up to the wagon south of Newtown at a little village called Four Lanes End right in front of an A.M.E. Church that had been founded in 1809.

"Hold up there! Where do you think you're going?"

The kidnappers still tried to bluff their way. "We bought this here wagon legal-like. You got no call to...."

"Help me!" Lang started yelling. The posse threw off the covering and pushed away the hay. By this time, several women who had been working in the church gathered around the wagon and began ministering to Lang. They recognized him from camp meetings they had attended up at the Wolf Rocks church. "Look! It's Langhorn Wellings from Buckingham."

"Get the sheriff!" someone cried, and the kidnappers were surrounded.

"We's only doin' our duty. This here's Henry Miller, an escaped slave…"

"This is Langhorn Wellings, and five hundred residents of Bucks County will attest to it. You're not going to get away with this one and you'll think twice before coming back to this county."

Lang passed out from pain coupled with relief at being rescued. The men used the oilcloth as a makeshift carrier and brought him carefully into the pastor's home next to the little church. A doctor was sent for.

The posse began escorting the kidnappers back to Newtown. Joseph and his group met them just north of Four Lanes End. Upon hearing the news that Lang had been rescued, the rest of the men went back home to inform the others and to resume their daily work. Joseph asked one of them to bring Mary back and rode on to Four Lanes End to be with his friend.

Of course, they knew the sheriff in Newtown would do nothing to the kidnappers, but it was worth the trip to watch them squirm for a few miles. Predictably, the sheriff let them go. "They claim official business, boys," he explained to Lang's rescuers. "Showed me a warrant for a runaway slave looks just like this Wellings fellow, and they've got Hubbard's support."

"Just so's they know," one of the Paxson boys warned. "We know who they are now and they'd be wise to stay out of our neighborhood. It's a good thing for them we're peaceable folks."

These particular bounty hunters did indeed stay out of Bucks County for a while, but others came quickly in their stead. Within months, Big Ben Jones was kidnapped and severely beaten and taken to a holding pen in Baltimore, where he languished for months before being rescued, a fate that easily could have been Lang's if not for the quick-thinking response of Joseph and the others.

His recovery from the injuries was not so immediate and swift as the rescue, however. After giving Lang copious amounts of liquor, the doctor reset his shoulder, and patched up the cuts. His left arm and shoulder were never the same again, and for the rest of his life he could not raise his left arm above his head. One of the blows on the back of his head produced a hematoma that in turn triggered a very small blood clot, just enough to destroy the nerve endings to some facial muscles. The result was his face would thereafter droop slightly on the left side.

Recovery from the psychological injuries took much longer, and there was no one he could talk to about it; they were all dealing with their own issues or busy blaming him.

Mary, for example, was initially hysterical, then relieved, then reproachful. She would never talk about it without criticizing Lang for his foolhardiness, thus widening further the gulf between them.

"How could you do this to me and the children? Don't you care about us?"

While supportive in a monetary measure, even his friends Mahlon and Andy and others were critical. "Hey, you know the rules, Lang, as well as the rest of us. In by dark, out in pairs."

"You gotta be out of your mind! What's the matter with your friend Joseph for lettin' you do that?"

Those words would come back to haunt Andy, as he himself ferried a woman and her children to safety in an emergency in 1852 when no one else was available.

Still, they promised financial help for as long as Lang was unable to work. His fellow limeburners all pledged to do his share of the work and give the earnings to the family. They knew he had done and would do again the same for any of them. "What goes around comes around."

Joseph had his own guilt issues to deal with. He came over so often that Lang finally told Mary one day to tell him he wasn't up to the visits any more.

There was a lot of residual pain that Lang had trouble dealing with, and he started to use liquor to smooth off the rough edges. The whiskey made everything better. If he was lucky he could drink until he passed out and then he wouldn't have to think about anything any more—black, white, slavery, Mary, the babies, money, his friends, work, kidnapping, the pain, the pain.

He began spending more evenings in New Hope than he spent at the Lacy farm in Lahaska, rationalizing that he was more trouble to Mary and Mother Lacy than he was worth. *She don't need me. I'm just a big, dumb yoke around her neck anyway.*

A couple of times when he did go home his hurt and anger turned their arguments into near violence. He never hit her, but came close, and Mary became hurt and fearful. She didn't understand what was happening to him and could not find a way of communicating with him about it other than by nagging. The vicious cycle was set in motion and continued spiraling downward for the rest of the year 1844 and well into the next.

The most frightening outcome of all for his friends and loved ones was that Langhorn began carrying pistols, two guns in holsters on each side of his body with straps running criss-cross across his chest. Despite everyone's exhortations and entreaties, Lang would not put the guns away.

"Nobody's ever gonna do that to me never again! Or he's gonna die trying, believe you me. And if I ever see those white-faced, mealy-mouthed bastards who done this to me in this county again, they're dead. You hear me? Dead!"

Mary became so desperate she wrote to her father asking for help and immediately regretted it. A few weeks later, she read his name in a list published in the *Intelligencer* of people for whom letters remained unclaimed in the Post Office at Doylestown, and she knew instinctively that it was hers. Within a few weeks after that, it was returned to her.

In the meantime, Mother Lacy's health continued to deteriorate. She would be eighty-seven at her next birthday and was for all practical purposes bedridden, although her mind was as alert as it had ever been. She rarely came out of her room any more, yet she remained aware of what was going on in the house and knew almost every detail about the turmoil that was overwhelming Mary and Langhorn and the children.

One day, she said to Mary, "Please go get neighbor Isaac. I need to speak to him."

"Of course," Mary replied. "Are you all right?"

"Yes, yes, as well as can be expected for an old lady." She smiled and patted the bed. "Come here, dear, for a moment. I wish to speak with thee."

Mary obediently sat.

Mother Lacy continued. "For the past many years, thee has become my spiritual daughter. I know there is a great deal troubling thee even though thee has scrupulously tried to keep me innocent. Thy husband is experiencing some terrible times. Thee may not know, I watched my own husband go through some severe trials. He did not take the deaths of our children easily. He was sorely torn for many years and even sought to blame himself in many ways."

Tears began to form in Mary's eyes as she internalized what Mother Lacy was saying. *How could she bear to lose her children? How could I bear to lose Ruth Ann or Elizzie?*

"Even though we had the Friends and the Word of God to comfort us, there was still a great void. I filled mine with the knowledge that they were departed from this world, but certainly not gone from my midst. Does thee understand?"

Mary nodded. "Yes, I think I do."

"My husband, on the other hand, was almost overcome with grief when our last son died. He would sit for days just staring and thinking. I had to do all the chores around the farm, and the crops were in danger. Lord forgive me, but I began to get angry with him for closing me out and shirking his responsibilities."

Mary sat in rapt attention. This was coming "close to home" for her. "What did you do?"

"I prayed. His spirit was broken, and I prayed that it be mended. Mind thee, if I had to send him to the Alms House as a melancholic, I was prepared to do so. But, first I tried to simply ignore it and treat him as if there was nothing wrong. Thee should have seen me. 'Twas as if I had a newborn all over again. I had to lead him around and dress him and feed him as if he was a child. We were too old to have more children, as if another could replace the beloved children we had lost.

"It took a lot of time. I kept talking to him as if he was still participating in the daily chores of life. 'Thee needs to plow the west field soon.' ''Tis time for corn planting.' 'Does thee think we will have a good peach harvest this year?' This and so much more, day after day."

"And? He got better?"

"Oh, yes, eventually, a little bit every day. Our sisters and brothers brought their children around, as well, and I told the children to pester him constantly." Mother Lacy smiled and chuckled at the memory. "In that way he was forced to pay attention to the children of today and gradually stop lamenting the children of yesterday."

Mary sighed and wiped the tears from her eyes. "Why is it," she asked Mother Lacy, "that I can cry about your situation of years ago and I cannot cry over my own problems?"

Mother Lacy smiled. "I know. 'Tis as if we are afraid somehow to give in to our troubles for fear we will be totally lost. If thee will permit an old woman the rights of sage advice, I will tell thee another secret." She looked at Mary's eyes, and Mary nodded and smiled through her tears.

"'Tis also a tendency of people to wallow in the bad things. 'Tis hard for us somehow to see anything else. But, always try to remember—look at the good things and overlook the bad."

"Just as you tried to overlook what your husband was doing?"

"Yes, and soon enough the good overwhelmed the bad. Now, I want thee to go get Brother Isaac and his wife, if she is available, as well."

Mary got Ruth Ann and Elizzie ready to go out and walked the quarter mile to the neighbors'. When they returned to the Lacy home, Mother Lacy was ready, sitting up in bed, and waiting for them.

"Thank thee for coming, dear friends," she said. "There is something important I need thee to witness. I feel my body slipping gradually day by day, yet, praise the Lord, He has blessed me with sound mind. My will has been made, and my nieces and nephews will inherit everything…everything, that is, except what I am about to do."

She turned to Mary. "Sister Mary, will thee get the little chest from the floor of the wardrobe?" Mary did as she was bid.

Mother Lacy gave the box back to Mary. "Brother Isaac and Sister Rebecca, thee are my witnesses that this box I place back into Sister Mary's hands. 'Tis my bequest to her and Brother Langhorn as a small measure of my gratitude for their kindness and caring over these many years. It is separate and apart from my estate."

Mary opened the box and saw that it was filled with gold and silver coins. Mother Lacy had never trusted bank notes, for very good reason. "Shin plaster" was what the newspapers called the sham issue of constantly-failing banks.

"Oh, Mother Lacy! I am moved to tears again."

"I trust thee will use it to secure the future shelter and comfort of thyselves and thy children when I am no longer here. Now, I am weak and tired. Please excuse me." She sighed and rested back into the pillows.

There was over one hundred dollars in the box, which, when added to what Mary had managed to save, came to almost one hundred and fifty dollars. Her dream of having her own home was finally within the realm of possibility.

The next time she was at Sarah Betts' house, Mary excitedly told her she was getting enough money together to buy a place.

"You know, Mary, it just occurred to me," Sarah said. "We have some property over in Solebury—at Canada Hill. Tom and I own it with our son Cyrus and his wife, Eliza. There's nothing on it now and the whole parcel is too big for you, but Tom and Cyrus might consider dividing off a piece for you to put a little house up."

Mary got the exact location and said she would go look at it first chance, which turned out to be several weeks later, and when she did, she was immediately taken with the area.

Canada Hill—no one remembers how the district got its name. It could have been because the Canady family lived nearby. Before 1833 it was called Somerville. It was located on York Road just a mile and a half east of Lahaska and about four miles west of New Hope. There was a small dirt lane intersecting that ran southwest to Buckingham Mountain and northeast to intersect Aquetong Road and access the farms.

Up on a hill on the northeast corner of the intersection was a small, still rudimentary Baptist church established a few years prior through the efforts of evangelists from Lambertville, New Jersey. Members of the church included the families of Walton, Smith, Hill, Naylor, Coffin, Evans, Kinsey, Cathers and Wright. The largest landowning neighbors were descendants of families that had been in Bucks County forever—the Pearsons, Naylors, Byes and Scarboroughs—and from the latter family the land for the Baptist church was purchased for seventy dollars in 1843.

The property in the neighborhood not being farmed was filled with old, tall trees—maples, elms, locusts. It was slightly hilly, enough to provide good drainage away from a house and down to a little creek that ran alongside York Road.

Mary was enchanted with the area, which she had passed several times on the way back and forth to New Hope, but had never really stopped and looked at before. *This is perfect! I could easily walk to Lahaska and Buckingham from here and the stage runs right down York Road to New Hope and Doylestown—not that I ever want to go to New Hope.*

But then the financial cost of such land brought her back to reality. The next time she was at Sarah's, she answered Sarah's questioning "Well? What did you think?" with a shrug. "It's perfect, Sarah. So beautiful. But there's no way I could afford it."

"We'll see about that. Come. Let's go find Tom. He's at the store."

Sarah had already spoken to Tom and Cyrus about her little scheme. Initially skeptical, they gradually became convinced, with Sarah's urging, that a little corner of the property could be carved off. Half an acre would be enough to put up a nice little house. In fact, they continued to reason, it might not be a bad idea to divide off more small lots to put up tenements and houses for farm workers, blacksmiths, and others. They could even make some extra money by renting.

Sarah and Tom explained the plan to Mary who was astonished to think it was possible she could really have a place of her own.

No, this is too good to be true. I know it. "But, what about Lang? He won't go along, and besides it's not legal for a woman—especially a married woman—to buy property, is it?"

Sarah and Tom had overlooked that little legality. "Well, maybe there's a way around it. Let's think about it for a while," Tom said, and Sarah reiterated. "You've got to protect yourself and the children, Mary. You do what you have to do to secure your future. That's what Sister Tamar wants for you."

Mary knew Sarah was right. She was terrified that Lang would find out about the money Mother Lacy had given them. Sadly, the way he had been acting lately, there was no question in her mind that he would take it and drink it away. As her husband, he had complete, unquestionable legal rights to everything—her body, her personal items, her children, her earnings, her savings—including the right to pour their money into a whiskey bottle if he wanted to. She had no rights or protection. None but her "smarts," that is, and a mother's determination.

Within a week, a way was worked out, but it meant talking Andy or Mahlon or some other man, preferably colored, into getting involved. Tom and Cyrus consulted with a lawyer who suggested, "Why not have someone else buy the property for her in trust and see if there's another Negro who can do it. That way, you will be protecting the husband with one of his own people, and you can never be accused of trying to take advantage of her."

Mahlon refused outright. "I don't want to get involved, Mary. Really, I don't want Lang getting mad at me. You understand."

No, she didn't understand. Next she went to Andy, who also was reluctant. "I just don't know,' he said shaking his head. "Lang is going to explode if he hears about it. He's going to think we're working in cahoots behind his back—and he's right!"

Andy's wife, Maggie, was more insistent. "Now, you listen here to me, Mr. Andrew Hartless. We got to protect this lady and her childrens. She got to hide that money somehow and you got to help her. You hear me? Besides, it's for his own good in the long run. When he come outa this trouble—and he will, you mark my words—he'll understand."

"All right, all right!" Andy relented. "But I know he's going to kill me."

The deed was done on March 5, 1845. Andrew Hartless received one-half acre in Solebury Township in trust for Mary and her children. Langhorn "or any future husband" was deliberately excluded from ownership rights.

Mary got the lot for two hundred dollars, with one hundred dollars down payment and a mortgage for the remainder, which she could easily pay off with her dressmaking and baking wages. Besides, she had another fifty dollars saved toward building a house, which she gave to Sarah and Tom Betts for safekeeping. The money was secreted legally and out of Lang's reach. That was the major objective.

Predictably, Lang was furious when he found out. He had been betrayed by his wife and his best friend—Andy, of all people, his closest friend for nearly twenty-five years!

He came to the Lacy side yard and hollered at Mary. He raged at the world, really, and vented all of his frustrations into this place and moment, while Mary clutched the crying girls in her arms and hid on the floor of the dining room.

"You've just sold me, Mary! You just sold your husband for a piece of property!"

"What's wrong with Daddy?" little Ruth Ann cried.

"It's all right, my sweet honey babe. Your daddy's got a bad sickness. Let's pray." And she began to teach her girls the Lord's Prayer.

But, it would take far longer for Lang's pride to recover than it did for his physical injuries from the kidnapping to heal.

COM. VS. LANGHORN WELLINGS—Surety of the peace on oath of Jacob McIntire. Langhorn, it appears had been rather intimate with the wife of McIntire; seeking every opportunity, in his absence, to visit her; took her out riding and said he knew as much about her as her husband did. McIntire forbid him coming to his house or having anything to do with his wife. Langhorn, then, and at various times afterwards, threatened that, if McIntire should say anything more to him about it, he would put a ball through him; said he would put him to sleep; that he had the instruments to do it with, and produced his pistols.

At another time he said if McIntire brought suit against him in relation to the matter of intimacy with his wife, he would put a ball through his heart and send him to h—l in a hurry. The parties were mulattoes, and there was quite an array of the colored *gemmen* present, who manifested considerable interest in the result of the matter. The Court, after hearing the parties, sentenced the defendant to pay the costs of prosecution, and required him to find security in the sum of $200 to keep the peace and be of good behavior for the period of one year. Carver for Commonwealth; Michener for defendant.

[*Bucks County Intelligencer*, Wednesday, February 13, 1853]

Chapter VIII

Canada Hill
1845-1853

Eventually, it fell to Bill Johnson to save Lang from his growing dependence on the bottle and convince him to come home. At one point several years before, surprisingly, Bill had his own serious problems with alcohol and, together with friends Elwood Longshore, Cyrus Buckman, Joseph Burton and others, formed the Bucks County Temperance and Total Abstinence Societies. Meetings were held every Sunday afternoon in the 1840s in Eli Carver's barn in Solebury. The men became very supportive of and concerned about each other and provided one another with a source of lifelong assistance and encouragement.

Bill, of course, had known Lang almost all his life and had employed him at his limekilns for many years. He began to notice that Lang sometimes did not show up to work for days at a time. At first he didn't think much of it because, of course, he knew about Lang's kidnapping and serious injuries; but, then, the absences became more frequent and the carelessness began whenever he was working.

"Hey, Lang! Be careful there! What're you tryin' to do, kill yourself?" Which may have been more than close to the truth.

Bill asked some of the other men what was going on with Lang. No one wanted to say anything. They all shrugged their shoulders and tried to brush it off by implying that Lang must still be hurting from the beating. Fortunately, Bill was not convinced. "You know, you men are 'living in hope and dying in despair' that Lang is going to get well on his own. This has been going on much too long. He should be over it by now."

Next, Bill went to the Lacy farm to speak with Mary who also was at first embarrassed and reticent to admit to their personal troubles. Bill told her point blank, "Sister Mary, Lang cannot fight this alone. He needs all of us. Even though he thinks he doesn't want our help, he needs us desperately, and we've got to work together."

Mary finally admitted that Lang had not been home for many weeks at a stretch and, when he was, he was sullen and withdrawn and fought with her constantly. He had not contributed to the family's upkeep for a long time, especially since hearing that Mary had bought the property and excluded him.

With Mary's help, Bill narrowed down all of the possible drinking and sleeping places and zeroed in on New Hope. He followed Lang there one evening to a particularly seedy establishment. As Bill looked around the dimly-lighted, smoky, dirty room, he couldn't help but notice the irony that here, at least, there was no color barrier. Liquor purveyors were equality-minded—they'd take anyone's money, black or white. In fact, there was only one bar in Bucks County—Strawn's Tavern, run by "Pappy Strawn" at the Court Inn in Doylestown—that did not admit coloreds. And "sutlers"—liquor purveyors—would so often show up at colored camp meetings that in July 1843 it was specifically advertised in the *Intelligencer* that none would be tolerated at that year's meeting in Brownsburg, and that if any showed up, "They will be dealt with according to the law."

Bill plunged right in, and the barkeep cringed when he saw him. This Quaker fellow was well known in the county for his crusade against "the demon rum." He posed a serious threat to the business and livelihood of every saloonkeeper for miles around.

"Hey, you there! I know who you are. You get on outa here. You got no business here!" he growled at Bill who stood his ground, told the man he had as much right to be here as anyone, and demanded a sarsaparilla soda. Actually, he didn't much care for the taste of it, but it was the only non-alcoholic beverage in the house, and as long as he was spending money, he figured the barkeep would leave him be.

He spotted Lang sitting in the corner with a whiskey and beer. He was alone and absorbed in his own thoughts and hadn't noticed Bill come in.

"May I sit down?"

Lang looked up at Bill with bleary eyes. "Suit yourself," he said. They sat in silence for a while.

Finally, Lang looked at Bill. "Why'd you come to this place? This ain't the right place for you."

"I came here for you, Lang. I'm going to take you home."

"I don't wanna go home. Got nothin' to go home for."

"There's Mary, Ruth Ann, Elizzie, and even old Friend Lacy needs you. You are very important to a great many people." Bill almost had to shout at Lang, the noise in the bar was so loud coupled with Lang's foggy, drunken hearing. "I need you! Mahlon and Andy need you! You are our friend!"

Lang stared at Bill in disbelief. "You're all better off without me. They shouldn'ta rescued me. Shoulda just let me go."

Bill's first inclination was to shake some sense into this fool, but he restrained himself and repeated calmly, with genuine feeling, "You are very important to us. We cannot imagine life without you, our friend. You are sick and hurt and need help."

They sat in silence for a few more moments. A mulatto barmaid came up and exchanged some banter with Lang and bumped her body against his shoulder in a flirtatious manner. Lang became embarrassed for Bill, an upright, moral person, who was obviously uncomfortable with the situation, and pushed her away. He had too much respect for Bill to push him away. He had worked for Bill for many years and knew about all of his efforts in the abolition and temperance movements. *To think this fine man came here for me,* he thought for a fleeting second, then gave in to depression again.

"There's nothin' you can do for me. Why can't you just leave me in peace?"

"I'm not leaving without you. It doesn't have to be home to the Lacy farm. I'll take you to my house if you prefer. We always have room for you."

For Lang, the effect of that simple, kind gesture was as if someone had lifted the dark shades of his anger, hurt and depression. Just a teeny bit. Just enough to let in a few rays of sunlight—hope. Bill saw it flicker in Lang's eyes for a split second and continued to press his case.

"I'm serious, Lang. You know you don't want to be living like this, spending all your money on booze and smokes and God knows what else. There's Mary and the children at home waiting and worrying. Think of the little girls, if no one else. They need their father. Is this how you want them to remember you?"

Lang was almost visibly sickened when he heard Bill's last comment. *Ruth Ann. Elizzie. My beautiful baby girls. What must they think of their daddy?*

Bill closed the sale. "Com'on, Lang. Let's go. I'll take you home with me." Lang looked up at Bill through eyes that were moist not just because of the liquor and smoke-filled air, and nodded in resignation.

An impromptu meeting of the Temperance Society was held that night and for several nights thereafter in Bill's office at the limekilns. Bill would not let Lang out of his sight. He made him get a bath, a shave and haircut, got him into a new set of shirt and pants—knowing that a "fresh start" sometimes makes all the difference in the world.

Slowly over the next couple of days and at the Sunday afternoon meetings, Lang began to understand how and why he was throwing his life away into the liquor. Compounded by the general troubles of life, part of it was that he was undoubtedly punishing himself for his foolhardiness the night of the kidnapping. The most critical point, they told him, was for him to accept that he had allowed booze to become more important in his life than God and righteousness, that he first had to give everything up to the Lord—all the hurt, all the pain, all the anger—and receive His grace, instead of "worshipping the devil" by pouring himself into a bottle.

The leaders prayed over Lang, preached and read the Bible. "Look what the Lord Jesus endured for us sinners on the cross. And He is with us always, ready to assist us with whatever suffering we are called upon to endure."

"There's nothing but the devil and eternal damnation waiting inside that bottle. Let us pray to follow the 'narrow path'—the Lord's path—instead."

With constant prayers, counseling, and support, Lang gradually gained the strength to face his troubles and deal with them one by one. He even came to understand why Mary had purchased the property without him and grudgingly agreed with Bill and the others that she probably had good reason to fear that he would have taken the money eventually when his own funds ran out. Though he agreed she did it for their future security, it still "stuck in his craw" for the rest of his life, but he didn't often let on that it bothered him.

The largest stumbling block was going home to Mary and apologizing. "Why should I apologize for things done to me? It's other folks who should be askin' my forgiveness."

Bill and the other men patiently explained that those other folks didn't exactly see it that way. "In fact, Lang, they feel they have been abused by you, not the other way around. For example, as your employer, I have every right to be upset with you for not showin' up to work half the time, for letting me down. But, you're angry that I don't understand how you been beat up and hurt and aren't feeling well enough to come to work. You see what I mean?" Lang nodded.

Bill continued: "But, even if they know how you've been hurt, they're not going to quickly ask forgiveness, if at all, so it's up to you to be the bigger man. You got to give eighty percent or even a hundred and ten percent, if you have to, especially to Mary. Another thing, you're going to have to prove yourself to her now, I mean that she can trust you again, and it's going to take a mighty long time if I'm figuring the depth of her German temper right."

This was all too confusing for Lang, but he did know the basics: He had sure made a mess of things, he wanted to go home to be with his wife and children, and he had to make some concessions in order to do so. There was nowhere else in the world he could go, or wanted to go, and life the way it was heading for him was a constant spiraling downward into the abyss of despair and death.

The thought of his precious little daughters was the final clincher. Bill was brutally honest. "You've seen how coloreds and mixed races are treated, Lang. Do you want that for your little girls? 'Cause there's little hope for them as it is, and without you there is definitely nothing, no one to protect them."

That was the key. Even if Mary didn't want or need him, he was the whole world and chief defender for his children, and he'd be damned if he was going to let his baby girls go through life alone, unprotected.

Finally, he was ready. He rode over to the Lacy farm loaded with gifts for Mary and the children, at Bill's urging, not of his own accord. In fact, he felt rather foolish all "gussied up and slicked down," but Bill kept reassuring him that he had to make a new start.

"Go to Mary as if you're courtin' her all over again…. And, don't be surprised if she kicks you clear off the porch the first time! And watch that temper—yours, I mean!" Bill shouted after Lang as he rode out of the yard.

Mary was still angry and fearful, but couldn't help giggling behind her hand when she saw Lang, clean-shaven, hair combed back, carrying a bunch of flowers, of all things. Bill was right about the gifts. Mary could not refuse letting Ruth Ann and Elizzie enjoy their new toys.

They sat on the porch as Lang stumbled through the speech he had prepared. "I'm sorry for all the pain I've caused you and the girls, Mary. I've done a fine turn of it, I guess, and I don't blame you for nothin'. I can't stand being away from you, and I promise to do whatever I can to make you trust me again."

Coached by Bill, Lang went through the cathartic litany of reconciliation that was essential for him to acknowledge his actions and forgive himself, let alone ask for Mary's forgiveness.

Even though Mary was skeptical and fearful, she knew in her heart she had no choice, that their lives were forever inextricably entwined with each other and with Bucks County. She and the girls could not survive without him. There was no one else in the world—certainly not her parents or even any of her brothers and sisters—who was willing or able to support them. She had no civil rights. There was nowhere she could get a job and support two children, and there was certainly nowhere else in the world she and the children would be accepted.

More importantly, she had shut down her youthful dreams and passions in the last few years. Her mother had been right. It was dangerous to love a man. Now their very survival was teetering on the brink of interdependence, and she used it as a tool to set the parameters of his acceptance back into the home.

Bill had warned Lang that Mary would undoubtedly vent her anger. "You just better sit there and take it and keep your mouth shut, if you know what's good for you. Just let her get it all out. Agree with everything, no matter if you think she's wrong. And, whatever you do, don't answer back. Just remember that whatever she says is like a butterfly that flutters away in the wind, and it can't hurt you no more than a butterfly can bite you."

It worked. Mary broke down in tears and let all of her hurt and frustration wash away from her soul while Lang gently held her and rocked her and said soothing words to her. "It's gonna be all right, old girl. We'll do better now. You'll see."

Mother Lacy was the easiest person to apologize to. Never in his life had Lang encountered anyone with a sweeter, kinder disposition. In his estimation, if the Quakers had saints, this lady would have been among the first to qualify.

He knocked on her door, and she called for him to come in. Even shut upstairs in her room, she knew almost instinctively he was there.

She was weak and sick, yet her face lit up with a smile when she saw him. "I am so glad I lived long enough to see thee has come home. Thou art like a son to me, and I feel thy troubles. If thee will allow an old lady to give some advice: Trust in the Lord always. Try to find His will for thy life and do not fight against it. He wants only what is best for us and will always take care of us."

"I am beginning to understand that, Mother Lacy." Lang knew that submission to the Lord's will and detachment from one's own desires were what had enabled Mother Lacy to accept and understand the deaths of her children so young in life.

"The Lord had another mission for them not of this world and certainly more important than my needs and wishes."

Joseph was another visit Lang had to make, and quickly. He realized that his friend had been consumed for many months with remorse for having been talked into letting Lang go on the underground mission with Henry Miller that fateful night over a year and a half ago. It was bad enough for Joseph to see men he hardly knew, like Big Ben Jones, beaten, kidnapped and hurting. Lang was his brother, his lifelong friend.

In a convoluted way of thinking, as long as Joseph saw that his brother Lang was happy and living well, he was reassured there was hope that all of the dark-skinned people of America could eventually look forward to the same prospects of happiness and well-being, thereby giving Joseph confidence that his work and struggles in the cause of abolition and human rights were worthwhile and would not be in vain. But, Lang being the barometer of Joseph's expectations for the black race, when he was down and out, Joseph was almost in utter despair for the success of his altruistic vision.

"Oh, Lang, praise God! I am so happy to see you looking well again! I can't tell you how sorry I am…"

"No, no, Joseph, it's my fault. I never should have talked you into it. It was a silly, stupid thing to do. Mary tried to warn me. But, I was bored and wanted adventure. Well, you know."

"I understand, but I will still blame myself forever."

Lang filled Joseph in on some of the happenings over the past year and a half, including the fact that Mary had bought some property over at Canada Hill.

"That's wonderful, Lang! Even though, as you say, you have been excluded from ownership, I don't think there is any court that would not recognize your claim if you chose to press the issue. Better yet, why not prove to Mary you are worthy of her trust. In the meantime, you can begin to build a home there."

The new home-building idea began to intrigue Lang, and he brought it up with Mary. "Joseph's idea makes sense, Mary. We should be preparing for the day when we can no longer live here after Mother Lacy goes."

But Mary was not yet ready to begin thinking about Mother Lacy dying, and she replied that they did not have enough money for building.

"We can start, Mary, a little bit at a time."

It was Joseph who cinched the deal. He saw an opportunity to make it up to Lang and Mary in a small way. He began by talking with some of the other men in the neighborhood and received from each commitments of support. He came over to the Lacy farm one evening excited about the results of his work.

"I have good news for you both! John Kenderdine has offered to let you have all the lumber and building supplies you need at cost. Buckman and Yardley have offered shingles, shutters and venetian blinds. Your other friends have offered help with the construction. Bill Ellis says he can get a gang together in a snap!" William Ellis, who had recently moved into the county, Perry Brown, Charles Lewis and Ben Wilson were among the blacks, in addition to Mahlon Gibbs and Andy Hartless, who had offered assistance. Even their children would get involved with small chores and painting.

Mary and Lang were overwhelmed and deeply touched by these gifts. At last her dream of having her own home was coming true, no matter how small and modest it must of necessity be.

Bill Ellis took over the design and construction of the home. It was to be a compact, "Cape Cod" style, with a half cellar for an icehouse and storage, two large rooms, being a parlor and kitchen, in the front and two smaller utility rooms in the back on the first floor. There were two bedrooms and a large storage area upstairs. The whole place had a pitched, tar-papered roof and dormer windows in the front of the house, one for each bedroom. It was covered with painted cedar shingles, and Lang would later add little embellishments like shutters on the windows, porches front and back, and a short white-washed, picket fence enclosing the front yard and flower garden.

At first, Lang would have only a corral and temporary lean-to for the horse and wagon until a small barn could be erected. There was no room on the half-acre lot for other animals except for a few chickens, maybe a pig and cow or two.

There would be no out-kitchen or cooking fireplace necessary since Mary was promised a new J.G. Hathaway's Patented Iron Hot Air Cooking Stove from Joseph Foulke's factory in Norristown. This wonderful new contraption promised that "a few sticks of wood will heat the stove both directly and by radiation, so that washing, baking, stewing, boiling, broiling and steaming may all go on together...." That, along with a smaller heat-stove in the parlor, provided all the warmth the family could ever need during the cold, snowy Pennsylvania winters.

Best of all, they were able to sink a well and bring the water pipe right up through the foundation into the house to a hand pump and into a large metal basin in the kitchen, which was emptied through a pipe into a drainage that flowed down to the ditch beside the road. No longer would Mary have to go outside in all kinds of weather and haul water from the well.

This also meant that Mary no longer had to take the laundry out to the back yard in all sorts of weather. Although she had to do it in smaller loads, she was now able to wash the clothing with hot water from the stove and rinse it with fresh water in the basin. This was a tremendous improvement.

Construction commenced in August 1845 and continued on weekends that were clement throughout the fall and into the spring of 1846.

Tamar Lacy died that winter. It was almost as if she had been hanging on long enough to make sure Lang and Mary and the girls were provided for. Every day, she ate less and less and seemed to wither away in her bed. She could no longer get out of bed to relieve herself, and it mortified her that Mary had to put diapers on her or try to lift her over a chamber pot.

"I'm so tired, Mary," she would repeat over and over as Mary would encourage her to eat something. "I just want to go."

As her mind was deprived of nourishment, she began losing her mental capacity. She would lie in bed for hours or sit in the big chair and stare absent-mindedly out the window.

Just before Christmas she developed a cough and fever that Dr. Cernea said was pneumonia. He did not offer much encouragement since she was unable to get out of bed or move around to loosen the phlegm. It would continue to accumulate in her lungs until she was literally asphyxiated. He advised Mary to just keep Mother Lacy as comfortable as possible. "Say whatever you have to say to her now. It won't be long before she won't be able to hear or understand or at least acknowledge."

Mary wrote to the nieces and nephews, a couple of whom were as far away as Ohio and Illinois, to let them know of the impending death. She consulted with the Quaker elders about the requirements of the church.

Most importantly, she spent every spare moment with Mother Lacy. She could not bear the thought of Mother Lacy passing out of this world alone. She would sit in the bedroom and knit or sew while Ruth Ann and Elizzie played in their room across the hall. And she slept on a pallet next to Mother Lacy's bed at night.

One afternoon, Mary had to go to Sarah Betts' shop in the village to bring a dress to a customer for fitting. She was nervous about being away from Mother Lacy and rushed to get back home. Almost as if she had a premonition that the time was near.

She ran upstairs with the girls and found Mother Lacy still in the same position, but her breathing was different—almost gasping like a "fish out of water." Dr. Cernea had prepared Mary that this would be close to the end. She picked up the Bible on the night table, opened it up and began reading at random from the Gospel John:

> Let not your heart be troubled: believe in God, believe also
> in me.

In my Father's house are many mansions: if it were not so,
I would have told you. I will come again, and receive you
unto myself; that where I am there ye may be also.
And whither I go ye know, and the way ye know.
Thomas saith unto him, Lord, we know not whither thou
goest; and how can we know the way?
Jesus saith unto him, I am the way, the truth, and the life:
no man cometh unto the Father, but by me.
If ye had known me, ye should have known my Father also:
and from henceforth ye know him, and have seen him....

Mary could not see the words any longer and was consumed with grief. She held the small, frail hand as Mother Lacy took her last earthly breath.

Ruth Ann looked down at the Bible on the bed and found words on the page that she could understand. "As the Father hath loved Me, so have I loved you: continue ye in My love," she read haltingly in her sweet, six-year-old voice.

Tamar Lacy, aged eighty-seven years, three months and fourteen days, was laid to rest beside her husband and children in the Buckingham Friends cemetery.

As soon as the funeral was done, the nieces and nephews moved in and took over. "They're like vultures!" Mary complained to Lang. "Just waiting to pick the body to pieces!"

One of the nieces who immediately assumed authority told Mary point-blank on the day of the funeral that she and Lang and the children would have to find someplace else to live since the property, house and furnishings were to be sold at auction on the first available date.

"She was so nasty about it, Lang. She would not even let me have our beds and things. I offered to buy them at a fair price, and she said we could buy them at auction just like anyone else! I'm stunned that these people could be any relation to dear Mother Lacy, and to call themselves Quakers no less."

"I don't know, Mary. Maybe they're jealous of you. That you were so close to her, I mean. And do you think maybe they've found out about the money she gave you?"

"Perhaps you're right. I can't believe—I don't want to think it could be because of you, our marriage."

The problem still remained that the house at Canada Hill was not ready and would not be until spring at the earliest. But, as soon as Mahlon and Elizabeth Gibbs heard about the situation they immediately opened their home for as long as Lang and Mary and the girls needed a place to stay.

Mary did indeed attend the auction and purchased all of their beds, bedding and many other items including kitchenware, cooking utensils, tables and lamps, practically for pennies. Everyone at the auction was aware of the situation, and no one would bid against her. Whenever she raised her hand, William Large, the auctioneer would cry, "I have a bid of two bits from Mrs. Wellings! Do I hear thirty?" He would wait a few seconds and then bang the gavel down swiftly, "Sold to Mrs. Wellings!" after a hasty, perfunctory, "going once-going twice."

Mary felt almost guilty with a naughty sense of satisfaction as she watched the niece fume with anger.

All of the items were stored in Thomas and Sarah Betts' barn until the Canada Hill house was ready.

March 21, 1846—Elizzie's fifth birthday and the first day of spring—was celebrated in the new home with a housewarming party attended by all the people who had helped build the house and the new neighbors—Frederick and Rachel Pearson, the Worthington widows, fellow lime-burner Amos White and his wife Lydia, the Shaws and Overholts and Thomases, the Fishers, Powerses, and Kees family, the Buckleys and Naylors, as well as the two large Betts families. These were all the people with whom Langhorn and Mary and the children were to form lifelong relationships—some good, some bad, but always considerate and respectful, because out in the country neighbors were important. You never knew when you might need their help in the middle of a dark, cold night.

Even wealthy landowner Allen Bye rode over to inspect the new house in the growing village of Canada Hill. And, much to Lang's horror, he brought along several of his prize hunting dogs. Bye was a member of a fox-and-hound hunting club that the idle gentry ran throughout Buckingham and Solebury and over into New Jersey. Because Bye was so wealthy and highly respected in the neighborhood, there was not much anyone could say about it, especially not a humble Negro limeburner who depended on him and other rich landowners for work.

On this auspicious occasion, however, a couple of dogs running about and sniffing the yard, wagons, carriages and horses could not mar the Wellings family's happiness with their new home.

And most everyone was happy to have the family in the neighborhood. They were very welcoming and complimentary of the house. Few, if any, of the immediate neighbors knew that Lang's name was not on the deed. It was a constant source of embarrassment to him nonetheless. It was almost like a giant, open wound on his face that everyone could see and judge, but he bore his disgrace stoically except for one occasion.

Neighbor Maria Chapman would testify years later that the only problem she ever knew about next door was early one morning when she heard yelling coming from the Wellings yard. "I went to the fence and heard Langhorn say, 'I work like a Negro all my life, and I can't even be master of my own house.'"

"Did he use the word 'Negro', Mrs. Chapman?" the District Attorney asked.

"No, sir, he said the other word—you know what I mean."

For Mary, the next few years were to be the happiest of her life. She finally had a home of her own. It was literally a dream come true. She threw herself into homemaking and motherhood with a joy and exhilaration she had not felt in years. She wrote to her mother, Jonas and Elizabeth, and a couple of the other siblings and invited them to visit—not that she expected any but Jonas to come if he could get away from his work in the locomotive yards six days a week, fifty-two weeks a year. Any so-called "vacation" had to be saved for family emergencies and deaths.

Gradually, day by day, month after month, Mary gathered the furnishings to make the little house a comfortable home for her family. She saved every penny she could find and earn and scoured estate sales in the neighborhood. She found a carpet, a large round table and chairs for the parlor, and a rocking chair that she upholstered, seat and back, and a little matching footrest.

One day in May 1847 she noticed a drawing of a sofa in an advertisement by the cabinet warehouse of David Kirk in Lumberville, who also offered coffins in addition to furniture from his shop. It was ornately carved wood with high, "S"-curved arms. The seat and back were upholstered in a deep red, velvet fabric, as were the tubular cushions on each end. It was perfect, but much too expensive. Mary struck a trade with Mr. Kirk. She would work off part of the price by sewing the linings for coffins.

Fortunately—or unfortunately for the departed—there were enough customers for coffins over the course of the summer so that by late fall, the beautiful couch was installed in Mary's parlor.

The rest of the room was tastefully finished with pictures—prints of bucolic, country scenes and flowers—two oil lamps that she had purchased from Mother Lacy's estate, and a small side table next to the rocking chair. The other rooms of the house were very simply decorated, leaving the best items for the parlor where guests would be received.

Mary envisioned the day when her daughters would have their friends visit and where they would eventually receive the young "gentlemen callers" who would ask for their hands in marriage.

The only thing left to get was a piano. That would yet take several more years to acquire, and Mary often worried whether she would remember how to play by the time she could get one.

Lang would shake his head at all this high-fallutin' folderol. "Kinda puttin' on airs, ain't ya, old girl?" he would tease. "You're gonna fluff 'n fancy your husband right out of the house!" Still, he was very happy with his new home.

Mary would fuss back at him. "Now, you listen here, mister. My children are going to have as nice a home as I can make. I don't care if you aren't interested." Lang would pat her ample bottom affectionately and nuzzle her neck with his rough-stubble beard, and Mary would wriggle away and feign indignation—"Lang! Not in front of the girls!"—but secretly dread that his attentions might suddenly turn serious. She was deathly afraid of becoming pregnant again, and that fear grew as her girth increased. Indeed, it might even be speculated that she was building a wall around herself in physical, as well as emotional, ways.

Truthfully, she would wonder sometimes why Lang was still attracted to her in that way. By this time, they had been married almost fifteen years, and the years of hard work and pregnancies had certainly taken their toll. Along with the considerable weight gain, she developed a condition akin to rosacea on her face that gave her chubby cheeks a perpetual reddishness. Her hair was beginning to thin and turn gray, and she no longer took much care with her toilette, but every morning simply parted her long hair and brushed it into a tight bun at the back of her head.

She sacrificed every pleasure and luxury for herself to give to Ruth Ann and Elizzie. All of her energy and efforts were directed to turning her daughters into immaculate, educated, well-mannered, well-dressed young ladies. She sewed all of their clothes from patterns she found in *Godey's Lady's Book* and fussed over them constantly, brushing and braiding their hair. She taught them all of the sewing arts and crafts she had learned at her own mother's knee when she was a child.

By the fall of 1847, when Ruth Ann was almost eight and Elizzie six and a half, Mary began taking them the mile or so down the road to the Buckingham Friends School. By 1850, there were so many children in the immediate vicinity of Canada Hill that the citizens erected a small one-room schoolhouse at the southeast corner of York Road and the dirt lane that was eventually to be named Upper Mountain Road. The school was directly across from the Canada Hill Baptist Church building that had been started in 1843 and was completed in 1851.

From the time her children were very young, Mary began teaching them how to read, and in the new house the family began a tradition that was to last for the rest of their lives together of reading the *Intelligencer* in the evenings after supper. By this time, the late 1840s, publisher John Brown had started a weekly feature called "Family Circle Discussion"—articles about current events, moral dilemmas, stories about ethics and virtues—in addition to printing full-length and serialized stories, poetry, and articles of scientific, geographic and religious interest.

Being published by and aimed mostly toward Quakers, the attitude of the paper was surprisingly, for that time, tolerant and respectful of most all beliefs and practices, so that the girls gained a well-rounded education undiminished by prejudice and bigotry. However, Mary still had to practice vigilance in what was read and not read, excluding anything about slavery, except what was written by abolitionists, news of anti-Negro riots, kidnappings and violence, and items about court proceedings, particularly those things she considered salacious and not proper for little girls' ears.

The years between 1835 and 1850 presented wave after wave of anti-Negro rioting in the Northern cities. The black population of

Philadelphia, especially, was frequently targeted; the burning of Pennsylvania Hall and the orphanage that Langhorn and Mary witnessed first-hand in 1838 were just two of many instances. Throughout those years, Mary would read about Negro homes, churches, schools and meeting halls that were burned, and blacks who were stoned, beaten and sometimes murdered.

In May 1844, a "Native American" political party meeting held in Kensington north of Philadelphia was attacked by a bunch of Irish men. Many blacks were killed and wounded during the fight. In retaliation, over the next two days, Catholic churches were burned and services had to be suspended. "City of Brotherly Love Disgraced," read the headlines in the *Intelligencer*. Indeed, it had been thusly disgraced for many years and was not about to have its former pride restored any time soon.

There was even a short time in the mid-1850s during which, for some reason inexplicable to Mary, the *Intelligencer* began using words such as "darky" and "Sambo" to describe Negroes instead of the usual, more respectful, "blacks," "coloreds," "Africans," "ebony-hued," "Africa's sable sons and daughters," among others. Someone must have spoken with publishers Darlington and Prizer because the tone changed considerably in the late 1850s, and those words were dropped unless the editors used them to make fun of the political and social stances of the rival *Democrat*.

Lang was half torn between his desire to protect the girls from anything hurtful and upsetting, yet wanting them to be aware of everything going on in the world, especially the condition of their fellow colored folks. In the end, he agreed with Mary that the girls would surely find out soon enough, and it was best to keep their childhood as innocent and happy and free of grief as possible.

It was during this time that Mary read about her brother, Amos, having been elected to the Doylestown Borough Council and being a member of the Doylestown Vigilance Committee.

"Why don't you join the Solebury Vigilance Committee?" she asked Lang.

"You got to be joking!" Lang responded and continued when Mary questioned him, "Why?"

"Because, you got to be upper class. Don't you get it? Look at the list. There ain't no colored names there and never will be."

"Well, that's ridiculous, and you should speak to your friends about it."

Lang just snorted and wagged his head. "There you go, puttin' on airs again."

Other than occasional letters from her mother and Jonas, and the visit with Elizabeth, Mary had not heard much about her family in twelve years when one day in June 1847 Lang brought home from the post office in Centreville one of the most extraordinary gifts Mary was ever to receive in her lifetime—a letter from her father, Jacob Stone.

She immediately recognized Jacob's handwriting on the envelope—crisp and well formed, almost delicate for a man.

Mrs. Mary Wellings
Canada Hill
near Buckingham, Penn.

She stared at it, afraid to open it. It was not a good sign that he had written "Mary Wellings" instead of "Mrs. Langhorn Wellings" as was the appropriate address for a married woman. On the other hand, that he had taken the trouble and initiative to write after all these years was overwhelming for her to conceive.

"Aren't you going to open your letter, Mommy?" Elizzie asked.

"Here, Mother, let me do it," offered Ruth Ann.

Lang quietly stood by the stove and watched his wife. "Now, let her be, girls. Let your mama take her time."

With shaking hands, Mary slit the flap of the envelope open and took out the folded sheet, written in small, tight script.

New Britain, Penn.
June 6, 1847

My dearest Daughter Mary,

"Oh!" Mary's throat caught with a lump and tears instantly welled up in her eyes. "'My dearest Daughter', he wrote! He called me dearest daughter."

"Read more, Mommy!"

"All right, I'll try." She began again.

My dearest Daughter Mary,

I have taken it upon myself to write to you to seek in whatever measure you are able to give your compassion for a sick old man who has come to see the errors of his life and asks redemption of his sins so that he may go to the Lord with a heart unburdened....

Mary could not read any further. She had to hold the letter up so that her tears would not spill onto the paper in her shaking hands.

"Shall I finish for you, Mother?" Ruth Ann asked. Mary nodded and handed it up to her.

I have been sheltered and saved into the grace of our Lord Jesus Christ through the ministry and friendship of my friend John Riale and Rev. Heman Lincoln of the New Britain Baptist fellowship. They have helped me to understand that the most important legacy of a man's life is his children. Most of my children have become estranged from me, I realize because of my dictatorial, heavy-handed ways. I ask your forgiveness.

Your father, Jacob Stone

Mary was stunned and could not stop crying. The girls were full of questions.

"Where do they live, Mommy?"

"Does this mean we can go visit them?"

"Will we get presents at Christmas now?"

"Hush, Elizzie," Ruth Ann admonished her sister. "We mustn't be greedy for personal gain."

"Well, why not? Becky Gibbs said all white people have grandparents who give them presents."

"Elizzie!"

Langhorn bent over and put his arms around Ruth Ann and Elizzie. "Here, now, why don't you go up to your room or outside to play and let your mama mull this over." The girls continued bickering as they left the room.

"What are you gonna do?" Lang asked Mary.

Mary sat with her head bowed. She dabbed her eyes with a handkerchief, would stop crying for a moment and begin to speak, then the tears would begin washing over her again. It was as if her father's conciliatory letter had opened a floodgate—a freshet, as the newspaper called the floods in the area—of hurt and anger pent up for at least twelve years.

She cried not only because she had not seen her mother in twelve years, not only because her father had refused to acknowledge her or her husband or her children. She cried because of the Irishmen in New Hope. She cried remembering the disastrous trip to Philadelphia, Lang's kidnapping and beating, and the uncountable personal slights and affronts that she and Lang and the children had had to endure over the years and would undoubtedly continue to suffer for the rest of their lives.

As the tears fell, they seemed to wash her soul with a protective coating. The fires were gradually doused, and the friction of all the past hurts could no longer burn her quite so badly. For most of her life, it was this natural defensive shield that allowed Mary to forgive and forget, sometimes instantly and sometimes over a longer time as in the case of her father, whoever came to her and asked it of her.

She looked up. "Does it bother you that you were not included in his plea for forgiveness? Or that he did not mention your name or address you properly as my husband?"

Lang thought for a moment. He poured a cup of coffee from the pot that was always kept just-right-warm on a corner of the stove. "Part of me wants to say 'yes'. On the other hand, I've never had his blessing or friendship, so I can't miss what I never had to begin with."

He sat down at the kitchen table and took Mary's hand, gently rubbing her fingers between his own. "I want you to be happy, and I want the girls to know their grandparents. For them to be accepted would make me happy."

Mary smiled and looked into Lang's big, brown eyes and fell in love with her husband all over again, as had happened and would continue to happen during all of their years together.

The next day Mary sat down and composed a letter back to her father. She said basically that her love was unconditional, that she had never held a grudge, and there was nothing to forgive. She closed the letter by saying that, with their permission, the Wellings family would like to visit on Sunday afternoon next, that unless they heard otherwise in the meantime, they would look forward to seeing them.

Then for the rest of the week Mary was almost frantically worried on the one hand anticipating the visit and, on the other hand, fearing that she would receive a note telling them not to come.

Throughout their life together, Lang could tell instantly whenever something was troubling Mary. If she was upset or worried, she would clean "with a vengeance" everything and everyone in sight. Even the family cat ran for cover! That week the house was spotless, that is, more than usual, the children were scrubbed, their clothing freshly laundered and ironed. And Mary was exhausted—too exhausted to think.

"It's going to be all right, old girl," he reassured her. "He's old and sick. He can't hurt you no more, even if he was inclined to try, which I very much doubt."

Mary nodded. "I know." But, still, everything had to be just so.

It was somewhat irritating to Lang, to be honest, this intensity with which Mary was compelled to excel to perfection. He didn't understand that it was Mary's way of maintaining some control over life. She couldn't do much about the outside world or the behavior of others, but, by golly, she could keep everything inside her little home, however modest it might be, in perfect order and cleanliness.

On a hot Sunday afternoon in June 1847, the Wellings family set out in their wagon over to Doylestown, on down the road to New Britain, and up Sandy Ridge Road to the Jacob Stone farm. The girls sat on boxes in the back, Mary up on the bench with Lang. As usual whenever she went out in public with Lang and the children, in addition to carrying her open parasol, even on cloudy days, she wore a bonnet that completely covered her head and obscured her face, and a long-sleeved dress with gloves. Anyone who didn't know them would not bother to look twice; they would simply assume this was just another colored family out for a drive.

Mary was startled when she saw her mother and father for the first time in twelve years. They had both aged a great deal in the interim. Each was almost completely gray; they were both stooped and moved about much more slowly than she had remembered. Mother Mary was still thin, but Jacob had begun putting on weight as he was slowing down and it was all in front in his belly. Jacob's heart was not healthy, Mary's mother told her later, and he could not work the farm as he used to.

The reunion with her father was strained but happy. He had never been an affectionate man with his children, always stern and aloof. Even with his spiritual epiphany, he was unable to change in that regard. He did admire Ruth Ann and Elizzie with grandfatherly attention as they stood shyly before him. He patted their cheeks and politely told them in his heavy German accent how pretty they were and, here, here's some candy for some sweet girls. Mary was so grateful for that attention to her children, she didn't care about her own reception.

Jacob nodded to Lang, but was not overly welcoming. Having this Negro in the family was still too much to accept, although since moving to Doylestown, Jacob had certainly come into contact with more coloreds. His grudging acknowledgement of the marriage and the children was about all they could ever hope for.

Jacob and Mother Mary's younger children, who were still at home, came to be presented—nineteen-year-old Camilla, who was engaged to be married to blacksmith George Garren, seventeen-year-old Rebecca, fifteen-year-old Hiram and "the baby," Emma, twelve. The younger children did not remember Mary at all and even the older children had only a vague memory.

On the other hand, Mary's reunion with her mother was tearful and heartfelt. After Ruth Ann and Elizzie went off with Emma and Hiram to inspect the farm, Mary and her mother went with Camilla into the kitchen to begin preparing the Sunday meal, leaving Jacob and Lang on the porch looking out over the fields in strained silence punctuated occasionally by brief comments about the weather, or the condition of the crops, or some political issue in the news. Jacob didn't show it much outwardly, but he was surprised and touched when Lang offered out of the blue to come over in the next couple of weeks and lime the fields.

As mother and daughter worked in the kitchen, Mother Mary filled her daughter in on all the family news, the comings and goings of her brothers and sisters—Reuben working as a shoemaker in Philadelphia; Amos married to Phoebe Smith and living in Doylestown; John, seventeen, living with Amos and Phoebe and working as an apprentice shoemaker for his brother; Aaron, also a shoemaker, married to Mary Ann Tyson; Harriet married just six months ago to John Hoff. Some of the siblings and their families were already beginning to move across the country—the first to leave were Mahlon to the far west, Chillian to parts unknown, Sarah and her husband William Page to Michigan. Eventually all but Amos and Mary would be gone from the area.

Mother Mary steeled herself from crying as she talked about her eldest daughter, Elizabeth, sick and weak, living in a hovel in Warwick, but unable or unwilling to leave her husband, and about her sons Mahlon and Chillian gone from home, their whereabouts unknown.

"Any news about Mahlon and Chillian?"

"Nothing since I wrote to you that we received a letter from Mahlon about four years ago from a place called Hardscrabble way out in the west that he was joining the Texas army in its war with Mexico. We have not heard a word from him since, nor from Chillian. We have no idea where he is."

Mother Mary sighed and looked away. "I suppose a mother has to expect that along with the joy and happiness her children bring will come some tears of sadness. It's inevitable, it seems."

Mother Mary spoke in German, which Mary had difficulty following, she had been away from it for so long. She asked her mother if she could talk in English, and Mother Mary agreed. "I vill try," she said. "Actually, I haff been getting much practice viss our neighbor, Lydia Svarts, and ze people at church."

Again on the subject of children, Mary told her mother about Mother Lacy and some of the other families she knew that had experienced heartaches with their children. She was grateful her girls were healthy and smart, well-behaved and devoted children. Except for a week-long bout with a mysterious fever when Ruth Ann was almost five, there had been little sickness in the family, knock on wood. She was reminded of the old saying about children: "A son is a son 'til he takes him a wife; a daughter's a daughter the whole of your life."

"I hope Papa will let me be a daughter once more, Mama."

"I sink so. At least I pray so. He is not vell and has done almost a complete change of heart becuss of ze church." Mother Mary smiled through misted eyes.

"Yes! Tell me, what precipitated this sudden transformation?" Mary asked. "It's a miracle!"

Mother Mary smiled and sighed. "Indeed it is. You haff no idea. It started vhen I begun going to ze Baptist church down ze road in New Britain. My neighbor took me there, knowing zat I vould receive ze solace of ze Lord in prayer and fellowship. You know, ve had not been back inside a church since you left home and married."

Mary's head bowed. "Yes, I heard. Jonas told me. I'm so sorry, Mama. I never…"

"It's all right. You know your father never really saw eye-to-eye viss Herr Pastor Miller. He never could replace Herr Mensch in our estimation. Zo, your father did not protest vhen I begun going to church. Even vhen Becky and me vhas baptized in April. I said zhen to Reverend Lincoln zhat I vhas sick at heart having some of my children and grandchildren avay from us and your Papa so zick and unhappy. Reverend Lincoln said, 'I haff just ze person for you.' It vhas John Riale, a fine, educated man. He come over und started talking to Papa, teaching and sharing ze spirit and word of ze Lord. Oh, it vhas vonderful to see zhem! Sometimes zhey vould get into zhese arguments about religion and ze Bible, but Mr. Riale persisted, and finally your Papa come around. He attended services and vhas baptized by Reverend Lincoln in ze Neshaminny on ze six of ziss monz. He calls it his 'new birthday', ze day he vhas born again in ze spirit of ze Lord."

Mary was thrilled. "That's a wonderful story, Mama! Did you know there is a Baptist church being built right near our house? I know some of the people going there. Maybe I'll talk to them about attending services. We don't have a church, you know."

Mother Mary came over to the table where Mary was laying out dishes and silverware and took both of her daughter's hands in hers. "Nussing vould make me happier zhan to see my children communing vhiss ze Lord Jesus and accepting Him as zheir Lord and Savior. I urge you to do it."

She smiled and hugged her daughter, who herself was visibly moved. Mary didn't dare tell her mother that Ruth Ann and Elizzie had not been baptized yet. *I'll take care of that as soon as we get home.* She found out later that she needn't have worried about the wait. She was pleasantly surprised to find out that Baptists did not believe in infant baptisms. They practiced only full immersion baptisms of adults.

Mary was able to enjoy just a few more visits with her father before he died suddenly, though not unexpectedly, less than a year later on April 30, 1848. She was very thankful for their reconciliation, and her grief was much eased as a result. She thought one time with a shudder how it might have been for her to hear about her father's death and still be estranged.

Several of the seventeen children and their families came to the funeral. It was the first time Mary had seen some of them since 1835, and the reaction to Mary and Langhorn and the children was mixed. Some of them still resented Mary for "breaking up the family." Some were humiliated that Mary had married a Negro, but kept it to themselves out of respect for Mama. No one, except Aaron and Jonas and his wife Lydia, was friendly beyond mere politeness.

Back at the house after the funeral and burial at the New Britain Baptist Church, the immediate family gathered for the reading of Jacob's will. Mary was grateful that none of the spouses was in the room.

> Item: I give and bequeath unto my beloved wife Mary one hundred and fifty dollars worth of goods of her selection to be taken at their appraised value. I further order that my said wife, together with any small children that may be with us at the time of my decease, be supported out of my estate for one year thereafter.

> Item: I direct that my remaining personal property be sold at public sale and also the farm whereon I now reside either at public or private sale as shall be considered by my Executors most advantageous to my estate; and the residue after the payment of debts I direct to be secured on the property at five per cent per annum payable to my said wife during her natural life and at her death to be equally divided among my children, the representatives of such of them as may then be deceased taking the parent's or parents' share. The shares of my daughters Elizabeth and Mary I direct to be paid to them respectively for their own sole and separate use whose acquittance shall be a sufficient discharge for the payment of the same.

By that seemingly innocuous wording, Langhorn as well as Elizabeth's husband, Aaron Height, had been deliberately excluded from the will! Mary looked questioningly at her mother, who came over after the reading of the will was finished.

"It vasn't just becuss he is schvartzeh, Mary. It vhas for your own protection. Papa vhas avare of your husband's problems and vanted to make
sure you and your children vould be ze only ones who could benefit."

She was still not fully convinced, although Mary had to grudgingly
acknowledge to her mother that was why she had purchased the property
at Canada Hill without Lang's participation.

"And Elizabeth, too," her mother continued. "He never showed it,
but your Papa's heart ached viss vorry for our two oldest children."

Mary did not tell Langhorn about the terms of her father's will. She
answered his questions about what the children would receive by saying,
truthfully, "Oh, we don't get anything until Mama goes. Everything is
used for her until then." It wasn't until years later, in 1862, when Mother
Mary died and Mary had to sign the Release of Dower along with all the
other surviving children and grandchildren, that Lang realized he had
been excluded. The law required the husbands of all the daughters to
sign the Release along with their wives, and Langhorn's signature was
not asked for.

Aaron, the third eldest son who was living close by in Doylestown,
and John Riale were appointed executors of Jacob's estate. The property
was sold on the 2d of November 1848 to John Foulke, and the residue of
the sale was to be used to care for Mother Mary for the rest of her life.

Mother Mary and the younger children stayed in the home until
after 1850, paying rent for the house to Mr. Foulke who continued to cul-
tivate the fields and orchards from his nearby home. Then, after all of
her children were married and gone off to live on their own, Mother
Mary spent the rest of her life living with one or another of them for
months at a time. She spent several years in Philadelphia with Jonas and
Lydia, then in Newtown with the families of Amos and Reuben.

Langhorn and Mary continued to live a reasonably quiet, happy life,
in their little home at Canada Hill. In 1849, Lang turned the spare room
behind the kitchen into a bedroom, and they took in a boarder for several
years, Burroughs Blackwell, a fourteen-year-old runaway slave who was
serving as an apprentice limeburner.

Mary was in a strange mood when the United States Census enu-
merator came around in August 1850. Even though there had been

articles in the newspaper preparing the people for the census, Mary resented his relentless questions about each person living in the home. This was the first time the census collected exact information on age, place of birth, sex, race, occupation, real and personal property values, if the individual attended school, was married within the year, could read or write, even whether someone was "deaf and dumb, blind, insane, idiotic, pauper or convict."

"Young man, why are you asking me all these questions?! This is the most ridiculous thing I've ever heard of! Excuse me, I've got bread in the oven!" She turned back to the kitchen.

"It's the law, ma'am." The young man called after her from the door. "The United States government has commissioned me to take an accurate count and description of all the citizens of this district."

Mary took the bread out and came back to the door. "I don't understand. Why does the government want to know all this personal information about me and my family? No, I'll not have it!"

The poor young man was so nonplussed that Langhorn and Mary were listed as "Williams," Ruth Ann and "May E." were shown as "Wellis," and young Burroughs was shown as "U"—unknown—in both "Sex" and "Color," in addition to having his name impossible to decipher. Mary was concerned the slavers and bounty hunters would somehow get hold of this information, and she was desperately afraid for the safety of her family, Burroughs in particular.

These days of relative happiness and calm, interspersed with moments of upset and fear, were too soon to be tilted irretrievably in the latter direction. Within two years Mary's life was to begin on a downward spiral so severe she would recover little of her former happiness of these few years. It started in early summer 1852 when she realized something that had been worrying her for months and she had been secretly dreading for years: She was pregnant again.

At first she had thought her monthly cycle had stopped due to the onset of menopause, and, mainly because of her added weight, by the time she found out it was really a pregnancy, she was well along, at least six months. *Oh, dear God, no! How can this be? I'm almost forty-two years old...* Her lamentations were loud. Her fear was almost tangible. Her hurt and resentment and anger with Langhorn were the worst yet in their sixteen years of marriage. She felt as if her life was falling apart and she was convinced she was going to die. At a minimum she feared life as she had grown to know and enjoy it was over.

Langhorn was confused, defensive and worried, with no small amount of guilt thrown in. Over the years, he had been forced by Mary's standoffishness into practically demanding his marital rights. It was either that or visit the prostitutes in New Hope, and that wasn't acceptable; many of them had diseases.

On the few occasions when Mary did consent to having relations, Lang at least tried to practice a form of birth control his friends had told him about called "coitus interruptus"—withdrawing just before ejaculation. It took just one time being a tiny bit too late. The only way he could show his worry and guilt was by not saying a word of protest about Dr. Cernea's intimate involvement again in their lives.

Dr. Cernea had his concerns, too. With Mary's added weight over the years, the apoplexy was more evident than ever. Her age and physical condition and length of time since the last child was born ten years ago all added up to a very dangerous situation. Yet, outwardly, he was calming and reassuring.

"It's going to be all right, Mrs. Wellings. Please don't worry. Just get plenty of rest." He knew it was useless to try to get her to lose weight. He knew the enormity of the underlying problems that caused the accumulation of weight was directly proportional to the largeness of her body.

In August 1852, Mary delivered their third child, a boy. Because of her almost hysterical fear, Dr. Cernea made a potentially dangerous decision and took a chance of drugging Mary with laudanum into a state of deep relaxation. While he understood there were tremendous risks associated with having a drugged mother, in this case, with her body so tensed up, the pros definitely outweighed the cons.

Thank God, the baby was healthy and, as Dr. Cernea had predicted, very large even for a boy. "As I suspected," he told Lang, "your son will take after you in size, but he is surprisingly light-skinned like his mother."

For the first time in her life, Mary was unmoved at seeing and touching one of her newborn children. She turned away and fell into a deep sleep. In fairness, it could have been the residual effects of the laudanum that caused her aversion, but the result was that she was unable to provide even minimal attention to the boy, and it fell to twelve-year-old Ruth Ann to take over caring for the infant.

Ruth Ann took up the job with a love and devotion that was, in a way, other-worldly. It seemed at times almost as if she had been born specifically to look after this baby. She adored him as if he was her own. She washed and pampered and cuddled and swaddled him. She carried him everywhere during her every waking moment. And, if she had been able to, she would have suckled him, as well. But, alas, she still needed her mother for that. Except for Ruth Ann having to go to school, she and her brother were inseparable for the next seven years.

Elizzie, still a child of ten, was just as happy to run off and play with her friends, but for Lang this new baby meant alienation from his wife and family once more. Mary's coldness toward him only increased after the birth. He tried to please her and cheer her up by suggesting that the baby be named Jonas after her closest brother, and it worked, but for a moment, to brighten her mood.

Since the Baptists did not practice infant baptism, the child Jonas Wellings was presented to the congregation and dedicated in service to God at the little Canada Hill Baptist Church on a lovely Sunday afternoon in September 1852.

Mary's recovery was long and very difficult. It was weeks before she could get out of bed and slowly resume even a small amount of her strenuous daily activities. Thankfully, Mother Mary came to stay for a while to be with her daughter and help out during her recovery.

One afternoon in late fall, Mary and her mother were in the front yard planting iris bulbs just behind the fence around the front yard. The girls were in school, and baby Jonas was asleep in a basket on the porch.

A young man rode up. He was colored, light-skinned, young, about twenty-five or thirty, Mary guessed. He got down from his horse and took off his hat.

"Mrs. Wellings?" he looked nervously at Mary, then at Mother Mary.

"Yes, I'm Mrs. Wellings." Mary got up from the ground and brushed her hands against her apron. "What is it?"

"Well, ma'am, I don't right know how to say this. I…" He looked so serious.

"Is something wrong?" Mary was alarmed. Ruth Ann! Elizzie! "My girls!"

"No, no, ma'am. It's… My name is Jake McIntire. Does that mean anything to you?"

"No, Mr. McIntire."

"Your husband, Mrs. Wellings, and my wife, Louisa…. Your husband has admitted being intimate…" Mary looked at him, puzzled. She didn't understand at first what he was trying to say.

Just then, Mary turned her head and saw Lang's wagon round the corner from York Road onto Upper Mountain Road. Jake McIntire noticed her movement and turned to look in the same direction. In that instant, Langhorn saw the young man and sped up the horse and wagon.

He jumped off the wagon and began yelling at Jake while Mary and her mother watched in stunned silence.

"You get on outa here, now! You got no business here! You stay away from my family!"

A look of anger quickly came over McIntire's face and he rose up to face his attacker. "'N I done tol' you to stay away from my wife! I warned you…"

"You be quiet now! You got no call comin' 'round here makin' your insinuations…"

"I ain't insinuatin' nothin' you ain't already 'fessed up to. I warned you to stay away from my wife or I was gonna take matters into my own hands. I hear'd you been snoopin' 'round my house already yesterday, and I done tol' you…."

"You better shut your smart-mouth flap, boy, or I'll put a ball through your heart and send you to hell in a hurry!" Lang opened his coat to reveal his pistols and puffed up his chest in a threatening manner. He greatly overpowered the younger man in size and weight as well as age. "You git goin'!"

Mary screamed and grabbed her mother. "Lang! Stop it! My God! What's come over you?!" This was a monster. The man she'd been married to for seventeen years had become a stranger, a bully, right before her eyes! She and her mother ran up to the front porch, picked up Jonas and went quickly into the house. She sat down on the red couch rocking and sobbing. Mother Mary sat beside her in stunned bewilderment. Mary could not decide whether she was more humiliated that her mother should witness this or shocked and saddened by her husband's behavior.

The women could not hear that the argument raging outside had stopped. As soon as young McIntire saw Lang's weapons, he backed away with both of his hands palm-out in front of him.

"Now, look here, there's no call for violence." He got up on his horse and turned toward York Road. "We'll just let the judge decide this…"

"Don't you dare go to the authorities!" Lang shouted after him. "I'll not have my family and good name drug through the mud with your dirty lies!"

But McIntire had spurred his horse and was gone down the road. Lang, still greatly upset, his large chest heaving and huffing, retrieved his horse and wagon and led them up the drive to the barn and corral in the back of the house, muttering to himself. "Stupid kid! Don't know what he's doin'. Puffed up, stupid pride, is all. Gonna be the ruin of me."

By the time Lang came into the house, Mother Mary had taken Jonas up to the bedroom she shared with the children. Ruth Ann and Elizzie were still not home from school, and Burroughs was working at the limekiln down the road. *Thank God for that*, Mary thought. *At least they weren't here to see this.*

Lang walked through the back door into the quiet kitchen. "Where's my supper?" he called out. "Mary? Where are you?" He walked through the door to the parlor where Mary sat on the red couch in a daze unable to speak.

He stood at the door looking at her for a moment, then said, "I told him to stay away from here with his wild accusations, but he wouldn't listen to me. Mary, you hear me? We been havin' it out for a coupla weeks now. He's just a stupid, young blow-hard, is all."

Mary shook her head back and forth as if trying to shake off what she was hearing. "You threatened him," she said in a weak voice.

"What?" Lang could not hear what she said.

"I said, you threatened to kill him. I heard you. He said you and his wife…"

Lang came further into the parlor and stood over Mary. "Now, you see? I tol' him not to bother you. Now he's got you all upset and for nothin'."

"Lang, you threatened to kill him! You've become a monster bully with those guns! I hate those guns!" She began sobbing. She careered through emotions, from shock and sadness at seeing Lang become so rough and threatening, to hurt that young McIntire's accusations might be true, that Lang and his wife, Lang and another woman…

Then humiliation and disgrace that this should have gone on in front of her mother and the neighbors. *Oh, God, the neighbors!* She couldn't remember whether any of them had been out or may have seen or heard the commotion.

"He asked for it, Mary! You ain't seen it all. He's been followin' me around for weeks threatening to call the authorities, to come and see you. I tol' him to leave me alone, but he won't. I didn't know what else to do."

Lang had already taken off his jacket and the guns and hung them on a peg at the back door as he did every night. He ran into the kitchen and fetched the holsters and guns off the peg and came back to the living room.

"Here, Mary, here! Take the gawd-damned guns! I'd never use 'em anyways, you know that! I couldn't do that. They was just for protection from the slavers." He put them on the red couch next to Mary.

"I swear, Mary, there ain't nothin' to what he's sayin'. He wouldn't believe me, or his wife when she tried to tell him. And he wouldn't leave me alone. I just didn't know what else to do to make him stop."

Mary could hear Ruth Ann and Elizzie come through the back door, chatting noisily and happily. *Oh, no! The girls! I can't let them know anything is wrong.* She quickly wiped her face and eyes with her apron. Ruth Ann came into the parlor, Elizzie continued up the stairs to their room.

"Hello, Mother…Father," Ruth Ann called out. "Where's Jonas?" She looked over at her mother. "How come the guns are on the couch, Mother? Are you crying?"

"It's nothing, dear. Just a little problem. Your father and I are having a talk about it. Be a dear and help Granny with Jonas while I make supper, would you?"

Mary got up from the couch. "Hang up your guns, Lang." She didn't need to add "for good." He understood. "We'll continue this discussion later."

It had been a cold past year for Lang. Even before Mary found out she was pregnant, she had been cranky and out of sorts. And, as soon as she learned about the pregnancy, she turned on him and shut him out.

She made him sleep on the floor, saying his snoring was keeping her awake, and claiming she couldn't get comfortable with him in the bed. And then, when the baby came, there was no room for him with anybody. He was pushed aside, hurt and very lonesome, though he tried not to let on.

It didn't take long before the first temptation to his weakened morale presented itself. One day in early spring, on his way to deliver some lime to a farm in Buckingham, he passed a small house just off the Durham Road north of York Road. On the porch sat a pretty colored girl, a mulatto about twenty-five years old, he guessed, and a little girl, looked to be about seven. The mother was snapping peas while the little girl played with a corn-cob doll. He doffed his hat and waved. They waved back, and the little girl jumped off the porch and ran to the gate. "Hi, mister man!" she called gaily.

The next day, Lang found himself in the neighborhood again. On the pretext of learning more about these new folks, he tied up the wagon and knocked at the door. And thus began his friendship with Louisa McIntire.

It all started innocently enough. She was such a young thing, young enough to be his daughter, really. She was alone and lonesome, too, just like him. She had no family in the area, no friends. Her husband, Jake, was off working on the new turnpike going through Falls Township and was gone for days at a time, bunking out in the work camps, coming home on his one day off a week.

"Why, he's just practically dumped me and Martha in the middle of nowhere's," Louisa complained to Lang. "I don't know a soul out here."

Lang started coming by more often, *just to see how Louisa and Martha are doing*, he told himself. He took her shopping to Doylestown for shoes for Martha and over to Lumberton where she needed to get some things for the house. Nothing more than that.

Later that summer, Lang took Ruth Ann and Elizzie down to a colored camp meeting in Brownsville. Mary was in the last month of her pregnancy and wasn't doing well at all with the heat and humidity; she couldn't come out of the house all summer. There he ran into Louisa, and this time Jake was with her, so he just nodded "hello" and tried to walk on. But, little Martha was delighted to see him. She jumped up in his arms. "Lang! I'm so happy to see you!"

The gossip started going around. Langhorn had been coming by often to visit Louisa, folks whispered, taking her out in his wagon and even renting a buggy one day so's he could take her over to New Hope in style.

Jake had been drinking and was emboldened. He cornered Lang around the back of the church when he went to the outhouse.

"I heer'd you been comin' 'round my house whilst I'm gone workin'," he growled at Lang.

"Yeah, I been seein' to the needs of your family while you been leavin' 'em alone all the time, if that's what you mean," Lang answered. He didn't like this boy's cocky attitude from the get-go.

"Now I don't rightly have a choice in that, do I? I gots to make a livin' now don't I, 'n support my family. And I don't care for you cozyin' up to my wife, you hear me?"

"Seems like I know about as much about your wife as you do. If you would take care of business, maybe she wouldn't need somebody else to...."

This infuriated young Jake even more. He rose up to his full height and jabbed his pointed finger at Lang's chest. Lang was not wearing his guns that day, in deference to the religious nature of the meeting, or Jake might have thought twice about his blustering manner. "You stay away from my wife, or else I'll..."

"Don't you dare threaten me. I'll do as I damn well please...."

"Not with my wife you don't. You think you're so big and tough. You're nothin' but a dirty old man!"

And the argument continued escalating until some of the other men separated them and took them off in different directions. Jake gathered up Louisa and Martha and left the camp meeting in a huff.

That fall Jake continued the argument by confronting Lang at the limekiln. This time he threatened to go to the authorities and to Lang's wife, and Lang was so furious he in turn shouted that, if Jake did anything like that, he would be sorry. "I'll put you to sleep forever!" he yelled.

"And that's it. That's how it all happened," Lang told Mary later that night. "The stupid kid just wouldn't believe me and wouldn't leave me alone."

"And did he have cause to suspect that you and she..."

"No, Mary. I swear. I felt sorry for her. Her husband is gone all the time and drinks. Sorta reminded me of us when we were young, you know? I thought maybe I could help her."

"You should have gotten Bill Johnson and the other men from the Temperance Society involved. You never should have tried to do it on your own. And how could visiting her and taking her out for drives help him?"

Lang couldn't answer that. More importantly, he could not admit to himself that perhaps it was a physical attraction to Louisa, that when he was with her he felt like he was young and attractive again and wanted and needed by a pretty young lady. With Louisa he felt alive again and welcomed, not old, useless and shunned like he was in his own home. He hung his head in defeat.

When the Sheriff came within a few days to deliver the summons to court, Lang and Mary went to see lawyer Michener and told him the story. It was agreed that there were so many witnesses to Lang's hanging around the McIntire home and the threats made to Jake that he didn't stand a chance in court. About the only thing he could do was apologize, swear that he had put up his guns forever, place himself on the mercy of the court, and take whatever medicine Judge Chapman handed him.

The McIntires packed up and moved out of the area, and Lang never saw Louisa or Martha again.

Mary tried to get back to some semblance of normal life, but her pretentions about being accepted into society were rapidly falling away, like leaves on the autumn breeze outside her window. She kept up the façade, covering her shame and disgrace with a bright smile, a jovial demeanor that hid the anguish inside.

Their marriage settled into an uneasy truce "for the sake of the children"—pleasant with each other in public, even overly considerate, but there were no more affectionate hugs, no intimacy or sharing of special moments in private.

Mother Mary left the Wellings home shortly after the confrontation in the front yard and never came back again. The article about the outcome of the court case that appeared in the *Intelligencer* on February 13, 1853, was cut from the paper and burned before Ruth Ann and Elizzie could see it.

Chapter IX

Buckingham, Pennsylvania, and Mount Holly, New Jersey
June 1865

It had been an eventful month for Mahlon Riegel. With Henry Darlington gone in the field inspecting the victorious Union forces as they entrenched themselves further into the South, Mahlon was gradually given more responsibility at the *Intelligencer*. Henry wired several instructions directly to him and expressed pleasure with the few pieces Mahlon had already written, especially about the Wellings case.

"Poison found. Wellings in for it. Too bad," Henry telegraphed from Georgia where he had gone in an attempt to interview Jefferson Davis, president of the vanquished Confederacy, who had been captured at Irwinville.

Mahlon got the distinct impression Henry thought Wellings was innocent and was being framed by H.P. Ross, the District Attorney. But, it was difficult to say. So intense was Darlington's rivalry at times with Ross and the *Doylestown Democrat* paper, Mahlon wondered at times if he was just hoping for something to show them up. On the other hand, Mahlon also kept feeling the same nagging thoughts, that Wellings was innocent, even though he was bound to print the facts as he learned them, and the facts didn't look good for the man.

The most important event of the past month was that Mahlon's wife, Nancy, told him she was pregnant, almost four months along already. She waited to tell him until she was absolutely sure, after she wrote her mother and described the symptoms and her mother wrote back confirming what she suspected was true. Nancy would not go to a doctor, as she was much too shy to ever allow a man to look at or touch her body. Her mother, Mrs. Evans, suggested that if she herself was unable to come to Doylestown to assist with the delivery when the time came, Nancy should look for a midwife. All of Mrs. Evans' children had been delivered by midwives, and that had suited her just fine.

Mahlon and Nancy had been looking forward to these few days for weeks, and Mahlon was quite concerned about whether his wife was up to making the trip. They were to travel first to Solebury, to the Canada Hill neighborhood, where Mahlon hoped to speak with the children of the defendant, and his neighbors and fellow workers. Then he intended to go back to Centreville to see Dr. Cernea. Cernea had written that he would be in his surgery all that morning unless an emergency called him away.

Then, that afternoon they would drive down to Bristol, across the bridge over the Delaware to Burlington, New Jersey, and south about twenty miles to Mount Holly to see Mrs. Wellings' brother, Reuben Stone, who had been a soldier with Mahlon in the 18th Pennsylvania Cavalry. Unfortunately, they would not be able to go to New Hope, since it was a little too far out of the way on this occasion.

"Are you sure you're up to this trip?" Mahlon asked his wife again, as he had in different ways at least seven times in the past week alone.

Nancy stopped brushing her hair and stood up to help Mahlon pin on his shirt collar. "Yes, my dear, and yes, yes, yes again. I've told you I'm fine. The sickness has worn off. I'm still able to fit into my clothes… well, with a little skillful pinning here and there." She looked at her husband soulfully. "Oh, Mahlon, I just know that if I don't take advantage now, it will be years before I will be able to get out of the house again."

"My dear, surely you are exaggerating."

"Well, almost such, once I am confined with children. And your mother. Since your aunt left, I have all the responsibility for her now, too."

Mahlon put his hands on his wife's shoulders in a loving caress, then pushed her long, thick hair gently back away from her neck. "I know, and I am so grateful for your help and relieved that we found a neighbor to come and look after Mother these few days while we are gone."

It was a beautiful late spring day. Mahlon sent a neighbor boy to Brower's to let them know he was ready for the horse and buggy he was renting from them for the trip.

"Here's a nickel. Now, be sure to tell them I want their most gentle nag. I don't care if she's slow, just as long as she's gentle." Mahlon's days of riding about with a prancing, young, high-spirited stallion in charge of the carriage were over and done with.

"A nickel! Thanks, Mr. Riegel! I'll tell 'em, just like you said."

It was just a couple of miles out to Solebury Township on the York Pike. Mahlon had no trouble finding the village of Canada Hill. There were the church and graveyard, the school, the limekilns down the road, just as he expected to see.

He went to find people to interview. In the meantime, Nancy got out of the buggy and walked up the road, admiring the budding tiger lilies, the irises and other spring flowers growing wild in the ditch along-side the road. Across the road a large field had gone to flower and was a sea of yellow buttercups. In one of the yards there was a lilac bush just going out of bloom. And up the road a few paces she saw a small peach orchard.

Mahlon was not sure where exactly the Wellings family lived, so he knocked on the first door—a small, one-and-a-half-story frame house with a whitewashed picket fence. The garden was unkempt, as if no one had been tending it for a while. This was indeed the Wellings house, but no one came to the door when he knocked. He went to the next house, where Maria Chapman answered the door.

"I can't tell you much, mister," Mrs. Chapman said when Mahlon asked about her neighbors, the Wellingses.

"But you were here. You've been neighbors, I understand, for twenty years…"

"No, not that long, but a long time. They's always been good people to me. I was sure sorry to lose Mary. But she was sick for a long time 'n they don't have no call to accuse Langhorn that way. He was a good hus-band and father. He's a good, steady man."

"So you think he's innocent, too?"

"Don't matter what I think. I know how they treat colored folks up in Doylestown. It's a real shame, it is."

"Do you know where the Wellings children are? I'd like to inter-view them."

"Well, now, I don't think that's likely. The boy is up t' Paxton Hill's working on the farm, and the girl is living with the Gibbses, I believe, and I don't think she'll talk to nobody. Me 'n my husband are tending to the animals."

And so it went up and down the road. None of the neighbors would talk. Mahlon and Nancy walked down past the Baptist church and grave-yard where Mary was buried, across York Road and to the limekilns a few hundred yards south. There they found Mahlon Gibbs who, while defen-sive, gave Mahlon the best background information on Langhorn's life he had yet been able to gather.

"So, I don't have to ask if you think Mr. Wellings is innocent?" Mahlon asked after Gibbs filled him in on Langhorn's history.

"Well, what do you think? He's my friend. We lived together when I was young. He's been my friend for so many years I can't count. There's no way he would have harmed anyone, let alone his wife." Gibbs started to tell the reporter how Lang had hung up his guns for good some years ago, then thought better of it.

"But they found the poison, apparently, in her stomach. You knew that?"

Gibbs hung his head and wagged it back and forth. "I just don't understand it. I would accuse the University of puttin' the poison there themselves 'fore I would think Lang did it."

"Well, that seems to be the key, then, as to how the poison got there if Mr. Wellings did not administer it. I don't suppose you can think of anyone else who would have wanted the Wellings woman dead?"

"Absolutely not! She was a good, gentle soul, a loyal wife, devoted mother when she was younger and not so sick. I can't say enough about Mary…and Lang. They've suffered enough, but not enough to suit some folks' needs, I guess."

Mahlon and Nancy were back at Centreville by ten o'clock in the morning, well ahead of schedule. Mahlon had not counted on folks being so reticent to talk. Perhaps Dr. Cernea could shed some more light on the matter. He found the doctor in his surgery measuring out medi-cines and packaging the powders into little envelopes to replenish the supply in his bag. Nancy was invited into the house by Mrs. Cernea where they chatted over coffee while Mahlon talked with the doctor.

"And you are of which Riegel family?" the doctor asked Mahlon immediately upon being introduced.

"Cross Keys," Mahlon answered.

"Oh, yes. I knew your family well, although I was not their physician. Absolutely tragic about your father's accident. What a terrible quirk of fate. I am so sorry. He was a good man."

Mahlon sighed and nodded appreciatively. "Yes, thank you, sir."

"And your mother? Is she still living?"

Mahlon filled the doctor in on his mother's status as well as briefly about his own education at Princeton, his teaching career and service in the cavalry during the war.

"I understand you have an interesting history yourself, Doctor," Mahlon said.

"What have you heard?" the doctor asked in return.

"Well, basically, that you are of French parentage, that you were orphaned and made your way to Bucks County at a young age. That you studied medicine and returned here to practice."

The doctor stopped measuring the medicine and sat back in his chair for a moment, thoughtfully, as if reminiscing. "Yes, all that is true," he said finally. "I was born in Philadelphia in eighteen oh-six. My father had been attached to the French army somehow. I found out later that my mother was French, also, and from the West Indies, where I understand her family had lost considerable estates during the troubles in those islands. I was never given the details, but I knew they had been here since before eighteen hundred. When I was about nine, they placed me in the Moravian School at Nazareth, Northampton County, saying they were going on a trip to France, and it would be too dangerous for them to take me. I remained there for three years with no word. And then the tuition stopped coming, and I was told abruptly one morning that I had to leave the school or work for my board."

"Good Lord! Just like that? They evicted a child from the school?"

"Well, they didn't have much choice, I suppose, when the money stopped. I went to Philadelphia and tried to find my parents. I found out they had left their previous address and the school tuition was being paid by a trust fund which had dried up. The bankers told me my parents had apparently been lost at sea, which accounted for the reason I received no letters from them in all the years I was there."

"Were you able to write to France and find out what happened to them?"

"Oh, heavens, no. France was in an uproar by that time in the aftermath of Napoleon raising armies, coming and going in and out of prison, Waterloo. It was not possible to learn anything more than that my father was in the military in some commission—it apparently must have been as a fairly high-ranking officer. But whether it was for Napoleon or against I am unable to ascertain. I assume he was ordered back to France and surely must have perished along with my mother, for I cannot imagine she would not have at least written to me were she still alive."

"Most assuredly so. My goodness! I just thought of something. Perhaps you are in truth descended from French royalty and you were brought here to America for your protection."

Cernea laughed appreciatively. "You certainly are a romantic fellow, aren't you!"

"Seriously, sir, you have the look of royalty, quite distinguished--looking, I must say. I should like to write a story about you some day...."

"No, no. Heavens, no. Save it for my obituary. Just tell them I'm a simple Quaker country doctor, and that will describe me sufficiently." He laughed again. "Although, I must admit I have often wondered whether it was possible my father was attached to General Jean Moreau who lived in Bucks County at one time."

"Was that Napoleon's General Moreau who was convicted as part of a plot to assassinate him?

"Yes, apparently he was pardoned by Napoleon and exiled from France. I've learned he came to live in Morrisville from eighteen oh-six to eighteen thirteen. He returned and died in Dresden during the battle against Napoleon in August of that year. But, then, my father had been here long before the Napoleonic Wars, and Moreau had returned to France at least three years before my father left."

"You were in school all that time?"

"Yes, for some reason, I do believe my parents felt it was dangerous for me somehow to be with them, because I do not remember very well any particular home that we lived in together, just the schools I attended. At a later time I wondered whether my father could have been connected to Joseph Bonaparte, Napoleon's brother..."

"The former King of Spain?"

"...Yes, you know whom I mean, of course. He lived in that grand mansion in Bordentown, New Jersey, for several years, but he arrived after his brother was defeated at the Battle of Waterloo in 1816, so apparently he and my father crossed paths and were not associated except perhaps as adversaries, if my theory about General Moreau is correct."

"Have you considered whether your father may have been a spy?" Mahlon asked.

"Oh, yes! My schoolboy imagination certainly conjured up several scenarios such as that. Oh, and I should tell you I recently found out that the name Cernea, or apparently as it should be 'de Cernea', is Romanian in origin. There is a town in Romania of that name, and the 'de' means 'of that place'."

"Fascinating. And if my history lessons serve me correctly, Napoleon conquered all of that part of the world around the turn of the century?"

"Yes. So it's possible that my father could have been a Romanian military officer who joined with Napoleon."

"Most interesting. You could be Romanian royalty!"

Cernea laughed again. "You surely do have quite an imagination, just right for a writer!"

Mahlon pressed on. "So, back to your childhood, what did you do when you could not find your parents?"

Dr. Cernea's face darkened a little with sadness as he remembered. "I was nearly overcome with grief and despondency. I can't describe to you how frightening the city was for a young lad, who had been sheltered in private schools his whole life, with no money and no prospects for even getting a meal together. I had been very fortunate to meet Eleazer Shaw from Plumstead at the Jenkintown Inn. He was on his way to market and gave me a ride to Philadelphia. He took interest in my story along the way and, when we arrived in Philadelphia, took me to the bank and my parents' former residence. When we learned what had happened, Friend Eleazer took pity on me and brought me home with him to Plumstead."

"And you spent the rest of your childhood with the Shaw family?"

"Yes. They were very good to me. Friend Eleazer recognized my former privileged station in life and my thirst for education. He allowed me to continue my studies and simply required small chores of me at the farm. They treated me almost better than their own. Eventually, there was a need for a teacher in the neighborhood, and I had shown myself fit for the job."

"How, then, did you become involved in the medical field?"

"I had always shown an interest in science and medicine in particular. I would go and sit as often as possible with old Dr. Wilson who lived close by in Plumstead, where George Maris now lives, as a matter of fact. You may know him…."

Mahlon nodded recognition of the name.

"…Dr. Wilson encouraged me to continue my studies. I read medicine with Dr. Hampton Watson for a few years, then applied to the University of Pennsylvania, was accepted and graduated in thirty-one. I came back home and went into practice with Dr. Wilson immediately thereafter. I stayed with him for several years, then took a part of Bill Johnson's house in Greenville. Then another short time in a house in Greenville now occupied as a store, and finally here to Centreville."

"And your family? You have children?"

"Yes. I've been married twice. Both named Sarah. My first wife, Sarah Ann Lester, died some years ago, along with two of our children when they were quite young. I have five children surviving, four sons and a daughter. My eldest son, Thomas, is a talented architect and artist. William is a merchant in Doylestown. I'm very pleased with all of my sons, Edward, James, William and Thomas, and my daughter, Anna."

"And you are a Quaker by faith?"

"Yes, I took the religion of my adopted family, although it seems my birth family were assuredly Catholics. I came to appreciate especially the gentleness, honesty and altruism of the Society of Friends and am not sorry a day since."

"Well, that brings me to the point of my visit, with your permission. I'm writing articles about the Wellings case for the *Intelligencer*."

Dr. Cernea nodded. "As you mentioned in your letter."

"I'm having a little trouble finding people who are willing to talk about the case, neighbors and friends."

"I'm not surprised. These country folk are a tight-lipped bunch. Even if they had anything bad to say about a neighbor, they would be hesitant to say so, especially to an outsider."

"Why is that?"

Dr. Cernea looked at Mahlon and smiled. "Undoubtedly, you've been in town too long to remember. These people count on each other in the country. It doesn't matter really what color they are, what religion. You never know when you're going to need help in the middle of the night. They may literally have to save your life some day, and it doesn't do to make enemies out of neighbors."

"I see. That makes sense. So, these people are figuring, if this fellow Wellings gets out of this murder charge somehow and comes home, they are going to have to continue to deal with him as a neighbor."

"Exactly. And the children. So no matter what they feel about him personally or his wife, it's going to be like pulling teeth to get them to say so. But, aside from that, the Wellings family was pretty well liked by just about everyone."

"So it seems. And you were her physician when she died, I understand?"

"Yes, I have been the family physician for, let me see now, almost twenty-five years since the first child. My goodness, Ruth Ann would have been twenty-five by now."

"Would have been? Oh, you mean she died?"

"Yes." Dr. Cernea's face turned sad, and it almost seemed to Mahlon for a second that the doctor's eyes moistened as he reminisced. *That's odd*, he thought, *for a physician who has seen people being born, getting sick and dying for over thirty years, including some of his own children.*

"She was quite a special young lady," Dr. Cernea continued. "Beautiful of face and feature, smart, talented, played piano like a concert virtuoso, self-taught, mind you. Absolutely devoted to her parents and brother and sister, especially the little brother. Her parents were devastated when she died. It's difficult for me to describe how much they suffered…the whole family did. I thought Mrs. Wellings in particular was going to perish right then and there, and, frankly, I'm surprised she lived so long afterward."

"What happened?"

Dr. Cernea settled back in his chair, folded his hands across his stomach, put his feet up on the little footstool next to his desk and began to tell the story. He purposely did not mention the Louisa McIntire phase of Lang's life in the early 1850s nor the kidnapping and beating and descent into alcoholism a decade earlier. That was a long time ago and no need for it to be brought up again, especially now.

He described some of Mary's physical problems, her obesity and difficulties having children, and the apoplexy that he had first diagnosed so many years before. "I saw the potential problems back then. People with that condition usually don't live as long as she did, especially under the more-than-usual stressful conditions of life that she was subjected to."

The years 1853 to 1859 were relatively quiet for the little family. Langhorn was appropriately circumspect in his behavior. As for Mary, she became even more reclusive than ever before, preferring to stay at home and sew, cook, and tend to her home and garden. It was rare that she went out beyond the neighborhood, especially after one day when she had to go to New Hope with Ruth Ann, who was fifteen or sixteen at the time. She would rather not have gone to New Hope at all, let alone with one of the children, but Ruth Ann had a toothache, and Mary had to take her to the dentist urgently.

After visiting the dentist, they had some time before getting the stage home, so they wandered into Miles Bennett's shop. Mary's attention was distracted for a few seconds by some just-stocked bolts of fabric, and Ruth Ann, thinking her mother was right behind her, continued out the door. As she turned around to see if her mother was behind her, she did not notice the group of men coming up the sidewalk. There were four or five of them. Immediately they began whistling and cat-calling.

"Whoo-whee! What a beauty!"

"Hey there, purty yaller girl, you workin' 'round here somewheres? I'd shor like to come see you!"

"Like to get my hands on some of that sweet chocolate." And other, even more vulgar remarks.

They surrounded her and some began pawing at her with their dirty hands. She cried out in fright, but was not heard.

When Mary raised her gaze from the table where she was examining the material and looked out the glass front door, she felt more than saw that something was very wrong. She could not even see Ruth Ann in the middle of the circle of men.

She ran out of the door in a panic, raised her parasol and began screaming in a rage. The men turned their attention from Ruth Ann to see this heavy-set, red-faced, middle-aged woman tearing at them, yelling at the top of her lungs and waving her parasol above her head.

"Sweet Jesus, it's a fat banshee!" one of them shouted, and they all laughed nervously, but backed off all the same, intimidated by this fury.

Mary kept coming at them, yelling, her pent-up anger finally finding a release. "You stay away from my daughter! Keep your filthy hands to yourselves! You good-for-nothing pigs!"

"She's a half-breed nigger!" one of the men shouted. "If they ain't good for slaves, 'bout all they're good for is whores."

This infuriated Mary all the more. She renewed her attack, and the men finally gave up and went on down the street, still calling back nasty comments. Mary sank down to the doorstep exhausted, heartbroken, and crying.

Mr. Bennett, the shopkeeper, ran out with a glass of water, and Ruth Ann tried to ease her mother's distress. She hugged Mary to her bosom like a mother would a child. "It's all right, Mother. I'm fine. I'm not hurt. People are not like that everywhere. It's just our misfortune to have run into these men." Ruth Ann always looked for the best in people and immediately forgave the worst.

But Mary never went back to New Hope for the remainder of her life and relied on neighbors or peddler Jimmy Acor to get whatever she needed there.

Other events going on in the world around them made life more difficult for the family, as well. In particular, the so-called "Dred Scott Decision" of the Supreme Court in 1857 signaled a renewed time of tension and fear among all blacks, slave and free, especially those living in areas like Pennsylvania, bordering on slave states.

The decision was the culmination of a lawsuit begun in St. Louis in 1846 by a slave, Dred Scott, who had been born in Virginia close to the beginning of the nineteenth century, to declare his freedom on the grounds that he had once lived in a free territory. The case was preceded for years by numerous "personal liberty laws" passed in several northern states designed to prevent slave owners from reclaiming runaways. Although the Constitution of the United States gave slave owners the right to pass into free territory to capture slaves, individual states sought to thwart the process by mandating stricter requirements, such as search warrants and jury trials for captured slaves.

The "ping-pong match" of Federal laws and court rulings and responding volleys of state laws continued throughout the 1840s and '50s. In 1842, the Supreme Court, in *Prigg v. Pennsylvania*, ruled that state laws obstructing the right of slave owners to capture runaways were unconstitutional. In response, several states passed new laws prohibiting the use of state officials and facilities in the apprehension of slaves, thereby forcing the slave catchers to rely solely on Federal officials. Then, in 1850, Congress passed the Fugitive Slave Act, requiring all citizens of the United States to assist in catching slaves or face imprisonment and fines. In response, Northern states passed additional, more restrictive laws designed to help runaways.

The situation was further exacerbated in 1851 with what has come to be known as the "Christiana Tragedy," when a Maryland slaveowner, Edwin Gorsuch, was murdered and his son Dr. Dickerson Gorsuch was seriously wounded by a mob of blacks in Lancaster County, Pennsylvania, when they came to collect runaway slaves and bring them back to Gorsuch's plantation near Baltimore.

The three slaves whom the Gorsuches were chasing fled to Frederick Douglass' home in Rochester, New York, and the remaining blacks claimed self-defense, further compounded by the fact that no particular one of them could be blamed for having held the weapon or weapons. In a desperate attempt to exact revenge, the Pennsylvania authorities were pressured into arresting several of the Quaker leaders in the county and indicting them with treason for having harbored the fugitives and for interfering with the execution of the Fugitive Slave Law, among other charges.

The resulting verdict of not guilty in November 1851 further infuriated the Southerners' wrath, and the ensuing political campaigns saw the downfall of several of Pennsylvania's abolition leaders and supporters, and at least indirectly influenced the election of Democrat James Buchanan to the presidency in 1852.

Meanwhile, the complex legal issues of *Dred Scott v. Emerson* dragged slowly through the Missouri courts for several years, finally landing at the United States Supreme Court where, on March 6, 1857, Chief Justice Roger B. Taney gave the majority opinion of the Court: Dred Scott should remain a slave.

If Taney had just left the ruling at simply that, history probably would have been much different. However, he chose the opportunity to promulgate additional principles that caused such a furor throughout the country, for and against, that many have said finally "drew the line in the sand" and precipitated the Civil War.

In particular, Taney wrote that slaves were the personal property of their masters and not entitled to the protections and benefits of citizenship in the United States, including the right to bring lawsuits in Federal courts. He further declared as unconstitutional the Missouri Compromise of 1820, which prohibited slavery in Illinois and the Wisconsin Territory, saying that the Federal government had no right to prohibit slavery anywhere in the new territories.

Public reaction was immediate and strong. Anti-slavery Republicans stepped up their campaigns for political control of Congress and the courts. Partly as a result of a split in the Democrat party, Republican Abraham Lincoln was elected President in 1860.

For individual American Negroes, the Dred Scott decision was the ultimate blow to their hopes for freedom from slavery. And it preceded a new wave of oppression and violence against them—rioting, burning, looting, and kidnapping. Blacks were not safe even on public streets in the North.

In Bucks County, the bounty hunters and slave catchers used the Dred Scott Decision as a renewed excuse to harass the citizens, knowing of the many numbers of homes in the area serving as way stations on the Underground Railroad. They literally swarmed everywhere in the county just watching and waiting to catch a hapless fleeing slave and would take anyone who looked weak and unprotected, even freed slaves, and sell them back into slavery.

The backlash against blacks from some white Bucks County residents was almost as bad. In 1858, a bill that was introduced by Rep. Buckalew of Columbia County narrowly missed passage in the Pennsylvania legislature. This law would have banned all Negroes and mulattoes from coming into the state with a view to acquiring a residence. Several men from Bucks and Philadelphia Counties signed a petition in support of the bill, stating that they were "subjected to trouble, inconvenience and expense, on account of a continual influx upon them of fugitive slaves and manumitted Negroes from other states":

"Old and broken down Negroes, set free by their masters on account of their utter worthlessness, seek our shores only to become a public charge or a prey upon individual charity; others still more objectionable commit petty and atrocious crimes, occupy the time of our Courts, and fill up our jails and penitentiaries, and thus in various ways increasing the already enormous burdens of our tax-payers."

Closer to the Wellings home, during the late 1850s, there was a wave of arson fires set at homes of Negro residents of Solebury Township, mainly in and around New Hope. Everyone was on alert, and several times Lang joined with others to patrol the neighborhood. He was forced to take the guns out of storage for a while, and Mary simply nodded her understanding.

If it weren't slave catchers and bounty hunters, house and barn burnings, there was always something else to worry about: Gypsies roaming the area, rabid dogs, burglars, runaway horses, fevers, illnesses and epidemics of every type and intensity, horse thieves, confidence schemes, and itinerant beggars, black and white.

In the midst of all this, Ruth Ann graduated from the little country school at Canada Hill and was asked to help teach at the Emlen Institute that had just been set up down the Aquetong Road in Solebury from the Wellings homestead.

The Emlen Institute for the Benefit of Orphaned Children of African and Indian Descent was established in 1837 with a $20,000 bequest from Samuel Emlen, Jr., a Burlington, New Jersey, Friend, who specifically designated that the school should teach basic education as well as agriculture, mechanical trades and arts. For the first twenty years, the school was operated for Negro boys in Carthagena, Ohio. Then in 1857, the trustees, who were almost all based in Philadelphia, decided to move the property closer to them, and a ninety-acre farm in Solebury Township was chosen.

Quaker John D. Balderston was immediately chosen to manage the school and property. Also involved were old family friends Joseph Fell, who had been elected the County's first Superintendent of Education in the late 1850s, and Bill Johnson, who had succeeded Fell for one term. Local children, including the Hartlesses and very large Gibbs family, also benefited from having the school close by in the neighborhood.

Langhorn and Mary were very concerned about allowing Ruth Ann to go at all and only agreed if Lang or another responsible adult, preferably white, could escort her morning and afternoon. But, that was difficult when Lang was away for days at a time at a jobsite. Finally, against his better judgment, he went up to see Aaron Fretz, the horse dealer in Plumstead, and bought Ruth Ann a small "Jenny Lind" carriage and an old mare. Still, he insisted she not go out alone, even to school. At a minimum, if no one else could be found to escort her, young Jonas would accompany his sister to school whenever Lang was not available.

"I'll be fine," Ruth Ann protested. "Really, you mustn't worry, Father. Everyone knows me and will watch out for me. It's just a mile or so down the road. For heaven's sake, stop babying me! I'm almost twenty years old."

"It is 'for Heaven's sake' that we do care about you," Mary replied simply.

Lang and Mary knew beyond mere parental pride that Ruth Ann was beautiful both of face and character—almost angelic—and attractive to the worst sort of attention, and they couldn't help but worry. Elizzie and Jonas were still too young to be so much of a concern. Elizzie, in particular, was quite shy and content being a homebody, and Jonas preferred to stay close to home where he was constantly surrounded by family and other neighborhood children.

To make the clothes to outfit Ruth Ann properly for her new role, Mary had recently purchased a Howe pedal-powered sewing machine and was beside herself with happiness over her new acquisition. The marvelous contraption had been introduced to Bucks Countians in an advertisement in the *Intelligencer* in July 1858, and within a few months Mary was able to save enough money to buy one. What a God-send it was! It meant she could sew within a day what had formerly taken her a week by hand, and now with much stronger, neater stitches.

She and Ruth Ann spent hours pouring through the *Godey's Lady's Book* magazines designing and creating beautiful outfits in the latest style—dresses with voluminous hooped skirts and puffy-sleeved blouses and jackets. "Not too fancy, though. We don't want to offend any plain Quaker sensibilities," Mary said. "They are your employers, after all."

They would read with amusement the articles in the *Intelligencer* in which the editors railed against this latest in ladies' fashions—"that abomination in fabric known as the 'hoop skirt'"—and laughed delight-edly when the paper reported solemnly one day how a woman's life had actually been saved by that very "abomination." The poor lady was thrown overboard into the Delaware River, and her dress and its under-garments had ballooned into a life ring that kept her afloat until rescuers could reach her. After that incident, the paper never said another critical word about the fashion.

It was a late winter storm that began on the evening of March 2, 1859 that kept everyone home the next day—everyone except Lang who was already away on a job over in Warrington and was stuck there by the storm. And Elizzie, who had just started working as a domestic in Doylestown, living with three elderly widows, Ellen Shaw, Mary Sharp-less, and Lovesia Heller. Whenever she could, Elizzie would come home on Sundays. Interestingly, Elizzie lived very close to her Aunt Sally Stone, first wife of Hiram, and Sally's daughter, Augusta, though they probably didn't even know they were related, if they knew each other at all.

For the children, the snow provided pure holiday spirit. More than a foot of fresh snow on the ground meant hours of blissful play—sledding (they called it "coasting" then), building forts and pelting each other with snowballs.

There was a field just up the road from the Wellings home that was perfect for coasting. It came to a long, flat high point, then gently sloped down for a hundred yards or so with several small hillocks along the way.

"Please, please, Ruth Ann. Go coasting with us," Jonas begged his big sister. Ruth Ann had long ago outgrown childish games and play. She was quite the grown-up lady now that she had graduated school and was actually working as a teacher.

But, Jonas kept asking until she finally agreed to go out with him, even though she had not been feeling well that morning—a tightness in the chest that she thought perhaps meant a cold coming on. She found an old pair of Long John underwear of her father's, some leggings and boots, coat, scarf, and gloves and off they went into the beautiful day.

The clouds had cleared and the view from the Wellings' doorstep was one of pristine, white perfection. Not even a horse or dog had come by to disturb the deep blanket of snow that had fallen all the previous night.

"Com'on, Ruth Ann!" Jonas called behind her. "Let's go!"

Ruth Ann stepped off the porch and immediately sunk through the snow past her ankles. She laughed with delight. "Here, give me the shovel, Jonas. Let's clear the walk while we're at it."

The two of them made quick work of shoveling the short, flagstone path from the porch to the gate, then they began trudging up the road toward the hill. Several other neighborhood children had joined them by that time. They could barely see the opening in the fence through which to get to the top of the coasting hill, it was almost completely covered by drifts.

Ruth Ann was almost out of breath by the time they got to the top of the hill. She thought it was rather odd, but, again, figured it must mean her lungs were congested and she was coming down with a cold. She pushed Jonas and some of the other children off on their first run down the hill and followed on her sled. The snow was so deep and soft that it was slow going down. It would take several runs down and as many trips back up side-stepping on snowshoes to pack it down for good coasting.

The third time up the hill, Ruth Ann had to sit for several minutes to catch her breath. Jonas threw himself on the snow beside her. "You okay, Ruth Ann? Hey, com'on," he urged after a few minutes of rest. "Let's go make angels in the snow."

They ran off to an untouched area a few yards away and laughed delightedly as they fell backwards in the snowbank, then waved their arms and legs, up and down, back and forth, to make impressions of "angels."

A few minutes of this activity, and Jonas was ready to go coasting again. He ran off, and Ruth Ann watched the children as they careered down the hill, landing in a pile at the bottom, giggling with joy.

"Oh!" Suddenly, a pain hit Ruth Ann in the chest and radiated down to the left arm. "Oh," she repeated and raised her right hand to call out to the others. They were too far away to hear or see her.

She grimaced again in pain, clutched her chest, heaved a great sigh and shudder, and fell back into the snow. When the children found her, they thought at first she was "playing dead," trying to fool them. But, to their shock and sorrow, they soon found out it was real, all too real.

"What happened?" Mahlon sat up and asked Dr. Cernea. "How did she die?"

"It was apparently her heart, although she had shown no symptoms prior. I remembered that she had suffered a mysterious fever when she was young, about four or five, and, in hindsight, I realize it was probably scarlet fever that undoubtedly weakened her heart. Perhaps that coupled with an undetected defect…"

"But, that's so sad. In the prime of her life. She sounds like an extraordinary girl."

"Yes, exactly. Her mother eventually came to accept it somewhat by saying, 'She was too good for this world,' and I agree, most definitely. It was the only thing that got Mrs. Wellings through."

Langhorn finally arrived home two days later to find a complete pall of mourning covering the house and neighborhood. Someone had sent word by the first coach that made it through the snow, and it had taken Lang hours to drive back home ten miles, all the time thinking only about Ruth Ann, his "precious baby girl." When he got home he kept it bottled inside, as so many men do, more concerned for the other mourners—Mary, in particular—than for himself.

Mary had been up for two nights, sitting at the kitchen table, crying and repeating over and over, "My angel, my baby." Little Jonas and sister Elizzie, who had arrived from Doylestown just ahead of her father, were equally upset and unable to solace their mother. The house was filled with neighbors and friends, sitting quietly with Mary, cooking, and undertaking a myriad of chores.

Their beloved Ruth Ann—so beautiful, clever and talented, filled with so much promise—was gone from them forever. Nothing anyone could say or do would relieve their suffering. Mary came out of her reverie and responded briefly only to old Mrs. Worthington from down the road who said sincerely, "We are truly fortunate to have had Ruth Ann with us, Mrs. Wellings, even for just a short time." Mary stopped rocking and crying long enough to take Mrs. Worthington's hands in hers and whisper, "Thank you."

The funeral was held three days later at the Canada Hill Baptist Church presided over by Rev. Dr. George Larison. There was no conversation among the congregants, only murmured somber greetings as they filed up the hill and into the little church.

The lines of black sleighs and dark wooden wagons up and down York and Upper Mountain Roads and the almost uniform dark clothing of the mourners were in stark contrast to the clear blue sky and bright white snow still packed on the roads and piled alongside on the banks, though much of it had melted already in the sun-filled days following the storm. The silent stillness was disturbed only by the horses. As they patiently waited, they would occasionally snort to clear their snouts, and the bells on their harnesses would tinkle as they shivered and shifted their weight.

Most of the neighbors and friends who had known Ruth Ann since she was a baby had lost children of varying ages to the numberless dangers of life, but not in recent memory had so promising a life been cut short so suddenly and tragically. None of Mary's family was there. They could not have gotten there through the snow, even if there had been a way to let them know in time.

In his eulogy, Reverend Larison repeated the sentiment expressed by Mary, "Our angel has been called home to be with Jesus. Her 'mansion' was prepared for her sooner than we, her family and loved ones here on earth, would have wanted or expected. But it is not for us to question the will of God. He wanted His angel home."

Because the ground was still hard from permafrost, it was not possible to dig the grave, and Ruth Ann's body was kept in storage in the basement of the church until later in the spring. At that time another small service was held at the graveside, and this time some of Mary's family were able to attend, including her mother and brother Jonas, his wife, Lydia, and their children from Philadelphia. Aaron and several of his children came over from their home in Chews Landing, New Jersey. Aaron's wife, Mary Ann, was not able to attend, as she was pregnant with their son, Hannibal Independence Stone, who was born on the Fourth of July 1859.

Mary was still deep in grief. She did not notice, and if she had she would not have cared any more, that the vast majority of her brothers and sisters were not there.

"What a sad story!" Mahlon exclaimed again.

Dr. Cernea nodded. "Particularly for those of us who had cared about the family for so long, colored and white. Mr. and Mrs. Wellings had a great number of powerful friends in the area—Joseph Fell, Bill Johnson, the Bettses, John Kenderdine—the list goes on and on...."

"And yourself."

"And myself. I don't recall anyone ever saying it outright, but I have often thought that at times we were all determined that they should have as normal and successful a life as possible."

"Because of the intermarriage, you mean?" Mahlon asked.

"Yes, almost like it was a 'grand experiment,' a laboratory for the future of mankind. That mixing the races could work." Dr. Cernea shook his head. "Oh, don't mind me. I'm waxing philosophical."

"No, no. I understand. Really, I do. They were certainly fortunate to live in the midst of yourself and your fellow Quakers. Try as I might, I cannot imagine any other place in the country they could have made a go of it."

"Oh, maybe out West somewhere. I understand unions between Indians and whites and blacks are more common out there."

"Yes, you're right. I guess 'conventions' are not so important when survival in the wilderness is at stake. Just like you said about neighbors in the country needing each other."

"Perhaps," Dr. Cernea agreed. "But it seems we were not so successful after all."

"What do you mean?" Mahlon asked.

"In protecting them, I mean. There's just some who could not leave well enough alone. Leave the dead lie in peace."

"Ah, you mean this murder charge. I take it you feel the charges are trumped up? I know you testified at the inquest that you determined Mrs. Wellings had died from an attack of apoplexy…"

"Frequent attacks."

"…frequent attacks, yes."

"Over a number of months and perhaps as long as a year or two," Dr. Cernea affirmed.

"Yes." Mahlon noted the doctor's remarks. "And, you know, of course, about the poison that Professor Rogers found in the body."

"Balderdash!" the doctor snorted.

"Beg your pardon?"

"I don't believe it. I found no evidence whatsoever of the effects of poison in Mrs. Welling's body. I'm positive about that."

Mahlon cleared his throat and looked at the doctor almost timidly. "As positive as you were in the Sanders case?"

Dr. Cernea looked up in surprise. "Oh, so you remember the Sanders-Rico murder trial, then?"

"Yes, I did a little research on the so-called 'Negro poisoning cases'."

"Well, then, no," Dr. Cernea said.

"I'm sorry?"

"No, I'm not as positive as I was in the Sanders case. I'm *more* positive there was no poison in her body."

"How do you explain its presence in the body, then? Do you have any other theory as to how it could have gotten there?"

"It will just have to remain to be seen whether there was, indeed, poison found, as you reported in the paper."

Mahlon looked puzzled. "Oh, but I got it on the best of authority from the District Attorney's office."

"As I said, we shall see."

"Yes, well, there's the other evidence—circumstantial, I will concede—that he had motive to murder her."

"Such as?"

"Well, that he was unhappy with her for many years…"

"Define 'happy' for me, please. And, tell me, how many 'happy' marriages are you aware of?"

Mahlon was at a loss for an answer.

Dr. Cernea pursued his point. "Besides your own, of course, but you're still newlyweds. Your parents? They were married how long before your father died? Twenty-five, thirty years? Were they happy?"

"Ah, I… I suppose not, now that you mention it."

"They occupied separate bedrooms, I assume."

"Yes. For as long as I can remember. Mother was always frail of health."

"That's the usual reason given. That and the husband snoring." Dr. Cernea chuckled. "Not sufficient cause, however, I trust, for your father to murder your mother. So, what is happy? What is a successful marriage? And this couple, Langhorn and Mary Wellings, faced with the unusual circumstance of having their very being together condemned by most of society, had to endure in addition the same trials and troubles of life that every other couple has to deal with. In addition, I don't think most people have any concept of the difficulties of caring for a sick person for many years. This is real life here, not some love story in a lady's magazine."

"So, you feel that voicing his unhappiness to friends and neighbors was…"

"…Simply sharing what every one of the rest of them would have undoubtedly said about their own marriages, if anyone had bothered to ask." Dr. Cernea finished Mahlon's sentence. "And that's certainly not motive for murder."

"I see." Mahlon nodded his understanding of Dr. Cernea's reasoning. "But the poison…"

"I've already told you, I don't believe there was any poison."

"No, I mean the poison Mr. Wellings purchased just before his wife died."

"I have it here. Elizzie gave it to me right after her mother died. And only a small amount is gone."

"But, why would he purchase this particular poison at all? What is it called, Quaker button?"

"Yes, terrible name. I don't know why they would call such a noxious substance 'Quaker button'. I've never been able to figure that out. 'Strychnos nux vomica' is the Latin term. It comes from a tree grown in India and Ceylon and is also called Dogs' Nut. And therein apparently lies the reason for Langhorn's purchase. When mixed with butter or other fat, it will be ingested by a dog and kill him within three hours, usually without any fuss or noise."

"But, why would he want to kill dogs? You mean because of the problem with rabid animals in the neighborhood?"

"Precisely. Mr. Wellings has been deathly afraid of dogs since he was a little boy. Tell me, young man, have you ever seen a child's face ripped off by a mad dog? Or had to tie up a person suffering from the effects of hydrophobia and watch them die in agony because there is no medicine known to help them? It's most horrible. The only time in my life I've ever considered euthanizing a patient, may God forgive me. I've probably seen a dozen cows ravaged by rabid beasts, and almost as many horses, having to be shot and the carcasses immediately burned or buried deep so that no human or animal could eat the meat and themselves become contaminated?"

Mahlon grimaced and his eyes opened in horror.

Dr. Cernea continued. "It's been a terrible problem in the area. There's been talk about instituting dog taxes and licensing requirements, shooting on sight any suspicious dog—any number of measures to control the problem."

"But why didn't he just shoot the offending animal? Why the poison?"

"Apparently because he suspected the dog belonged to Allen Bye, a very wealthy landowner in the neighborhood. Probably one of his hunting dogs. Put yourself in Langhorn's place. A Negro living at the behest of close-by gentry, shooting one of their prized dogs."

Mahlon nodded. "I see your point. So, you think this was just a coincidence, that the poison was ordered to kill the dog just at the same time as Mrs. Wellings was ill and dying?"

"Absolutely."

Mahlon looked at his notebook briefly. "Well, that's all my questions, I think. This has been most enlightening. I certainly appreciate your taking the time to speak with me." He closed his notebook, leaned on his cane and stood up. "If you think of anything else that's important, please write to me."

"It was a pleasure to meet you," Dr. Cernea replied and stood to shake hands. "I wish you the best of luck in your new endeavors. And, here, by the way, here is something that might help your leg mend faster. I noticed you having some discomfort. No charge, just my small gesture of appreciation for your service in the war." He went over to a cabinet and pulled out a blue bottle with a white lotion inside and a label that read "Dr. Watkins' Palliative Balm."

"Thank you," Mahlon said as he accepted the bottle. "I appreciate that very much." He in turn presented Dr. Cernea with a calling card, one that he had printed during the past month with his new title of "Reporter" and reading simply "Mahlon Riegel, *Bucks County Intelligencer*, Doylestown, Penna."

"Oh, I just thought of something," Dr. Cernea said as they walked over to the house to visit with Nancy and Mrs. Cernea.

"What's that?" Mahlon asked.

"We were talking about 'happy' marriages, and I just remembered Thomas and Anna Paxson—happily married for almost fifty years. Both still in good health and cheerful and social folks and still affectionate with each other."

For most of the way down to Mount Holly, Mahlon thought about what Dr. Cernea had said regarding what made a marriage happy. He wondered several times if he and Nancy would be able to remain as happy as they were now in the years to come, especially after one of the carriage wheels broke in a particularly nasty rut, and they had to wait by the side of the road for assistance.

Nancy became quite vociferous about her discomfort and inconvenience—the dust, the heat, Mahlon's inability to drive properly, the inferior quality of the carriage he had rented, how late they were going to be getting to Mount Holly, and on and on. Several times Mahlon stifled the impulse to tell her to *Just please be quiet, for God's sake*! Out of respect for her "delicate" condition, he simply listened and murmured "Yes, dear," several times.

As a result of the delay, the usual three-hour ride became five hours, and they did not arrive in Mount Holly until well past five o'clock, too late to go and see Reuben Stone.

After dinner at their hotel, the Washington Hotel at the corner of Water Street and Main, Mahlon and Nancy strolled up and down the streets of this quaint little town that for years had so many connections with Doylestown and Bucks County. For two hundred years, there had always been a great deal of travel back and forth between Burlington and Bucks Counties, and the respective county seats, Mount Holly and Newtown, then Doylestown. The first ferry across the Delaware, from Bristol to Burlington, had been operating continuously since 1713.

As they walked up Main Street past the county courthouse, with its large buttonwood trees in front, and the county jail, with its massive iron-bolted door, the most prominent feature of the town that they noticed was "the mount," rising off to the right to 185 feet above sea level. Turning back down Main Street, they walked past the old Friends Meeting House and cemetery and the offices of the *Burlington County Times*, to the intersection of Mill and Main, where Mahlon noticed immediately the sign announcing "Love & Stone Shoes" painted on the window of a small shop with a green and white awning hanging over the sidewalk. Mahlon knew that Reuben was engaged in the business with his brother-in-law, James Love.

Reuben's wife, Emily Love, was descended through her mother, Rebecca Gaskill, directly from Edward Gaskill, one of the first settlers of Mount Holly, originally called Bridgetown. Gaskill had arrived in Burlington, New Jersey, on the ship "Kent" with John Cripps and his son Nathaniel in 1677. Gaskill, along with more than half of those early settlers, who eventually built this little community south of Burlington along the banks of the Rancocas Creek, were Quakers.

The next morning, right after breakfast, Mahlon walked back down to Reuben's shop. As soon as he entered, he recognized his man sitting at the cobbler's bench in the back of the store that was lined with boots and shoes, some for sale and others having been repaired.

About five feet four inches in height, Reuben had thin, light, almost blond, hair combed to a curl that formed a slight peak at the top of his head and curling almost shoulder-length at the nape of his neck. He was wearing an eye patch over one eye and was clean-shaven except for a long, thin chin beard, which he had started growing since the last time Mahlon remembered seeing him in the Wilderness swamp near Spottsylvania, Virginia.

James Love, who was standing toward the front of the store, saw Mahlon first. "May I help you, sir?" he asked, and at that moment Reuben looked up.

"Lieutenant!" He stood and walked toward Mahlon. "Sure is good to see you, sir!" He introduced his brother-in-law, and the men chatted for a few moments.

"What brings you over here?" Reuben asked.

"Well, I have some family in the area and I wanted to see you. Is there somewhere we can go to talk?" Mahlon asked.

"Yes, there's a restaurant just at the corner," Reuben said. "You don't mind do you, Jim?"

"Of course not," Love replied. "Take your time."

"So, how has life been treating you since the war?" Mahlon asked Reuben after they sat down and ordered coffee.

"I s'pose I can't complain much, Lieutenant, seein' how a great many of our boys didn't make it at all."

"Please, you don't have to call me 'Lieutenant'. That's all over with now. And, besides, I was chosen by default, really. I didn't do anything to deserve the commission."

"That's not the way I seen it, sir." Reuben looked at Mahlon with intense seriousness in his good eye. "In fact, me 'n some of the other boys even suggested that you get a medal for what you done."

Mahlon looked puzzled. This was the first he had heard of that. "What do you mean?"

"In the swamp sir, at the Wilderness. When you took the bullet."

Mahlon shrugged, still confused. "I don't remember much about it, really."

"Well, I seen it all. Do you want to hear?"

"Sure, I guess," Mahlon said.

"It was after comin' through the pine thickets and then the swamp. You remember that?"

Mahlon nodded.

"And we had just come onto dry ground and was turned around to fire back on the Rebs. Took us some time, and some of us had weapons that was useless. They got wet and all. Jenkins was struggling with his gun. He couldn't get it cocked proper, so he weren't payin' attention to anything goin' on around him. All of a sudden, this Reb sniper stands up from behind a tree, pretty close he was, and takes aim at Jenkins. I saw you look up, and in that split second you realize what's happening, and you dive."

"You mean I ran for cover?"

"No! No, sir. You cried out and turned around and dove for Jenkins! You were tryin' to push him out of harm's way." Reuben looked down, and said sadly, "But you was too late. The bullet went through you and right into Jenkins' head."

Mahlon was stunned. "I don't remember that, honestly. It all happened so fast. I just remember the face of that soldier when he stood up to fire, he was that close. I'll never forget that face. It will haunt me in my dreams forever."

"Well, like I said, I seen it all. And I have no doubt you was tryin' to save Jenkins."

"So, what's this about a medal?"

"Yeah. We tried to get Colonel Brinton to recommend you for a medal, but you know how things get tied up in war. I don't suppose we'll ever hear nothin' more about it, but I will look after it…"

"No, please. It's all right. I'm sure there are thousands who deserve it more than me. Especially since I was unsuccessful in saving Jenkins."

"Well, if you say so, but at least I'm glad I got to remind you of what you done."

Mahlon looked down, somewhat embarrassed, and decided to change the subject. "So, what happened to you after Wilderness? Your brother Amos tells me you got sick?"

"Yah. I took sick with a fever pretty bad in September. You might remember, I had only been in the Eighteenth since February of sixty-four. Me 'n Emily had five little ones by then. I knew my number was gonna come up sooner or later, so I found family for 'em to live with, and I joined up."

"I think I remember you joining us. Was that before or after that hair-brained scheme of General Kilpatrick's to attack Richmond?"

"After. I was spared that fiasco, thank goodness, but I seen my share no less."

"Back up to May, what happened after I was taken to the hospital in Washington?"

"Well, let's see. After we joined up with the main division, and they took you and the other wounded away, we proceeded on down the road towards Spottsylvania. There was some pretty heavy fighting all the way. When we got into the place, we managed to capture a lot of the cavalry, about fifty of 'em, and drive the rest back into their own artillery. But it was there that I found my nephew dead."

"Amos' son? Thomas, was he?"

"Yes. Shot right off his horse in the middle of town. It was sad, 'cause of all of my brothers and brother-in-laws and nephews in the war, the only one killed had to have been an only child. We were real close, you know. We all lived in Newtown right up until the war. Tom was almost like one of ours, he was in our house so much when he was growin' up."

"I'm sorry, Reuben…. May I call you Reuben?" he asked in deference to the older man.

"Of course."

"We'll make an agreement. You call me Mahlon. Try not to say 'Lieutenant' or 'sir'." The two men smiled.

Reuben continued. "So, anyway, I had to see to the body getting back home. He's buried up in Doylestown, I understand. I haven't been able to get over there since I got home. Then, after that, let's see, I think that's when we struck out towards Richmond. By that time, we was linked up under Sheridan's command. We had several skirmishes along the way— Yellow Tavern, Haxali's Landing.

"End of June, I think it was, we crossed the Pamunky and moved up towards Hanover Courthouse. The Rebs held all the roads. We managed to drive in the outposts, but the main force was securely behind barricades made from torn-up railroads. We stopped for the night and picked up the charge first thing in the morning. You should've seen us, Lieu... Mahlon. We was greatly outnumbered, and the Rebs was well covered by the breast-works, but we succeeded in routin' 'em from the town. Unfortunately, Colonel Brinton was wounded, Major Phillips, too, and Captains Kingsland and Hamilton."

"Sorry to hear about Brinton. I don't think I knew the others. Oh, wait a minute. Captain Kingsland, I remember him. He was wounded at the Rapidan the year before."

"Well, he was out of commission for the rest of the war after Hanover."

"What happened then?"

"Let me think. We followed Johnny Reb on towards Ashland, but they was too much for us, and we had to fall back. We joined up the main body at Old Church Tavern on the road from Richmond to White House. We had to provide rear guard for the main regiment when they crossed the James River, and, let me tell you, that was somethin' fierce! Nearly five hours of non-stop shootin'. Bullets 'n cannonballs flyin' every which way. We finally got across the river, and I think it was then we was ordered to destroy the railroads south of Richmond. We had one more serious battle 'fore I was taken out. In July, us and some sharpshooters from another division was able to drive the Rebs back from Yellow House, and we did manage to tear up some track, but then we was forced back and rejoined General Wright's division at Prince George Courthouse where we was ordered into the pits to rest.

"It was pretty quiet the rest of July. Hot as blazes, though, I remember. And muggy. Them bugs was all over us—mosquitoes and gnats, millions of 'em! Then, in August, we moved out towards Winchester, and the regiment started gettin' real messed up."

"Oh! Yes, I heard about that from some of the boys who came to the hospital in Washington. I heard Brinton was taken prisoner there."

"Yup. That's what I heard, too, but by that time I was down with the fever real bad. Don't remember nothin' much. I was in the hospital for a long time, then they sent me home. I just got mustered out at Mower Hospital in Philly a coupla weeks ago. I had to go over there when my wife got a letter askin' my whereabouts. They got the paperwork all messed up, I guess."

"Oh, yes, I know how that happens. Be careful, though, I know one fellow who was taken off to jail. They had him mistakenly listed as a deserter!"

"Oh, my. Well, I got my discharge papers all right 'n proper now."

"So, were you wounded in the eye?"

"No, it was the fever. The doctors said, it 'ulcerated' my eye, or some such. I was blind in both of 'em for a while, then the sight come back in this one." He gestured to his good eye. "I'll just have to wait 'n see if I ever get the sight back in the other one."

"I think we were pretty lucky," Mahlon said. "I heard a lot of the boys of the Eighteenth who survived the battles but then came down with typhoid later and died."

"Yeah, so I heard. Bad enough gettin' shot at without all them diseases. So, how 'bout you? How're you doin' with your leg?"

Mahlon filled Reuben in on his hospitalization and recovery, meeting Nancy in Washington, and moving back to Doylestown. "And that brings me to another point of my coming to see you. I'm working at the *Intelligencer* now as a reporter."

"Oh, good for you. I still get the paper, you know. Couldn't get by without my *Intelligencer* every week."

"That's nice. I'll tell Henry Darlington we have another loyal reader over here." He smiled, then said hesitantly, "I have to ask, though, it doesn't bother you reading about your sister?"

"Oh! So, you know..."

"…that Mary Wellings was your sister, yes. Amos told me when I went to see him."

"Well, I was so young when she left. I hardly remember her at all, really. I did see her at Papa's funeral. Let's see, that was April, eighteen forty-seven, no, forty-eight. Almost twenty years ago. Oh, and then when our mother died in eighteen sixty-two, Mary was there with the girl. What's her name? The crippled one…Elizzie. But not her husband. I ain't seen him since forty-eight."

"So, you didn't go to Ruth Ann's funeral?"

"No, we didn't get up there. Like I said, I really didn't have much to do with her after she left. I have to say, though, she sure did look bad when I saw her at Mama's funeral. Awful sickly-lookin' she was. Real heavy, too."

"Yes, her doctor said she had been ill with apoplexy for a long time before she died. He still insists that she died of natural causes."

"You mean to say Langhorn didn't poison her?"

Mahlon shrugged. "Well, that's what Dr. Cernea says."

"But I thought the paper reported that the professor found poison in her stomach."

"Yes, that's what I was told by the prosecutor's office. So, what do you think? Do you think your sister was murdered?"

"I honestly don't know. I haven't heard too much good things about him in the family. Whenever I saw him, when I was young and then at my father's funeral, he was always quiet. Not too talkative, you know. I'm sure he weren't too thrilled about being around us. We weren't always so friendly, you know?"

Mahlon nodded. "Yes, I understand. It was a big shock for you all, I'm sure."

"Right, and I suppose we didn't always behave so nice. I ain't proud of it, but…"

"But, you've been put in a very awkward position. The family is embarrassed."

"Yeah. It ain't right, you know, this mixing the races. I just don't go for it. Not that I would wish them any harm, mind you. But, they got their place…"

"I understand how you feel. You fought in the war and understood the cause, I'm sure. That it's more than states' rights, like the South tried to say. It is affirming that Negroes are human beings entitled to the same rights as other human beings."

"Right. I don't want to see anyone, black or white, slave to nobody. That ain't right, neither. But, there's a line. We should keep the races pure. Blacks and whites."

Mahlon smiled and snickered a little. "I'm sorry. I'm not laughing at you. I'm trying to understand how you feel, really, but it just struck me that it almost sounds like we're talking about cows. You know, keep the breeds pure. I remember my father talking like that about his animals."

"Yeah. You're right. But, that's the way I see it."

"Well, it certainly would be simpler that way. If we could draw the lines and everyone stays within their line. The only thing is, though, I wonder, where do we draw the line? Say, Irish and German? Or, Italian and English. America is becoming a mish-mash with folks intermarrying. It's not just blacks and whites, or Indians and blacks. Down in Texas, for example, there are Mexicans intermarrying with whites and coloreds. And most of them are half Spaniard or French and half Indian themselves. I don't know. A great part of me just says live and let live, you know, if they're attracted to whoever, another race, it doesn't matter. Let 'em get married and live in peace and quiet."

"But, it ain't right. The children suffer…"

Mahlon felt himself becoming increasingly irritated. "But, don't you see? The children suffer because we make them suffer! Society doesn't accept them kindly and they are terribly mistreated! If we'd just mind our own business and let them be. Practice the Golden Rule…" He stopped short, realizing he was taking unfair advantage, both by education and rank. "Oh, I'm sorry. Please excuse me."

"That's all right, Mahlon. You got a right to your opinion. And you certainly got a lot more education than me. Sometimes I don't look at things intellectually like I should, I guess. I just go on gut feelings."

"I suppose you and I are not going to solve this problem in one morning sitting over coffee, are we?" Mahlon smiled at Reuben. "So we'd better change the subject, I guess. Tell me, I've been wondering. What was it like growing up in such a large family?"

Reuben took a sip of coffee. "Well, there was only a short period of time when there was a lot of us home. Just before Mary left, as a matter of fact. It was interesting, I'll say that. The house was always full, what with the cousins running around the place, as well. Sometimes it was very funny, especially when us kids would get Papa all mad at us. He would chase us around the house with his strap, all red in the face, calling off the names—'Johannes! Mahlon! Jonas! Amos! Aaron! Reuben!' Sometimes he'd have to go through ten or more names 'fore he got the right one!"

Mahlon and Reuben laughed at the image. "And we used to confuse him by telling him things like, 'No, Pop, weren't me you saw chasin' the chickens. I was down by the pond. Must've been Chillian.' It was great growing up on the farm, though. I can see that now that I'm grown, though I guess I didn't much appreciate it then."

"And I understand your family moved to Doylestown right after Mary left. Tell me about that."

"Yeah, that was somethin'. Let's see. I was almost eleven then, but I'll never forget that day. I think that's the day I really grew up. Pop was so angry when Mary run off. Angrier than I had ever seen him before or since. I thought he was gonna keel over right then and there. And that was nothin' compared to his fury with the preacher who told Mary she 'n Langhorn could get married legal-like."

"I heard. Apparently he didn't step foot inside another church until he became a Baptist?"

"Yeah, practically the whole family become Baptists once we seen that! Any church that had the power to bring our Pop back to God was the one for us!"

Mahlon smiled appreciatively at the sentiments Reuben was expressing.

Reuben continued. "And Pop wrote every one of us kids letters askin' for our forgiveness. Can you imagine! And 'most all of us come back home. But there's still a bunch of 'em not talkin' to others. Some of the sisters found out that Mary 'n Langhorn were visiting Mama and Pop and refused to go over when they was there."

"And you? How did you feel about that?"

"I don't know. I didn't purposefully avoid them…. Well, I guess I did at times," Reuben said, remembering Ruth Ann's graveside service. "It was just real awkward, if you know what I mean. The family was in a real upheaval for many years. Still is."

"I understand. Every family has its share of 'black sheep'. But, I'm an only child, so I have no choice in the matter!"

"So you got two sides to you, huh, good boy, bad boy?"

"No! I never had a choice but to be good, 'cause I was the only one my parents could blame!" They laughed.

Mahlon paused for a moment and sipped his coffee, then asked, "I understand you all eventually left Bucks County? Only Amos and Mary were left by the time she died, and he's the only one there now?"

"Yeah. A couple of us stuck around 'til after Mama died in '62. Course, that was during the war, too, and there was a lot of us had to go in the army. But there was a bunch of 'em who just plum took off, early-like, twenty, thirty years ago. My brothers Mahlon and Chillian, for example. One by one, and sometimes two by two, we left the farm, and some of 'em I ain't seen since."

"So, where are they all now? Do you know?"

"Gosh, I don't know…. Say, you got a piece of paper?"

"Sure." Mahlon ripped a page from his notebook and handed it to Reuben along with his pencil. "Here."

Reuben started writing. "I used to pride myself that I had memorized all us kids and our birthdays. Let's see if I can still remember." Reuben started writing. Every once in a while he would stop and look off vacantly as if trying to remember, then start writing again.

A few minutes later, he presented the list to Mahlon[4]. "There, that's the best I can remember. I might have a couple of 'em wrong."

Mahlon scanned the list.

Elizabeth, born July 19, 1808		Chillian, born Nov. 26, 1820	
Sarah,	" " 12, 1810	Harriet,	" Sept. 6, 1822
Jonas,	" " 18, 1812	Reuben,	" Sept. 30, 1824

---

4   This was a list that seventy years after this meeting, Reuben's grandson, William McIlhenny Wilkinson, son of his daughter Olive Griffith Stone Wilkinson, found among his grandfather's papers and transcribed into a two-page family history chart that, in turn, a yellowed, onionskin copy of which would be found sixty years after that by the author among the possessions of her uncle, Reuben's great-grandson, James Johnson Goodenough Stone, Jr. Neither Reuben nor his grandson, William Wilkinson, noticed that Aaron and Amos were shown as having been born six months apart.

Mary,			Camilla,	"	Mar. 1, 1827
Elisa Ann	"	Aug. 30, 1813	John,	"	Dec. 13, 1829
Mahlon,	"	Nov. 24, 1814	Rebecca,	"	Aug. 31, 1830
Rachel,	"	June 21, 1816	Hiram,	"	Mar. 11, 1832
Aaron,	"	Oct. 6, 1818	Emma,	"	May 16, 1835
Amos,	"	Mar. 11, 1819			

"You don't have a date for Mary," he said when he finished reading. The lack of any notation about Mary in the midst of all the other children was almost glaring.

Reuben looked down and frowned. "Yeah, I know. Mary had left 'fore I set myself to memorizin', and Mama wouldn't tell me nothin' about her, not even her birthday."

"Oh…the 'shunning'?"

"Yes."

"That's too bad."

"I know, but you gotta understand how the folks took it, 'specially Pop. I think she was even erased from the family Bible."

"Oh, my! But she was accepted back, after your father's conversion, that is, isn't that right?"

"Yes, sort of, and kept in the will, though her husband was not. Neither was Elizabeth's, for that matter. Pop didn't much care for Aaron Height, neither." Reuben had a second thought. "Say, you ain't gonna write none of this in the paper, are you?"

"Oh, no, no," Mahlon assured him. "I don't think any of this is really relevant to the murder case. I'm just curious, is all. I hope you don't mind. As an only child, I find this fascinating, such a large family."

"All right. Glad to hear that."

"And, getting back to my question. Do you know where they all are now?"

Reuben took the list back. "Let's see. Let's start with Elizabeth. She's dead. She died back in the late forties, I seem to recall it was. She got married late, you know, run off with Aaron Height when she was near-about thirty, too old to be havin' kids, I guess. She had three of 'em, Elizabeth, Edward and Charles, 'fore she died. They never come around much, even though they was livin' practically just down the road in

Warwick. Of course, like I said, she was pretty much shunned, too. Pop weren't too happy about her husband, neither."

"What became of her children and husband, do you know?"

"I think the kids was raised by some of his family. I do know Aaron joined up in the war first thing and served all four years as a farrier and ambulance driver. He may've got married again, but I'm not sure. Last I heard he was living up in Mercer County, New Jersey."

Mahlon looked at the list. "Sarah?"

"Sarah was the first one to get married. She married William Page way back in eighteen thirty-one or so. I was just a little kid. I ain't seen nor heard much about her over the last coupla years. I heard they went to Michigan, but I think maybe they're back. They run in a different social circle, if you know what I mean. She's probably trying to distance herself from us. Can't say as I blame her."

Reuben laughed and looked down at the list again. "Jonas. Jonas 'n me are a little closer. He married my wife's aunt, you know, Lydia Gaskill. They got three kids, Jacob, Richard, and Margaret. Jonas was a boilermaker at the shipyards in Philly, and recently got into makin' gasometers...."

"What's a gasometer?" Mahlon looked confused.

"You know. It's the contraption that meters the gas that goes into the houses. So's the gas company knows how much to charge."

"Oh, of course! I should've known that."

"He's prob'ly been the closest to Mary of any of us. You should really talk to him, but he's been away workin' in New York for the past coupla years, doin' pretty good for himself, I guess. I heard both his boys was in the war, too. I haven't been able to find out if they come out all right."

"Oh, I hope so. We've lost so many men."

"Yeah, we seen our share of killin', I hope forever," Reuben agreed. "I'll tell you, sir, I don't have much stomach for it. To be honest, I'm kinda glad I took sick. Now, I don't mean to sound like a coward or nothin', but I just had my fill of it, you know?"

Mahlon nodded. "Believe me, Reuben, I understand. There were times when I hoped I would just get shot and killed, get it over and done with. Because I knew that even the pits of hell could not possibly be worse than the carnage we were going through."

"Yeah, my feelings exactly. But, we weren't killed. We got to stick around here a while longer and think about it." He looked up at Mahlon. "Do you still have bad dreams?"

"Oh, yes, especially about Gettysburg." Mahlon told Reuben briefly about the Confederate boy he had seen gathering violets after the battle at Gettysburg and the ambulance wagon train that went down the mountainside.

They reminisced some more about the war, and then Mahlon looked back at the list. "Back to your family. Mary, I know about, of course. Elisa Ann is next."

"Elisa married John German, and they lived over in Plumstead for a long time. They had at least four kids last time I heard, but I've lost track of 'em. For all I know, they went West like so many of the others."

Mahlon smiled when he saw the next name on the list. "Oh, Mahlon, same as me. I think it was a pretty common name back when we were born."

"Yeah. Mahlon was born in eighteen fourteen, kinda ahead of you, though, I think. When was you born?"

"Eighteen thirty-six," Mahlon replied.

"Oh, just about the time our Mahlon took off," Reuben said. "His story is great. We found out after he run off, much later, that he went out to the West and become what they call a 'mountain man', a guide and fur trapper."

"Really. Interesting."

"Yeah, and that ain't the half of it. Mama and Papa got a letter back in forty-three or so that Mahlon had joined up the Texas army and fought in the war of independence from Mexico. Then we didn't hear nothin' from him for years. Word of Pop's death finally got to him sometime after eighteen fifty, and suddenly we get a letter and find out that he's been working in the Gold Rush in Californee. Must've made himself a tidy sum, 'cause the next thing we hear is he's buyin' up land there in California. He's a rancher now, got himself quite a spread."

"Wow! The stories he could tell! I'll bet he's seen it all, American history all across the country."

"Uh-huh. I don't suppose I'll ever see him again, though. I sure don't 'vision myself ever gettin' out to Californee, but maybe he'll make a trip home some day."

"That would be nice." Mahlon looked at the list. "What about Rachel?"

"Rachel married Mr. VanSant—Aaron VanSant from Bensalem. Just before the war they moved down to Talbot County, Maryland. They was offerin' land down there real cheap, do you remember?"

"Yes, there were lots of advertisements in the *Intelligencer,* I recall around that time. Maryland in particular, for some reason, as well as Illinois, Indiana, and other points West."

"Well, they found themselves smack in the middle of the war just a coupla years later. And there they were with two grown sons, Mahlon and Aaron, Jr., and Maryland was goin' back and forth—Confederate, Union. I guess they was tugged every which way. Finally, I hear, they pulled up, left their property and moved out to Missouri, which weren't much better, far's I can tell."

"Yes, depends on what part of Missouri one was in, but certainly with Quantrill's Guerillas, Bushwackers, Jayhawkers and others, it was not a particularly safe place to be."

"Yup. I hear the Civil War was goin' on in Missouri and Kansas long before it started official-like at Fort Sumter. It's a miracle those two boys survived. I just thought of something: I've heard stories about where folks would disguise their boys as girls to try to get 'em away from having to serve in the war."

"Yes, I've heard some of those stories, too. But, on the other side, I've also heard of girls masquerading as boys just so they *could* join the army!"

"Yes! There was a girl from Trenton I just read about, Mary Jane somebody, who was serving as a clerk to a general. She said she wanted to see the world. And the article said she was just one of some hundred and fifty who had joined up disguised as boys."

"Amazing." Mahlon shook his head and looked down at the list. "Aaron's next."

"Aaron was probably the closest to Mama and Papa of all of us, the anchor of the family, I guess you could say. He's a shoemaker like me. He married Mary Ann Tyson from Montgomery County. They lived for a while in Doylestown, had a small four-acre farm there. Then they moved to Manayunk, near Philly, and then to Chews Landing over in

Camden County in Jersey. They had a bunch of kids, a coupla twin girls, Esmerelda and Alexcenia…"

"What interesting names! Your brother must've been a fan of the classics."

"Oh, yes! We was all raised on that. Did you hear about my Pop's fascination for Shakespeare?"

"No, tell me." And Reuben told Mahlon a bit about the book of Shakespeare's works that had been given to Jacob so long ago and from which the children would playact.

"And, wait 'til you hear what Aaron named his other kids. There's Leonidas, Cyrenius, Cleopatra, Clayudine—there's two of them, one of 'em died young. And Hannibal Independence Stone. He was born on the fourth of July. Oh, and Mildred Mary."

"Mildred Mary? That's rather a plain name after all the illustrious ones before."

"'Tell you the truth," Reuben said with a laugh, "I think Mary Ann just finally put her foot down and insisted that at least one of her kids would have a common name!"

"That's funny. Those are quite some names."

"It's real sad about Hannibal, though. I gotta tell you. My brother joined up in the war right away and was in it almost the whole time. He was called home on furlough last year. Little Hannibal had died. He was just four years old."

"That's a shame. I guess there are so many children dying."

"We counted up one time. We figured that my folks had seventy-two grandchildren that we know about, and several of 'em got sick and died from one thing or another. But, me 'n Emily, my wife, are real lucky, I guess. We got five healthy kids, knock on wood." Reuben rapped the table three times. Mahlon didn't say anything, but he was reassured somewhat about his own wife and expected child.

"So, you say your brother Aaron was in the war, too?"

"Yah, practically the whole time. There's a story I gotta tell you 'bout Aaron and his boy, Cyrenius, too. Aaron joined up, like I said, right away, first in the Fourth New Jersey Volunteers for three months, then in the Sixth. He was in the war that time for twenty-two months and told me he was in twenty-one battles. He was wounded and captured at the second battle of Bull Run, and then was let go. Somewhere along the way, he meets up with Cy and they both get home at the same time. He says when they got there, Mary Ann wouldn't even let 'em in the house 'til they took off all their clothes in the back yard and burned 'em!"

"They were full of lice, probably, and who knows what other vermin. Can't say as I blame her."

"Yeah, but my brother looks at his boy and says, 'Son, I think they treat us better in the army than what we can get at home. What d'ya say? Let's go!' So, off they go into the United States Marines for another four-year enlistment!"

"Yikes! That's a born soldier there!"

"Yeah, well, not so smart. He was wounded again in the marines. He's back over in Manayunk now, near Mary Ann's family, recuperating. I heard Mary Ann was real frugal. Saved almost all the money that Aaron sent home, and they're talkin' about buying a place up in Monroe County, near Stroudsburg."

"That's nice country up there."

"So I've heard."

Mahlon looked back down at the list. "Amos is next," Mahlon asked. "I've met him and his wife at their shop."

"I guess Amos and me was closer than any of the other brothers. Let's see, he married Phoebe—she was Phoebe Smith from Spring-field—way back in forty-one. He started out havin' a shoe store in Doylestown, then moved out to Chicago for a while. When they come back, we all lived in Newtown for a long time, and our Ma come to live with us just before she died in sixty-two. She's buried with our Pop down at the New Britain churchyard. Amos was probably the most civic-minded of all of us. When he was livin' in Doylestown, he started to get all involved in that business—you know, town councils and vigilance committees and all that."

"You mean one of the 'Self-Defence Horse Companies for the detection and apprehension of horse thieves and other villains'?" Mahlon asked laughingly, repeating the wording of the many announcements of membership that were published in the *Intelligencer* year after year.

Reuben nodded. "Oh, yes, of course, you've seen the lists in the *Intelligencer*."

"Are they really vigilance societies, or…?

Reuben frowned. "Naw! Shucks, they're just excuses to drink and carry on away from the wives, far's I can tell. I ain't never seen a thief that's been caught by any of 'em!"

Mahlon laughed. "That's what I thought. Did you ever get involved?"

"Oh, back in Newtown they tried to get me, but that's not for me. Then, in fifty-five, they appointed me tax collector. What a job, you can't imagine! I never had so many people hatin' me personal-like 'cause they had to pay their taxes. It weren't me; t'was the guv'ment, but they took it out on me all the same." Reuben laughed, then frowned and waved his hand down. "Bah! on that."

Mahlon laughed. "Well, that wasn't exactly the type of job that would win one friends."

"I know. I didn't think about it at the time. Stupid me, I thought it was such an honor to be asked to do somethin'. Now Jim, my brother-in-law, is tryin' to get me to join all these Knights of the Carpathians and Loyal Order of Philozathians and Royal Orders of Mooses 'n I don't know what all else—all that nonsense. He says it's good for business, that we got to get established in the community. I s'pose he's right."

"And you're all Baptists like your parents became?"

"Yes, we go to the Mount Holly Baptist Church. Oh, speaking of, our pastor, Samuel Aaron, was from the New Britain church. He just died here not a month ago."

"Sorry to hear that. I don't think I knew the man, but, then, I didn't attend any church much until I married last December."

"Yeah, me, too. After the folks left the Lutheran church in Tinicum, we didn't attend church at all. It vexed my mother for a long time, and she finally went to the New Britain Baptist church on her own."

"Yes, I heard. Then your father was converted. That must've been quite an event."

"You got no idea. Most of us kids was so shocked, we joined up, too. We figured anything that could have that much affect on our Pop.... He just basically turned himself around, you know."

"And you said he wrote letters to all of you? And you got one, too?"

"Oh, yeah. Nearly knocked my shoes off to get it, I'll tell ya! But he had nothing to apologize to me about, really. I was a hellion when I was a kid and probably deserved everything he dished out, and then some!"

"I can't imagine what it could have been like trying to raise seventeen children. And even the girls appeared to be high-spirited and head-strong. And you say all the children lived to adulthood?"

"Yes. Well, except for John. He's the only one that didn't marry, and he died when he was twenty-four in Chicago. He got cholera in an epidemic in about eighteen fifty-four." Reuben remembered something else. "Oh, and Chillian."

"What about him?"

"We don't know what happened to him. When I said that we had all lived to adulthood. Chillian just up and run off one day and we never heard from him since. I can't believe if he was alive somewhere he wouldn't write to us or we wouldn't have heard somethin' in the last thirty years."

"One would think, yes."

"Chillian always had a fascination for foreign places and travel. It wouldn't surprise me if he signed on one of them sailing ships out of Philly, and who knows where he ended up?"

"I hope one day you will be able to find out what happened to your brother."

"Yeah, at least to know…."

"And, he was next on your list, so after him is Harriet."

"Harriet married John Hoff from Montgomery County, but they were living over in Bristol. She died just a coupla years ago and left three boys: Rutledge, John, Jr., and Daniel. The guardian appointed for the three in Orphans' Court was Moritz Loeb."

"Moritz Loeb? The Jew?" Mahlon asked in surprise.

"Yes. Publisher of *Der Morgensterner.* That's him."

"But, was your brother-in-law Jewish then? That's highly unusual, isn't it?"

"No, I don't think so. I'm not sure whether the court even takes that into consideration. It's just a formality, you know, and anyone can be chosen. Besides, I think my brother-in-law always respected Loeb greatly. I think they served together in the war."

"As I recall Loeb, he was renowned as a great speaker in the German language, regardless of his religion. Whenever there was a debate with Loeb scheduled, the hall was always packed. Did you ever hear him speak?" He looked up. Reuben shook his head and Mahlon continued. "He had very strong facial expressions and marked ges-tures—very dramatic. I didn't really understand much of what he was saying and wished I hadn't let my German go. So, what happened to the three boys and their father, do you know?

"I know that Rutledge for one served in the Army, both in the Regu-lars and the Volunteers, first in Penn, then in Jersey. Harriet's husband, I'm not sure what happened to him. I read in the *Intelligencer* a coupla years ago that a fellow by the name of John Hoff living up in Milford Township went and hung himself, but I don't know if it was him."

"That's a fairly common name in Pennsylvania, I think. So, did any of the girls have as many children as your mother did?"

"Yes, as a matter of fact, Camilla was the only one. And she's next on the list. She married George Garren, a blacksmith. You may know him."

"Was he big, barrel-chested? Kind of colorful character who played the bugle?"

"A cornet, yes. That's him."

"Yes, I sure did know him. He played in the Doylestown brass band for a number of years before he left for…Illinois, wasn't it?"

"Yup. They moved out to Kane County west of Chicago in the late eighteen fifties."

"I didn't know him for long, so it must've been shortly after I moved back to Doylestown. But, I remember hearing the funniest story about George. He was practicing with the band one afternoon and appar-ently made some rather unusual chords, and his bandmates looked at him oddly each time. Finally, he stopped, made a slap at his sheet music and spouted, 'Get away from there, you damned bug! I've played you three times already.' He had mistaken the bug for a note in his music!"

Reuben laughed. "I can sure picture that! He's somewhat near-sighted, you know, so he probably couldn't tell the difference between a gnat and a note!"

"What a character he is. Where are they now?"

"Back in Kane County. He's back to blacksmithing. He was in the war, too, the whole time, eighteen sixty-one to just a while ago, he was finally released from service. Camilla come back East during the war and stayed with family. You know, a lot of the women were forced to live together whilst us menfolks was gone."

"Yes, I experienced that somewhat in my own home with my mother."

"I think they're back in Kane County. Last I heard, she'd had a boy, named him Ulysses after General Grant…"

"Who was also from Illinois, by the way."

"…I imagine a lot of folks are gonna be naming their kids after Lincoln and Grant and Sherman, just like they did George Washington, who George Garren is named after, I think. So, let me think now, Ulysses was number nine or ten for George and Camilla. She's the only one of the girls who had a lot of kids."

Mahlon looked at the list again. "Which brings us to John, and you already told me about him. What was he doing in Chicago, by the way?"

"He was staying with Amos and Phoebe, actually. They had gone out there in about fifty-three or fifty-four to try their hand at keepin' a hotel, and John went out to help. When he took sick and died in the epidemic, Amos and Phoebe got concerned for their boy and brought him home."

"And that was Thomas, the one who was killed in the war."

"Yes, very sad."

"How ironic." Mahlon frowned and shook his head and looked off briefly, remembering. He gave a little sigh and looked back at Reuben. "Well," he said, "it looks like some of your brothers and sisters caught the 'Western fever' like so many other folks. Everybody movin' West."

"Yep, including the next three: Rebecca, Hiram and Emma. All of 'em moved West."

"Tell me about Rebecca, then."

"She married Owen Swarts, our neighbor in Doylestown. He was quite a bit older than her, about twenty years maybe. He was widowed by first wife Lydia Bruner with a coupla kids, and Becky was just twenty when they married. They had three or four kids and moved out to Princeton, Illinois—it's in Bureau County, I think—in about eighteen fifty-seven. Owen and the boy named after him both died before eighteen sixty. Very sad. Becky's been left a widow with little kids to take care of for about five years now. But, we just got a letter from her recently that she's plannin' on marrying an English fella, a widower by the name of Jim Hubbard who she met workin' on a farm out there."

There's another typical situation we're going to find more often—widows, thousands and thousands of them. She's lucky to have found another husband, I think. Not to mention men missing limbs…"

"Yeah, like I said, the family's very fortunate that none of us brothers or brother-in-laws was killed in the war. Although a couple of my sisters have become widows, like Becky. And Emma, the baby." Reuben looked hesitatingly at Mahlon. "But, Hiram's next on the list."

"Oh, Hiram!" Mahlon remembered. "I've heard he had two wives at the same time."

"Then you know. I didn't want to say nothin', but as long as you know about it."

"What happened? Do you know?"

"Not really. I was gone from the house by eighteen forty or so, doin' my apprenticeship in Philly. Hiram was just a little fella when I left. Then, Emily 'n me got married in eighteen forty-nine in West Kensington, a little less than a year after Pop died. Hiram would have been, let's see…" Reuben looked down at the list. "…only fifteen or so then. Then I hear he's married Sally Closson in about eighteen fifty-three, I guess, and they moved out to Illinois, Kane County."

"Before or after Camilla and George Garren moved there?"

"Oh, way before by six years or more. In fact, next thing I know, Hiram's back in Pennsylvania, and in eighteen fifty-five, I'm sure it was, he marries Hannah Roberts and they've already had a kid, Ellwood, born six months before. Then Sally shows up back in Penn, with her little girl, Susan Augusta."

"By the way, this first wife is now housekeeper for my pastor, Silas Andrews."

"So I've heard. It was real touchy there for a while. Hiram and Hannah had been livin' in Doylestown, but when Sally showed up, they moved just across the river to Lambertville, New Jersey. He was workin' in the shoe factory there. They just recently moved back out to Kane County."

"You don't know how or what caused him to be married to two women at the same time?"

"Nope. Never would talk to me about it. Not that we saw each other often enough to even get into a conversation. And, after our mother died in sixty-two, you understand, most of us really lost track of each other.

She was like the focal point, if you know what I mean. Every once in a while, we would receive word about the others through her. Each letter she received when she was livin' with us or the few times a year we were able to visit with her when she was not, she would list off all the kids and grandkids she had heard from. But, to tell you the truth, there was so much of an age difference between most of us that we was like strangers, really."

"I understand. Almost like your parents had several, almost separate families?"

"Yeah, kinda like. Then, too, was the shunning. Both Elizabeth and Mary was shunned. And Hiram caused himself quite a scandal, too."

"I can well imagine. You know, the Reverend Andrews and I were speculating whether Hiram got himself involved with the Mormons. They have multiple wives and were active in Illinois."

"Oh! I never thought of that. I don't think so. But, now that you mention it, I do remember the *Intelligencer* used to print a lot of stories about them Mormons back in the '40s. I think it was John Brown publishing the paper at the time. And he was real sympathetic to them, too, I recall. Made it sound all romantic and adventurous."

"Yes, then when Prizer and Darlington took over the paper, the tone changed. The paper became much more derisive, especially about the polygamy aspects and when the United States Army was threatening to march on them out in Utah Territory."

"I remember. But, again, I don't think Hiram was mixed up in any of that. Although, whatever possessed him, I can't imagine. You know, our Pop used to say all the time, 'There's only two ways of arguin' with a woman, and neither one of 'em works!' So I sure wouldn't envy anybody havin' more than one wife!"

Mahlon laughed and nodded, thinking of his own very dear, but sometimes exasperating, Nancy. "You said it!" he agreed. "Well, that brings us finally to Emma. You said she went West, too?"

"Yes. Emma was the baby of the family. Real special, too. I sometimes think her sweet nature done more to soften Pop and turn him around as the Baptist Church. She was definitely the 'apple of his eye'. She was just twelve or thirteen when he died, just the sweetest kid. When she was seventeen, she married George Rue…"

"Rue…that's a well-known name in the area."

"Yup, some of 'em used to be 'LaRue' years ago, I think. They moved out to Chicago, too, like Amos and Phoebe and John. And, just like John, George died, I think eighteen months or so after John. There was a lot of sickness going around at that time."

"Oh, yes, and still," Mahlon agreed emphatically.

"Emmy was left a widow with a couple of kids. The youngest was born after his father died and then the poor little fella died himself. Next thing I know, Emmy's hooked up with our brother Mahlon in California. How she ever made it out there across this country on her own with them little kids, I just can't imagine. We've never heard the full story."

"Like thousands and thousands of other pioneers going across the plains in wagon trains, I imagine. You sure got to give them credit for hardiness and bravery, especially these women, like you said. I hear some of them walked the whole way."

"Uh-huh," Reuben agreed. "Apparently, once she got there, she met up with a Major Emanuel McMichael from South Carolina, who, so told, did very well for himself in the gold fields and took up ranchin' and farmin'. I hear they got themselves a real nice place outside of Monterey. She's had a couple more kids with him, but I don't know much more beyond that. It takes so long for news to travel from California, and we just recently found out where she and Mahlon were. We'd been lookin' for them ever since our mother died."

"Are all of the children required to sign the Release of Dower from your father's estate?"

"Yes, I signed mine right away, and the lawyers have been lookin' for several of the others and the children of the ones who've died. Them lawyer fees sure is eatin' away at whatever we got left in the estate. But, with sixteen of us still alive or who had children, I guess we don't have much choice."

"You know, I think the miracle of your family is not so much that your parents had a lot of children, but that a lot of you lived beyond childhood. That didn't happen until the early part of this century. Before then, people lost more children to disease."

"Yes, I know what you're sayin'. I've known folks that lost five or six, and more. It must be that pure Bucks County air and water." Reuben smiled and laughed.

"I know you're joking, Reuben, but I think you might have a point there. At least at your home, and I know in mine, the quality of life—good food, cleanliness—may have been the key to our survival. Especially the almost fanatical cleanliness. Was your mother like mine? Always scrubbing and cleaning? Made you wash up before every meal?..."

"Oh, yes!"

"...As if the very lives of her family depended on it? And, indeed, perhaps it did."

Mahlon took his pocket watch out of his vest and checked the time. "My goodness, I've kept you away from your shop for far too long. This has been extremely fascinating, and I do appreciate it." He looked up at Reuben. "Are you coming to the trial in September?"

Reuben shook his head. "Oh, no! I couldn't get away from my business, and besides...."

"You haven't told me one way or the other whether you think he's guilty, if you think Langhorn really did murder your sister."

Reuben frowned and put his head down. "I'd rather not say. Really, you got to understand that my sister has been dead to me, for all practical purposes, for almost thirty years. When she left our home that day, she was gone forever. And even our Pop's sudden 'see the light' and conversion couldn't change that. It was too far gone for most of us kids to come around."

"I understand." Mahlon thought of several other things he wanted to say—such as how, as an only child, he hoped Reuben and his brothers and sisters would appreciate each other all the more and become closer because of their shared experiences—but he knew that the forces of human nature and the realities of sibling rivalry would probably not work in favor of any of his high ideals.

Mahlon groaned unconsciously as he struggled to get up and pick his weight up on his cane.

"You all right, Mahlon?" Reuben asked, concerned.

"Yes, I'll be fine. I've just been sitting too long." He suddenly thought of something and laughed. "We're quite a pair between the two of us. Tell you what: You let me lean on you and be my crutch, and I'll guide you and be your eyes! Then we'll be the lame leading the blind supporting the lame!"

Reuben laughed. "You got a deal there, sir!"

LANGHORN WELLING—As was briefly alluded to in our column several months since, this defendant was arrested upon the crime of murdering his wife. He is now in our county prison, awaiting his arraignment and trial at the coming September sessions of the court of Oyer and Terminer, and as it has been authoritatively stated that an analysis of the stomach of the deceased, made by Professor Rogers, disclosed the presence of poison therein, the case assumes more than ordinary interest and importance to both the accused and the public. Lang, as he is generally known and called, is a stout, stalwart mulatto, now in his fifty-first year, born in the alms house, the son of a colored woman named Welling and his first name given him after his reputed father. Left alone in early life to provide for himself, he earned a scanty subsistence by doing small chores for neighboring farmers until at the age of fourteen he bound himself to Joseph Carver, in Solebury Township, to learn farming, and remained there until after attaining his majority. Since that time he was of good report for industry, and has been actively engaged in burning lime in kilns which he leased. Thirty years ago this August, he married [Mary] Stone, a white woman, by whom he had three children, two of whom, a son and daughter, are now living. He lived some years in New Hope, removed to Lahaska, and thence to a lot near Canada Hill, where he resided when arrested. He is kept locked up both day and night, being allowed reasonable recreation outdoors in presence of the jailor. He can write his own name, but not read, is averse to strangers seeing him; is quiet in demeanor; and evidently realizes the serious nature of the charge preferred against him.

Bucks County Intelligencer, June 20, 1865

Chapter X

The Trial, Doylestown Court House
Friday, September 15, 1865

Langhorn woke earlier than usual. This was the day he had been waiting for and yet dreading at the same time since his arrest on February 4th—the trial. He had already gone through this agony a little less than a week ago, when he was brought to the Court House on Monday, September 11th, along with all the other prisoners at the regular term, and had to sit in the courtroom while some of the other cases were calendared and disposed of.

How humiliating it was for Lang to be manacled and chained to the most wicked and desperate bunch of ruffians and criminals he had ever seen in his life. There were burglars, horse thieves, even an arsonist. There was a surfeit of crimes and criminals to be dealt with, including a manslaughter trial arising out of a train collision in Bristol on the Philadelphia and Trenton railroad in March. Then there was the gang of four outlaws from New York who came to an abrupt halt in their nefarious activities behind the walls of "Fort Wilkinson," the Bucks County jail.

It was going to take all week to dispose of these cases, and Judge Chapman knew this Wellings murder case promised to be a long one in and of itself. The defendant adamantly swore his innocence, and H.P. Ross, the prosecutor, and George Lear, the defense counsel, indicated there were to be sixty or more witnesses called.

"September 15th," Judge Chapman pronounced, and banged his gavel on the little wooden block on the bench. Lang was brought back to the jail to await the week's end and his trial's beginning.

Presumably within the next two days, Langhorn would learn whether he was to live or die. He closed his eyes and hung his head and murmured a prayer. *Please, Lord, don't leave me....*He still couldn't believe what he had been hearing—enough poison to kill two persons.

"Mr. Lear, if that poison was found in my wife's body, I swear I don't know how it got there. It was none of my doing. You got to believe me."

"I do, Lang. We'll get to the bottom of it. But you got to understand, the finger of blame is pointing straight at you. You bought the poison off of Jim Acor..."

"I tol' you fifty times! It was for that gawdamned dog of Bye's comin' 'round my house!"

"I know. I know. Calm down, Lang. But it don't look good all the same."

"You tellin' me! 'Cause I try to protect my home and family. 'Cause a colored man buys poison, there ain't no other reason folks can see 'sides killin' somebody. Seems I ain't got a friend left in the world. They all believe it. 'Cept a few die-hards, I guess, and even them are actin' kind of stand-offish."

Lear stood up and patted Lang's back. "And me, Lang. I believe you. And Fell and Johnson and Kenderdine, to name just a few of the whites. And your colored friends, Gibbs and Hartless. And your children. You got more friends than you know. We'll do our best to get to the truth."

Lear's reassurances did little to ease Lang's agonized, sleepless worry. He knew most often the truth didn't "'mount to a hill o' beans" if folks believed what they wanted to. They would hang a man just as fast on lies as they would look for the truth. He tried not to worry about it: *'Til they actually put the rope around my neck, there's no sense in frettin' on what might never be,* he would tell himself. But it was hard not to wonder, and wonder led to worry. And there was nothing to do in jail but sit and think.

He stood up and looked out the barred window to see if he could tell what kind of day it was going to be. So much had happened outside the prison walls all spring and summer, including the strange weather. On April 11th a tornado had even ripped through the county causing tremendous damage. On July 16th there were heavy rains and flooding all along the Neshaminy Creek. Eight covered bridges were washed out. There was apparently no damage to his little house at Canada Hill. The

Chapmans (distant cousins—"poor relations"—it turns out, of the judge) and other neighbors were looking out for his animals and property and reassured him everything was fine, just a few sheets of tarpaper off the roof, which was easily fixed.

The emotional damage to Lang and his children over the past couple of years was not so easily repaired. Elizzie was forced to leave a domestic job in Doylestown that she took to try to pay off some of the expenses of her mother's sickness and funeral, since Lang had to borrow from neighbor Fred Pearson to pay for the funeral and the doctor. She had been there only a month when her father was arrested, and her employers told her they didn't want any scandal associated with their house and help.

But, of the three of them, the events of the past years were hardest on little Jonas, just thirteen years old. Bad enough he had to lose his precious sister Ruth Ann when he was just a boy. Lang had tried his best to ease the pain and pay extra attention to Jonas, but Ruth Ann was more of a mother to him than a sister, and Mary was so caught up in her own grief that she pretty much shut everyone else out. Lang realized she must've been getting the sickness even way back then. She "weren't right in the head"—as folks say when they can't put their finger on the exact cause of a malady—for a long time really before she died.

Then to have his mother die and his father arrested and carted off to jail! It would be a miracle if the boy came out of this all right.

As soon as it was light enough, Lang got up to put on the shirt and pants his lawyer had brought. He tried to clean up as best he could, and one of the guards was kind enough to come and shave him so he would look at least a little more presentable. They were certainly not going to allow him to have a shaving razor, even though he had been a model prisoner.

"Them's the rules, Lang. How do we know you ain't gonna use it to do yourself in," the guard said in an exaggerated, teasing manner as he pretended to rake the razor across his own throat.

And save you the trouble of hangin' me? That's not a bad idea if I could figure out a way to do it.

When Sheriff James M. Wilkinson himself came to take Lang, shackled and manacled, to the Court House in the prison wagon, Lang could almost imagine what it was like going to the gallows. Hanging was such a horrible way to die, he'd heard. Sometimes, the neck snapped like a chicken bone. Other times, if the knot wasn't tied just right, the poor fellow just kind of hung there, suspended, body twitching and legs flailing every which way....

Lang unconsciously put his hand up to his throat and shuddered with a wave of revulsion whenever he thought about it.

This was the second time he had stood before this judge in this courtroom as a defendant. He pleaded *nolo contendre* the first time and would not be testifying in his own behalf this time. Attorney Lear said, as far as he knew, no one had yet remembered or found out about his little problem of threatening Jake McIntire, but if Lang were to be questioned he would be obliged to answer truthfully any question such as, "Have you ever run in with the law before?"

"That won't do, Lang," George Lear said. "Do you understand how it wouldn't look good for you?"

Lang agreed, but still he wanted to have his say, tell them the truth about the poison and Mary being so sick for so many years. But, then, why would they believe him when they'd already made up their minds.

"We'll have your friends and neighbors and Dr. Cernea tell that," Lear reassured him.

Lang looked around the large, square-shaped, white-washed courtroom. The judges' bench was the most dominant feature, large enough for the three judges to sit side-by-side at one time. It was certainly imposing, set high up on a platform in front of twin frame-and-sashed windows, with twenty-four panes each, set about five feet apart in a bay-shaped extension outward that broke up the otherwise squareness of the room.

A gaslight chandelier with six tulip-shaped bowls hung from the high ceiling. About twenty feet directly in front of the bench were two large wooden pillars, and the traditional rail, or "bar," extending out from either side. Behind the rail was the gallery containing five rows of high, straight-backed benches on which the spectators, prospective jury members and witnesses sat. The floors of all the galleries were littered with peanut shells, the residue of refreshments brought in little bags every day by spectators to enhance their enjoyment of the entertainment.

The Negroes always sat upstairs in the small balcony, although in cases involving Afro-Americans, the audience usually became so large they most often overflowed downstairs and even into the hallways outside the courtroom, and the whites didn't protest on those occasions when there were no other seats available.

The lower seating area was invariably filled with a sampling of the inhabitants of every section of Bucks County, drawn by duty or idle curiosity. It was quite a spectacle: The high-collared, brass-buttoned, swallow-tailed blue coats of the residents of the upper ten townships; the broad-brimmed, low top hat and black suits of the staid Mennonite; the long, luxuriant, flowing beards of the venerable Dunkards; the pale faces that peculiarly distinguished the followers of Penn and their descendants; and the ruddy complexions and corpulent bodies of the German stock. Sometimes they looked like actors gathering for an elaborate costume drama.

Until recently, at least two languages—English and German—were routinely heard in the courtroom. Even as shortly as two years ago several draft-dodging cases from rural climes of the county required German translators. Neither the defendants nor their witnesses could—or would—speak English. Judge Chapman was not amused, and, as a result, the court had just decreed the official language of its proceedings would henceforth be English.

On either side of the room were small wood-burning stoves that were used to keep the courtroom warm on cold days. This day, heaters were definitely not needed, as it was hellishly hot, unusual, in fact, for a fall day in Pennsylvania. But, for some ungodly reason, someone had fired up the stoves early that morning, and the room was quickly becoming unbearably warm.

The walls of the courtroom were bleak and bare and, as he looked up, Lang was visibly surprised to see they were festooned with draperies of cobwebs hanging from high ceilings that were almost saffron-colored after years of dust and smoke wafting up from the wood-burning stoves, candles and now gaslight.

The whole room was bereft of decoration of any type—not the usual great seal of the Commonwealth of Pennsylvania nor even the ubiquitous statue of the blindfolded "Lady of Justice" with tipped scales—found in most other courtrooms around the states. All in all, a pretty dismal looking place.

Spaced around the center of the room were four tables—one each for the defense and prosecuting attorneys, the clerk of the court and the sheriff. The sheriff's table was closest to the prisoner's dock, which was up a few steps against the wall to the left of the judges' bench surrounded by a short balustrade. The prisoner was normally required to stand whenever someone was testifying—to "face his accusers"—but in deference to Lang's age and arthritic legs and shoulder, he was told he could sit whenever he felt the need. To the right, as one looked at the judges, was the witness box, and to the right of that, across the room from the prisoner, was the jury box in which would sit the twelve white men who would decide his destiny.

At eight o'clock on the second, a long, loud peal of the bell atop the Court House rang out, announcing the beginning of the court session. Lang looked around at the people, all white men, who were beginning to gather in the room: Hale and hearty Sheriff Wilkinson stood just in front of his table chatting amiably with the clerk. George Lear, District Attorney Henry P. Ross, almost jubilant and jolly with one another, it seemed to Langhorn—the complete antithesis of the fear and depression he had been feeling for the past many months as he awaited the unfolding of his fate. A few men were sitting in the gallery, one of whom he recognized as the young, lame reporter from the *Intelligencer* who had tried to talk to him at the jail a few months ago.

His children were not here yet. The witnesses had been advised not to show up at court until the afternoon of the first day, and Elizzie was coming with Mahlon and Elizabeth Gibbs who, along with Andy and Maggie Hartless, were subpoenaed by the defense to testify. Lang told them to leave Jonas at home with the Paxton Hill family where he had been staying and working since Lang's arrest. No need for the boy to hear all this, and he especially didn't want him to see his father in chains.

"Tell my son he can best help his old man by goin' about his regular routine as much as possible. And praying…ask him to pray mighty hard."

The venerable old crier, John D. "Johnny" James, rose solemnly and majestically to stand before the witness box. "Silence!" he pronounced, and banged the floor three times with his tall staff.

"Oyez! Oyez! Oyez!" His voice boomed out so strongly that the walls and windows nearly shook. "All ye good people who have anything to do before the Judges of the Courts of Oyer and Terminer, the Courts of Quarter Sessions, Orphans' Courts or Courts of Common

Pleas, held this day in and for the County of Bucks, draw near and give your attendance if you wish to be heard!"

James had been opening every session of this court with those exact words for almost forty-four years, having been appointed in December 1821 to succeed Stephen Brock who was elevated from crier to sheriff. Johnny James had seen probably fifteen hundred criminal and civil cases come before this court. If he wanted to, the crier could very well have recited book and verse the defendants, their crimes, outcomes, and the sentences of nearly every case that had come before this esteemed judiciary in those years. If he recognized Langhorn from his previous visit twelve years before, James never let on.

Needless to say, he and his aide-de-camp, David Maulsberry, who had been here just a few years less than James, also knew more than a little about the peccadilloes and proclivities of most of the members of the Bucks County bar, though they would never tell. If the eyes of the Lady of Justice were blindfolded, ironically, the lips of the criers were sealed.

Judge Chapman, the president of the court, entered the room with an almost regal stride, followed by associate justices Henry Troxel and Joseph Morrison. At sixty-one, Henry Chapman still had a little over six more years to serve on the bench. He certainly looked the part: Tall and handsome, with silver-gray hair. The *Intelligencer* described him as a man who was "worthy to wear the ermine and has redeemed the district from the reputation of having from time immemorial the homeliest judges in the state."

As soon as the judges were arranged in their seats, Judge Chapman banged his gavel, announced the opening of the case and stated that the process of choosing the jury would begin at once. The doors opened again, and the lower gallery began filling as the traverse jurors who had been chosen last January—men from every corner of the County, from all ages over majority, and engaged in every walk of life—filed in and took their seats. Almost fifty additional men crowded into the already stifling room.

At the beginning of each year the sheriff and commissioners of the County met for the purpose of selecting and placing names of qualified white, male citizens into the "wheel." Those chosen would serve as jurors for the twelve months following. One hundred and twenty jurymen were required for each regular term of Court—twenty-four grand jurors and ninety-six traverse jurors, the latter of which were divided in half into "first week" and "second week." Lang's jury would be chosen from among those who were serving for the first week.

There were four regular terms of Court, making it necessary for four hundred eighty names to be drawn during the year. To be prepared for emergencies, however, enough names were put into the wheel for another complete jury meaning there were usually somewhat over six hundred in all selected.

Each man's name, occupation and residence were written on a small piece of paper—"John Smith, merchant, Doylestown borough"—and the slips of paper were then folded up and put into the wheel, which was turned several times to mix them together before any were drawn out. The twenty-four names first taken out constituted the grand jury, and so on. If any of the men failed to attend court as required, their names were put back into the wheel, and they were given another chance to serve before the sheriff was sent out to "politely inquire as to the reason for their absence."

In choosing the names to be submitted, the number of voters in the various townships and the votes polled by the respective political parties were considered. Therefore, in the eastern and southern districts of the County, where the Republicans prevailed, a majority of the jurymen were of that political persuasion, and in the Democratic townships of the upper end, it was the reverse.

Lang scanned the faces to see if he recognized any of the men. There were farmers, merchants, drivers, cobblers, tailors, and even gentry—a complete social and economic cross-section of the Caucasian men of the County. A few of them were familiar to him, mostly farmers from the lower County for whom he had worked over the years.

The jury panel was questioned *voir dire* in turn by Ross and Lear during a preliminary examination to determine the competence of the prospective jurors. Several men were eliminated in that round, even though very few of them admitted to knowing anything about the case or having made a judgment as to the guilt or innocence of the defendant.

Lear then made sixteen challenges of those left, and Ross three, and the final twelve men who would comprise the jury were named: J. Paul Knight from Southhampton; Samuel S. Gilbert, Bensalem; Charles

Jamison, Richland; Philip R. Brunner, Warrington; Pierson Mitchell, Middletown; James M. Paist, Buckingham; Henry A. Moyer, Hilltown; Daniel Hibbs, Newtown; Ephraim Shank, Springfield; Jacob Delp, Bedminster; James C. Clark, Jr., Buckingham; and Jesse W. Knight, Bristol.

Lang tried to look at them squarely without emotion in his face so that no one could read his unease with the knowledge that in the next few days, these men would decide literally whether he lived or died. Most disconcerting was the fact that of all the traverse jurors called and questioned *voir dire*, only two of them declared conscientious scruples against rendering a verdict in a case where the penalty would be death. That meant that at least forty-five men sitting in that courtroom, potential judges of Lang's living or dying, had no reluctance to sentence him to hang.

The empanelment of the jury took all morning. After the lunch break, when court reconvened at two o'clock, the proceedings began by the reading of the lengthy bill of indictment that was filed by District Attorney Henry P. Ross after the inquest on February 4, 1865. The jurors at the inquest—John S. Bailey, John G. Palmer, Joel Worthington, Morris H. Large, Pearson Good, and James M. Reynolds—had found simply that Mary came to her death from the administration of poison "by the hand of some person to us unknown." Yet, based primarily on the testimony of James Acor that Lang had ordered poison, and even before the results of the chemical analysis of the contents of Mary's stomach were received from the University of Pennsylvania, Ross ordered that Lang be arrested and taken to jail that very day. He then used the inquest's findings as the only evidence to prepare and file the indictment.

"The Grand Inquest of the Commonwealth of Pennsylvania," James read, "inquiring for the body of the County of Bucks upon their oaths and solemn affirmations, respectively do present that Langhorn Wellings, late of the County aforesaid, Yeoman, not having the fear of God before his eyes, but being moved and seduced by the instigation of the devil, and of his malice aforethought contriving and intending a certain Mary Wellings to deprive of her life, and has the said Mary Wellings feloniously to kill and murder on the first day of November in the year of our Lord one thousand eight hundred and sixty-four, and on divers other days and times between the said first day of November in the year last aforesaid and the third day of January in the year of our Lord one thousand eight hundred and sixty-five, such force and arms to, at the County aforesaid and within the jurisdiction of this Court did knowingly, willfully, feloniously and of his malice aforethought mix and mingle certain deadly poison, called *nux vomica*, but commonly known as ground Quaker buttons, in certain food which had been at diverse days and times, during the time aforesaid, prepared for the use of the said Mary Wellings to be eaten by her, the said Mary Wellings, he the said Langhorn Wellings, then and there well knowing that the said food, with which he the said Langhorn Wellings did so mix and mingle the said deadly poisons as aforesaid, was then the there prepared for the use of the said Mary Wellings, with intent to be then and there administered to her for her eating the same. And the said food with which the said deadly poison was so mixed as aforesaid afterwards, on the said first day of November in the said year of our Lord one thousand eight hundred and sixty four, and on the said other days and times last mentioned at the County, and within the jurisdiction aforesaid, and delivered to the said Mary Wellings…"

Lang closed his eyes. *Oh, dear Lord, this is awful! How can I keep myself from yelling for him to stop!*

On and on Johnny James droned through the four felony counts— administering poison in food, administering poison in liquid, murder generally, and murder by poison. *How many times can one kill a person? This is ridiculous.* Lang groaned unconsciously. He held onto the railing of the prisoner's dock and swayed back and forth, the ordeal made even more unbearable in the hot closeness of the courtroom. Thankfully, Sheriff Wilkinson noticed and told him to sit.

Lang rubbed his sore shoulder and decided it would be best if he didn't listen. He deliberately caused his thoughts to wander. *They say Mary started dyin' in November sixty-four? No, she begun dying long before that. And her love for me… When did that die? Was it that stupid thing with Louisa? Or gettin' her pregnant with Jonas? Was it when I got lost in the bottle? Or even as far back as New Hope right after we was married? Was she sorry then she'd run off with me?*

No! Lang frowned, and almost spoke out loud. *There was good times, lots of good times. Lahaska. Canada Hill. Even just before she*

died, she was almost sweet and loving to me again. It was the strangest
thing. But it was too late…

Lang could almost pinpoint the day Mary began dying to the world,
at least in spirit, if not in body. It was March 2, 1859—the day the children found Ruth Ann dead. Like a beautiful bronze angel lying in the
snow, with her scarf and dark brown hair falling all around like a halo, as
they described the scene to him.

Mary never really recovered from the shock, and nothing any of
them could say or do would console her. In her grief-induced delusion,
aggravated by change of life, obesity and her apoplectic condition, she
turned particularly cold and angry to Lang and shut him out of her life
and bed. She moved permanently to the little room behind the kitchen.

"It's too hard for me to get up and down the stairs anymore," she
explained. Though no one believed it, they did not argue, and she grew
even heavier from the lack of that simple exercise.

Grief swirled around Mary like a maelstrom and consumed her
every waking hour. Life in the little house in Solebury would never be
the same again. There would be no more sitting in the parlor of an evening, listening to Ruth Ann play the piano, with everyone joining in
happy song. For Mary, there was no longer pleasure in sewing or knitting, gardening or cooking, or even reading *Godey's Lady's Magazines*
or the *Intelligencer.*

It almost seemed as if she had been created solely to mother that
one, very special child, and when that reason for living was gone, there
was no more use for her. Unfortunately, by this time, Mary could not see
her relationships with Lang and Elizzie and Jonas as being particularly
compelling. She had never bonded with her other children in quite the
same way. She and Jonas were almost strangers. Elizzie was grown and
much too self-sufficient, and, besides, she was shy and wasn't interested
in any of the things Mary and Ruth Ann used to share.

The day after Ruth Ann was buried, Mary stood in the empty parlor
staring at the red velvet couch. Suddenly, with a realization that welled
up in her body like a fountain, she knew it was finished. All of her
dreams and aspirations had been for naught. Her depression flooded
over her and tainted everything with gloom.

She finally understood that no matter how much her neighbors might smile at her in public, and tip their hats and parasols politely, they would not welcome her to their quilting bees or socials. Her Negro husband would never be invited to join their hunting clubs, Masonic temples, agricultural societies, Vigilance Committees or Self-Defence Horse Companies.

There would be no gentlemen callers for her shy, crippled daughter, certainly no balls at the Masonic Hall, and no young friends coming to their house for gay musical entertainments now that Ruth Ann was gone. And, simply because of his race, no matter how much she tried to educate her son, he would never be eligible for employment at anything more than manual labor.

The red velvet couch stood bigger than life in mute mockery of all of Mary's dreams. Elizzie came running at the sound of her mother screaming and crying and found Mary on her knees tearing at the couch with her sewing scissors. She was able to restrain her, fortunately, before too many irreparable cuts had been made.

But, from that day on, Mary rarely went into the parlor. For the most part, she maintained a stony, stoic silence, although, the family was to learn within a few years, her rage had not yet been completely spent.

Life continued for the rest of the household, despite the pall that Mary's grief laid over the entire neighborhood. Elizzie took over most of the household duties, and quietly and without complaining went about her chores. Lang and Jonas found more reasons to be gone from the house for a great portion of each day, and by the time the war came two years later there was plenty of work around the county, as the farmers stepped up farm production and animal husbandry to supply the soldiers with food and horses.

Perhaps the most affected by Ruth Ann's death, however, and most overlooked in the months and years following, was young Jonas. His grief turned inwardly to guilt. For the rest of his life, he blamed himself—somehow, he thought, his insisting that Ruth Ann take him coasting that fateful day had spelled the death of his beautiful, devoted sister. Even many years later, when he finally told the story to someone—his wife, Winifred—he would not listen to her protestations that he could have had nothing whatsoever to do with his sister's untimely demise.

"Now, that's outright ridiculous, Jonny," Winifred, an Irish Catholic immigrant whom he met in Philadelphia, cried out when he told her the tale. "Ye could've had nuthin' to do wi' yer sister's heart condition 'n ye know it."

Jonas shook his head. "No," he insisted. "It was much too strenuous for her to be doing. She'd still be alive if it wasn't for me."

With few variations, such as church on Sunday, the rest of Mary's days were spent, in temperate weather, sitting on the front porch or in the yard, absentmindedly cleaning and paring vegetables and fruit, and in rainy weather and winter, sitting on a settle by the stove, just as absent-mindedly doing needlework, usually knitting socks and sewing other articles of clothing for the soldiers during the early years of the war. Her hands had never been idle in her half century of life, and she could not break the habits of a lifetime. Yet, more and more often, the vegetables or the needlework would gradually fall to her lap, and she would sit for many hours staring aimlessly, seemingly in a trance.

In the beginning, Lang comforted and counseled Elizzie and Jonas. "Let your mother be. She's had a terrible shock. She'll be better someday soon. We must be patient."

He would not let on his own misgivings about her recovery. He and Mary never discussed it—indeed, she rarely spoke more than a perfunctory response when spoken to—yet he somehow knew it was more than Ruth Ann's death. This was the culmination of a lifetime of bearing up 'til she could bear no more.

"It's like a breakdown of her system," Dr. Cernea told Lang. "Her mind and body are broken."

"Will she ever get better, Doc?" Lang asked more than once.

At first Dr. Cernca was encouraging. "Oh, yes, Lang, I do think so. She's a good strong German woman. We must maintain hope and a positive attitude." Lang continued giving Mary the tonic recommended by Dr. Cernea that was supposed to build her blood, but was actually laced with laudanum, which suppressed her nervous system and kept her fairly much in a prolonged stupor.

Despite all their best hopes, the months and years went by with little sign of improvement. In October 1862, they received the news that Mary's mother, Mary Trullinger Stone, had died while on an extended visit with the families of her sons Amos and Reuben in Newtown. Mary took the news quietly, yet inside her heart was crushed with grief once again.

Lang decided it was best that he not go to his mother-in-law's funeral, which was held at the Baptist Church in New Britain. In truth, he did not much care to see any of the family again. Even Mary's brother Jonas, the friendliest of the bunch, had not been very forthcoming in the past few years. It was agreed that Elizzie would accompany her mother on the stage over to New Britain to the funeral and then a couple of weeks after that to the lawyer's office in Doylestown to sign the Release of Dower.

Once again, Aaron took charge of the estate, and, as did all the other brothers and sisters or their surviving children, Mary received the sum of sixty-nine dollars and seventy-two cents as her share of the accumulated estate of her father and mother. She gave it to Lang. She had no use for money any more. How ironic, he thought, that he had been purposely excluded from old Jacob's will, yet the bequest wound up in his hands anyway.

Lang, Elizzie and Jonas eventually resumed the family tradition of gathering in the parlor in the evening and reading the newspaper. The piano sat idle, since none of them could play as well as Ruth Ann did, and Mary could not tolerate hearing it. Eventually it went out of tune.

One evening in 1863, while reading the paper for Lang, Elizzie got downright silly and began reading an article with exaggerated eloquence, mimicking the ladies of the "hoity-toity society" she had seen while working in the house in Doylestown.

"The propah uses of fertilizer," she read, raising her eyebrows, elongating her chin and holding up feigned lorgnette eyeglasses. "The successful fah-mahr will diligently economize on his use of man-uah in fertuh-lizing his field, and the labour of applying it to the soil...." Langhorn smiled and chuckled, and Jonas rolled on the floor giggling.

Suddenly Mary was at the door, red-faced with anger. "What are you doing! Stop it!" she cried out. "How can you laugh? There's nothing to laugh about. The war! My mother is dead, Ruth Ann is dead...." Her voice became hysterical, then trailed off as she leaned against the doorjamb. It was the first indication they'd had that she could hear what was being said and read aloud in the parlor.

Elizzie and Jonas stopped still with stricken looks on their faces. Lang jumped up and put his arm around Mary and led her back to her bed off the kitchen.

"Don't be upset, old girl. She was just havin' a little fun. Gotta have a little fun now 'n then. Not to worry, Mrs. Wellings, not to worry." He sat her down on the bed and held her in his arms, talking, soothing. "It's gonna be right as rain 'fore you know it."

Mary laid her head on his shoulder. It was one of the few times in many years that she allowed him to hold her for more than a brief embrace. It almost made her feel safe again for one of the few times in her life, but, then, she had long ago given up caring about being safe.

From then on, Elizzie kept up the practice of reading the papers, but lowered her voice. In fact, it had become imperative to Lang that she continue reading the newspaper to him. By that time, he was deeply involved and interested in the progress of the war and the whereabouts and experiences of the Bucks County soldiers, in particular.

He listened intently as Elizzie read letters from the soldiers as they ventured forth and penetrated further into Rebel territory. He rejoiced with their victories and cried with their defeats. He followed with excitement as Elizzie read the news of the battles—Fair Oaks, Antietam, Fredericksburg, Murfreesborough, Chancellorsville, Vicksburg, Gettysburg, Charleston, Cold Harbor, Chickahominy, the capture of Atlanta, and more. He mourned the wounded and killed, including John Simpson Hartley, George T. Magill, and Samuel A. Watson, all young men he knew from Solebury, who died in June 1862, members of the 104th Pennsylvania Regiment.

All of these men were lamented, but by far the most devastating loss for Langhorn personally and Solebury Township and Bucks County generally was Robert Kenderdine, the twenty-three-year-old son of John Kenderdine, Lang's benefactor so many years ago who had donated much of the building materials for the house in which they sat.

A member of the 114th Pennsylvania Regiment, also called Collis' Zouaves because of the flambouyant uniforms they wore at the beginning of the war, Kenderdine was in the midst of the hardest fighting at the Gettysburg battle. His father and brother-in-law left immediately for the area as soon as they heard about the battle and found Robert in a hospital tent at the battlefield. They removed him to the home of Alexander Poland in Leesburg, Virginia, who was a Southerner and Confederate by political persuasion, but who comforted the sick and wounded from both sides.

Young Robert's wound should have not been fatal. It was a musket ball that had lodged in the right buttock. When his father and brother-in-law found him, he was still awake and able to converse, but he had lain on the battlefield for two days among the dead and wounded before being removed to the hospital. By that time, the wound was much inflamed and closed up, preventing discharge of the infection and forcing the tainted blood to course throughout his body. Careful and timely nursing could probably have saved his life, but his was a typical fate of thousands upon thousands of soldiers, both Union and Confederate.

Langhorn went over to the Friends meeting house in Solebury to pay his respects to the family at the solemn and impressive funeral, where many of the mourners gave praise to the life and exemplary deportment of the young man who "fell in defence of a holy cause." Robert had two brothers still in service in the army who could not attend—Thaddeus, a lieutenant in the 174th Regiment in South Carolina, and Watson, a member of Captain Hart's State Militia on duty on the southern border of the state.

Another example for Langhorn of John Kenderdine's kind and virtuous character was the stirring tribute he wrote for the *Intelligencer* when his son's benefactor, Alexander Poland, was killed by Rebel soldiers in his own home just six months later in December 1863. Although a Confederate, Poland's home was open to solace the suffering—whoever was sent to him was welcomed and given aid and comfort. He was thusly entertaining two Union soldiers with a meal one evening when two Rebels pushed their way into his home and demanded the surrender of the guests.

Poland stood to face the defilers of the peace and safety of his house. "Not in my house!" he pronounced and made toward the attackers. He grabbed the gun of one of them and started to push it aside, and the other Rebel shot him through the heart, killing him instantly. They then turned on the helpless Federal soldiers, who had laid down their arms when coming into Poland's house, and severely wounded one of them before making their escape with the Union soldiers' horses.

"Though professing to feel and act with the rebels himself," Kenderdine wrote in tribute to Poland, "he and his wife and kind daughters did everything within their power to make us happy and comfortable, with a manifest disposition, if need be, to protect us, also manifesting a deep interest for my afflicted son, by offering and doing every kindness within their reach for his relief and comfort, for which I will ever hold them in grateful remembrance."

As the Union armies proceeded south, and casualties mounted up, in early June 1863, the draft rules were changed to include Negroes, and the so-called "Colored Regiments" began forming. Eighteen names were procured in Buckingham and an additional fifty-five in Newtown, Attleborough (formerly Four Lanes End), and Bristol.

Recruiter James K. Morris of Buckingham reported that at first there was some talk among the colored boys of dodging the draft, but most of them came out in the end and agreed that it was perfectly right that they should be required to do some of the fighting in this war. A number of them, including Lang's neighbors Richard Wells and Joseph Peaker, joined up without waiting for the draft. By June 1863, there were two hundred volunteers. Most of those recruits went to Hawley's Brigade as part of the 8th U.S. Colored Infantry and distinguished themselves in bravery and courage.

One officer described the scene at a recruiting camp: "Our camp thronged with visitors, and darkees who wanted to enlist. There are hundreds of them, mostly slaves, here by now, anxiously waiting for the recruiting officer. The boys are singing:

'Rally round the flag, boys, rally once again, Shouting the battle cry of freedom. Down with the traitor, up with the star.'"

Unfortunately, the enthusiastic fighters were ill-prepared and poorly-equipped and suffered terrible losses during their tour of service in Florida and, later, Virginia.

In February 1864, the *Intelligencer* published a poem by Edna Dean Proctor, "Response of the Colored Soldiers," reprinted from *The Independent*. So beautiful, so stirring, was this poem for Lang that he cut it out of the paper and had Elizzie read it to him again and again. It eventually was placed in the family Bible.

RESPONSE OF THE COLORED SOLDIERS
BY EDNA DEAN PROCTOR.

To God be the glory! they call us! we come!
How clear rings the bugle, how bold beats the drum!

Our "Ready!" rings clear; our hearts bolder beat,
The strongest our right arms, the swiftest our feet;—
No danger can daunt us; no malice o'erthrow;
For country, for honor, rejoicing we go.
How watchful, how eager we waited for this,
In terror lest all were betrayed with a kiss!
Yet, weary in cabin or toiling in field,
The sweet hope of Freedom we never would yield,
But steadfast we trusted, through sorest delay,
That the beam on our night was the dawning of day.
'Tis dawning! 'tis morning! The hills are aglow!
God's angels roll backward the clouds of our woe!—
One grasp of the rifle, one glimpse of the fray,
And chattel and bondmen have vanished for aye!
Stern men they will find us who venture to feel
The shock of our cannon, the thrust of our steel.
The bright Flag above us, exultant we hail;
Beneath it what rapture the ramparts to scale!
Or, true to our leader, o'er mountain, through hollow,
Its stars never setting, with fleet foot to follow.
Till, shrill for the battle, the bugle-notes blow,
And proudly we plant it in face of the foe.
And then, when the conflict is done, in the gleam
Of the camp-fire at midnight, how gayly we dream,
The slave is the citizen—coveted name
That lifts him from loathing, that shields him from shame;
His cottage unravished; and, blithesome as he,
His wife by the hearthstone—his babe on her knee.
The cotton grows fair by the sea, as of old;
The cane yields its sugar; the orange its gold;
Light rustle the corn-leaves; the rice-fields are green;
And, free as the white man, he smiles at the scene;
The drum beats—we start from our slumbers and pray
That the dream of the night find an answering day.
To God be the glory! they call us! we come!
How welcome the watchword, the hurry, the hum!
Our hearts are aflame as our good swords we bear—

"For Freedom! for Freedom!" soft echoes the air;—
The bugle rings cheerily; our banners float high:
O comrades, all forward! we'll triumph or die!
—*Independent*

Lang was so proud of "my Boys" as they acquitted themselves very well in their first big fight at Port Hudson. At the same time, he was more than a little grateful that he was fifty and Jonas was just shy of nine years old when the war began, too old and too young, respectively, to have to march off to battle.

"Even so," Lang told Mahlon and Andy one day, "we colored folks been fightin' this war for centuries. 'Bout time we don't have to keep lookin' over our shoulders all the time." Ironically, the beginning of the war marked the first time in his life Lang and his friends did not have to live in constant fear that they and their children might be attacked and kidnapped at any moment.

How especially proud Lang was when a member of the Carver family—Lieutenant James M. Carver, of the 104th Pennsylvania Regiment—was appointed Captain in Colonel Montgomery's Second Regiment of South Carolina Colored Volunteers. He received his commission directly from President Abraham Lincoln himself! Lang delighted to hear the letters that Capt. Carver sent home that were printed in the *Intelligencer*. Captain Carver wrote in the newspaper that the colored troops performed admirably and were "uniquely qualified for service as they are accustomed to the climate and able to withstand any amount of exposure and fatigue."

In addition to news of the soldiers, Lang loved to hear the stories about blacks who vindicated themselves nobly, especially the article in July 1864 of a couple in Virginia who had discovered and buried the body of a white soldier:

> ONLY A NIGGER.—Lieut. Hunt of Utica (U.S. regular artillery), recently fell overboard from a tug in the James River, and was drowned. His body not being recovered by the tug, some relatives went down and dragged the river for it in vain, being afforded every facility by our naval officers. Finally, they inquired along the river bank, and found two negroes who told them of another negro who had buried the body of a

Federal soldier which he found on the river bank. Proceeding to that negro's hut, they met his wife, who showed them the clothing, spurs &c., of the buried officer, which they readily recognized as Lieut. Hunt's. She also produced and gave them $57 in cash with his wallet, which her husband had taken before burying the body, decently shrouded in coarse cloth, in the best coffin he was able to make. In a little while, the husband returned, and, before aiding them to exhume the remains, produced $300 more, with certain important papers, which he had also taken from the body, but which he had carefully concealed even from his wife, because (he said) the guerrillas often came there, and they might frighten her into giving up to them documents and money which they ought not to have. All those were brought away with the body. Of course, the negro only proved shrewd, thoughtful, and strictly honest, but there have been instances of white men doing considerably worse.

Earlier in the war, Elizzie read a story about a slave who had fled to Western New York and asked a clergyman for shelter. Two or three persons in the neighborhood came to look over the runaway and began to suspiciously ask questions:

"S'pose you had plenty of hard times down South, licking plenty?"

"No—never was whipped."

"Wa'nt? Well, you had to work most awful hard?"

"My work was light."

"I guess your clothes were not very nice?"

"I am well clothed, a good house servant."

"I reckon your victuals were not uncommon fine?"

"As good as I desired."

"Well, I should give it as my opinion that you was a mighty big fool for running away from such a place as that, just for the sake of shirking for yourself."

"Gentlemen, my place down South is vacant. Any of you can have it by applying for it." The former slave nodded graciously and ended the conversation.

"Ha! I'd like to see any of 'em go for it!" Lang laughed over and over.

On a rainy spring Sunday in April 1862, Lang and Elizzie and Jonas, and a few others in Solebury and Buckingham, rode over to New Britain for the funeral of Violet, a ninety-nine-year-old former slave. The *Intelligencer* reported:

When Doylestown was in the chrysalis state of only tavern and blacksmith shop, John Hough, a wealthy land-owner, while at the latter place having some work done, purchased as his slaves: Violet, her mother Tamar, and her sister Sylvia, from a traveling trader in human cattle, and removed them to his farm. Tamar, who, it is asserted, lived to the advanced age of 105 years, attended to the domestic duties of his household; while Violet, of more robust constitution and masculine temperament, was for many years engaged at the heavier out-door farm work—during which, she entirely eschewed the bonnet and donned the old-fashioned beaver hat—and there are many grand-parents now, who can remember in their early school days, her quaint apparel and queer appearance. As years brought on their bodily failures, she became the faithful nurse and guardian of her owner's children, possessing the affection of the household, who regarded her as a member of their own family. They became separated, hither and thither and with a most commendable regard for her comfort, procured her a comfortable room and boarding, where her declining years glided peacefully away within sight of her early home. Respected by all who new her, her funeral was respectably attended by white friends, who buried her on Sunday last, at the New Britain Baptist grounds. From the time she became, in early girlhood, the chattel of John Hough, her world was bounded by the horizon on which she gazed; and she knew no other sphere than duty to those of whose family circle was an honored and unobtrusive member; while at her funeral, those who had been her early care, gave to her memory the tribute of tears as sacred as can be except over those of fairer skins but not more spotless hearts. Her sister, Sylvia, is, as we are informed, still living near Hartsville, at a very advanced age."

Then, in July of 1862, another tragic personal loss to Lang and Solebury Township occurred. Old friend William Ellis, who had designed and helped build the Wellings' home almost twenty years before and had

remained a good and true friend throughout the years, died in a construction accident, leaving a widow and six children. All of the colored
families of the area especially gathered round to mourn his loss, including the large Peaker family, Burroughs Blackwell and his wife Katy and
children William and Claude, Elias and Lydia Woods, in addition to
Mahlon and Lizzie Gibbs and Andy and Maggie Hartless. Also attending were Benjamin and Elizabeth Wilson, Ann Griffith, Henry and Jane
Wright, Perry and Julia Brown, Charles and Maria Lewis and their six
children, Morris and Ann Frost, his brother Maxwell and wife Elizabeth
Frost, and Henry See.

Among the mourners was fifteen-year-old Robert Earle Kohl (also
spelled Cole in later years), a mulatto orphan who was working for
farmer John Roberson and his wife, Rhoda, in Solebury. This was the
first time the Wellings children met Bobby, who was to become Elizzie's
husband six years later.

Just a year after Bill Ellis' death, in April 1863, Lang learned about
the passing of another well-known colored resident of Bucks County:
Morris Bake, who had a small cake and apple shop in Doylestown.
Morris had been ill for some days, and under the care of Dr. Hendrie, but
was alone when death found him. The paper went on to report:

"When quite young, Morris was afflicted with white swell-
ing, which distorted his limbs so much that he walked with
difficulty, and rendered him unable to perform much labor.
Still, Morris was useful in his humble way, and by his correct and honest deportment set an example to many of far
higher pretensions. Everybody in Doylestown, down almost
to the smallest child, knew and respected him. For some
time, we believe, he was the only representative of the sable
race among us. His remains were interred in the Presbyterian church-yard, in the presence of a number of persons
who were his friends in life and in death did not cast him off.
He was about fifty years of age. In the brief funeral services
held, it was observed, 'We bury an industrious man—a man
of honesty, of truth, respectful toward others, non-complain-
ing, constant reader of his Bible, and who leaves no stain on
his character as a professing Christian.'"

All of this was inter-mixed with disturbing news of the war, as well, such as in November 1862, when over two thousand fleeing slaves were taken captive and shipped back South after the terrible battle at Harper's Ferry, not to mention the devastating loss of over fourteen thousand Union Troops killed, wounded and taken prisoner. This was one of the first and worst Union defeats of the war.

Then, in February 1863, a very sad case was detailed from Cincinnati, Ohio, where slave traders from Henderson, Kentucky, had arrived after purchasing a number of Negroes in Lexington. Among them were a woman named Harriet, about thirty years old, and her infant. The slaves were placed in the basement of the Capital Hotel for the night. Harriet apparently became crazed with the thought of being separated further from her husband and older children. She waited until late at night, and dashed into the hall. Finding the door locked, she raised her hand, and with powerful blows, smashed the lights surrounding the door, severely lacerating her hands and arms. Then she used the glass to somehow cut through the door and, streaming blood, fled for her life.

They found Harriet, with her infant clutched to her bosom, exhausted from loss of blood and almost frozen to death, crouched in the corner of a stable, where she had been traced by the blood upon the snow.

"The door-sill and wall at the Capital Hotel are saturated with this slave-mother's blood," the paper concluded, "mute but eloquent appeal, and there it will remain, 'for not all Neptune's ocean can wash this blood clean,' and senators and law-makers shall see it as they go and come from the legislative halls, another evidence of instinctive and ineradicable love and aspiration for freedom."

In July 1863, the *Intelligencer* reported sadly about the draft riots that had occurred in New York City, during which a colored orphan asylum was burned and many innocent Negroes were murdered in the streets. The riot was instigated by Copperheads, who whipped the local immigrants to an impassioned frenzy, and was quelled only when United States troops were called in.

Throughout the war, and for many years before, as early as 1838, there had been reports of the debates raging about Negro repatriation to Africa and colonization, especially to Liberia. Lang didn't want to hear any of it, and he spoke for millions of his fellow Afro-Americans when he stood up and stated firmly in church one Sunday: "Now all this talk about 'goin' back to Africa', all us black folks are supposed to jump on ships and 'git on back home'. I got one thing to say about it, and that is: This soil I'm standin' on right this minute is my home! I was born here, and my mother was born here. For all I know my father was born here, and his father before him. My wife and her family are Americans, and, most importantly, my children are Americans. I don't care if they never give me citizenship rights or allow me to vote. I am an American, always have been, always will be. My people may have been African before, just like yours are English or Irish or German, but I am an American. This is where my bones was born, and this is where they'll be buried!"

He sat down to rousing applause and many pats on the back. The subject was never mentioned again in the Wellings household or neighborhood, and word of the prevailing sentiment among the colored people in Bucks County must have got back to the *Intelligencer* because there were no more articles about repatriation and colonization.

Then, in January 1864, the famous Negro orator Frederick Douglass himself came to Bucks County. This was perhaps the most exciting thing that Lang had ever experienced. His hero—the champion of the colored folks (even more so than Abraham Lincoln)—was coming to Bucks County. Lang, Elizzie and Jonas traveled over to Pineville, where Douglass gave a talk on "The Mission of the War" to a very large audience. Even so, Langhorn felt such a kinship and affinity with Douglass, it was as if he alone was in the room, and Douglass was speaking directly to him and only to him.

Douglass was born Frederick Baily in February 1818 at Holmes Hill Farm near Easton, Maryland. After his escape in 1838, he changed his name in New Bedford, Massachusetts, to "Douglass" after a character in the book *The Lady of the Lake*, by Sir Walter Scott, which a friend was reading at the time.

Douglass' mother was Harriet Baily, a slave on the large plantations of Edward Lloyd V managed by Aaron Anthony. It was rumored that Douglass' father was white and could have been Anthony himself, who was well known to be a "slave breeder."

As a child, he rarely saw his mother, who had to work long hours six days a week in the fields far away from her children, and Douglass was raised by his maternal grandmother. One of the most horrible, traumatic features of his life was as a young man seeing his beloved grandmother evicted from her cabin and forced to go into the woods alone to die, since she had become too old and feeble to be of use to the slave master any longer.

Douglass spent his childhood and young adulthood being pulled back and forth from the fields of the plantations, where he was beaten regularly in an attempt to break his spirit, to the City of Baltimore, where he was exposed to the finer things in life and where his longing for education was enkindled by reading and writing and learning the Bible. Whenever possible, even though it was an extremely serious offense, Douglass continued his education. He quietly set up clandestine schools and church services for the field slaves on the plantations, and joined secret educational organizations for blacks while in Baltimore.

By the time he was twenty, Douglass had apprenticed in the craft of ship caulking and was earning a good wage for his master, Hugh Auld, and at the same time honed his hatred of slavery. He was indeed taking on the very characteristics of an educated man of which the slave owners lived in fear—knowledge, dignity, courage, and self-respect.

By posing as a free sailor and using a friend's documentation, Douglass went north to Philadelphia, just months after the catastrophic riots in Philadelphia that Langhorn and Mary had witnessed in May 1838. He immediately took a train to New York and wandered around for several days, afraid to talk with anyone for fear of the slave catchers and bounty hunters who were prowling about the city streets looking for runaways.

By September of that year he made it to New Bedford, Massachusetts, a place of relative safety, where he was forced to work as a common laborer, despite his training as a caulker, since the Northern white shipbuilders would not allow blacks to work at anything else. He brought his fiancee, Anna Murray, a free woman, up from Baltimore, and they were married.

It was in Massachusetts that Douglass came into contact for the first time with William Lloyd Garrison, anti-slavery leader and publisher of the *Liberator*. While Garrison was a pacifist, believing that the slaveholders could be convinced through education and rhetoric to abolish slavery, yet he was also controversial even within the abolition movement because of his commitment to equality for women as well as for Negroes and for his attacks on churches for refusing to take a stand against slavery.

Douglass quickly and firmly aligned himself with Garrison, attending conventions and traveling on speaking tours in the early 1840s throughout the North and West where he talked about his early life, even introducing himself as "a piece of property" and describing himself as "a graduate from that peculiar institution, with my diploma written on my back." In his speeches he refuted the lies perpetrated by the slaveholders that the life of a typical slave was benign and happy, that they worked short hours, were well fed and clothed, and enjoyed job security that would be envied by white factory workers in the North. He successfully used humor in several places in his speeches to get his point across to the audiences, and in this measure was especially derisive toward clergymen who warned the slaves they would be offending God if they disobeyed their owners.

He was an immediate success on the lecture circuit and also began speaking out about racism he had witnessed and encountered in the North such as the fact that blacks could not stay at all-white hotels, were not allowed to work at skilled labor, and were forced to sit in segregated train cars, even segregated churches. He did this bravely in the face of retribution and retaliation from not only pro-slavers, as in Indiana where he and his associates were beaten, but also from Northern racists who did not extend their humanitarian sentiments beyond merely freeing the slaves.

In 1845 Douglass published his *Narrative of the Life of Frederick Douglass, an American Slave*, naming names and places, although friends and associates tried to talk him out of it, thinking for sure the slave hunters would find him as a result. Douglass insisted that he wanted his story authenticated, regardless of his personal safety. As a result, he was forced to leave his wife, Anna, and their four children in Massachusetts, where Anna supported the family by working in a shoe factory, and go to England for almost two years. While there, his friends raised enough money to purchase his freedom from Hugh Auld.

After returning home, Douglass took the family to Rochester, New York, where he began his four-page weekly paper, *The North Star,* on the masthead of which was proclaimed: "Right is of no sex—Truth is of no color—God is the Father of us all, and we are all Brethren." He took up the fight for women's rights, along with abolition of slavery as well as temperance. As a slave, Douglass had been appalled as he witnessed the use of alcohol by slave owners to pacify and subjugate the slaves.

What a compelling and inspiring man Douglass was for blacks and whites alike! Langhorn himself was mesmerized by this forceful man who spoke so eloquently about all of the things that were important to him: Equality, justice and rights for blacks and for women, and temperance. But, Lang was sad to realize that apparently Douglass did not have universal appeal, as he overheard a conversation between a white man and woman leaving the hall.

"I still say there's no way that man was ever a slave. You can't convince me. He talks too good," the man said. "Why, he talks better'n me!"

"But he was self-educated, I understand," his companion answered. "He learned to read and write at a young age and then joined a debate society run by free blacks in Baltimore."

"Well, then, he did all that as a slave, you're tellin' me, so what's so bad about slavery, then, if they take care of the niggers so good? I never got no education, 'n I'm white!"

"Oh, Horace, you just wouldn't understand!" the lady frowned and shook her head in disgust.

It did cause Lang to ponder the obvious comparisons—that here Douglass was born a slave, and his hunger for education was so keen as to cause him, through the worst opposition imaginable, to learn and develop himself, whereas Lang, who was born and living all his life as an unbound black with free education easily accessible, was not particularly interested in even learning how to read and write. For the umpteenth time in his life, he kicked himself for resisting Joseph Fell's efforts to educate him so many years ago.

He put his arms around the shoulders of his children as they walked to the wagon. "Now you kids, you be sure never to slack your education and reading. You listen to your old man. You'll never be sorry."

It was just a month or so after Frederick Douglass came to speak that Mary had her first bad attack. She'd suffered from terrible headaches for years, and the tonic that Dr. Cernea was giving her didn't seem to help any more. She would sit for hours on the settle next to the stove in the kitchen with a warm compress on her head. She would hold the same piece of sewing or knitting on her lap for months at a time, not quite finishing anything anymore.

One day—it was in March or April, Langhorn recalled—he was walking around the kitchen preparing a bite of lunch for himself. The kids were both away, Jonas at school and Elizzie at a neighbor's. Mary, complaining of a headache as usual, had just came back from the outhouse and was sitting next to the stove. It was difficult for her to even walk around the first floor any more, let alone up and down the back stairs leading out to the convenience.

Lang began chatting with her, hoping to interest her in conversation about plans for their future. But, they didn't seem to have conversations much any more, and especially not ones that weren't liberally laced with acrimony.

"I'm gettin' older, you know, old girl. We're going to have to think about what to do in our old age. I can't be workin' at the limekilns lifting all them heavy things. And the farm work and construction labor is takin' its toll on me, too. Not to mention the new fertilizers are comin' in and takin' over the lime business."

Mary said something; it wasn't exactly a word, more of a grunt, and picked up her knitting.

Langhorn sat down at the table, began eating his lunch and resumed his conversation.

"I know you don't like to talk about it, but I was thinkin' we'd sell this place…"

Mary suddenly became agitated. "Stop it! Stop talkin' about selling my property out from under me!" She rubbed her forehead with her palm. "Oh, my head! Why do you keep after me with this nonsense about selling the lot?"

Lang put his sandwich down and looked at her intently. "Mary, I thought you understood. I can't be workin' the kilns any more, and I can't take care of you and support us without more area for farming. We need a bigger lot. I'm only thinking of our future, so's we can have some stock and raise enough produce to feed ourselves and maybe a little extra to sell up at Rice's Market…"

Mary stopped rubbing her forehead and looked at Lang through pain- and drug-glazed eyes. She stared at him in silence, almost vacantly, for several seconds. Lang looked away for a moment, just time enough to miss something that passed over her eyes. And, he never knew that in that instant something had touched her so deeply, so profoundly, it was almost as if a bolt of lightening had come into the house and struck her—just as it had those thirty years ago when their eyes had met for a brief glance over the washtub at her father's farm. It cut like a knife through the accumulated layers of pain and sorrow, and as she knew in that encounter thirty years ago, so she was confirmed now.

This is my man. He is my life and the father of my children... Scenes from her life came flooding back over her, and this time it was the good things that outweighed the bad.

As she looked at him, tears welled up in her eyes that Lang would later mistakenly conclude were tears of pain or, worse, tears of anger at him. He never knew they were tears of joy at the remembrance and rekindling of pure young love.

For in that instant, Mary's spark of enlightenment coincided with the first major stroke to afflict her already overburdened body. A small blood vessel burst in her brain. She jolted up off the couch and fell to the kitchen floor, her massive body thrashing in convulsions.

Lang looked up in shock. He dropped his sandwich and jumped up to see if she was all right, waited until the convulsions subsided, then ran to the neighbors to get Elizzie and others to help get her into bed and to send someone for Dr. Cernea.

The saddest part of these final months of Mary's life was that he never knew her thoughts just before the attack. Indeed, he carried guilt with him for the rest of his life, thinking that their argument over the sale of the lot had caused her attack and sickness.

"A serious attack of apoplexy," Dr. Cernea concluded. "There's nothing we can do to prevent it or to cure it, I'm afraid." He felt Mary's pulse and did the only thing medical science had taught him to do in this situation: He bled her. It was erroneously thought that removing some of the blood from the body would eliminate the pressure on the vessels and arteries, though, in all fairness to medical science, it probably worked for a very short term.

Mary was up and walking again within days, but this was just the first of a number of strokes, big and small, that would jolt her body over the course of the next ten months, each one hitting her a little harder and keeping her down in bed a little longer. She was unable to communicate much more than a few words, usually in response to a question—"How are you today, Mrs. Wellings?" "'Well as common," she would reply, if she responded at all beyond a nod and a half smile.

The sudden rap of the judge's gavel woke Lang from his daydreaming. Judge Chapman announced it was time to begin the trial with the opening statements of the lawyers for the Commonwealth and the defense. Lang looked up and realized several more people had entered the gallery during the crier's reading of the indictment, including Elizzie, the Gibbses and Hartlesses. He perked up a little when he saw Elizzie and his friends, and they smiled shyly back at him. Elizzie raised her hand slightly in greeting.

He hoped she had not heard all of the indictment. *Such awful things to say about your father… Seduced by the devil, indeed!*

Following the opening statements, Dr. Cernea was the first witness called. Under questioning by District Attorney Ross, Cernea gave the background of his professional services to the family over the years. Then he talked about the last days of Mary's life.

"I was called upon on the thirtieth of December, eighteen sixty-four, in the evening to attend her. At that time, I found her in a state of coma-insensible. When I first saw her, her eyes were closed, so I did not examine them. She did not protrude her tongue, and from her condition it was not possible, or scarcely so, to examine it. The woman who was attending stated that the deceased had had two convulsions. I inquired whether she had vomited, and was informed that she had been sick at the stomach, but had not vomited. Her breathing was slow, but regular. She had a strong, full pulse, and her face was very much flushed—she suffered from erysipelas generally…"

"What is that, Doctor? Erysipelas?" Ross asked.

"That's a condition of the skin usually associated with broken blood vessels near the surface of the skin. It gives an overall inflamed, reddened appearance to the face, mainly."

"I see. Thank you. Did you notice that she was paralyzed at all?" Ross asked, apparently referring to the usual symptom of an apoplectic stroke being paralysis on one side of the body.

"Well, she motioned one arm—her left—frequently up to her head and face. I did not observe any motion in her right arm or right side, and I simply took for granted she was paralyzed. Though I was told by those in attendance that she had moved her right hand."

That was me who told him that, Lang thought. He remembered sitting to the right side of the bed. He was leaning forward with his elbows and forearms resting on his legs when Mary did a most uncommon thing. She gradually inched her hand over—it had to have been her right hand—and weakly caressed his fingers.

Not being used to showings of affection like this from Mary, Lang was startled for a second. Finally, he said, a little nervously, "I guess we done it up okay, hey, old girl? Thirty years we made it through thick 'n thin. I hope you forgive me for all the troubles…" He was too embarrassed and choked up to finish. He didn't know what else to say or do or whether she even heard, though he could swear a slight smile came to her lips. Then, again, maybe it was a grimace of pain.

"What did you do then?" Ross asked.

Dr. Cernea replied, "I attempted to give her some water, to ascertain if she could drink, tried to introduce a teaspoon into her mouth, but found her jaws were stiff. After two or three efforts with the spoon, I finally introduced a teaspoon full of water into her mouth. After giving two or three teaspoons full, imagining she had swallowed it, I introduced the fourth, and the water ran out the side of her mouth. I realized then she did not swallow, and I did not attempt to give her any more. It was not possible to administer medicine, in my opinion."

He stopped and looked at Ross. "So, what did you do then?" Ross prompted.

"Well, not being able to give her anything, there being small force of pulse, the only remedy I saw probability of relief from, was bleeding…."

"Bleeding. You mean you cut into an artery and took blood from the woman's body?"

"Yes, very common practice, the object being to relieve the force of the pressure upon the brain, which I supposed to exist. I bled her moderately, scarcely making any impression on her pulse in this instance, however. She had another convulsion about the same time she was being bled, and I directed ice to be applied to her head."

"And the reason for that to slow down the blood flow to the brain?"

"Yes, just so. But, I knew this was her last sickness."

Lang remembered that day very well. Of course, he had thought about it many times over the past few months sitting in jail. After examining Mary, Dr. Cernea came out of the bedroom and told everyone that

it was very uncertain whether Mary would ever regain her consciousness, and if she did at all, it would not be until the lapse of some hours.
Lang had been going through this up-and-down uncertainty and waiting
for wellness or death—something!—for so long now that it was beginning to take its toll. Until people go through it, they just don't understand
that friends and family—especially close family and caregivers—can
experience one or more of the stages of grief—disbelief, depresssion,
anger, anguish, and acceptance—sometimes all the way to the end and
back over it again even before death comes.

"Did you prescribe any other medications?" Ross asked the doctor.

"Yes, I mixed a teaspoon full of the extract of valerian and told the
attendants if she became capable of swallowing, to give her two teaspoons full of that every hour. I then told them I would call the next
morning, and left."

"And you came back the next day?"

"Yes. The next morning when I called there—about noon, or
later—I found her very much, or almost exactly, in the same condition
she was in the evening before and was informed she was not able to
swallow anything. I directed cold applications to be kept to her head, but
I deemed the case of so desperate a character, that it promised but little
benefit from any prescription I could make."

"And, in fact, your predictions came true?"

"Yes. I saw her again the next day—I think in the morning…

"That would be January 2nd then?"

"No, January 1st, I believe. Maybe I'm getting my days confused,
but it was every day for two or three days."

"Very well. What did you find then?"

"The next I saw her the only change was a more depressed condition of the system, and not so much activity of the pulse; she was apparently gradually sinking. She was said to have had another convulsion. I
saw her again on Monday—that would be the 2nd—not far from two
o'clock. The only change about her showed that her constitutional force
was yielding, and, comparing it with the first visit, had greatly yielded. I
passed by the same day, in the latter part of the afternoon, and asked
someone by the fence if she was still living, and learned that she was.
That day was the last I visited her."

"So, after you found out she had died, what happened then?"

"Well, I attended the funeral. Mrs. Wellings had been my patient for many years, you understand. And then I was called upon, at the inquiry by the coroner, about a month after, to make an examination, and to cut out her stomach and send it to Professor Rogers, to have the contents analyzed."

"What did you find in the examination, then, briefly, if you will?"

"May I consult my notes?"

"Of course."

Dr. Cernea studied his handwritten papers for a few moments, then put them down on his lap and began. "The deceased was of very full habit, having an unusual development of fat about her. Because of the winter cold, her body was in a kind of semi-frozen condition. I removed from her body her stomach and duodenum, and eight or ten inches of the rectum, and placed them in a jar. The stomach was perforated at the extremity nearest the heart. The perforations were ragged and a portion of fluid had escaped. With a crooked spoon, I took it up, and placed it in the jar. The jar was stopped up, and sealed with wax.

"As the cerebral symptoms had seemed to be most prominent, I opened her head, as well. The brain was not frozen, it exhibited some congestion, and on the right side and posterior portion of the perebrum, I found a mass of extravasated blood, amounting, as near as I could judge, to a full fluid ounce of volume. There were other small specks of blood in the brain, and in the same portion of the brain there was serum near the base of the brain in a diffused state. The serum was independent of the blood entirely."

Lang looked up and noticed Elizzie leaving the room in some distress. He could well understand it must not be pleasant hearing your mother talked about in that manner.

"Let me stop you there for a moment, Doctor. You used some words that might need explaining to the jury. Perebrum, extravasated blood? Could you explain that briefly?"

"Yes, the perebrum is a portion of the brain, sort of here…" He motioned with his hand up to the back of his head. "'Extravasated blood' means blood that has been forced out into the surrounding tissue as if by a small burst or explosion."

"Thank you. Please continue."

Cernea picked up his notes and studied them for another second or two, then continued. "I have noted here that in my examination of the brain, I found that it was softer around the mass of blood than in the other portions, and the brain at the base exhibited some signs of the effect of decomposition. So far as the blood is concerned, there was no probability that it had been extravasated after death. As to the serum, that may have taken place while she was dying, but the fact that the blood was not extravasated after death agrees with the symptoms of cause of death."

He stopped suddenly. "Oh, I made a mistake as to the side. The blood was on the left side."

"So what did all of this mean in the autopsy examination?" Ross interjected.

"My examination of the brain confirmed my previous diagnosis of the cause of death, and the disease that diagnosis was based on, what I saw when I first saw the patient, strengthened by conditions which she had exhibited at other times prior to the last attack."

"Apoplexy?"

"Yes. I had been called to attend her repeatedly previous to the time of her death. She had complained generally of her head, and, at one of those times, some degree of numbness of the arm, and lower extremity of the right side. This, however, was not serious; it only exhibited a tendency. Her mind seemed obtuse, and she answered questions slowly. That condition might have arisen from congestion of the brain, but if from effusion it was very insignificant."

"And could those symptoms have been caused by any other condition?"

"Well, the slight paralysis might arise from various causes, effusion, congestion, et cetera. The former symptoms were also on the right side."

"And this had been evident for a long time?"

"Oh, yes. I judged and feared at the former attacks she would continue to be liable to attacks from paralysis or apoplexy. With the same condition and quantity of blood several months before, she would not have lived. These diseases may be anticipated for months, or may come like a flash. In Mrs. Wellings' case, it was expected for a long time."

"Now, you say the stomach was perforated. Was that something that was manifested in her last illness?"

"No, I don't believe so. If her stomach had been perforated before death, it would have been attended by pains, peritoneum inflammation, which would have been manifested. Oftentimes, such perforations take place after death, and I believe that to have been the case in this instance. The perforation was not surrounded by extravasated blood, and from that I infer that it took place after death. It is said to take place from the acrid condition of the gastric juice, the stomach being flat—empty—or nearly so."

"And not by the effects of poison?"

"Oh, certainly, there are poisons which would have a tendency to perforate the stomach. Anticipating your question, nux vomica would have a tendency to produce such a perforation." The doctor frowned and wagged his head. "A large quantity of it could act as an irritant and tend to perforation, but I think it would have taken a very large amount, and, as I said, I did not see any evidence of the effects of poison in this case."

"What about tetanus? Could that have produced the symptoms?"

"I saw no peculiar tetanic symptoms connected with the convulsions. I do not recollect any motion of her right side and the convulsion expended itself mostly upon the side not affected. A tetanic action might affect the paralyzed side of the body and not be seen, however."

Ross paused for a moment to look at his notes, then turned back to Dr. Cernea. "Just some minor housekeeping now. What did you do with the stomach after you removed it from the body?

"I gave vessel containing the stomach to Harman Yerkes who, in turn, I understood, was to take it to Philadelphia…to Bob…I mean, Professor Rogers at the University laboratory."

"Thank you, Doctor. That is all I have for now."

During cross-examination by defense attorney Lear, Dr. Cernea testified more about his relationship with Langhorn over the years and during the last days of Mary's illness. If he knew that Lang and Mary had been at odds for years about her dependence on him and his role in their lives, Cernea didn't let on. He remained adamant that the cause of Mary's death was apoplexy.

"I saw no symptoms during her life, or condition of her body after death, inconsistent with her having died with apoplexy," he concluded.

By the time Cernea finished testifying, it was late in the afternoon and Judge Chapman was inclined to adjourn for the day, but Ross reminded him that Professor Rogers had arrived from Philadelphia and could go back on the evening train if the Judges were not averse to having him testify into the early evening. Otherwise, he would have to stay overnight, and there was no need to inconvenience him.

"If you think you can get through the testimony quickly," Judge Chapman said.

"Yes, Your Honor, before six o'clock, I estimate."

Judge Chapman looked at Lear, who affirmed his agreement. "Very well, then. Proceed," he said.

Professor Rogers was well known to this courtroom's judges and lawyers for a number of years. He had testified in poisoning cases since almost the time forensic science at the University of Pennsylvania had progressed to the point of identifying various chemicals in human tissues. Robert E. Rogers had been a professor in the University of Pennsylvania and had occupied the chair of chemistry in the medical department for at least twenty years prior to the Wellings case.

He was so well known it was not necessary for the court to inquire about his experience and qualifications. He began directly by testifying about his introduction to this case and how he went about the performance of the chemical analysis.

"In the latter part of the winter, Mr. Yerkes presented himself to me, with a vessel purporting to contain human remains, which he informed me he had brought to me from Mr. Ross, the District Attorney of Bucks county, and that I should examine the same for poison, and report myself to him...Mr. Ross...yourself, sir."

"And can you describe for us what you found upon examination of the jar," Ross asked.

"The vessel was a glass bottle of wide mouth, sealed, and upon opening it, I found it to contain a human stomach, a small portion of the appended bowels, and a small length of the lowest portion of the bowels, along with a few tablespoons full of liquid."

"And you then proceeded to examine the stomach and bowels?"

"Yes. Upon opening the stomach, which had not yet been cut open, I observed it to be entirely empty. In fact, its sides were completely caved in and came in contact with each other somewhat closely. The curved end of the stomach, which in life is nearest the side where the heart is, had in it a large perforation or tear of the tissues. Upon laying the stomach thus cut open flat upon a large porcelain plate, I examined carefully the texture and appearances. Its texture was soft and easily torn and bore evident marks of decomposition…."

"Just a moment, please. Back up for a second, if you will. Can you tell us what you believe the perforation was caused by?"

"The perforation was evidently the work of organic decomposition. I concluded that there were no marks of decided inflammation over the surface of this organ. Where fat usually accumulates about the stomach and bowels, it was here found in abundance. No marks of disease especially presented themselves in this organ, although I must add it is not always safe to conclude when a stomach is in a state of far decomposition, what was its original condition immediately after death."

"I see. Now, please describe for us your remaining examination and analytical procedures."

"Yes." Professor Rogers continued, glancing occasionally at his notes. "Having thus made this physical examination, I next proceeded to the chemical investigation, which I had been requested to conduct. Not knowing how extensive the field of inquiry over which I would have to travel might be in that search, looking to the possibility of having to seek for either arsenic, corrosive sublimate, tartar emetic, prussic acid, some preparation of opium, or strychnia, or brucia—all of which are poisonous and are sometimes given for poisoning purposes—I necessarily divided the materials which I had received from Mr. Yerkes into so many separate portions, and then proceeded as follows: In one of these portions I laboriously sought to find, through all the appliances of chemistry, arsenic. I failed to find the slightest indication of its presence."

A slight murmur was heard in the courtroom.

"With equal care I examined another portion for corrosive sublimate, which is a preparation of quicksilver, or mercury, and failed to obtain any trace of its presence. The search for antimony and prussic acid likewise led me to no suspicion that they were present. It takes a very long time for some of these chemicals to make themselves manifest, and after weeks spent in these unavailing efforts, the question narrowed itself down to the possible presence of some preparation of opium, or strychnia, or brucia. Every care was bestowed to get rid of the substance, or animal matter of the stomach, and methods were adopted, which, while they should destroy all the substance of the stomach, and of all the liquids which were with it, there should live undestroyed and uninjured morphia, which is the poison in opium, and strychnia, and brucia, which are the poisons in nux vomica, or what is commonly called the Quaker-button. It will be observed therefore that if, by these steps, we have any poison left, it must be either morphia, strychnia, or brucia, or a mixture of two of them, or three of them.

"Coming down to this point, I had next to determine whether the minute spot of material, which was the remnant remaining as a result of all this chemical treatment, contained or consisted of any, or all of these substances. I would mention here in parenthesis that it required the destruction of ounces of liquid and solid substances before we could get down to this minute residuum; and, even with all the refinement of the science, when the quantity is so very small, it is next to impossible to destroy the very last trace of the animal substance.

"Now it is important for me to say to the Court and jury that when we test for arsenic, corrosive sublimate or antimony, we can preserve the results of our testing and can take them where we choose, to exhibit them to a court or a jury, for example, because the results of those testings are permanent; while in the instances of morphia, strychnia, and brucia, we only get an effect. That effect then vanishes under observation, and passes from the narrative of its existence.

"Now I would mention that after all this experiment, I obtained only the minutest possible spot, which might be the residuum of a small drop of dried spittle, to which I could apply the test for either of these poisons. And when I did apply the test, so little was the quantity of any substance, that the mere contact of the material used with it, produced, as it were, a flash and was gone never to be repeated.

"To be accurate in giving to the minds of the jury, exactly the impression which it had on my own mind, I must ask, what was that? It was not of a distinct bright purpose nor an equally bright color— red—due to brucia, but a sort of undefined color, approaching something intermediate between them; not however clearly defined. With my mind directed to the subject of poison, and having failed in detecting all others, especially looking to these, this is the impression, the sum total of the effect produced upon me a suspicion that there might be these poisons, strychnia, or brucia, or both, and therefore I regret that I had not more of that small amount of material to corroborate or refute that suspicion, and otherwise to settle the point. I closed the investigation, feeling in my own heart, that the result obtained would not permit me where the important issue pends, to say that strychnia, or brucia, or both of them, did or did not exist…"

The murmur in the courtroom became more agitated, and Judge Chapman perked up from the lethargy to which he had succumbed. He had heard this technical, scientific evidence many times before. He and the other justices exchanged glances, then he banged the gavel on the wooden block.

"Silence! What's the problem here?"

George Lear stood. "Your Honor, if I may. I believe there is a bit of confusion among the court and gallery…"

"Well, what is it?"

"I…ah…sir, Your Honor, it appears that Professor Rogers was unable to find any residue of poison within the deceased's stomach, and…"

"Yes, yes."

"Well, it had been generally reported some months ago that actually there was enough poison found to kill two persons. I believe that's what it was." He rifled through the papers on the table before him. "Yes, here it is. An article in the *Intelligencer* of May 16th of this year. With your permission…" He looked up at the justices.

"Yes, go ahead," Judge Chapman answered.

"'We understand that the District Attorney has received information from the Professor that the stomach of the deceased woman contained poison enough to kill two persons,'" Lear read. He looked over at Ross, who appeared perplexed.

"Well, Mr. Ross, do you know anything about this?" Judge Chapman asked.

"Ah…no, sir. Your Honor, I never said anything of the sort. I… As you know, I was not in the office a great deal this year owing to the death of my father and my accident."

"Yes, yes, of course." Judge Chapman looked at him sympathetically and nodded, almost deferentially. "We are all aware of your terrible loss, and that of this court, as well. Your father was a greatly esteemed member of the bench. Well, let's get to the bottom of this." All eyes then turned to the gallery and toward Henry Darlington, who looked rather stricken. Mahlon sat in shock.

Darlington rose and took a few steps. "Your Honor, I believe I can say that we had it on the best of authority…ah, I believe it was…" He looked down at Mahlon, who roused himself somewhat and stood.

"A…law clerk," he said weakly.

"I'm sorry, young man, I can't hear you," Judge Chapman bellowed down from the bench. Mahlon wished he could melt away into the wood-work, but endeavored to compose himself.

"An acquaintance of mine, Your Honor, from Princeton. He is a law clerk for District Attorney Ross." All eyes went back to Ross, who nodded and shrugged.

"I think I know who they mean, but he is no longer employed in my office. For this and other reasons, I believe he has shown himself to be unworthy of the profession."

I should have known! Mahlon thought. *It was a set-up!* He immediately looked over to the prisoner. Lang sat with an ever-darkening mood over his countenance. *How angry he looks,* Mahlon thought sadly. *My God! What have I done to him by stupidly trusting that fool law clerk?*

He looked over at Darlington whose face was definitely redder than usual and perspiring immensely, and not just because of the close heat in the courtroom. *Oh, no! There goes my job.* He sat down dejectedly, humiliated. *So Cernea was right. Where is he?* He looked around the gallery, but the doctor had left as soon as his testimony was over. Mahlon never knew that Cernea and Rogers were old friends from the University and had been in contact about the case for some time; Cernea knew there was no poison found because his friend Bob Rogers had told him.

Judge Chapman looked sternly back at Mahlon and Darlington, the latter still standing at the bar. "We trust this will convince you to consider carefully before printing something like that in the future."

Henry smiled and half-bowed. "Of course, Your Honor, as always, we will endeavor to report fairly and truthfully," he said and sat down. He took his handkerchief out and mopped his brow.

Lear suddenly seized the opportunity. "Your Honors, with all due respect, I have to move on behalf of the defendant for a directed verdict of not guilty." He walked a few steps closer to the bench to press his point. "If there was indeed no poison present in Mrs. Wellings' stomach, then the case is moot."

All three justices looked at Ross. "Well, I'll have to respond," he said, "and insist that the trial continue. For, I understood Professor Rogers to say that there very well *could have been* poison present, but he had too little matter left for testing, isn't that right, sir?"

Rogers nodded affirmatively. "Yes, unfortunately, because of all the prior tests which had destroyed the tissue, there was so little left. That is not to say there was no poison present."

There was some further legal arguing between the lawyers, in which Ross pointed out that there was still ample evidence as to the motive and opportunity for the accused to have murdered his wife and, besides, there were so many witnesses gathered, not to mention the jury, who would have to be put up for the night at Brower's Hotel anyway.

Darlington turned and looked at Mahlon, who had ceased writing in his shorthand notebook. Darlington looked momentarily puzzled and whispered and at the same time gestured. *"Why aren't you taking notes?"*

Mahlon looked shocked. *"You mean you want me to continue after…"*

Darlington nodded earnestly and wrote a note on his pad and passed it to Mahlon.

> *You've just gotten one of the best lessons you'll ever learn in life as a newspaperman. Trust no one! Now get to work. Trust me!*

He smiled encouragingly, as if to say, "Buck up and get a grip!"

The three justices conferred for a few moments, after which Judge Chapman rendered the decision. "Motion for directed verdict is denied. The case will proceed."

The day's proceedings ended with Professor Rogers giving a recitation on the usual symptoms of poisoning by strychnine, as he had done countless times before in innumerable cases.

"The initial symptoms usually appear within fifteen to thirty minutes after ingestion, which are tightness and twitching of the muscles, agitation, and hyperreflexia. Convulsions and hyperreactivity to stimuli are also characteristic of strychnine poisoning. The patient is usually conscious and has intense pain. The body arches backwards in hyper-extension. The eyes are usually widely opened, and the pupils are dilated. The facial muscles contract producing a characteristic expression known as 'risus sardonicus'. Long-term complications include lactic acidosis, rhabdomyolysis, and acute renal failure. The convulsions may recur repeatedly and each episode is followed by a period of relaxation."

"And to sum it up, Professor, death eventually comes by....?"

"Death is caused by asphyxia or medullary paralysis," Rogers concluded.

"Thank you, Doctor, I believe that is all I have for you," Ross said and looked over at Lear, who half rose and said, "No questions, Your Honors. We can adjourn for the evening, if you like."

As soon as the justices dismissed the courtroom, Mahlon rose and walked quickly over toward Langhorn, who was having the manacles and shackles put back on by the Sheriff before being led away. He stood stoically, staring straight ahead with an angry scowl darkening his face.

"I'm so sorry," Mahlon gestured more than said, but Lang was still too stunned and angry to pay attention. It was as if this massive, almost life-long, conspiracy was unfolding before his eyes, and this boy was just a small part of it. Even his own attorney, George Lear, had just walked out of the courtroom practically arm-in-arm with District Attorney Ross, chatting amiably as they all left for their homes and waiting families and dinners. Lang had nothing but a cold, empty cell to look forward to. *And never again, if these people have any say about it, will I ever know the warmth of family and home...not that I ever did have much of it in my life.*

Next morning, Saturday, September 17, 1865, the trial continued with a veritable parade of people. For Lang, it was as if his life was flashing before his eyes. Like he'd heard people say happened when you came close to death. And most of these folks didn't tell it the way he remembered it happening, either.

First was Jimmy Acor, the peddler. "I am in the commission business," he said. "I was running the wagon down Canada Hill when Wellings come out and applied to me to bring an article from Philadelphia."

"And what was that?" Ross asked.

"He asked me if I could get him any Quaker button. Then, he came to my house on Sunday following, and asked me if I got it. I told him I had not, and he asked me to get it the next week."

"And did you get it for him then?"

"No, sir. I did not. But, he came the third time, and I finally promised to get it the following week. I went to a drug store and asked for it and he came the next Sunday again, and I gave it to him."

"And how much would you say there was?"

"I got ten cents worth. It made about the size of a quarter of a pound of pepper, or a quarter of a pound of tea."

"And was that close to the time his wife took sick?"

"Yes. He got the poison on Sunday before she was taken sick."

"Did he give any reason for wanting the poison?"

"No, sir. He gave no reason for wanting the poison, but on other occasions he told me had, or thought he had, a purchaser for his property, and his wife said she would not agree to sell it as long as she lived, but after she was gone, she said he might do as he pleased with it. He said one time that he wished she would hurry up and leave." Acor put his head down with a sad expression on his face.

"And your suspicions were thereby aroused?" Ross asked.

"Yes, sir. That 'n other things he said didn't set right with me. I don't like to hear nobody talk like that."

"I understand."

Next was Jimmy Acor's wife who testified: "I remember Wellings coming to our house. We live about a mile and a half apart. I think it was on the Sunday before New Year. It was definitely a Sunday, and it was just before his wife was taken sick. He said, 'Jim, did you get that for me?' And Jim brought it to Langhorn and said, 'This is poison, be careful.' I then said, 'Whose dog are you going to kill?' And he replied, 'I said nothing about killing dogs, did I?'"

"Do you think he was… Let me phrase this another way. What do you think he meant by that?"

"I don't know, sir. Whether he was telling me he didn't want anyone to know who done it if a dog did actually come up dead or…"

"Whether he meant it for something—or someone—else."

"Yes, sir."

"What happened then?"

"Well, I think I then asked him how Mary was doing. He said she was pretty well today. She seemed better than common."

"And did he mention anything about selling the property that day?"

"It wasn't that day, but sometime before he had said he had an offer for his property, but his wife would not let him sell it. She said he should have it after her death, and he said in a joking manner, 'I wish she would hurry up and die,' or something like that."

"Were you surprised or shocked by that?"

"Well, yes. I said, 'Tis better not to speak the truth sometimes, even in jest.'"

Neighbor William Samsel came up next. He testified briefly about how long he had known the Wellings family and in particular about a conversation he had with Langhorn some four or five weeks before Mary's death.

"Langhorn told me that he and his wife had not lived together as man and woman ought to live for the last nine years, and he was tired of it. He said he was going to have a woman that was a woman."

Upon being questioned on cross-examination by Lear, Samsel told the court and jury that he had first told this to someone about a month or two ago—"it was after Mrs. Wellings' body had been brought up"—and that, when Langhorn had said, "Nine years, I took it to mean it was since the boy, Jonas, was born, which was really more like twelve years."

The next witness was a young man who was somewhat acquainted with Langhorn, though not closely. Charles Coates testified that Lang came to his father's place just following Mrs. Wellings' death and, finding the elder Coates not at home, had a conversation with young Charles:

"We talked about my upcoming marriage. He inquired as to where we was going to live and other small talk. He said I would find it much nicer living a married life than running over the country a single man. It was teasing, like, winking—an older man to a young man about to get married, you know?" Young Coates looked down and blushed a little.

"Yes, I understand. What did the defendant say next?"

"Well, he said, 'I buried my old woman the other day, but she has not been of any use to me to sleep with for three years.' He said she had been sick a great deal in her life and had been a great expense to him.

Then he said, 'When she was taken this last time, I knew she would never get up again.'"

"And what did you understand that conversation to mean?"

"I took it, and I think he actually said, that people should not think strange of it if he got another wife pretty soon. We was talkin' as if man to man about gettin' married."

Several other prosecution witnesses testified briefly, including Allen Bye who said he had lived peaceably all these years with Wellings, had even employed him on occasion, and claimed that none of his dogs had ever been loose or missing.

On cross-examination by Lear, Bye admitted there had indeed been a number of running dogs in the neighborhood over the years, some of which were rabid. "Oh, yes. It's been a terrible problem, I know. That's why I take such care with my hunting dogs, that none of them gets out of the yard. I can't speak for my neighbors, though."

Then came the three neighbor women who had taken care of Mary in her last illness: Julia Brown, Maria Chapman, and Rachel Pearson. They had been close friends and neighbors for nearly twenty years.

Julia Brown testified particularly about tending to Mary on the Saturday after she was taken sick with her final illness. "He—Langhorn—told me Mrs. Pearson and Mrs. Chapman were there when she was taken; they helped to wait on her. She was lying quietly in bed when I first went there, but she got very restless several times."

"Did she respond to you in any way?" Ross asked.

"She could not speak, but looked at me as if she knew me. I think she could hear."

"And what was her general condition?"

"Well, in appearance, her face was very red when I went, but after that she turned pale. Her teeth were clenched. Julia Anne Yeomans told me how to administer the medicine, which was there prepared at the time, but I never saw that she could take it."

"Did she particularly favor either side of her body?"

"Yes. She seemed to be paralyzed on the right side, and when she became restless, the side which she had the use of she would throw her limb, and use her hand at her head. Then, during the attack, she would draw her arms up and clench her hands. When her feet and legs were straightened out, she would draw them immediately back up."

Ross then asked her about the medicine in the sickroom, and Mrs. Brown replied, "When I first went, Langhorn said, 'This is the medicine for her to take,' and he showed me two cups sitting on the bureau. There was a dark medicine, I think, he said she was to take every two hours, but I could not be positive, and a lighter-colored medicine I think every three hours."

Ross produced a cup with a dark liquid, sort of like coffee or dark tea and asked the witness if this resembled one of the medicines that was at Mrs. Wellings' bedside.

"No," Mrs. Brown said, "the liquid was darker than this and this does not smell like the mixture given to Mary. I saw Langhorn try to give her some medicine once, but Mary lifted her hand and pushed the spoon away, or turned her head away. That was on Sunday forenoon. He took the spoon and poured it in her mouth, but she did not take it willingly."

"Now, as to the defendant, what was his general mood? Did he speak to you at all about his wife's illness?"

"Langhorn said she had suffered very much, and would not get over it. He seemed to be cheerful. He was talking to everyone there. I said to Mrs. Gibbs he did not appear to mind it much."

The next witness, Mrs. Chapman, described what she had found on the Friday evening she was sent for. "It was between sundown and dark on Friday evening. The little boy came and said his mother was sick. I went in right away and found Mrs. Wellings sitting on the side of the bed. Her daughter, Elizzie, was by her, bathing her throat and breast."

"Will you describe for us Mrs. Wellings' general condition when you found her?"

"She appeared oppressed for breath. Someone said she had had one of her bad spells—I think it was Langhorn said she was taken in the kitchen. She sat on the edge of the bed and appeared very uncomfortable."

"What did you do?"

"I asked her daughter if she did not think she would be more comfortable sitting in a chair. Elizzie said her mother could not breathe well while lying down. She asked her mother if she would have a chair, and Mary made an answer, which I did not fully understand. I sent Langhorn over to my house to get a chair, and while he was gone she fell or laid over upon the bed, on her left side. When he came back, we lifted her upon the pillow. Some time after that she had a convulsion."

"Did she say anything to you?"

"Yes, she was conscious when I first went there, knew everything that was going on around her, but after she fell over, I never heard her speak again."

"And she was not paralyzed at the beginning?"

"I do not think she was paralyzed at that time, at least she appeared to use her hands and arms and limbs for anything I could tell. It might have been a half hour or an hour after I got there, when she had the convulsion after she was laid upon the pillow. The first we noticed the convulsion, she commenced moving her mouth. Next she commenced moving her arms." Mrs. Chapman demonstrated how Mary's arms moved during the attack. "She would throw her arms about and clench her hands, and we endeavored to open them."

"Why is that? Why did you try to open her hands, that is?"

"Well, I had heard that opening the hands would break the fit."

"How long did the attack last?"

"It lasted five minutes. It might have been longer and might not have been quite so long."

"And what was her general condition after the attack—was she conscious? Did she know you?"

"I cannot say whether she was conscious or not after the convulsion went off, and I don't remember whether she knew me or not after the convulsion. In fact, I cannot tell whether she knew anyone after she laid over on the bed. Before that she did."

Mrs. Chapman went on to describe the next attack, which occurred about an hour from the first. "It came on the same as the first. We first saw it in her face, then she straightened out her arms and clenched her hands. We opened her hands easily. She then threw her arms about. I think I took her hand in mine and opened it with the other. She remained on her back, but I seem to recall she raised her body a little from the bed."

She said Langhorn tried to minister to his wife by putting the handle of a tablespoon in her mouth.

"Why did he do that?" Ross asked.

"He said he was afraid she would bite her tongue. Doctor had advised him what to do, he said."

Mary apparently had the third attack after Dr. Cernea arrived. Mrs. Chapman was not by the bedside at that time.

Ross asked about Langhorn's overall demeanor during his wife's illness, and Mrs. Chapman responded, "Langhorn appeared very sorry, I thought. I saw him shed tears at times, and I believe he acted as any other man would, I suppose. I think I heard him say that they might look for it—Mary's death—at any time, what with her going off in one of those spells, and I think he said he told the children when they helped her in, that that would be the last time they would have to help her. He said it sorrowful-like, final."

Next, Ross questioned the witness about her observations of her next-door neighbors. The homes of the Chapmans and the Wellingses were separated by a small yard.

"I never saw anything to the contrary but what they lived agreeable, as far as I know."

"Did you ever hear Langhorn say something about getting another wife?"

"Yes." Mrs. Chapman said quietly. She seemed reluctant to continue and had to be prodded by the District Attorney to tell the details.

"It was sometime before his wife's last sickness. I don't recollect all the conversation, but he was in our house and conversing with my husband. He spoke of his wife being sick a great deal of the time. That was the time he said Dr. Cernea had attended her for many years and he wished her to have another doctor. He said he would employ any doctor she wanted. In particular, he wanted her to let him call Doctor Fell in, who was attending at our house."

"Why did he want her to change doctors, do you know?"

"Well, for one, Mary didn't appear to be getting any better, and Langhorn said we should call in another doctor to see if something else couldn't be done for her. For another, Dr. Cernea was so far away over in Centreville—it took us near an hour to fetch him—and Dr. Fell was closer. And I think he had a special affinity for the Fell family, as well."

"But Mrs. Wellings was not willing?"

"No, she was not willing to have any other doctor than Cernea. He had attended them so long she said she would rather have him than a stranger."

"And this was the occasion when he spoke of getting another wife—even before Mrs. Wellings had suffered her final earthly trial?" Ross exaggerated the final phrase dramatically.

Mrs. Chapman looked down, embarrassed. "Yes," she said finally. "It was during this conversation I heard Langhorn say that he would take all the care of his wife while she lived that he could and bury her as decently as he possibly could when she died. And then he said he did not think he would do long or a great while without another wife, if he could get one."

"Oh? Is that so? And did he say anything else about this 'other wife'?"

"Well, he said he would not marry a woman darker than himself and as much lighter as he could get her."

"Interesting. Are you aware of whether he had anyone in mind at that time?"

"He did not indicate any person as being then in his eye."

"Were there ever any women who came around the house of the prisoner?"

"No. I cannot recollect any female in particular who visited, and I don't recollect ever seeing a strange female staying at his house. There was no one snoopin' around to move in and take over, if that's what you're referring to," she said and frowned at Ross.

On cross-examination questioning by Lear, Mrs. Chapman's demeanor softened considerably. She testified that Langhorn's attention to his wife "was tender and careful, for all I could see."

Rachel Pearson reaffirmed the previous testimony of the other neighbor women as to Mary's last days and final illness. When asked about the relationship of Mr. and Mrs. Wellings in all the years she had known them, she said, "They lived agreeably together during the twenty years that they lived near us, for anything that I know."

All that morning the prosecution witnesses came: Neighbors, peddler Acor, and several men that Langhorn had worked for and to whom he had made statements about his life and marriage—he thought in the act of sharing confidences with friends. Never in his life did he dream these "friends" would turn on him. He remembered something Joseph had told him years ago, that when someone is truly your friend, you can't do anything wrong in their eyes, and if someone does not like you, you'll never be able to do anything right.

Joseph. Joseph Fell, his dearest friend and supporter in the world, was absent.

"Mr. Fell's an important man, Lang," Lear explained. He's got business to attend to. In fact, I think he's even in Philadelphia or Harrisburg right now consulting with people about setting up schools here for orphans from the war. Besides, in my opinion, it's not a good idea for him to testify. He knows everything about you. Bill Johnson, too. They've known you too long, if you know what I mean."

Lang tried to understand. True enough, Joseph and Bill both had come to the prison quickly to comfort their friend. True enough, Joseph had gathered contributions from his friends and assured Lang not to worry about the money for the lawyer.

But, as he gazed at the sea of faces in the gallery, he couldn't help but feel a profound letdown. *If only I could see Joseph, I could get through all this. I could face anything.* As many of us do, he had grounded himself in one human being, which Joseph would be the first to tell him was not a smart thing to do.

"We come into this world alone, and we will go out alone," Joseph would have said. "If we have friends and loved ones along the way, we are truly blessed. But, in truth, we must learn to rely on God alone, not fallible fellow human beings, for our spiritual support and sustenance. And that is deep within you, in your heart, if you only turn your inner eye to it.

"Be strong, Brother Langhorn."

"Besides, Lang," Attorney Lear had reassured him, "Joseph has sent John Balderston in his place, and I think you will agree that Squire Balderston is an excellent choice for a spokesman in your behalf."

Lang, of course, was well acquainted with Balderston, who was director of the Emlen Institute in Solebury and had been Ruth Ann's employer just before her death. Lang himself had limed the fields and helped out in other ways on numerous occasions over the years at the school. He understood after Balderston testified why he had been chosen and acknowledged that Joseph had made a brilliant choice.

On Saturday afternoon, the parade of defense witnesses began, which lifted the mood of the trial and made the proceedings a little brighter for Lang. These people were truly his friends—Maggie and Andrew Hartless, John Balderston, neighbor Fred Pearson, and Mahlon and Elizabeth Gibbs.

Balderston probably was the most impressive and important of all the witnesses, prosecution or defense. In his sixties, a tall, dignified man with a large build and calm demeanor, Balderston was a well known and highly-esteemed member of the Society of Friends and a successful businessman as well as superintendent of the Emlen Institute. It was generally understood that he was to be chosen the next Justice of the Peace in Solebury Township, a fact not lost on the justices and jury in the courtroom.

"I've known Langhorn practically all his life, but closely for near on to fifteen years now," Balderston said as he testified about how Lang lived in Lahaska and moved to Solebury so many years ago and how he had worked at the Emlen Institute over the years. "I know for a fact that he's not had an easy life. He's worked hard since he was a child to provide for first himself and then his family. He's an exemplary father and was a devoted husband as long as Mrs. Wellings was in our midst. He's suffered more than his fair share of tribulations along the way, but I've never seen him give up, as weaker men would have done in his stead."

"Do you think he is capable of murder?" Lear asked.

"Absolutely not."

Fred Pearson told of a conversation he'd had with Lang when they were shelling corn toward the end of December last year.

"It was sometime during the afternoon when the conversation started about dogs, and their trespassing on his property. He stated that people found fault with his shooting them, so he would have to take a more quiet way to put them out of the way."

"Did he mention any dogs in particular?" Lear asked.

"He named no particular dogs, with the exception of one, and that was Allen Bye's. He said the dog was in the practice of chasing cattle and running upon his lot. But, he said the powder he got from Acor was of little use. He saw the dog running around after he had supposedly eaten the poisoned meat."

On cross-examination by Ross, the problem of ownership of the property was brought up.

"Did the defendant ever speak to you about selling his lot?" Ross asked.

"I have heard him say he would like to sell the lot, but she would not agree to it. The property was hers, so…"

Ross stopped and looked at Pearson. "I'm sorry. Did you say the property was hers? You mean sole and separate property? They didn't own it jointly?"

"Yes, her property. She apparently bought it in trust, oh, twenty years ago or more."

"And do you know why it was done that way?"

"I understood she bought it with an inheritance or some such. And that it had something to do with protecting Lang, actually—that folks could never say he married her for personal and financial gain."

Ross jumped in. "But, it would certainly give him additional motive to murder her."

"Oh, no! I wouldn't say that. The kids inherited the property when she died. It was according to the deed, I'm sure of that. He wouldn't have any say after she died."

Ross' expectant balloon suddenly deflated. He sent a clerk over to the recorder's office to look at the deed and, sure enough, Langhorn Wellings "or any future husband" was specifically excluded from ownership. That was certainly curious, Ross thought, but he did not pursue it any further.

Lear changed his mind right then about calling Andy Hartless as a witness. No sense giving Ross a chance to delve into this property situation any further. Mahlon Gibbs would be a good witness, and he had known Lang for as many years.

Mahlon testified for a long time about his relationship with Lang, then Lear asked him about the poison.

"Langhorn told me in December he was going to get some Quaker button to dispatch some dogs which ran over his premises."

"Did he say whose dogs?" Lear asked.

"No, he did not tell me whose dogs. But he afterwards said he shot a dog and that he had got the poison, but that he had tried the poison on a dog, and it never fazed him. He said he saw the dog living afterward and that he thought the poison was 'good for nothing'."

"Did he tell you what he did with the poison after?"

"Yes. He told me he kept it in a bureau drawer, where his papers were kept."

"And did he say how, if at all, his wife could have taken any of it?"

"He didn't say nothing about his wife having taken it until after he came to prison, and then he said Mary could not have taken any of it, for the box it was in was full, and none had been taken out."

Mahlon actually provided the only light moment of the whole two-day trial. It was on cross-examination by Ross, when Ross asked him whether Lang had mentioned anything about remarrying after Mary died.

"Well, I don't remember anything specific. He may have said something. But, I naturally assumed he would have to find another wife. It's a matter of fact. No way he could be alone and take proper care of the house and the boy 'specially."

"So, if I hear what you're saying, then, it sounds like he was eager for his wife to die so's he could get himself a new bride?"

Before Lear could object that Ross was leading the witness, Mahlon shouted, "No! He didn't say nothin' like that." Mahlon looked over at Lang with a pained expression in his eyes, then up at the judges. "I didn't mean it like that, Judge. Lang was lonesome-like. Mary had been sick for many years…"

Ross walked closer to the bench and in an imperious tone of voice said, "Perhaps you could explain to the witness, Your Honor, that he has no way of knowing what was in his friend's head or what he meant by his words."

"Then neither do you, seems to me!" Mahlon shot back at him, causing the courtroom to break out in laughter.

Judge Chapman banged the gavel lightly to bring the room back to order.

The final witness was Elizzie. Shy, frightened Elizzie.

"I should like to call the defendant's daughter now," Lear said.

"Mary Elizabeth Welling!" crier Johnny James' voice rang out. (The clerks continually cut the 's' off the end of their name throughout the whole trial and even wrote "Welling" on all the court documents.)

Elizzie froze in her seat, and Elizabeth Gibbs gave her a hug of encouragement. She rose and, with all the courage she could muster, walked to the witness box. Her long skirts covered the special-made, raised shoe that made her legs an even length, but, even so, she had a slight, noticeable limp.

Lear patted her hand and apologized. "We're sorry to have to put you through this, dear. We'll make it as brief as possible."

Under questioning, Elizzie told a little about the family and home and how her mother had been sick for many years before her final release in January of this year. She spoke so quietly that Judge Troxel, who was closest to her, had to lean over several times and ask her to "Speak up, child. We can't hear you."

Shortly, Lear got down to the real point of her testimony. "There was an occasion last December, just before your mother died, was there not, that your father brought home some poison? Would you describe that for us?"

"Yes, it was in December, I think, about two weeks before my mother died. Father brought the poison home from Acor's. He set it on the table and asked for a tin box, one with a lid on it."

"Did he tell you what it was?"

"Yes. He said he had some poison he wanted to put in it. He said, 'I have some poison here.' He held it in his hand and showed it to us all—mother, Jonas and I—and said he was going to put it in the bureau drawer, where he kept his papers, and that we should be careful and not touch it because it was poison."

"And do you know what happened to that poison?"

"Yes. Dr. Cernea took it away."

"And how do you know that?

"Because he asked me for it, and I gave it to him."

"Do you think your father poisoned your mother? That he could have murdered her?"

"Oh, no, sir!" Elizzie's voice became more voluble and quivered with emotion. "My father would never have done that. He cared very much for my mother. I know he did." She looked over at Lang with love and fear and tears all readily apparent in her eyes.

Jesse Knight, foreman of the jury, told Mahlon Riegel later that every man on the jury probably made up his mind right then and there. Every one of them undoubtedly would have wished to have a daughter look at them as lovingly and sure of his uprightness and innocence as Elizzie looked at her father that evening. Even Ross was moved and declined to cross-examine.

"The defense rests, Your Honors," Lear announced, and there was some discussion about how the trial would proceed. Since it was close to dinnertime, after conferring briefly, the justices decided to continue with closing arguments, then break for dinner at Brower's and come back to begin the jury's deliberations that evening. A nod to and from the jury confirmed their agreement.

There was something about the mood of the courtroom that Lang found disconcerting. He could not directly put his finger on it, but these men were awfully relaxed—almost jolly—to be preparing to put a man to death by hanging. He could swear, as well, that some of them imbibed a bit too much at dinner. It's like the trial—his life and death—had turned into some sort of party to which everyone but him had been invited.

Before the dinner break, as Lang was being manacled and chained to be taken to the holding cell for his dinner, Lear had patted his hand and said, very confidently, "Don't worry, Lang. Everything's going to be fine." Then he strode out of the courtroom to go to dinner, apparently, with everyone else.

It had been like this for Lang for the past nine months. *They're going to hang me. No, they're going to set me free. No, they've made up their minds I'm guilty....* and so on, back and forth.

But, when they assembled back in the courtroom at eight o'clock, and Judge Chapman gave an almost perfunctory charge to the jury—"If you feel there is a reasonable doubt that the defendant murdered his wife, Mary Wellings, by the administration of poison..."—the speed with which the jury went into the deliberation room and filed right back out with the verdict was almost dizzying.

Five minutes.

It might even have set a record for the fastest jury verdict in Bucks County history. Five minutes.

"We find the defendant not guilty, Your Honors, of all charges," Jesse Knight proclaimed.

Lang closed his eyes and shuddered with relief. He turned to accept handshakes first from Lear, then, surprisingly, the Sheriff. He glanced up at the justices, as Judge Chapman banged the gavel.

"Not guilty. The prisoner is released. The jury is dismissed with our heartfelt gratitude for your selfless, sacrificial service..." Blah, blah. "Court is adjourned." Bang!

It's a good thing the thought process takes as long as it does sometimes. It would take Lang another several days, sitting alone in the privacy of his home, before he would get angry again. By that time everyone had scattered all over the County, back to their homes and families and businesses.

Why'd they put me through that for all those months if they knew there was no cause, no evidence... No answer would ever come. That's just the way it was. Some people were truly your friends and others never would be.

And it's a good thing Lang didn't overhear Knight, as he was being interviewed by Mahlon Riegel, when he said, "Oh, we made up our minds this afternoon. It was just a formality, but some of us knew we would have to stay in Doylestown one more night anyway, and we wanted to have dinner."

LOCAL AFFAIRS

Trial of Langhorn Wellings for Murder. —This case, mentioned by us in our Court reports last week, and of which we publish the evidence given at the trial this week, is one that excited a great deal of public attention at the time the defendant was first arrested. The defendant is about three-fourths colored, while his wife was entirely white. They had lived together in Solebury township for 20 years or more, and had raised a family of children. Public opinion then set decidedly against him, but the result of the trial now seems to prove that their opinion did him injustice. For the evidence, as will be seen, entirely failed to show that Mrs. Wellings was poisoned. But the defendant's conduct in rather many remarks made by him shortly before and after his wife's death, was improper, and highly calculated to cause him to be suspected of having caused his wife's death. Then it was known that he had sent to the city for a quantity of poison-sometimes called Quaker Button-only the Sunday before his wife had taken sick. And the general belief was that the symptoms of her sickness were those commonly caused by this poison. She had long been in bad health, but near the end of December last she was taken much worse. On December 30th, Dr. A.D. Cernea was sent for, and January 3d, she died. About a month afterwards her body was exhumed, and the stomach and contents sent to Prof. R.E. Rogers, of Philadelphia, for examination. He found slight indications of something resembling poison, but, if it was poison, it was not in quantity sufficient to destroy life. But the story was currently reported in this county, after Prof. Rogers had finished his analysis some two months ago, that he had found a large quantity of strychnine, which is the poison found in nux vomica, or what is commonly called the Quaker Button. The defendant was thereby rendered very miserable, for however innocent he might be, if poison in considerable quantity had been found in his wife's stomach, he would almost certainly be hung. But now the story as to the poisoning proved untrue, and the previous fears have been wasted. The Commonwealth failed to make out a case, and the jury almost without a moment's deliberation, rendered a verdict of not guilty. H.P. Ross & G. Ross for Commonwealth; Lear, James and Harvey for defendant.

[*Bucks County Intelligencer*, Tuesday Morning, Sept. 26, 1865]

Chapter XI

Bucks County
November 1880

The five-thirty train from New York to Philadelphia was late getting into the Lambertville station, and as Mahlon stepped onto the platform, he worried whether he would be able to catch the coach to Doylestown. Luck was with him this evening. The coach had waited for the train since the driver knew there were several passengers on board for Doylestown, and Mahlon was relieved to know he would be at Brower's Hotel in Doylestown within an hour and a half in time for dinner.

"It's called the Fountainhouse or Corson's now, sir," the driver said.

"Of course, I knew that," Mahlon laughed. "I just can't get used to the new name." The hotel had been purchased by William Corson and, in May 1872, the well in front was topped with a large public fountain, thus the new names. In 1876, a fourth story and mansard roof were added.

Mahlon continued a brief conversation he had started with a man on the train who was also going to Doylestown, and as he settled back into his seat and looked out the window he realized they were shortly coming up to the steep incline known as Canada Hill. The coachman slowed the pace of the horses somewhat as they went easily down the hill. Even so, it was already dark, and Mahlon had to strain to get a glimpse of the little white Baptist church and the cemetery where he knew a new grave contained the remains of Langhorn H. Wellings.

He had learned of Wellings' death from one of the Paschall brothers, cousins of Henry Darlington, who along with Darlington's widow, Susan, were running the *Intelligencer* since Henry's death in 1878. Paschall was visiting Mahlon in his office in New York City.

"Hey, an old friend of yours died last Saturday," Paschall had suddenly remembered as he was getting up to leave.

"Oh? Who's that?"

"That Wellings fellow. The black guy who poisoned his wife."

Mahlon hung his head and wagged it back and forth. He was more than a little vexed that his initial hearing of the news, and thus his ability to be appropriately surprised and then mourn for Wellings, were ruined by this man's ignorance.

"He was acquitted, Al. He didn't kill his wife. Ross kept him in jail and raked him over the coals for nothing. Remember?"

"Yeah, well, whatever. That's the guy. Apparently dropped dead the other day."

"I hope you get your news stories more accurately than your memory serves you," Mahlon teased. On the other hand, this was a minor example of a serious problem he had lately noticed—a tendency on the part of editors and publishers to taint news stories with their own interpretations and prejudices. It was developing into a disturbing trend in his opinion and he hoped it would not infect the *Intelligencer*, too.

"Hey, I'm the business partner, remember? I worry about paying the bills, you reporter guys worry about getting the facts straight," Paschall joked back.

The moment Mahlon heard the news about Wellings' death was one of those that would be forever etched in his mind. Mahlon would remember for the rest of his life that just before he heard Paschall say that Wellings was dead, he was looking at a dispatch on his desk stating that Lucretia Mott, life-long champion of women and African-Americans, had died the same week in Philadelphia. The irony did not escape him.

Fifteen years had gone by since that day in the old Bucks County Court House when Jesse Knight proclaimed, "We find the defendant not guilty." A great deal had transpired, including the fact that there was now a new Bucks County Courthouse, and it was even spelled differently. Across the street, the old frame *Intelligencer* office was torn down and replaced with a three-story brick building in 1876. That was the same year Darlington started publishing the paper twice a week. The new *Intelligencer* building was the last life work of architect Thomas Cernea, son of the doctor.

For Mahlon personally, the years had been an eventful time, almost from the moment he stepped out of the Court House on that September

Saturday evening and watched the vindicated accused walk away with one arm resting on his daughter's shoulder and with the sleeve of his other arm wiping away spontaneous tears. Mahlon remembered thinking at the time, *I want to learn how to describe scenes like this so completely and accurately that people will think they are there watching it. No...that they are there feeling it!*

He began at once to hone his new craft, so much so that others started to sit up and take notice. Within five years, he was approached by Dr. Edward Morwitz, publisher of the *Philadelphia Democrat*, a German--language paper, who informed Mahlon he was going to set up an English-language newspaper in New York that would be managed by a fellow named Mierson, an old friend Mahlon knew from the *Intelligencer*. They wanted Mahlon to come to New York and work for them. There would be a substantial increase in pay, not to mention the incredible stories in the city just awaiting his pen to be told.

The only drawback was that Morwitz was a Democrat, although he assured Mahlon he would not have to deal with political issues and would be free to write stories and articles on the social issues of the day that he felt strongly about. Mahlon promised to at least think about the idea.

By that time, there was nothing very compelling to keep him any longer in bucolic, remote Doylestown. His mother had passed away in 1867, within months of the birth of Mahlon and Nancy's second child, a daughter, in July of that year. Nancy had delivered their first-born, a son, in November 1865.

In 1870, real estate agent Andrew J. Larue had helped him sell the Cross Keys farm. Interestingly, it was a member of the new wave of German immigrants fleeing conflict in Europe—this time the Franco-Prussian war—who bought the place. Mahlon received five thousand dollars for the farm, a fair price, and a windfall for him since the family had owned the property outright for close to a hundred years, and there was no one with whom he had to share the inheritance.

After talking the offer over with Nancy, who expressed her willingness to get back into big city life—and was even excited at the prospect of living in New York—in the summer of 1871, they packed up the children and the household and moved to a brownstone on West 49th Street in Manhattan.

Mahlon began the New York phase of his newspaper career across the street from the new City Hall in the Bowery in a brick building that was built by fellow Bucks Countians Ben Solliday, Hank Livesay, and "N.B." Hubbard. Morwitz imported the masons from Bucks County to erect the building because housing and paying them was cheaper than using New York laborers.

That newspaper venture was a bust, and within a few years, Mahlon was looking for a new job. Fortunately, during those years he had made the acquaintance of several reporters and editors; one of them, George Jones of the *New York Times*, helped him secure a position on that paper, and his career continued after only a month or two of concern about his future.

His financial fortunes continued to increase, as well. Despite the advice of humorist Mark Twain to "Invest in one basket, and then watch that basket!", Mahlon decided to invest the money from the sale of the farm in three "baskets"—railroad stocks, bonds, and bank savings. He knew that if one of the portions foundered, the others would probably succeed and make up for it. To credit his good judgment, with the exception of one minor bank failure, all three generally prospered, and he was assured of having a substantial nest egg with which to educate his son, marry off his daughter in a wedding ceremony appropriate to her station in society, and eventually retire with Nancy some day, he hoped, to a small place back in Bucks County.

If only his marriage was as happy and successful as the other components of his life. *I guess one can't have everything*, Mahlon sighed whenever he thought about it. Nancy never did become convinced of the "bliss" part of "marital," and after their daughter was born, she informed him one evening that she would no longer indulge his carnal desires.

"But, what am I supposed to do? You're my wife! A man has needs," Mahlon protested.

"I don't know, dear. Do...well, do whatever other men do." She smiled with a sweet innocence and kissed him with a peck on the forehead. Shortly after, she moved into her own bedroom. "I need my rest. My days are so full and busy."

There were the children to care for and the household to run, with its one live-in and one full-time-daily servants. There were church functions and social affairs, in addition to numerous societies and committees a woman of Mrs. Riegel's position had to attend to. There was family to entertain sometimes for months at a time—her parents from

Virginia, where her father had retired from government service, and numerous friends, brothers, sisters, spouses and children.

Not to mention the plays, operas, symphonies and balls that proliferated in New York, which people of their social status were expected to attend.

Mahlon began frequenting "Casey's," a bar in the Bowery, along with many of his colleagues, and attending baseball games as often as possible. He was smoking cigars and drinking too much and his belly was beginning to fall over his belt, but he was otherwise in fairly good health for a man over forty.

It was at a company Christmas party a couple of years ago that Mahlon met a woman a few years younger than himself who worked in the society section of the paper, a widow whose husband had died in the war and left her with a small son to support. It was an instantaneous attraction. Shortly after, Mahlon set her up in a small apartment on the lower east side and arranged for her son to attend a prestigious private military academy, thus beginning a mutually-beneficial arrangement for everyone concerned, including Nancy who never asked what it was that "other men do."

In the meantime, he had risen to be a writer and editor of some importance on the paper, no longer expected to attend court sessions daily or follow down stories with his own shoe leather. He was writing pieces of substance—long, "in-depth" articles in which he could use his skills of description. He had traveled across the country several times—one especially memorable trip being a hunting expedition just last year to Dakota Territory with an affable young man named Teddy Roosevelt—and had paid for the trips by writing articles about them. Several of the pieces about New York were purchased by Darlington and printed in the *Intelligencer* under the headline "New York Correspondent."

Everything was generally going very well for Mahlon, but, for the past several months, he had been longing to get out of the city, and this news from Al Paschall provided the ticket. Maybe there was a story or two here. At a minimum, he could write about celebrating the holidays in a Pennsylvania Dutch village or some such.

He had been back to Doylestown several times since leaving in '71, most recently just two years ago for Henry Darlington's funeral in November 1878. That was a complete shock, and there was nothing much in life and death that shocked Mahlon anymore.

After the Wellings case, Henry Darlington and the other citizens of Bucks County were immediately off and involved in other things. Old feuds were patched, though never completely mended, and people got on to business at hand. Because they had to live together in a small community, there was no choice.

Henry and his *Doylestown Democratic* antagonist Col. W.W.H. Davis always came to "literary and verbal blows" during elections, and again when a scandal erupted in 1876 when the County Commissioners were arrested and put on trial for fraud. However, at the same time their respective newspapers carried on the political debates of the times, especially around the issues of suffrage and higher education for blacks and women, they often laid down their sometimes vitriolic pens to work together on various projects.

At once after the war, there was a committee formed to relieve famine and disease in the South and another group that banded together to build a large memorial dedicated to the 104th Regiment, which was erected in front of the Court House in 1868. Rev. Silas Andrews also joined in that effort, in addition to his many other community services.

Col. Davis donated the remainder of the moneys collected for the memorial to build a new public fountain in front of the Court House, and Henry noted in the *Intelligencer* that was nice, but somewhat like trying to "paint up an old lady." He began in earnest campaigning for a new courthouse and almost weekly made some comment about how disgraceful, rundown, and inadequate the old place had become.

Several times the *Democrat* offered its presses to Henry, as problems plagued his old and outdated machines, especially in October 1868 when Henry was trying to print the County Fair Journal.

Henry and Col. Davis cooperated again in 1872 on a committee to prevent visitors to the county fair from being fleeced by gamblers and "sharpers." There were veterans societies, another group to form the first Bucks County Fire Company, and they worked together on the Centennial Committee to plan befitting celebrations around the County for America's one hundredth birthday.

One of the most interesting corroborations between the two was in April 1876 when the Guernellas, a husband-and-wife team of escape artist and magicians, came to entertain. Col. Davis and Henry, along with H.C. Michener and William Harr, were called up to the stage to ensure against deception and to prevent the possibility of aid from parties concealed about the stage. They watched as Dr. L.W. Closson tied Signor Guernella with ropes and locks and placed him in a box. The gaslights were put out for a few seconds and the men all watched in astonishment as Guernella appeared outside the box, unshackled, when the lights came up again.

By that time, escapes from the old, dilapidated jailhouse had become so common that it was a standing joke in the County, and someone stood up and yelled from the audience, "Hey we got a jail full of these escape artists! Sheriff Reinhart ought to hire this fellow Guernella to 'shore up' the Fort!"

Beginning with the Wellings trial, Col. Davis bought and printed several articles from Mahlon in those years. Not having a court reporter of his own for the *Democrat* for a time, Davis provided to Mahlon a much-needed, additional source of income. Mahlon quickly discovered in those years that one can easily put aside one's political differences if it meant paying for the doctor (or in their case, midwife) and putting food on the table. This was particularly true after both the *Intelligencer* and the *Democrat* published a very lengthy article on the County Teachers' Institute in 1867—just in time to pay for his new baby daughter.

Davis was elected to the Town Council in 1868 and basically turned over the day-to-day operation of the *Democrat* to others while he became involved in writing, first, the history of the 104th Regiment and, next, the large and impressive *History of Bucks County Pennsylvania From the Discovery of the Delaware to the Present Time* and giving speeches at "Tea Drynkes" and other functions in honor of the country's centennial celebration.

He successfully fought off an extortion conspiracy by several colored people in 1870, who tried to charge him with fathering a child by one of the women while in North Carolina in 1863. They claimed the woman with the child had followed Davis north to Bucks County after the war, but, in the end, it was proved beyond doubt that the woman had never been out of Bucks County, while Col. Davis had been almost continuously away during the war.

That was a real tragedy and especially a serious setback to Henry's cause of improving race relations and raising the social status and welfare of the coloreds in Bucks County. This incident, along with other crimes committed by blacks ranging from vagrancy and petty theft to murder, did not do much to endear members of the Negro race to the white people of Bucks County, and Henry made a special measure to highlight in the *Intelligencer* positive accomplishments by the county's colored residents in an effort to mitigate the damage.

It didn't occur to anyone that the far more prevalent criminal activities of whites, including a burglary of Col. Davis' home in 1876 which netted the thieves two hundred dollars' worth of goods, did nothing whatsoever to affect the Caucasians' overall social status and perception in society.

After the war, Henry immediately commenced work on several municipal committees, including one dedicated to preserving and improving the Doylestown Cemetery and the Doylestown Water Works, a group devoted to the enormous task of bringing piped water from a reservoir to all of the homes and businesses in town.

He became actively involved in the Bucks County Agricultural Society and regularly printed almost verbatim that Society's consultations, as well as the deliberations of other farmers' clubs, so that farmers all over the county, and elsewhere, where former Bucks Countians continued to maintain their subscriptions, could benefit from the combined experience and knowledge.

In September 1869, Henry and Susan took a six-week trip to Wisconsin, Iowa and Kansas to inspect the Indian agencies of the Northern Superintendency, mainly the Santee, Winnebago, Omaha, Pawnee, Otoe, Missouri and Great Nemeha tribes. Immediately returning, he wrote several articles on his findings and joined with Joseph Fell and others concerned with the welfare of the indigenous peoples to form Indian Relief Societies.

Several agency superintendents and physicians were chosen from among the members of the Society of Friends. In 1870, Dr. Cernea sold his practice to one such returning home and retired to a small house in Buckingham to pursue his study of the area's botany.

In 1874, Henry was elected a Director of the Doylestown Library Company and Director of the Normal School at West Chester in his old home of Chester County. The district included Bucks, Montgomery, Delaware and Chester Counties and took Henry away from home on several occasions for meetings and school inspections.

The problem of wild and rabid dogs still continued throughout the years after the Wellings trial. Several people were bitten, and at least two children died of hydrophobia. Many animals were destroyed, including at Emlen Institute where hundreds of chickens and turkeys were killed by a pack of dogs. In counteraction, numerous townships followed the example of Doylestown when, in March 1869, the council mandated licensing and muzzling of dogs. A bounty of two dollars was offered for killing an unmuzzled dog running free in the town.

There was, in addition, a devastating horse disease epidemic in the mid-1870s, and many hundreds of valuable animals were lost. A chapter of the Society for the Prevention of Cruelty to Animals was set up in Doylestown, with Henry, Rev. Andrews and Col. Davis all appointed as charter members. Their mission was not only to protect animals from depraved humans, but also to study and hopefully eliminate these animal diseases once and for all.

As for H.P. Ross, in April 1869, he was nominated by most of the members of the Bucks County Bar to fill the position of Associate Law Judge for Bucks and Montgomery Counties. Though Governor Geary failed to make the appointment at that time, Ross was eventually elected to the position by the voters in October of that year. In 1871, when the two counties split their judicial districts, he elected to stay in Montgomery County and moved permanently to Norristown.

Ross' life was certainly not without its share of troubles, as well. He was personally plagued with poor health, and his first wife died rather young of consumption in November 1873. He was robbed by pickpockets in Philadelphia, and in 1874 sustained a severe cut on his head when a train he was riding in lurched suddenly. Still, he managed to fulfill his professional responsibilities, "admirably," as the *Intelligencer* remarked on more than one occasion, probably in respectful acknowledgement of his struggles to overcome the many vicissitudes of life.

In December 1874, H.P. married Emily Genung of Brooklyn, New York, and, after a long honeymoon in Florida for the winter season, they returned to their home in Norristown, H.P. being "much improved in health," the *Intelligencer* happily reported. Within two years, in November 1876, their firstborn, who died shortly after birth, was buried on a cold, rainy morning in the Doylestown Cemetery.

Perhaps the prime example of altruistic work in the face of personal tragedy was Rev. Silas Milton Andrews. There was hardly an event, committee or cause for the common good in Bucks County that Rev. Andrews was not involved in from the time of his appointment to the Doylestown Presbyterian Church in 1831, despite the death of his wife and several children, including his only surviving daughter Mary, married to a Mr. Thompson of Philadelphia, who died of consumption at the age of twenty-six in 1877.

The most fulfilling activity for Rev. Andrews personally was divided between overseeing the renovation and expansion of the Presbyterian Church, the cornerstone of which he laid in June 1871, and the fact that he accomplished more than eleven hundred wedding ceremonies in his fifty-year career, especially including that of his son, Robert, who came all the way from Denver just to be married by his father.

George Lear, in addition to practicing law for many years, took up a new vocation: Politics and public speaking. He toured the county giving lectures at Republican meetings and entertainments at lyceums and schools on the rather interesting subjects of "Humbugs" and "The Heroes of Private Life." He and H.P. Ross' brother, George, were both elected representatives to the Constitutional Convention in 1874. And, in December 1875 Lear was appointed by Governor Hartranft as Attorney-General of the Commonwealth.

Thinking back on his experiences with all of these individuals, Mahlon observed how often personal adversarial relationships seemed to flare up and die down, ebb and flow, over the years among people who are forced to work together in a small community. He also concluded that no one on this earth is either all bad or all good, that humans are capable of joining hands to work for a great common cause one moment and the next will be at each other's throats. He had seen it happen literally, as Town Council and municipal committee meetings turned into "free-for-alls," yet the next day the combatants would stand side by side speechifying and turning over shovels full of dirt to dedicate a new building or monument, all the time smiling ingenuously for the public.

A prime example of the overwhelming propensity of humans to work together for the common good was the razing of the 1812 Bucks County Court House and the design and construction of the new 1878 Courthouse, a feat for which Henry worked long and hard and lived long enough to witness from his office in the newly-rebuilt *Intelligencer* building across the street.

It was a Saturday morning in November 1878 shortly after the dedication of the new Courthouse that Henry left his home for some early morning exercise before breakfast. Although he had been suffering for several years from apoplexy, he was feeling rather well this November morning, a brisk, cold, fresh-air day. He walked among the produce markets for a few minutes, exchanging pleasantries and greetings with everyone, and purchased a flower for his lapel, as was his custom every morning except Sunday.

He returned home, feeling refreshed and invigorated. He "breakfasted heartily," the paper later reported, spoke with his children, and, in the company of his youngest son, left for the office. As they passed the new Courthouse, Henry spotted janitor William Harr and crossed over to speak with him about bringing some soil for the flowerbeds at the Darlington home.

As they were talking, Henry suddenly said, "My hand!"

"What is it, sir?" Harr asked, immediately concerned.

"My hand has gone numb. Here, feel." He extended the hand toward Harr who remarked, now alarmed, how cold it felt.

Henry leaned against a maple tree. He turned to his little son and said twice, "Go tell your mother I need help. But don't alarm her. Run, now."

Harr attempted to help him into the Courthouse to sit and rest, perhaps the attack would pass, and Henry leaned on Harr to go, but could not move his right leg. He sank heavily down to the ground dragging Harr with him with his weight.

"I am very sick," he said solemnly. And these were the last earthly words uttered by Henry Townsend Darlington.

At that moment, Joseph Hawk was passing by, and Harr called for him to run and get Dr. McCoy, who came quickly. Darlington was placed gently propped on pillows in a wagon and borne to his own bed at home. Family physician Dr. Kirk was called, and he and Dr. McCoy quickly realized this was a fatal paralysis.

Susan and the other members of the family sat vigil all night by his bedside. Henry never regained consciousness and died at four o'clock on Sunday morning.

"And has he gone, the bravest and purest.
He who upheld our bright banner the surest."

So acute was the shock, and so greatly loved was Henry Darlington, as the news passed along the streets of Doylestown and into the far-flung corners of the County, women openly sobbed and normally strong, emotionless men dabbed their eyes with their handkerchiefs.

Henry was forty-eight years old when he died on Sunday, November 24, 1878. Immediately on Sunday afternoon, the telegrams began flying out—to Chester County, Henry's birthplace; to Harrisburg, the State Capitol; to Washington, D.C.; to the newspapers in New York, particularly to Mahlon Riegel, one of Henry's most prized journalism apprentices, who immediately rushed home to attend the funeral on Thursday, November 28, and burial in the Doylestown Cemetery.

Mahlon was stunned when he learned at the funeral from Sarah Prizer, widow of Henry's partner, Amos, who had died in 1864, that Henry had only the equivalent of an eighth-grade education. Before coming to take over the *Intelligencer* twenty-five years ago in 1853, he and Amos Prizer had served their apprenticeship together at the *Village Record* of West Chester. Henry combined the qualities of natural-born newspaperman and writer, astute businessman, and devout Quaker dedicated to working for the highest ideals and concepts of his Christian faith.

Now, just a little over two years later, here Mahlon was again in Bucks County saying goodbye to another pivotal person in his life, although Langhorn Wellings died probably never knowing of the important place he held in Mahlon's heart and memory. It was doubtful he even knew any more about Mahlon than that he was "that crippled young man from the *Intelligencer.*"

But it was Langhorn Wellings who helped Mahlon define his feelings toward African-Americans and his views on slavery, equal rights, interracial marriage, and the terrible, sometimes violent, prejudicial attitudes and behaviors with which all of those were treated in the years following the Civil War.

Mahlon spent the rest of his life writing about and celebrating the successes and advances of the colored people in American society at the same time spotlighting and censuring the appalling post-War, Reconstruction attitudes and crimes against humanity of racist individuals and groups such as the Ku Klux Klan in both the North and the South. His name and body of work would become associated with what was much later labeled the "liberal press" in America. And he would forever acknowledge with gratitude his initial training at the right hand of Henry Townsend Darlington.

Following a rather restless night fighting bedbugs that had unfortunately invaded his mattress at the Fountainhouse Hotel, Mahlon emerged from the hotel after breakfast and walked around downtown. The crisp November air reminded him fondly of many years before when Henry and Susan invited the *Intelligencer* staff and families to their home on Thanksgiving for a sumptuous banquet. It was a happy tradition that would be forever associated in Mahlon's mind with November.

He stood for a few moments gazing around town. He noticed that the long porch on the Court Inn where Joseph "Pappy" Strawn used to recline on summer evenings was gone.

Probably the most prominent feature next to the new Courthouse and the war memorial was the Lenape Hall and town market building at the corner of State and Main Streets, designed by Thomas Cernea and Addison Hutton. The beautiful, ornate building was hugged on the two street sides by a wooden awning supported by posts and rings for tethering horses. In addition to numerous shops and offices, it housed a large meeting hall that held up to a thousand people.

As he walked down Main Street, Mahlon also discovered that Amos and Phoebe Stone had moved their shop over from West Court. He chatted briefly with them, got caught up on the news of Reuben Stone, who he knew from veterans' group communications was still living in Mount Holly, but was not doing well physically, presumably suffering the residual effects of the fever he had contracted during the war that eventually permanently took the sight in one eye.

Amos and Phoebe were delighted as Mahlon bought an expensive telescope for his son and a stereoscopic viewer for his daughter. They promised to have the packages delivered to the hotel tied up neatly with twine and a wooden handle so that Mahlon could easily carry them home on the train to New York.

He stopped in at the *Intelligencer* office and visited with a few of his old mates. Mrs. Darlington was not in, but had sent a note to the hotel inviting Mahlon to dinner that evening. The Paschall brothers were both on hand. Otherwise, he hardly knew anyone there, so complete was the turnover in staff in the past nine years. He'd heard years before that one of the printers had gone to Philadelphia and become Chief of Police. A printer, with no police experience. Mahlon puzzled over that one for years and, for him, it became a classic example of government cronyism.

He walked down the street to the Presbyterian Church to visit with Pastor Andrews, but Sallie Stone, who was still working for Rev. Andrews as his housekeeper, said he was not at home, so Mahlon took a turn around the new church, which had been built just after he and Nancy left in 1871, and admired the building and gardens.

Then he walked over to the Doylestown Stables and rented a carriage. He took a leisurely drive out State Street to the York Road. As he drove along, he noticed all the changes in the landscape, the most prominent being the presence of many more houses at the villages, Centreville and Lahaska, in particular, and alongside the roadway. It looked as though several of the farmers had sold or rented most of their land fronting the road and new homes were going up all along the way.

Yet the farms beyond were still as beautiful and prosperous and serene-looking as he remembered his entire life. Every time he came home his heart swelled with pride. Bucks County. Daresay there is none other place like it in the country.

Canada Hill had bloomed, as well, except, surprisingly, for the little Baptist Church, which looked somewhat rundown. The grounds of the cemetery were covered with fall leaves and fallen brush, and it looked as though no one had attended to the graveyard in some time. Mahlon noticed he had to be careful of the poison ivy vines, as well.

He found the new grave for Langhorn quickly enough. It was toward the Upper Mountain Road to the far left as he stood looking at the church. There was no stone yet, but there was a new grave on the right of a stone that read, "Mary Wellings, wife of Langhorn H. Wellings, d. Jan. 3, 1865, aged 53y & 6m." To the left of that was another stone reading, "Ruth Anna Wellings, dau. of L. & M. Wellings, d. 3 Mar 18—, aged 19y 4m 14d." The letters and numbers were already beginning to wear away on the older stone, but Mahlon remembered it had been sometime around 1859 or 1860 that their eldest daughter had died.

Mahlon looked up the road and saw someone at the Wellings' home, a thin, frail-looking lady with graying blond hair walking out to the vegetable garden. He watched her for a few moments and debated whether he should try to speak with her. He knew it was Caroline Wellings, Langhorn's second wife.

In the end, he decided not to bother her, but to leave her in peace. The many questions he had and things he wanted to know were too personal and private, none of his business really.

He sat on the short stone steps that someone—maybe even Langhorn himself—had built on the York Road side of the graveyard and lit a cigar. He sat for many minutes just smoking and thinking and watching a cat as it stalked something for dinner in the bushes.

He thought how strange it was that he was drawn more to this man's graveside than his own father's, and from that the thought process led to the acknowledgement that sometimes relations, even casual, with people other than one's close family can be the most important and pivotal in a person's life. There's an attraction and connection there that cannot be easily explained nor is it wise to treat it with disdain.

It's almost like we're "spiritual" relatives, he thought, among other things in line with the metaphysical thinking that was becoming popular lately.

Then, "Yikes!" he yelled out loud. The peaceful moments of being lost in thought were instantly and irritatingly interrupted by a large coach led by three horses that was traveling much too fast down the York Road hill, kicking up rocks and pieces of macadam.

Mahlon jumped up and ran as fast as he could away from the edge of the York Road to where his horse and carriage were parked on the church drive off Upper Mountain Road. It was time to get going anyway.

He drove up to Aquetong Road, turned left and meandered his way over the quiet country farm roads back to Doylestown, by way of the little graveyard at Cross Keys where his mother and father were buried.

If he had spoken with Caroline, he would have learned that it didn't take long for Langhorn to take the next actions following his release from jail on that Saturday evening in September 1865. Then, again, Caroline probably would not have talked to him at all.

Outrageous Affair at Lambertville—A Company of Colored People Assaulted and Beaten by a Mob of White Ruffians.—On Thursday last the colored people of the surrounding country celebrated the adoption of the Fifteenth Amendment by a grand demonstration at Flemington, New Jersey. Extensive preparations had been made beforehand for the event, and an immense concourse of people of this class was gathered together, including some hundreds from Buckingham, Solebury and other portions of Bucks county lying near the Delaware. The affair passed off very satisfactorily, the exercises of the day consisting of a procession, followed by speeches, with music, &c. Good order prevailed throughout the day, and no disturbance or disorder occurred until a portion of the company were returning home in the evening. As a delegation of about one hundred, including a number of colored residents of Buckingham and vicinity, who were in wagons with their wives and children, were driving into Lambertville, about eight o'clock in the evening, the fire bells were rung, on which a crowd of men and boys rushed into the streets. The wagons containing the colored people were at once surrounded by a crowd of white persons, armed with clubs, stones, and pistols, some of whom attempted to seize their horses, while others poured a volley of stones into the wagons containing the defenceless people. Those at the head of the procession, on seeing they were surrounded by a mob, made every effort to push forward their horses and urged those following to do the same. Some of the men jumped from the wagons to try to extricate the horses from the hands of their assailants. One of these, Edward Jackson, of Buckingham, while trying to get his team through the mob, was shot through the hand, inflicting a painful wound, which will disable him for months. His companion, Tobias Thomas, of the same township, was struck in the side with a stone and severely bruised. Among the others injured was Philip Peterson, who was knocked down with a stone. An old woman was struck on the back with a stone, but was not seriously hurt. A son of William Bensing, while sitting in a wagon, received a severe cut on the side of the head. His sister, who was near him was knocked off the seat by a stone, but escaped without much injury. Philip Taylor received a severe blow from a stone, but was not badly hurt. All these parties live in Buckingham. By a determined effort on the part of the drivers of the wagons they succeeded in breaking away from the mob in a few minutes, and crossed over into New Hope. The outrage was a premeditated one on the part of the members of the "white man's party" engaged in it. The ringing of the fire bells was the signal for the attack. It was an unprovoked and outrageous assault upon a peaceable and inoffensive company of people quietly passing through the place. While this was most likely the work of the rabble of Lambertville and probably of New Hope, such proceedings are the legitimate fruits of the teachings of the Democratic leaders for years past. We have not learned whether any measures have been taken to bring the perpetrators of this outrage to punishment.

[*Bucks County Intelligencer*, Tuesday, September 20, 1870]

Chapter XII

Solebury, Bucks County, PA
1865-1880

The celebrations began on Sunday, September 17. Church service. Folks coming over to the house to congratulate Lang. A few more on Monday.

Those who did not come by the house Lang went to see to thank them for their support and participation in his defense, including John Balderston at the Emlen Institute off Aquetong Road, Joseph Fell, Dr. Cernea, and Bill Johnson.

Fell, it turned out, had been very busy over the past six months traveling to Philadelphia and all over the County with Capt. Alfred Marple establishing the new schools for orphans of soldiers and sailors who died in the war, including the School for Colored Orphans that would be set up in the large property called "China Hall" in Bristol.

"Sending John Balderston was probably the best thing you could've done for me," Lang told him, acknowledging Joseph's decision not to participate in the trial. "And I expect to pay you back for Lear's expenses."

Fell put his hand on the big man's shoulder, as he had done repeatedly for almost fifty years. "'Tis not necessary, Brother Lang. Friend Lear significantly lowered his fee for you."

"Then let me give you a donation towards the new colored orphans' school."

"*That* would be wonderful and very much needed. We have to feed and clothe these children, so many of whom are from the most pitiable situations, and there are a great many still on the waiting list."

Lang drove down to Centreville to pay his respects to Dr. Cernea, who was not at home. He asked Mrs. Cernea to please convey his appreciation for the doctor's support.

"I hope he understands that I wasn't trying to get another doctor for my wife because…well, 'cause I thought he weren't good enough."

Sarah Cernea smiled. "I'm sure he understands that, Friend Langhorn, and I know thee understands that my good husband only had the welfare of thyself and thy family in his heart at all times."

"Yes, ma'am. I do know that now."

Bill Johnson had retired almost ten years before to his son-in-law, Stephen Janney's home near Newtown. A widower himself now, he spent his time reading the Bible in Greek for an hour each morning, then walking the two miles into town. The rest of the day was devoted to correspondence and writing articles for the *Intelligencer,* the *Practical Farmer* and *Farm Journal.* Bedtime was early, preceded by a few minutes with Byron or Burns, Whitman or Longfellow, his favorite poets and writers.

"I'm near onto seventy-five now and just about wore out," he said when Lang sat with him.

"I won't hear none such!" Lang retorted. "You're as fit as ever."

Bill smiled contentedly. "But we got to see the end of slavery, didn't we, old friend? It was worthwhile living long enough just for that. Now, we have to get suffrage back for you, just like we tried to do so many years ago. My heavens, can you believe it was thirty years ago!?"

Everyone gradually got back to their own work and lives. There was plenty of work whenever Lang wanted it. The lime business was petering out and the kilns were gradually closing up as new fertilizers were imported. But Thaddeus and Watson Kenderdine were talking about beginning a new business to make superphosphate of lime at the mill near Lumberton, and there was no end of help Lang could give them, especially during the winter when the fields and crops were dormant.

There was sporadic work at the Emlen Institute, as well, and a new operation beginning in Solebury that looked promising. It was just down the York Road from Canada Hill, called Beaumont's Deer Park. It boasted buffalo, deer, and other exotic animals and park-like grounds, with streams and ponds stocked with fish, and even its own small paper mill.

Within weeks, Lang's children left him alone, too. Jonas went back up to the Hill farm where he had been staying during the trial. Paxton Hill had plenty of work for him, laid out good food and paid a fair wage, and there were some other boys there whom Jonas enjoyed being around more than he wanted to be in this house that had known only sickness and sadness for so many years.

Elizzie left to find work in New Hope at Vanhart's Hotel where she was provided a small room on the third floor that she shared with another maid. She, too, wanted to be around her friends, and there were so many more exciting, interesting things going on in New Hope. She wouldn't have admitted it if you asked her, but she was also beginning to form an attraction to Bobby Kohl who was by then working as an apprentice barber in a shop in New Hope.

And she would have shrugged shyly if you had asked her if her father's mood didn't have something to do with her leaving. When other folks weren't around, Lang would just sit in the rocking chair in the living room for hours in the dark. Or down at the churchyard. The whole atmosphere of the house and neighborhood had been oppressive for years and was even worse now than when her mother was sick and dying.

It was Bobby who tipped Elizzie off that something was up. It was a Friday afternoon in mid-November and he had come over to the hotel kitchen to get some lunch. Elizzie was often in the kitchen at that time of the day, too.

"Hey, what's up with your father?" he asked as soon as he came in the door.

"What do you mean?" Elizzie looked puzzled.

"Oh, you didn't see him? He was just at the shop, gettin' a shave and haircut—the whole works! Lookin' mighty fine. I asked him if he was goin' to a wedding or a funeral." Bobby laughed.

"What did he say?"

"'Didn't. He just smiled and gave me a big tip."

Years later, Elizzie would think back on that time and wonder why she reacted as she did. In her old age, she would eventually come to understand that she had undoubtedly compacted into that time and place all of the pent-up grief and heartbreak associated with her mother's death, worry and fear for her father, probably mixed with no small amount of sibling rivalry with a sister who was now ultimately perfected in death over six years ago. She jumped up, grabbed her shawl, and ran to catch up with Lang, but she was too late.

Lang had thought about it for weeks. Alone in the house. Alone in the world—even his friends seemed to be standoffish. He didn't talk with anyone. And just like that he made a decision.

He got up that Friday morning, took a bath in a big tub in the kitchen with water heated on the stove, hitched up the wagon and went into New Hope for a haircut and shave. Then he drove up to Rice's Market where he bought some pretty fall flowers—mums, zinnias, and carnations—from a stall supplied by Mahlon Moon's greenhouses in Morrisville. From there, he drove out to the Moore farm where he knew Caroline Barrett lived and worked as a servant.

Caroline was born in Philadelphia in 1838, as close as anyone could figure, though no one knew anything about her very early years. She was found wandering the streets, practically still a toddler, and placed in an orphanage. No family or neighbor ever came asking about her.

She would never know her birth name, as she was given the name "Caroline Barrett" by the directors of the institution. It was speculated that her mother was undoubtedly a prostitute and that it was of no use to try to find her.

When Caroline was eight she was "farmed out" to Bucks County where she was immediately put to work on the Moores' place. That was probably infinitely better than the alternative in the city, being forced to work for twelve hours a day, six days a week, in one of the many factories and mills that used child labor. In the smoky, filthy atmosphere of the city, she undoubtedly would have been dead from consumption before she was twenty.

The Moores were childless, yet it never occurred to them to adopt Caroline. In fact, they would have been shocked if anyone had even suggested it. Why, her mother was probably a prostitute, after all, and one could only imagine what her father was! Nor would they have thought of giving anything to Caroline beyond her basic room and board and the few pennies a week that constituted her pitiful wages.

The Moores were devout Christians of the "hell, fire and brimstone" variety. Morning and night they gathered everyone in the household to read the Bible and pray as fervently and loudly as possible that their souls would be saved from the devil. About the only thing of lasting value that they gave to Caroline was to teach her to read.

"This is your place in life," they had told her very shortly after she came to live with them twenty years before. "We have rescued you from a certain terrible fate." They didn't exactly say it, but implied that that place was to serve them for the rest of their lives. "We expect you to bloom where you are planted," they would have added sternly, since that was their way as long as she knew them. "It's God's will." Yet, people like the Moores would not understand that, just like plants and flowers in a garden, it takes nutrients (love, praise), rich soil (healthy environment), sunshine (spiritual training), water (music) and constant nurturing (hugs) to make the individual blossom.

Lang knew that Caroline Barrett had nothing in life to look forward to but hard work, day in and day out, sunrise to sunset, for the rest of her life. It was unlikely there would be any suitors for her. She was not particularly pretty. Her teeth were crooked and already bad. She had a slight humpback caused by curvature of the spine. The years and unending toil had already done their damage. No one ever remembered her smiling, and she appeared even older than her actual age of twenty-eight.

But, every time he thought about her, Caroline reminded him of the little, thin bird that Mary had been years ago when they had fallen in love and run off together. And thinking about that and remembering made him successively happy, then lonely and bereft for human companionship.

It was a gamble, but he decided to take his chances. He walked right up to the front door of the Moores' farmhouse—the important visitor's entrance—and rapped the doorknocker sharply several times.

Caroline came to the door, followed closely by Mrs. Moore, who was at first puzzled, then outraged that this colored man was at the front door. She knew this Langhorn Wellings. She knew all about him.

"What are you doing here?" she asked indignantly from behind Caroline. "Go out to the back where you belong if you want to speak to my husband." Then she noticed the bouquet of flowers. "What is the meaning...."

Lang removed his hat. "Pardon me, ma'am, but I'm here to see Miss Barrett, if you don't mind. I'll ask her kindly to step outside for a moment."

Mrs. Moore was stunned beyond shock. She ran as quickly as she could considering her old age and rheumatism to the back door. "Mr. Moore! Mr. Moore!"

Caroline stood in the open doorway and stared at this big, muscular black man, all clean-shaven, spiffed up in his "Sunday best," and still mighty handsome after all these years, not a wrinkle in his face, except for a very slight droop, certainly not looking at all like he was over fifty. She knew instantly why he was there.

"Miss Caroline," Langhorn stammered. "I…ah. I know you don't know me very well, but I been thinking about you for a while now. A lot while I was sittin' up in jail, in fact…. I'm awful lonesome since my wife died. My kids are goin' off on their own…."

Caroline stepped out onto the porch and shut the door behind her. She could hear Mr. and Mrs. Moore coming in through the back of the house, and she wanted to slow them down somewhat. The fact that she did not slam the door in his face gave Lang more courage.

"What I'm tryin' to say, ma'am, is I would be mighty honored if you was to become my wife…. I ain't a rich man, but I'm an honest, hard-working Christian man, and I can offer you a neat little house and I'll take the best care of you I can for the rest of my life…."

Mr. Moore opened the door and immediately began yelling at Lang. "What's the meaning of this?! You got no right here. You git on down the road, now, you hear!"

Caroline turned around and held a hand up to Mr. Moore, which flustered and infuriated him all the more. She turned back to Lang and said quietly, but just loudly enough for him to hear.

"Yes."

She decided to leave with him right then and there before he changed his mind. She quietly turned around, took off her apron, went upstairs to get her few belongings, all the while with the Moores at her heels yelling that she had no business running off with this colored man—"This nigger who'd kil't his first wife."

"You're runnin' straight to the devil! Satan'll have your soul by sunset!"

Then, as she was walking out the door and to Lang's wagon, they hollered after her, "Don't you never dare try to come crawling back to us, young lady! You got no gratitude for all we done for you, that's for sure!"

The next morning, Caroline was sitting in the little bedroom off the kitchen, where Lang had put her until they could be married proper-like, when three people, two young men and a woman came right through the back door to the kitchen. The woman was leading the pack and took charge.

She looked at Caroline sitting on the edge of the bed on which Mary Stone Wellings had died not eleven months before.

"Who are you? What are you doing here?" she demanded.

"Caroline," Caroline answered quietly.

"Where is my father?" Elizzie shouted before Caroline could continue.

Lang was down in the ice house putting away the meat from a hog he and Fred Pearson had just butchered and split between them. He heard the footsteps above him and recognized immediately Elizzie's distinctive gait. Then he heard the loud voices—or, really, just one loud voice, Elizzie's.

By the time he could get upstairs, Caroline had closed the door and was sitting in trembling fright that she was about to be put out. Whatever would become of her, she could not bear to imagine. She sat on the bed praying that she had not made the most serious mistake of her life, next to being born at all, by running away with this man.

Elizzie proceeded around the house, up to her old room, grabbing things along the way. This shy, crippled young girl had seemingly in an instant turned into a "she-cat from hell."

Lang came into the kitchen and looked at Jonas and Bobby. "Hello, son, Bobby. What's going on?" Both young men shrugged and looked upward.

Elizzie came back into the kitchen and thrust her burden onto them.

"Hello, daughter," Lang greeted her. "That's a nice way to visit your old man."

"Don't you call me daughter! What's *she* doing here? In my mother's room? Using my mother's things!" She approached the door of the bedroom, and Lang positioned himself in front of it.

"You wait up, here. This is Miss Caroline Barrett, and I've asked her to marry me."

"Marry!? My mother is hardly cold in her grave! You couldn't even wait the proper mourning period! You never loved her, did you?!"

Lang's temper began to rise. "Now, you just look here. You don't know what I been feelin'. You don't know nuthin' 'bout sittin' in jail for seven months! I had plenty of time to mourn, believe you me, little lady, and worry about my own neck in the process! And it's none of your business, 'sides. You got no right tellin' me what I can and can't do!"

Elizzie's lip and chin began trembling. She tried to fight her tears, but everything came rushing out.

"How could you do this?" she cried.

"How could I do what? Be lonesome? My wife dies. My children leave me and you blame me for being lonesome?"

Elizzie started for the door of the bedroom again. "I want my mother's things! You let me in there!"

"No." Langhorn stood firmly in front of the door. "Not the way you're behavin'. You go on home and calm down."

"No, I will not! This is my home, this is my house! I want you out of my house!" She looked at Jonas for reinforcement. "This is our house. Jonas, tell him!"

Jonas shook his head. "Com'on, Elizzie. Let's go. It ain't worth it."

Lang became furious at the suggestion that Elizzie would assert her legal rights to the property and try to put him out. He came toward her menacingly. "You listen up, girl. This is my house and property, and I will not have you comin' in here threatening me. I don't know what's come over you, but I want you gone, now!"

He looked at Jonas and Bobby. "You better take her now 'fore I spank some sense into her." He turned back to Elizzie. "You ain't too big for a good spankin'!"

The young men did as they were ordered. "Come, Elizzie," Bobby said. "This is no good. We should go."

Elizzie went, but not quietly. She yelled back at Lang that she would be seeing a lawyer about the house and her mother's personal property. And Lang yelled something back that in later years he would regret having said, among many other things in his life.

Lang went back into the house and opened the door to Caroline's room. "I'm sorry about my daughter," he said awkwardly. "I don't know what's come over the girl. She'll come around, soon I hope."

But those hopes would be long in realization.

The next day Lang took Caroline to church where he introduced her as his fiancé to the other worshippers, most every one white. Then he brought her to his friends, Mahlon and Andy. On the surface, everyone seemed polite and congratulatory, and Lang was too elated and preoccupied to notice or hear the undercurrent of shock and repugnance on the part of more than a few of them. Nor, for a long time, did he hear any of the gossip that immediately began.

On Monday they drove over to Lambertville to Rev. Larison's home to be married, but, while Larison was all smiles and politeness at the church, in private he demurred.

"I'm not sure it's legal, really, Lang," he said with embarrassment evident in his manner.

"But, that's ridiculous!" Lang replied. "I was married to Mary for thirty years and no one said nothin' about it not bein' legal."

"I know, but times have changed. I think the law's been changed in the meantime, as well. Why don't you check with Squire Balderston. That would make me feel better." John had just been elected Justice of the Peace for Solebury Township.

So over to Emlen Institute they drove where John said, as far as he knew, the law remained the same: Whatever was acceptable to the church was legal in the Commonwealth.

"In fact, I have power to marry you now that I am Justice of the Peace, and I would be honored to do so," he affirmed.

And so, in a very short but pious ceremony, widower Langhorn Wellings took orphan Caroline Barrett as his second wife.

The couple settled into domestic life over the winter. Caroline had never before been touched by a man and was very delicate in physical nature. Unfortunately, Lang did not have the slightest concept of the delicacies of some women's nature, so it could be said that in the balance of life the physical aspect of their relationship was something Caroline endured because the rest of her life was reasonably contented.

She had her own home and only one other person to cook and clean for, and, most importantly, she was saved from the Moores of the world. One had to make compromises in life, after all. For a while, she never asked or thought about what would become of her should anything happen to Lang. She didn't know that Lang did not legally own the house and assumed that, like other widows, she would be entitled to inherit or at least live in the house for the remainder of her life.

Lang continued to attend the Canada Hill Baptist Church, while Caroline begged out of more Sunday and evening services than not. She'd personally had enough of those hypocrite Christians to last a lifetime, and she had seen something in the manner of some of them that reminded her too much of the Moores and their fellow religionists.

After a few months, Lang went to New Hope and tried to speak with Elizzie, but she refused to talk to him. Jonas, as well, didn't have much to say and refused to come home as Lang asked him to do.

"But, I got married so's to provide a home for you, son. I want you to come home now where you belong."

"Aw, Pop, I got my friends here and a good job. I'm savin' up my money so I can buy my own place. This is my home now. 'Sides, you don't want us around all the time anyways. I'll come and visit you sometime soon."

He was awfully mature for a fourteen-year-old kid. Yet very shy. And light-skinned. Surprisingly so. His hair was almost blond, especially in the summer when he was outdoors in the sun all the time. Truth be told, when he was away from his family he didn't have to think all the time about the fact that he was half Negro, half white. Other fellows left him alone when they would have normally picked a fight with a black. And there were even some white girls who had flirted with him before their friends told them he was mulatto.

The days and months passed relatively quietly for Lang and Caroline. Caroline immediately settled into the practice of reading the weekly *Intelligencer* to him. After a while, she tried to scan ahead as she read and skip over certain items that were almost guaranteed to upset him. But, Lang noticed what she was doing and demanded to hear everything, even the bad news.

"I'm gonna hear about it from my friends eventually," he reasoned, "so you mind's well be straight with me and not try to hide anything."

One such article was the report in February 1867 about Mr. and Mrs. Miles Robinson, "a very respectable colored man…with his wife and young infant," who were ordered off Car 25 of the Spruce and Pine Street Line in Philadelphia. When they refused to leave, the conductor took all of the other passengers off the car to another, and left Car 25, with the Robinsons still sitting inside, on the tracks, thus "obstructing both lines of railway travel for an hour or more, collecting a large crowd of people and exciting much disturbance in the neighborhood.

"Mr. and Mrs. Robinson retained their seats in the car," the article concluded, "and the brutal conductor then proceeded to freeze them out, by opening the doors and windows and removing the cushions and thus, at last, driving these very respectable and unoffending people to vacate the car and walk home through the cold."

This was in contrast to reports from most Southern cities where it was mandated by Union military governors that Negroes be permitted to ride in all of the street cars. Even so, most blacks waited for the special cars marked with a star, and, of course, things changed drastically again as soon as the occupying Northern forces withdrew.

Then in June 1868, there was an article about "[a]n inoffensive man, whose great crime consists of his color, [who] was followed by a gang of rowdies…waylaid and injured near Clemens' buildings, opposite Ashland street" right in Doylestown. Lang already knew about that incident, having heard it through the colored grapevine.

In fact, he learned more from his friends and at colored camp meetings than he did through the *Intelligencer.* All things considered, both sources were undoubtedly at least partially incorrect and biased in their own way—the average African-American being somewhat pessimistic and the *Intelligencer* being more "ivory tower" optimistic. When Lang considered them together, they probably provided him with a fairly balanced view.

At the same time, Lang saw the dichotomies of crimes against blacks in the North going unpunished, such as the beating in Doylestown, which was actually only one of many incidents that he heard about, while in the South extra, stepped-up efforts were made to exact justice for such attacks and, worse, rapes and murders committed against coloreds.

That is, until the Union troops and military overseers pulled out of the South and returned government to the locals and the Northern "carpetbaggers." Then, gradually, reports began arriving North of the formation of such groups as the Ku Klux Klan in April 1868, ostensibly "for the protection and advancement of the white race," and the ensuing atrocities perpetrated by them as they gained more members and more power. Gone forever, it seemed, was any hope of protection and justice Southern blacks would ever have.

Things quickly returned to pre-war normalcy, where the killing of a black man by a white was considered an "unfortunate affair," whereas the same act of a black on white was "diabolical murder." More often than not, the accused colored offender was tried, convicted and hung within a matter of hours, on the slimmest of evidence, and with no judicial authority ever involved.

On the other hand, one very pleasant event occurred for Lang on a spring day in 1867. Lang was working out in the barn when he saw Dr. Cernea and a young man he knew to be the doctor's architect son, Thomas, drive up. They carried a package. It was rectangular and flat, wrapped in brown paper and tied up with a string.

He nodded hello as they walked up to the corral and asked politely, "You comin' to see the Chapmans' or Pearsons'?"

"No, Lang, we're here to see you and Mrs. Wellings."

"Oh! That's right nice of you." Lang wiped his right hand on his overalls and extended it to each of them. "Com'on in the house. I'll see if Caroline can brew up some coffee or tea."

They sat in the parlor chatting mainly about the news of the day. Caroline made tea and quietly served it with fresh cookies. She sat stiffly, with arms folded across her chest, in a straight-back chair she brought from the kitchen. Lang somewhat nervously glanced around and noticed for the first time things were looking a little the worse for wear. Still, he was thankful that Caroline took good care of the place.

Finally, Dr. Cernca extended the package toward Lang. "My son here painted a picture of the Buckingham Valley. We had photographic copies made of it, and I know how much you love the place of your childhood, I thought you'd like to have one."

Lang unwrapped the picture and found a true-to-life drawing of the Valley from a point just west of Centreville looking eastward. He was stunned and so touched he was moved to tears. This was probably one of the nicest presents anyone had ever given him.

He took out his handkerchief and wiped his eyes and blew his nose, somewhat embarrassed.

"Looks like it was drawn from Palmer's property," he said trying to recover his composure.

"Yes," said Thomas. "He has a beautiful hill that overlooks the whole Valley. I've always admired the view."

Lang nodded. "And here's your house, Doctor. And the Watsons, and all the others. This is wonderful…" He lost his composure again momentarily.

"I guess things have certainly changed in our time, haven't they, Lang?"

Lang nodded as he thought nostalgically about the truth of those words and so many of the important events that had taken place in the course of the last fifty years.

As Dr. Cernea and Thomas were preparing to leave, the doctor turned to Lang and said, "I've been meaning to ask, one of the last times I visited with Mary before she died, she said something in German. It sounded like verses or poetry. I had a suspicion of what it was, but I wanted to ask you."

Lang nodded. "Shakespeare."

"So, it was! *Romeo and Juliet*, if I'm not mistaken. However did she come to memorize Shakespeare in German?"

Lang explained.

"I never knew that about her. It's amazing how long you can treat a patient and never really know everything about them."

Immediately after they left, Lang hung the picture over the red couch where it remained for almost fifty years until Elizzie's death, when the furniture and personal property, most of it long tattered and worn, were thrown out or sold at auction.

Every time he looked at it, Lang would remember the friendship and good will of this gentle and distinguished Quaker man, of whom he had been so suspicious and jealous at the beginning and during the course of their relationship.

Later in that year, in the summer, Lang heard that Elizzie and Bobby Kohl were married at the Mt. Moriah A.M.E. church in New Hope. He was deeply hurt that he, especially, and Caroline had been excluded, and the emotional gulf between them was further widened.

Shortly after, she and Bobby showed up at the house demanding her mother's hope chest and other personal items. Caroline was home alone and became frightened and would not let them into the house. When she told Lang about it, he went immediately to New Hope. He found Elizzie at work at Vanhart's Hotel. They got into a terrible argument and this time, when Elizzie threatened to exercise her ownership of the property, Lang made responding threats that were overheard by others.

Terrible things they said to each other. Everyone who heard about it shook their heads sadly. For weeks afterward, the gossip traveled.

"Father and daughter, can you imagine? How sad."

"Why is it that those we love the most seem to turn on us so quickly?"

And worse, "Isn't it just like those colored people?"

And worst. "Stupid nigger's prob'ly drinkin' again. I happen to know he had hisself an awful problem years ago, and you know *their kind* never change."

Elizzie immediately went to the constable and insisted on filing charges. He tried to talk her out of it.

"No, I've got witnesses. He's gonna do somethin' terrible to me. I know it."

The constable then went and tried to talk to Lang, who was still fuming, sitting in a colored bar drinking a glass of water. The constable unfortunately assumed it was gin and roughly proceeded with the arrest, and the constable's treatment of him made Lang even angrier, telling him like a child to "Stay out of New Hope" and "I don't want to see you nearabouts your daughter."

When the case came up for hearing in December, Judge Chapman was visibly alarmed. "You! I thought we'd seen the last of you!"

As he pronounced the sentence to Lang of a year's probation and to pay the costs of prosecution, he added, sternly: "I don't want to see you in this courtroom again. Do I make myself clear?"

A small article appeared in the "December Term Court" section of the paper on December 8, 1867:

> *Commonwealth vs. Langhorn Wellings.* Surety of the Peace on complaint of his daughter Elizabeth Wellings, who testified that he had threatened her personal injury. They had some difficulty about some goods claimed by her about which a law suit is now pending. Sentence, to pay costs of prosecution, and enter into his own recognizance to keep the peace for one year.

Lang was humiliated and infuriated at the same time. Now everyone in the County knew. No matter how much he had tried to assert his innocence in the murder trial, and despite the fact that he was found not guilty, this was only going to further convince people of the worst about him.

"Look at that," they'd say to each other. "Now he's turned on his daughter. Poor little crippled girl. Prob'ly did kill his wife, after all."

Lang understood he had to straighten this terrible mess out, but he had no idea how to go about it. He was beyond reasoning. He and Elizzie weren't getting anywhere. There was no middle ground. Even the lawyers couldn't or wouldn't communicate. Elizzie had moved into the "revenge" stage of her hurt and was demanding her rights to the property and insisting on putting Lang and Caroline out in the cold in the process.

A few weeks later, the answer came shortly after New Year's Day 1868. Lang answered a knock on the door and found John Balderston standing on the porch.

"Good day, Friend Langhorn. Can you see me?"

"Of course! Come in, please. Come in. Caroline! Would you make some tea for us…" He turned back to John, "Would you like coffee or tea?"

"Tea, please, yes," John answered.

The men talked amiably for several minutes as John explained one of the reasons for the visit.

"You know the Chapmans are selling out and moving into Doylestown?" he asked Lang.

"Yes, they mentioned something like that to me."

"And Sarah and I will be buying their place. So, we're going to be neighbors!"

"Oh!" The Justice of the Peace of Solebury Township living right next door. "Aren't you going to live at Emlen?"

"As you know, I've been superintendent at Emlen for ten years now. It's been wonderful. We've had some great successes. I would say we've educated and graduated hundreds of boys over the years. Some of them have gone on to become teachers themselves. But, it's time for me to retire. Sarah and I have been looking for a small place to move to, and the Chapman property is perfect."

Lang never knew that several Quaker leaders, including Joseph Fell, Eastburn Reeder, and the Kenderdines had visited John specifically to ask him to take Lang under his wing and be a true "Friend," as the old saying went, "A true friend is someone who doubles your joys and halves your sorrows." John's retirement and the purchase of the Chapman home, right next door to Lang's, dovetailed perfectly with their needs.

"What's going to happen to Emlen?" Lang asked.

"William Isaac is coming from New York to run it from now on. But I understand they're going to be looking for a new property. This one just isn't producing."

"I know. For as many years as I been limin' the place, it just ain't improving, and I don't know what's to be done."

John laughed. "Perhaps they can use it to build a big country mansion for some rich fellow from Philly who doesn't need to farm it. That seems to be the thing in Solebury."

After a while John asked Lang to come outside to look at something at the Chapman home he wanted to improve and needed Lang's advice on.

As they walked around the property, John said, "You know, Lang, I have another reason for coming to visit you. I'll be straight up with you. I've received a letter from Judge Chapman about this little problem you have with your daughter."

Lang looked at John and wagged his head. "I am so embarrassed. I don't know what's come over the girl...."

"She's heartbroken, friend. Look at it from her perspective. She undoubtedly feels that by marrying again so soon, you have betrayed her mother, therefore, you have betrayed her."

"No. It had nothin' to do with Mary or with Elizzie. I was lonely and..."

"And angry, admit it."

"Yes, I s'pose…and angry."

"And your marrying Caroline had almost as much to do with anger at what people—life—had put you through with not a little 'I'm going to show you all' thrown in?"

"Could be."

"But, you had every right, my friend, to marry again. Just because you didn't wait another month or two has nothing to do with it, really, I don't think."

The two men stood at the corral for a few moments mulling over the situation.

"So, what do we do?" Lang finally asked.

"I've been thinking. You say Mary took the deed to the property through Andrew Hartless as trustee and that you were specifically excluded from ownership."

"Yes." Lang kicked himself for the umpteenth time for never straightening out the property ownership problem.

"Well, I don't think there's a court in the land that would uphold that deed. This is your property. Even by the process of what they call 'squatter's rights'. You've lived here for what, twenty years?"

"Just over, yes."

"And you've built the house and made improvements and paid the taxes. No, relax, my friend, there is no court that would put you out."

Lang breathed a sigh of relief. "Well, that's sure good to know. But, what do we do about Elizzie?"

John thought for another moment, then turned to Lang and asked, "Would you let her have her mother's things? What is it? A hope chest? Anything else?"

"Yes. Mary's brother Jonas made it for her. Some little pieces of jewelry, I guess. We don't have much. Oh, and the sewing machine, though Elizzie never did seem much interested in sewing, I s'pose she'd want it."

"And, most important?" John looked earnestly at Lang. "An apology? Would you do that?"

Lang suddenly began to remember so many years ago when Bill Johnson had made the exact same suggestion and insisted that it be delivered with flowers for Mary and toys for then babies Ruth Ann and Elizzie.

And he remembered, but did not voice to John, his objection then: *But I got nothin' to apologize for. I'm the one that's been done wrong.*

Instead, he looked at John and nodded his head. "Yes. I'll do that."

"Wonderful! Now all we have to do is convince Elizzie. But, I think she'll be much easier than you were. In the meantime, we're going to work on your temper, my friend," John said teasingly.

"Too bad they won't print *that* in the *Intelligencer*!" Lang observed wryly as they walked back to the house.

As John took his leave, he turned to Lang. "I'm delighted we're going to be neighbors. I want you to know I look forward to being your friend, and I hope you feel the same."

John went immediately to New Hope and found Elizzie at work at Vanhart's. She was puzzled, then a little apprehensive, when Mr. Vanhart came to tell her that the Justice of the Peace himself was waiting for her in the dining room.

She sat down nervously across from Squire Balderston. He was a big man—even bigger than her father—and very important.

Albeit gentle and kind. "Dear Elizabeth," he said. "I think we have a solution for your little problem." As he explained it, she gradually, though grudgingly, came to realize that, as long as her father was alive, she would not have the property.

"Even the laws of intestate spousal inheritance call for your father to remain in possession of the house as long as he lives."

All these big, confusing words.

"And you understand," John continued, "that he had every right to marry again whenever and whomever he wished and that he has no obligation to give you anything from the house that isn't your personal property...."

Elizzie sat up, "But..."

"...Now, now. I have talked with him, and he is willing to let you have your mother's things. He always was, but you seem to have inherited a double dose of your father's anger and your mother's German temper. Am I right?" He looked at Elizzie and smiled as she nodded shyly and grimaced.

"So, it's settled, then." John reached across the table and patted Elizzie's hand. "Come, let us tell Mr. Vanhart that we'll not be disturbing the peace of his little establishment any further."

The next Saturday, Lang packed everything he thought Elizzie would want in the wagon and drove to New Hope, first stopping at Rice's Market to get a large, lovely red poinsettia plant.

The reunion was tense and awkward, but at least they were speaking civilly to each other again.

"You be sure to tell me if there's somethin' I missed," Lang said as he left Bobby and Elizzie's rooms in the tenement house. "Better yet, you com'on over and visit us sometime."

But that would be a long time coming. It was too late and too far gone for Elizzie to ever have any kind of relationship with Caroline but one of respectful distance.

From the day of her birth, life dealt Elizzie a number of crosses to bear, and she shouldered each with increasing strength and determination, cleaving first to her family, then to her husband and ultimately to God alone, for support. In the process over the years of her lifetime, she developed into a wise and incredibly strong and steadfast woman, the likes of whom are found in almost every community. But they are usually eccentric loners, and very few folks take time out of their busy lives to get to know and appreciate what these people have been through and the lessons they have learned along the way.

The most sorrowful aspect of the life of Mary Elizabeth Wellings Kohl is that she left no heirs—only distant cousins—to tell her story and celebrate her praise for future generations.

For Lang, once the problem with Elizzie was resolved, at least on the surface, life got back into a more normal routine. Having John Balderston next door became the high point of his life. It was wonderful having someone to talk with. Lang became somewhat of a permanent fixture at the Balderston home and took on a great deal of handiwork about the property, as well as running errands for Sarah Balderston and driving and accompanying John on occasion as he went about his business as Justice of the Peace and as founder and president of the Solebury Farmers Club. Caroline took over much of the housekeeping chores for Sarah.

Lang would never accept wages for the things he did for John and Sarah. One just didn't do that with friends and neighbors. Instead, the Balderstons found every opportunity possible of sharing food items and gifts of clothing and other luxuries and necessities with Lang and Caroline. In addition, he made sure that Lang always had work on the farms and in the businesses of his friends.

The relationship became truly a cherished friendship, and it ended much too soon. Within four years, John Balderston was gone.

In the meantime, an immediate loss of a good Friend for both Langhorn and John came on January 23, 1868, when John Kenderdine passed away from complications of pneumonia. As Lang drove John and Sarah over to the funeral on the 26th at Kenderdine's large "Laurelton" estate that he had built in 1855, he told them about his one disastrous Underground Railroad experience taking Henry Miller to Kenderdine's and the kidnapping, beating and subsequent rescue.

Come to find out, John knew all about it. He had been business
partners with Kenderdine in the late 1830s with his brother, William
Balderston.

"The firm was called Kenderdine, Balderston & Co. for many
years," John explained. "We eventually sold our share to Lukens Thomas
in eighteen forty, and I think he's had several other partners since then.
But we've always been in close contact with the Kenderdines ever since.
John Kenderdine was one of the finest men I've ever known."

"He certainly was a fine man," Lang agreed, "and I will never forget
his kindness and generosity to us when we was building the house."

In the summer of 1868 there was an incredible, once-in-a-lifetime
infestation of locusts in Eastern Pennsylvania. The swarms were sometimes so large they shut out the sunlight. Crops that were not devoured
by the dreaded insects had to be burned in an effort to kill or drive them
away. Terrible damage was done and human lives were lost. Several
people, mostly children and the elderly, were caught in the sudden
swarms and died, probably either by suffocation or fright, although the
paper incorrectly reported that they were bitten or stung to death.

The next spring, on April 12, 1869, Lang's world turned around
with joy. His first grandchild was born—William Stone Kohl—the only
one, it turns out, he would ever know. What a wonderful time it was for
Lang to see his beautiful little grandson. Dark brown, curly hair. Long,
thick eyelashes over sparkling brown eyes. What a precious boy!

Now that Elizzie had found new love and joy in life as a wife and
mother, her feelings toward her father softened considerably. She still
did not like to come to the house at Canada Hill. No matter. It was an
easy four-mile ride for Lang to New Hope, and every time he was in
town he made a point of visiting Elizzie, Bobby and especially little
Billy. He proudly stood with Bobby and Elizzie as Billy was dedicated to
the Lord before the congregation of the small Mt. Moriah A.M.E.
church. The church building itself was still in the stages of construction,
and the meetings were held in the meantime in a borrowed church.

The church had been operating continuously since its creation in
1818 just two years after the A.M.E. denomination was created, making
it one of the earliest congregations in the country. In 1837 they built a

church on the western edge of New Hope, near where Stoney Hill and Sugan Roads converge in the section of town known as "Darkeytown" on maps. Until the early 1870s, the congregation was housed in a small wooden church building.

Shortly after the war, a colored preacher from Trenton had come over to address the African-Americans of New Hope on what it meant for their people to be free and the importance of elevating their position by means of dress, behavior, cleanliness, upkeep of their homes and surroundings, and establishment of churches, and such. Almost immediately, a new lot was procured and the Mt. Moriah church building was started, and gradually the small brick church was built, albeit with several setbacks, including the destruction of one of the walls when a tree fell on it during a severe blizzard in the mid-1870s.

The fifteen hundred dollar mortgage was completely paid off in 1874, and the *Intelligencer* noted in a lighthearted manner that the colored Methodists of New Hope "can now worship without fear of the sheriff."

There were two sad events that happened during the year 1869. Lang learned that young James Martin Cernea, aged eighteen, youngest child of Dr. Arthur and Sarah Cernea died on May 25. Then twelve-year-old Margaret Hartless, orphaned niece of Andy and Maggie, whom they had raised since she was a baby and loved as if she were their own, died on September 10.

In later years, Lang would often look back and think that young Cernea's and "Little Maggie's" deaths were almost like the "Twin Trumpet Blasts" preceding or announcing the earthly end of many of his friends, white and colored alike. There were at least six funerals a year after that, many of them very dear and close life-long friends or their children.

For many years after the war, devastating climatic problems, diseases and plagues were prevalent throughout the country, and Bucks County was certainly not spared, even though most of its residents were lucky enough to boast an almost privileged lifestyle with plenty of wholesome food generally available and clean, fresh air.

Bucks Countians were, for the most part, living in a veritable parkland, free from the sickening squalor and stenches of the city with its factories, rundown tenement squares, inadequate sanitation, and tens of thousands of citizens jammed together in close quarters. Still, blizzards, thunderstorms, freshets, and diseases such as apoplexy, consumption, cancer, smallpox, measles, meningitis, Scarlet and other fevers, relentlessly stalked them and their children.

Elsewhere during these early months and years following the war, events were taking place very rapidly, both good and bad, that would have a lasting impact on America and Bucks County in particular. Most important was Negro suffrage and the debates leading up to and passage of the 15th Amendment to the Constitution of the United States granting the right to vote to all adult males, black and white alike—those who could pay the poll tax, that is.

The arguments that raged in Congress were reprinted in the newspaper beginning immediately after the end of the war. Letters went out to Presidents Johnson and Grant and Pennsylvania's representatives in Congress. Caroline sat down one day and painstakingly wrote one of the few letters Lang ever sent in his life. It took several tries and many sheets of precious paper to get it just right. And then Lang had to bring it to one of the teachers at Emlen to copy because, although Caroline had learned how to read, she never had any lessons in penmanship.

The letter was just one page. In it he talked about how proud he had been to vote thirty years before in 1837 and how he had waited for so many years to receive the full benefits of his birthright in the United States of America that now showed glimmerings of its true potential as the land of freedom and opportunity for all of its people.

The Amendment was proposed on February 26, 1869, and ratified almost a year later, on February 3, 1870. "The right of citizens of the United States to vote shall not be denied or abridged by the United States or by any state on account of race, color, or previous condition of servitude."

All summer the Assessors went about the county registering the colored men eligible to vote. In all, about four hundred stepped forward to be counted, all Republicans. It was said later in the fall that the Democrats had paid the poll tax of one man, but in the end he voted Republican, as well.

The townships with the largest populations of colored voters were Middletown with sixty, Bensalem with forty-five, Buckingham with forty-three. Bobby was counted in New Hope with a total of only nineteen men who enrolled. The number in Solebury was twenty-six, including Mahlon Gibbs, Andy Hartless, and Langhorn Wellings, each of whom could remember having voted at least once before in their lives in the infamous 1837 election.

The celebrations began immediately all over America, and especially in Philadelphia where, at one, Robert Purvis presided over the last meeting of the Pennsylvania Anti-Slavery Society in May of 1870, as the group was disbanded amid great happiness. "Our work is done!" Purvis announced as he rapped the gavel for the final time, and immediately announced that he would continue in full force his work on securing suffrage and equal rights for women, another issue he had felt strongly about his whole life.

The people of lower Bucks County went over to Trenton to join the celebration there. And the folks in middle Bucks—Doylestown, Buckingham, Upper Makefield, Solebury—made preparations to go across the river on Thursday, September 15, to Flemington, New Jersey, to join with blacks and friendly whites from Princeton, Trenton, and Lambertville.

There was no premonition that anything would go wrong. The only backlashes they had heard about were far away. There were, for example, some protestations by whites over having to serve on juries with the now-eligible blacks. One white man in Philadelphia was fined two hundred dollars for refusing or told he would be taken to jail. He chose jail and tried to get his release on a writ of *habeas corpus* but failed. He eventually paid the fine.

That and the evil workings of groups such as the Ku Klux Klan were the only incidents of which the celebrants were aware that could mar their exultation in victory. And those people and events were far removed from Bucks County.

Lang brought his wagon, which he decorated with garlands and red, white and blue banners. Caroline begged off, as usual. She just didn't like the crowds and especially the speechifying that reminded her too much of the years with the Moores listening to their haranguing and preaching. Unfortunately, her fear and shyness was misinterpreted by many folks as being haughty and standoffish.

Elizzie and Bobby insisted on going and bringing the baby, too. Jonas didn't want to take off work and miss getting his meager one dollar a day wages. He had inherited his mother's determination to own his own property someday and was saving every penny. He had nearly thirty dollars saved up already in a trunk that he kept locked in his room.

It was a beautiful fall day. A sudden frost a few days ago had started the leaves turning early, and the ride over to Flemington went through several areas where the trees formed canopies of sun-dappled gold, red and yellow leaves.

Elizzie had taken up sewing since Billy was born and made the eighteen-month-old baby a darling little shirt and brown tweed suit. The boy was so precious toddling about the campgrounds. He especially had the heart of each and every woman he smiled at.

Everyone brought "enough food for an army," they joked. There was certainly plenty to go around. Lang was contentedly full and had trouble staying awake as he sat listening to the speeches and musical entertainments. He finally gave up and went back to the wagon for a short nap in the afternoon.

One time during the day, Lang thought he caught sight of the young crippled fellow from the *Intelligencer*. He debated whether to speak to him, but in the end decided against it. He was still a little put out about the "poison" article. In addition, the *Intelligencer* had not printed the announcement of his marriage to Caroline, even though he had inquired at least twice at the offices when he was in Doylestown. The clerk kept saying it had to be submitted by a "qualified authority."

"Well, what the heck does that mean?" Lang asked grumpily.

"The authority who married you is the only recognized source of information for the paper."

Whenever he asked about it, John would say, somewhat vaguely, "I'm sure I sent it in, Lang. Perhaps it got lost somewhere."

By sunset, after another little bit to eat, it was time to go. Everyone was exhausted. It was going to be late by the time they got back to New Hope, and Lang had a wagon full of people to deliver to their homes in New Hope and Solebury. The Bucks County group formed up a line of about twenty wagons and carriages, each with two lights mounted on the rear, and proceeded toward home.

Someone started up softly singing hymns. Others gradually joined in, and the voices melded and carried beautifully in the cool night air. There was something ethereal about hearing music that you can't see people singing, like angels crooning lullabies to them. Lang's was the third or fourth wagon and he was in a good position to hear. Bobby sat with him up on the buckboard. Elizzie was just behind them with little Billy asleep on her lap.

Lang was thusly lost in the music when they rolled into Lambertville. Later he would remember thinking for a fleeting moment that there was something wrong. Even at eight o'clock at night, the place was too quiet, deserted-like. And at all the other little towns along the way, folks had come out and waved as the parade of conveyances went by.

Maybe there's a town meeting or dance, Lang remembered thinking, then immediately dismissed it as unimportant. Bobby would later say that his suspicions were aroused, as well, but, by the time they got through town, it was too late.

Suddenly, the fire bells began ringing. Everyone in the wagons was startled and the singing stopped immediately. Then the gang of white men and boys fell on them from both sides of the road, throwing rocks and yelling.

"Go home, niggers!"

"Get out of our town!"

The women screamed, rose up, then immediately recoiled and tried to cover each other and their children from the rain of missiles. The horses began bucking and rearing in fright, and Lang and the other drivers had to stand up and try to control them. He could see the wagons ahead and hear behind him that other drivers were having the same problems.

Some of the white gang tried to grab the reins, but Lang expertly flicked the whip and caught one of them right on the head knocking the man's cap off in the process. Bobby jumped down and took the reins and tried to calm the horse.

Lang yelled out, "Go for the bridge!" several times. The wagons in front were trying to do the same.

Then he could hear several gunshots, and the general pandemonium was increased. There was so much yelling and confusion and noise that Lang did not hear Elizzie screaming, "Billy!" "Billy's been hit!" until he was over the bridge with Bobby running alongside guiding the horse to safety. Lang could only drive and pray there was not another mob waiting for them in New Hope.

By that time, Elizzie had turned around. "Daddy! Billy's been hit by something!" He turned around and could see there was blood on the bodice of her light tan dress. It was too dark to see anything else.

Oh, God! The baby! Not the baby! Got to get to Dr. Foulk! "Bobby, get in the wagon! Hurry!"

Fortunately, there was only quiet and curious bystanders waiting for them in New Hope, and Lang drove unimpeded to Dr. Foulk's where Elizzie rushed the baby inside the house with two of the other women. Lang checked the rest of the passengers, who included some of Mahlon and Lizzie Gibbs' children, and they seemed to be okay, thank God. Shaken up, but okay.

Then they spent a very stressful, worried half hour wondering about the welfare of little Billy. Apparently, one of the first rocks thrown had struck him right on the forehead before Elizzie had a chance to cover and protect him with her body.

Finally, Elizzie came out. "The doctor says it's a superficial head wound that bled profusely, but it doesn't look to be serious, and there shouldn't be any lasting effects other than perhaps a small scar."

Lang was relieved, yet still so angry he was shaking. Bobby, too. It was one thing to be attacked oneself, but when the innocent babies were hurt...

Several of the men, including Lang, had to be restrained from going back across the river to "finish the fight."

"No, that won't do. That's revenge, don't you see. Let the authorities take care of it. They've all scattered by now anyway."

But, of course, the authorities never did. Oh, everyone was indignant and swore justice at first. The constable in New Hope promised he would get to the bottom of it and find out who was responsible, but as the days and weeks went by the rhetoric changed gradually.

It started out: "I've got my men out sniffing the neighborhood. We'll learn who those gangsters are soon enough, don't you fear."

Then, "Well, nobody's talkin', I'm afraid. And, seems like it was mostly New Jersey people, and I don't have no authority over in Jersey, you see."

And finally, "Oh, they was just tryin' to have a little fun, and it went bad. It was just a little joke, don't ya see? Just tryin' to shake you up a bit. Nobody got killed, now did they? You just go on home now and forget about it."

But, Lang could not go home and forget about it. The hurting of baby Billy was the "final straw" for him. He talked about it constantly. He stood up in church almost every Sunday that he was there and asked them repeatedly what they were going to do about it to the point that nearly everyone would sit with a glazed look in their eyes, and no one would speak to him any more for fear "the crazy old coot will start up again."

And that just made Lang angrier. He didn't know which was worse, to be persecuted and attacked or to be ignored. A proverbial vicious circle was started that would eventually culminate in Rev. Larison taking Lang aside and speaking to him about it in early December 1871.

All summer and fall the church had been having several times weekly very successful revival meetings. At least forty new people had been baptized and welcomed into the flock. Rev. Larison was at the same time undertaking a building project to expand and beautify the edifice of the church. This was quickly becoming a vibrant, active Christian community, and this Wellings fellow was turning people off.

Lang went immediately afterwards to see John. As usual, he walked in the kitchen door of the Balderston house, which was immediately across the yard from his own. He knew by now there was no need for him to knock and wait for the door to be opened. He found Sarah in the kitchen.

"Good morning, Sister Sarah."

"And the same to thee, Brother Langhorn. Is thee well this day?" Sarah, like many of the older Quaker women, clung steadfastly to the old ways and never could learn how to change her speech.

"Thank you, Sister, fair to middlin'." No sense bothering this sweet, gentle lady with his troubles. "Is the old man in?"

"Aye, my 'old man' is in the study, himself 'fair to middlin'," Sarah laughed. She always found these odd little idioms so humorous.

Lang stood at the doorway of the study and watched for a few seconds his friend sitting at the desk reading. John looked suddenly old and tired, even after just getting up in the morning. He was, what, just seventy?

"Are you okay?" Lang finally asked.

John looked up and his face immediately brightened. "Good morning, Friend Lang! Come, sit down with me for a spell. I'm just reading some papers on the Shaddinger estate. I have to go over to Centre Bridge tomorrow and inventory the property."

Lang sat down. "I've got somethin' most interesting to tell you."

John put the papers down and looked at Lang with interest.

"I was just down at the church, cleaning up the grounds, and the good Reverend Larison took me aside for a little talk."

"What is it?"

"Well, he said basically, that several people in the church had come to him, 'with their concerns,' was how he put it."

"What, you mean concerns about you?"

"Yup. Finally, he told me, in so many words, that I would be happier attending another congregation. 'You'll be more comfortable with *your own people*,' were his words."

"Oh, my." John closed his eyes and stroked his lips with his forefinger. "Frankly, I've been waiting for something like this to happen. I'm afraid these folks just don't know what to do with you." He looked up. "You're an anomaly, my friend. Do you know what that means?"

"No."

"It means you don't fit into their prescribed boxes or patterns of behavior. They don't have the same issues as you do, and they cannot see or understand your passion. The attack at Lambertville, last year, when little Billy and the others were hurt, is typical. I doubt whether any of them had anything to do with it, and if you were to ask them, every one of them would undoubtedly condemn it, but…"

"By their silence, they…what's the word, they condone it."

"Yes. You understand. Then, as your indignation—and righteous indignation it definitely is, in my opinion—as your indignation grows they turn away from you even more."

Lang frowned and nodded. "I've seen it in their eyes every time I try to bring it up."

"I daresay you won't find a sympathetic audience there. They had no part in it and feel as if they're being unfairly punished for it every time you speak."

"Yes, I s'pose they would feel that way."

John frowned with dismay. "But, even beyond that, Bucks County is changing, my friend. The old timers like Joseph Fell and Bill Johnson and John Kenderdine are getting old and tired and dying off. Their passion for equality and justice for all humankind is being extinguished, and there are few to take their places. I'm watching a new dynamic coming in, and I'm mighty concerned."

Lang agreed. "It's as if they're sayin', 'Well, you got your freedom now, you got your vote. Go on, now, and leave us alone.' But I think it's gone beyond slavery and voting rights, 'specially in the factory towns like Lambertville and New Hope. It's now all about money and survival itself. We blacks are competing with these new folks for our very lives and jobs. Meager and demeaning what is given to us as it is. They are afraid of us, and they are on the attack."

John was visibly impressed by his friend's learned reasoning. "I think, my friend, you have hit it square on the head. I've often wondered, though, why it is that the coloreds have been singled out for so much hatred and persecution. Oh, in the beginning, I understand it was economic, as well, only there it was the vested interest of the slaveholders to keep the perception of blacks as subhuman, thus justifying their enslavement and treatment like animals."

"And now?"

"Now? I suppose part of it is that those perceptions have been ingrained for centuries, and it's going to take a long time to turn people's thinking around. And now it's being perpetuated by people, like you said, who have a different vested interest—that is, in taking over your jobs and pushing you out for fear that your people will do the same to them."

"And they're doin' the same thing to the Indian people out West now. Killin' 'em off and pushin' them out."

"You are right. It is most shameful, but all of our protestations go unheard. They claim it's the Indian who is on the warpath and they who are exacting justice. Terrible."

"Henry Miller—you remember, Henry was the runaway I ferried up to Kenderdine's back in '44."

"Yes."

"I remember something he said at the time, that God had chosen us Africans to suffer. He meant it almost like a badge of honor, that by suffering here on earth, we would be 'the chosen people' for heaven."

"That's an interesting way of looking at it. But, then, one would think you would all rush to become martyrs, and that's no answer, either. Besides a tremendous number of whites—and others—have suffered, as well."

"Yes, but I've never seen a white person suffer simply because of the color their skin."

"Good point. You're right. That was unthinking of me." John looked at Lang and smiled in apology. "You know something?" he said. "I've just noticed that you're not angry. Seems to me if I had just been told to find myself another congregation to worship in…"

"Well, I am angry, but not at you. Never at you. You're just about the only white person in the world—well, besides Joseph and Bill—I can talk to and 'share' my anger. You understand it and don't tell me I'm crazy or try to talk me out of it." He thought for a few seconds, then looked to John and asked, "So, what do we do?"

"You mean about the right Reverend Mister Larison and his flock?"

"Yeah, for starts."

John shrugged. "Stay away from them, I suppose, as much as you can. Be pleasant and courteous if you run into them."

"In other words, give in and give up and perpe…what was that word you used?"

"Perpetuate."

"Yeah."

"No, not exactly. But it makes no sense to go where you've been asked to stay away and continue to escalate the situation until they feel they have no choice but to take drastic measures." John shook his head. "No, why not try showing them you're the bigger man? Continue to care for the church and the cemetery as if it's still your religious community. It's still hallowed ground, after all, to you. It contains the remains of your wife and daughter and many of your friends."

"And where do I go to church? Even the Quakers don't want me. They make me sit in the back or upstairs in the balcony. And, speaking of, there's the Good Templars, the Elks, Moose, Harvest Home celebrations, not to mention even your own farmers club. I could go on and on listing off all the organizations that don't want no part of us black folks."

John hung his head. "I know, and I am immensely ashamed of that. I suppose, in all fairness to my brethren, they *do* feel you would be more comfortable with your own people."

For the first time during the conversation Lang became agitated. "Tell me, John, just who are *my own people*? I've lived most of my life in Quaker homes. I just barely remember my mother. I was married to a white German woman. My children are half white. I've attended a 'white' Baptist church for twenty years...."

"I know, I know. The minute I said it... That was again insensitive of me."

"The simple truth is, *they* would be more comfortable if I was with *my own people*!"

"Out of sight, out of mind. Yes, you're probably right." He nodded sadly. "What do your friends Andy and Mahlon say?"

"They call me an 'Uncle Tom', say I'm an 'uppity nigger'."

"Oh, my! That's awfully harsh."

"Naw, they only mean it half joking, teasin' like."

"Pardon my ignorance, but what's an 'Uncle Tom'?"

"You know, the character from that book—*Uncle Tom's Cabin.* Mrs. Stowe's book."

"Oh! Yes, of course. It's required reading for the children at Emlen. And you say it has come to signify a behavior on the part of a Negro of what..."

"Suckin' up to the white man, curryin' favors."

"How does that make you feel?"

"Aw, they're just pokin' fun at me. Mahlon, 'specially, tried to warn me years ago about marryin' a white woman. 'Ain't nothin' but trouble,' he used to say over and over. 'You mark my words.'"

The men sat quietly for a few seconds, and Lang spoke up again. "Tell you the truth, John, and I've never said this to nobody else in the world. But I am not comfortable with most of the black churches. And 'specially not some of those preachers."

"I've heard some of that preaching at colored camp meetings a couple of times. It's definitely...ah, very interesting."

Lang nodded. "Yup. I've never been comfortable with it. It sounds... 'ignorant' is the word I'm lookin' for. Not that I'm all educated myself, hear. I never did learn to read nor write. But I suppose after over thirty years of havin' the *Intelligencer* and Godey's magazine read to me almost daily..."

"You certainly have a tremendous amount of good, old-fashioned 'horse sense', seems to me."

"I'll never forget when I was just a little kid, I remember there was a funeral. It had to be, oh, 1820 or so. It was at the Buckingham burial grounds. A colored fellow. The pastor was Daniel…. I can't remember his last name…"

"Yemmans. I remember him, too. What a colorful character he was. He was especially happy at funerals."

"Yes, that's him. One hot day in summer there was this funeral at Buckingham grave yard, as I said. Yemmans was late, and the people had partly lowered the coffin into the grave. Yemmans arrives, pushin' through the crowd, and wipin' the perspiration from his brow, he yells, 'What you niggahs about? Would you bury a man like a dog without a blessin'? Lower him up! Lower him up!' Then he proceeds to preach a sermon about 'Adam was de fust man, and Eve was his brudder'.'"

"Yes, whatever did he mean by that? As I recall, Pastor Yemmans also used to say often that he felt 'umbrage fur de Lord'."

"That's what I mean. I was never around that kind of talk, and I don't like it."

"But you can't blame the fellow. He was not educated, yet filled with the spirit…."

"Filled with the spirit or filled with himself?"

John laughed. "Could be a little bit of both. Regardless, he spoke a different dialect of English than you were used to. Don't blame yourself, either. You had been taught what you thought was the proper way of speaking, and that's what you were used to."

"But I've held these feelin's my whole life. Like at the camp meetings, 'specially the ones over at Guentner's campgrounds near Hatboro. Do you know where that is?"

"Yes, I think I know the place."

"I can't stand it when the white folks come and make such fun of the preachin' and the music. I'm ashamed. You know, anymore, there's more white people there than coloreds. It's all a great entertainment for them! They sit there gettin' drunk and hollerin' back at the preacher, 'You said it, brother! Ayyy-men!'" Lang waved his arms in the air to illustrate the behavior. "And the coloreds have to sit and try to ignore the insults and not say a word. They don't want us in their churches, and they won't let us alone to worship in peace in ours!"

John shook his head sadly. "I am so sorry. And ashamed of these supposedly good Christian people who show their ignorance by making fun instead of looking at the beautiful richness of spirit that animates the sermons and the music! Do you see? It's not the behavior we're each ashamed of, but the ignorance behind it."

Lang raised his eyebrows and nodded to signify that he would at least think about John's explanation.

John continued. "You know, old friend, I'll tell you a secret, too. I've always been ashamed of most of the immigrants, especially the Irish, and the way they behave and speak. And it's simply, like I said, we're accustomed to certain speech and behavior. I imagine that's one of the reasons you wanted another white woman when you were looking for a wife?"

"I s'pose. I was certainly used to Mary for a lot of years. To be honest, I chose Caroline 'cause she reminded me of Mary when she was young. We were so happy then, despite them shunnin' her and our troubles. Until she got sick…"

"Yes, when love was new. Anyone who's been married for a long time will understand that."

"But, Caroline isn't like Mary at all. Oh, she's a good cook and takes care of the house fine 'n all. But, 'tween you and me, there ain't much affection there."

"I can imagine not, with her upbringing. I doubt she was ever touched in an affectionate way in her whole life until she married you."

"And she sure is quiet. She don't talk much at all. Almost like she's deaf 'n dumb. Just sits in the corner with her arms folded."

"Tell me, do you find yourself comparing Mary and Caroline?"

Lang nodded and frowned.

"You're frowning because Caroline is coming up short?"

"Yes, again. Just between us, I'm wonderin' why I married her at all."

"I ask that because I know there's a tendency in old men, and I know that because I'm an old man myself…"

"Naw! Don't go talkin' like that!"

"No. I'm almost seventy, now. I've got a good ten years on you. But I've also found myself thinking, remembering, and sometimes I can remember the old days long ago clearer than I can recall recent events. Even what I had for lunch yesterday!" John chuckled.

Lang exhaled in a kind of laugh. "Oh, yeah. I can sure liken to that!"

"So, what I'm going to suggest for your consideration is based on those reminiscences. And it's rather convoluted, so bear with me."

Lang looked up in puzzlement. "What is it?"

"As you remember the good times, the happy days you had with Mary, and you are renewed with love for her, know that she loved you, too. She loved you so much that she left her family, her home, her comfort and safety—everything she had ever known just to be with you."

Lang nodded wistfully as John spoke.

"And you had several good years together, happy times with the children and your little home here."

"Until Jonas was born and she started gettin' sick real bad. And I guess I didn't always behave the way I should of." Lang lowered his head.

"Now, there you go blaming yourself again. That won't do any good unless you learn from your mistakes. And that leads me to the point of what I'm trying to say. You know until the veil of illness was pulled over Mary's eyes that those eyes looked on you with love. And loving you, she would want you to be happy, am I right?"

"Yes. She always did want me 'n the house 'n kids and everything to be just so."

"So, what I am suggesting is that you treat Caroline as a gift from heaven—from Mary—as a show of her love and wanting you to be cared for properly for your remaining days here on earth."

Lang was so moved by John's words that his eyes began misting. "I...I never thought of it that way."

"Well, there's some reason you thought of Caroline, and thinking that an angel whispered her name into your ear is as good an explanation as any!" John laughed.

"You're right."

"And if you think of Caroline as a precious gift, you can best show your love for Mary by treating her earth-bound sister, who has had such a terrible life until she met you, with kindness and respect. Try to ignore Caroline's irritating idiosyncrasies and concentrate on her good qualities."

"Mother Lacy used to say that! Overlook the bad, concentrate on the good, and you won't even notice the bad after a while."

"Anyway, it's worth a try. And perhaps you can expand that to our Baptist friends here." John cocked his head toward the southwest. "And stick with me. I would never turn you away, you know that."

"Yes. I see what you mean. But, that still leaves the problem of Lambertville and other things I keep hearin' about. The Ku Klux Klan 'n all. Gawd-damned bastards... Oh, I'm sorry, 'scuse me for swearin', but they make me so mad!"

"I understand, really. And certainly I don't suggest that we ever give up fighting for what we believe is right, speaking out against injustice and evil. But we must do so in a way that is not violent or confrontational. Just like that rabble who attacked you in Lambertville last year. We must rise above them and persevere."

"But, they will never get the justice they deserve. The cowards strike and run. We don't even know who they were. Just like the Ku Klux Klan uses them white sheets to cover their faces."

"No, we don't know who they were. And we may not, not today or tomorrow or maybe ever. And we may not have the satisfaction of seeing them brought to justice, either. But we will rise above it and succeed. And the way to achieve that is by continually speaking out, as I said, in the *Intelligencer* or wherever we'll be heard. In the meantime, I think it's very important that we forgive them and pray for them."

"Pray for *them*? You got to be kidding!"

"No, hear me out. Think about this: Even if the authorities were to find and arrest every one of them and prosecute them to the fullest extent of the law, do you think that would suddenly make them 'see the light' and understand their errors and reverse their ignorance?"

Lang shook his head. "No, prob'ly not, if they're set in their wrong thinkin'."

"No. So where is our next source of justice?"

"God."

"Exactly. All that leaves is Divine guidance and justice, and that is out of our hands. We must pray that God will somehow be enabled to enlighten their hearts. Just like Paul in the Bible. You remember, when he was Saul and persecuting the Christians. God suddenly spoke to him, 'Saul, Saul, why do you persecute Me?' and blinded him until Saul looked deep within his heart and understood his wrongdoings and begged for forgiveness."

"Yes. And we humans cannot *force* that understanding on anyone, that's what you're saying."

"Exactly."

"That's a tall order. But you've made me think. And realize I've been most fortunate to live near folks like you, good people. And I know there's millions of black folks who have suffered far, far more than me."

"You may be feeling a little guilty about that? I mean that 'your people', Negroes, have suffered under slavery for so long, while you have been relatively free?"

"Could be. I never really thought about it other than I remember I was very much afraid of Henry Miller and the other runaways, what they represented, what they was runnin' from."

John struggled to his feet, unsteadily.

Lang rushed to take his arm. "You okay, John?"

"Aye. I've got to go to the convenience. I have been mighty tired lately, though."

"You gonna be all right goin' over to Centre Bridge tomorrow? I can't go with you. Williams asked me to come over to Beaumont's to work some special party that Mr. Stavely's puttin' on."

"Yes, I'll be fine. John Betts is going with me. He was kin to Shaddinger anyway."

The two men walked out to the kitchen. Lang was alarmed to see how his friend walked slowly and seemed more bent over than usual.

As they got to the kitchen, John looked out the window and noticed the wind was kicking up.

"Oh, look," he said, "Someone very special has died. A great spirit is winging its way to heaven."

Sarah looked up and smiled. Lang had never heard that before and was somewhat alarmed. "How do you know that?" he asked.

"The old saying goes that some souls have trouble getting used to their wings and stir up a great wind as they leave." He laughed. "It's just an old wives' tale, really. Still, whenever the wind comes up, we can pause to pay respects to those who have passed on and wish them God-speed on their journey."

As Lang prepared to leave, John turned to him and said, "I think we are all very fortunate, my friend, that we have been given the time to live so long to have the chance to think over our lives, ask forgiveness, and prepare to meet our Lord. I, for one, am ready."

"Oh, dear husband! Why does thee talk so?" Sarah asked, alarmed. "Thee knows I cannot bear to hear it?"

"Now, now, good wife, thee wouldn't want me to remain here if it meant suffering any longer." He embraced her in a little hug and smiled at Lang over her shoulder. "And we will be together again, I promise thee, my dear."

How prophetic were John's words, Lang would come to realize within hours. The very next day, during the trip to Centre Bridge, John was struck by paralysis and carried home.

The watch began as he lay on a chaise in his study next to the window. Word got around quickly, and a notice was printed in the *Intelligencer* on Tuesday, December 12, that John had been taken severely ill. The visitors began coming almost immediately. For five days, friends and Sarah sat with him. His mind was alert to the end, although half his body was paralyzed and he had difficulty speaking.

Lang was sitting with Sarah late one night when John awoke and asked for water. While Sarah went to the kitchen to refresh the carafe, John spoke with effort and slurred words. "Brother Lang, you…care Sarah…"

"Yes, yes. You know we will."

"Don't want her suffer…"

Lang tried to arrange the blankets around John, but John patted his hand as if to say, "I'm fine." Then he said, slowly, with effort to form the words, "You do what I told you?" And Lang knew it was a reference to their previous conversation last Friday.

"I'll try, John. You tryin' to make a saint outa me, but I'll try."

In return, John tried to smile, but half of his face was limp.

"Do that…I promise…be remembered. Maybe not…your lifetime… not Billy's.…Future generations will honor you…won't even know this old white man.…" He started a chuckle that turned into a cough.

"They will, if I have any say about it," Lang promised.

John died just before dawn. As Lang walked across the yard toward home, he stopped in stunned grief, even though it was bitterly cold, and watched for several minutes as a spirited wind kicked up leaves and debris and formed whirlwinds that played among the houses and trees.

The funeral and interment were held on Monday at the Solebury Meeting House. A great number of people were present. Sarah insisted that Lang and Caroline sit up front with her.

The Quaker leader who delivered the eulogy gave a synopsis of John's life and accomplishments, then summed up, "Certainly there are few private citizens who pass from our midst, who have deservedly held so large a share of the confidence, esteem and affection of the community as has John D. Balderston. Generous to the extent of his means pecuniarily, he gave to all whom he could assist that which is better than money—earnest sympathy and sound counsel."

"*Amen*," Lang whispered.

Another speaker reiterated those sentiments when she said about John that, "As a friend and neighbor he was kind and just to all, without regard to creed or color."

Lang didn't know that one of John's final visitors was Henry Darlington and that John had made a special effort to tell Henry about Lang's problems with the Baptist church and his observations about the other "white" churches and the ill-behaving white people who went to camp meetings. It took Henry awhile to mull over what he could do, but, eventually, several articles appeared in the *Intelligencer* that made Lang wonder for the rest of his life how they could have known so completely what he was experiencing and feeling. Or was it a general concern that was being complained about by other blacks in the County of which he was unaware?

One article, in May 1873, was about the death of Sarah Stewart, "Aunt Sally" as she was affectionately known in the Doylestown area, a former slave from Maryland. The article read: "In religious faith she was a Catholic, and her funeral on Sunday at the church was largely attended by members and others. During the services Rev. Mr. George referred to the fact that the Catholic church made no distinction of color or race among its members—that all stood upon an equal footing in its presence, and that none could be deprived of a full share of its attention."

Henry apparently couldn't resist adding a further little "dig": "This was a new feature in a funeral address, and one that might be adopted by all Christian denominations without doing any harm."

Later that year, in August, Henry happily reported that at a colored camp meeting at Beaumont's "[t]here was no disorderly conduct, and everything passed off in a becoming manner," even though the "white audience was considerably in excess of the colored."

Unfortunately, a few weeks later, while Henry was away from the office on a visit to West Chester to inspect the schools as they were preparing to open that year, a long article, very derogatory and almost mocking in tone, was published in the *Intelligencer* about the colored camp meeting at Goentner's. It was overall most definitely disrespectful toward the preaching skills and musical style.

The article noted that the pastor was called "Doctor" by his brethren, "we suppose of divinity, though to what high institution of learning he owed his honored degree we were not informed." After reading a few verses of Ezekiel from the Bible, the preacher closed up the book and proceeded with his discourse extemporaneously. "Gifted with copious speech, an easy delivery and a ready, retentive memory, as pertains to his race, he left his text to take care of itself, whilst he poured forth a constant stream of narration in the most quaint and grotesque language; his exuberant fancy breaking forth in nearly every sentence, in pictures, comparisons and similes, often apt, but oftener most ridiculous and absurd."

The reporter was even more derogatory about the music, stating that "[t]he hymns written under the inspiration of religious fervor by Wesley and Newton would be hardly recognized by their authors; as the brain of the African has changed and modified their pure diction to the bent of his own capacities, inspirations and fancies."

Henry was furious when he came home and gave the reporter a good dressing down, but the damage had been done. It would take another two years to soothe somewhat the hurt feelings.

In September 1875, Henry printed a report on the camp meeting at Fisher's Woods near Doylestown where Mrs. Frances E.W. Harper, a well-known lady sometimes called the "Negro Poetess," "delivered a lecture which was worthy of a much larger audience. Her subject was 'Character,' and in her remarks she introduced fine sentiments and excellent language. She pictured the glorious possibilities of knowledge, and cited illustrations of renowned men who had either used to advantage or abused the power of their culture. The aristocracy of character, and its treasure and value, were pointed out and illustrated by fine rhetorical figures. Reverence and respect were discussed, both in relation to God and man."

The paper concluded that while the gathering on that September Sunday afternoon numbered from eight hundred to a thousand and "scarcely more than one in ten [was] of African descent…there appeared to be no disorderly or unseemly conduct."

Lang also never knew that John and Henry had consulted and decided against printing the announcement of his and Caroline's marriage because of several threats against Lang's life the paper had received following the trial. They came to the understanding that certain evil sentiments would undoubtedly be enraged if notice of this second interracial marriage, so soon after his first wife had died and his trial for her supposed murder, was published.

"I may be doing this behind Langhorn's back," John concluded, "But I'd much rather have him alive and mad at me if he finds out."

Sarah Balderston became so lonely and brokenhearted without her beloved John that she died within months, despite the careful ministrations of friends and neighbors such as Lang and Caroline. John and Sarah had no children surviving, and all of their estate was given to the Emlen Institute.

The property was sold to Thomas Ely and Moses Eastburn who rented it out to a succession of neighbors, with none of whom would Lang ever have a special friendship and affection as he had with John Balderston.

In July 1873, the Emlen Institute was moved to a ninety-five acre property in Warminster purchased from William Lyle, and the Solebury property was, as John predicted, bought by a rich man from Philadelphia who built a country mansion and had no need to farm the land beyond "show."

Meantime, Lang's work at Beaumont's increased. Except for the deep winter months, there were almost year-round festivals, school celebrations, mass meetings, and picnics to set up and serve. In 1876, a new pavilion was built to hold two thousand people theater-style. As he was aging, his arthritis progressively worsened, especially in his left shoulder, where he had been injured so many years ago. The duty at Beaumont's was light, not so strenuous as hauling and shoveling coal and limestone.

One of the side jobs Lang especially liked was working occasionally for Joseph Hough over at Buckingham. Mr. Hough was an ingenious and inventive mechanic who was constantly coming up with one and another of the most magnificent machines and contraptions. Hough was always putting up shows of his reapers and steam engines and the like, and he especially liked to have Lang, "this handsome, strapping Negro," posing at the controls, then Hough would step up and make a great show of the piece of equipment, "oohing and aahing" the crowd every time.

On several occasions, Lang got to drive the reapers. One especially memorable time was a show and competition of a number of different machines on Stavely's farm in Buckingham.

Mahlon Gibbs also invited Lang to work on his farm and large peach orchard and shared a portion of the garden so that Lang could grow the vegetables he and Caroline needed and have some left over to offer occasionally at a stall at Rice's.

Those and other odd jobs sustained the couple for the next nine years. Lang even managed to set some money aside toward his needs in old age, though he probably needn't have worried. In their small community, everyone looked out for each other and took care of most of the sick and elderly and never once considered taking reimbursement or pay. *What goes around comes around. Do for others, and they'll do for you and yours someday.*

Lang continued to tend to the Canada Hill church and graveyard, as John had suggested, and did not attend meetings, as Larison had requested. In an interesting twist of fate, one evening in early January 1872, shortly after John died, in fact, Lang was able to show in more tangible ways his friendship and good will, though it's doubtful that any of the recipients immediately understood the significance of it.

It was about ten o'clock on a Wednesday night. Lang was coming home from visiting Elizzie, Bobby and Billy in New Hope where they had attended Wednesday night services at Mt. Moriah. As he was coming up on the Canada Hill church, which he knew was having more revival meetings, a dedication of the new church building that night was just letting out. Several carriages and wagons passed him on York Road heading east, and others were going down the back driveway to Upper Mountain Road and then onto the pike.

Just as he was passing the church, Lang watched in alarm as a terrible commotion suddenly began at the crossroads. It was difficult to see in the dark, but apparently a wheel of a falling-top carriage had broken off just as the carriage was rounding the corner, bringing a sudden halt as the carriage fell over and scraped the road by the hub and the occupants cried out in alarm.

The horses, two young and skittish colts, became frightened. They sprang aside and started on a run at top speed down York Road toward Lahaska. Lang immediately took off after them and could see vaguely in the dark, and definitely by the debris that was being thrown on the road, that the carriage was breaking up. The driver was thrown over the front somehow and dragged for several yards, then finally dropped to the ground, where the carriage passed over him without harm.

Then Lang noticed two women jump out of either side of the twisted carriage and roll on the ground, their landings thankfully cushioned by their voluminous skirts and heavy coats. He pulled up to see what assistance he could give the ladies and gentleman. Many people soon joined him, so he and others began giving chase to the horses which, by this time, had galloped down the road at break-neck speed.

The horses raced past Judge Paxson's and Dr. Stavely's homes, then turned up toward Greenville, then back to the right toward Lahaska, all the time with the remnants of the carriage banging up and down on the road at their heels, frightening them all the more.

Meanwhile, Joseph Fell was just returning from a meeting and dropping folks off at Daniel Smith's home when he heard the commotion. He turned to look, but could not see in the dark. He procured a light from Daniel and ran to the bridge where he found the runaways with just the tongue, neck yokes and checklines of the carriage remaining. They had apparently started to run over the bridge, but one of the colts went into the creek and the other on the stone bridge, so that they were stopped short and wedged in place.

Joseph quickly took his wife, Harriet, home, and on the way called to Jane Hill to awaken Gilbert Maris and his son to help extricate the horses. Unfortunately, Jane had fallen asleep in her chair in the living room and became so confused when Joseph knocked on the door that she opened the door to the cellar instead of the door to the upper rooms and fell all the way to the bottom, fracturing her arm.

Joseph and Daniel Smith returned to the bridge and began working to free the animals. Meanwhile, Lang and the three or four others who had followed the trail of debris arrived. Lang immediately grabbed a blanket from his wagon and began drying and rubbing down the horse that had fallen in the creek, while others checked for injuries.

Once it was determined that the colts were not in the least injured by their escapade, they were returned to the church. Lang tied one of them to his wagon and when he handed it over to Rev. Larison two hours later, he learned that the occupants of the carriage were none other than the Reverend's brother, John, their sister and a friend.

Reverend Larison nodded, "Thank you, Langhorn. That was mighty good of you."

Lang tipped his hat. "I'm just glad the animals are safe and sound, and I hope no one was hurt?"

"No, thank God, just a swollen ankle on one of the ladies. It seems that the carriage is the worst victim of the incident."

Lang turned to walk home, and the Reverend called after him. "I trust everything is well with you?"

"Yes, thank you for asking."

"We sure do appreciate everything you're doing for the church. I want you to know."

"My pleasure. I'll tend to my wife and daughter especially as long as I can.

"Whenever you're in Lambertville, I hope you'll stop and see me."

Lang smiled. "Well, I don't get over there too often, Pastor. But, yes, I'll do that."

They say deaths always come in threes but, for Lang, the year 1872 the loss of friends came in at least fours. During the first six months of 1872 alone, there were four funerals, all colored friends. Bill Murphy of Buckingham, died on February 27, 1872. He was buried up at the Mt. Gilead Church at Wolf Rocks.

Then, less than two months later, on April 10, 1872, came a particularly sad blow when Lang learned that Andrew Hartless had passed away, aged sixty-five years and twenty-one days. He was buried at Mt. Gilead. Andy was the first to depart of what they had called the "Black Solebury Triumvirate"—Lang, Andy and Mahlon.

Young Richard Hopkins, who was employed by Charles Atkinson of Solebury, was kicked and fatally injured by a horse in May and also buried at Mt. Gilead.

Then, in June, came the death of a particularly beloved old lady named Ann Girton who had lived with and cared for the Stacy Brown family of Brownsburg for upwards of forty years. "Auntie Ann" had never married, but was content to be a faithful servant her entire life, and the Brown family returned that devotion by giving her a large, respectful funeral and placing a long, glowing *memoriam* in the paper in her honor.

In December 1873, Lang learned that Joseph Fell's son William was gravely ill and "home for good"—not expected to recover. William was Joseph's first-born of the four surviving children. He had studied law with George Lear, and was instrumental in engaging and paying for Lear's services when Lang was arrested and tried almost nine years before.

Lang knew that young Bill had left the church of his ancestors, having come through study and searching his heart to a deep dislike for dogmas and creeds, and especially for hypocrisy in any form. That is not to say he was not a deeply spiritual man, but a man whose soul could not be confined to the principles of a single man-made creed, however much Divinely-inspired it might be. A friend later noted that some may have called him "infidel" for his beliefs, but many who would apply that term to William Fell were not worthy to carry his shoes.

Bill shared his father's love of education, and when Lang went to Lahaska to visit, he found him on a makeshift bed in his father's library surrounded by the fruits of people who had truly inspired and delighted him his entire all-too-short life: The playwright Shakespeare, first and foremost, then English poets Byron, Tennyson, Shelley, and American writers Lowell, Whittier, Holmes and Longfellow. He loved to read history, both ecclesiastical and social, and had recently expanded his study into the metaphysical.

He was very weak and barely able to talk above a whisper, yet he was able to clearly show his delight to see "Uncle Langhorn" once more. He spoke candidly about death, what he called the "Mystery of tomorrow," and voiced his optimism that he would be reunited with all of his loved ones some day.

"I am confident that I can entrust my spirit to the Power that gave it to me thirty-eight years ago."

Just before Lang left, Bill took his hand and said, "Let's not say goodbye, Uncle; rather, I'll be seeing you again some day."

"You think they're gonna let me in the same heaven with you?" Lang tried to half joke with trembling lip.

Bill looked at him with loving eyes. "They had better, Uncle, or I'll tell them I want no part of it."

With a heavy heart, Lang took his leave and went to the parlor to visit with Joseph and Harriet.

"We have all experienced the loss of children, haven't we, Brother Lang," Joseph observed. "No parent should witness the death of a child. It's not in the natural order of things, but I know scarcely anyone of our acquaintance who has not."

Then they talked for a while about their mutual disillusionment with their respective churches. Joseph summed up his and Harriet's feelings. "Unfortunately, none of the established churches fares well under the light of educated scrutiny. There is none we have found that can truly claim it is completely free of pretense or hypocrisy or that purely reflects the Divine nature of its foundation. Personally, while we have remained Quakers, as that faith embodies most of the high ideals we hold dear, we are profoundly disappointed that it has not embraced people of all races with open hearts and helped to assimilate them fully into society."

"Don't feel bad," Lang answered. "It ain't just the Quakers. Coloreds are being pushed out everywhere. 'Why don't you build your own churches,' they say. And they even give us money and help to build 'em. 'Just go away and leave us alone' is the message they're really giving."

Joseph agreed, sadly. "If only my fellow religionists had not 'run out of steam,' as they say, when slavery was finally abolished. As I saw it, the 14th Amendment was just the beginning of our work, not the end result. We then had the tremendous responsibility of clothing, feeding, educating and training these poor wretches who had lived for centuries under the yoke of slavery. Instead, except for a few pockets of stalwarts who established schools, the rest of them had no 'steam'—no passion—left to do the job that needed to be done."

"In all fairness to Mrs. Mott and the others, they was tired. They'd been fightin' the good fight for nigh onto fifty years, some of 'em."

"And had failed to light the spark in fresh recruits, young people who could carry on the work. It's as if the young men who came home from the war and their wives have said, 'We've had enough of this suffering and struggle. We only want good times and to amass property and possessions.'"

"John Balderston said something like that before he died. The old fighters are getting sick and dyin', and there's a new…'dynamic' was the word he used, comin' in who don't have the caring you all do."

"I'm particularly concerned because we will have to close China Hall within a few years. There was only enough money to educate each orphan for a couple of years. We cannot take any more students, and when the last of them graduates, we will have to close up the place."

"That's a shame. And I know there are thousands and thousands more folks comin' up from the South all the time lookin' for work and prob'ly just to get away from the terrible conditions there. They come up here and find themselves packed in the cities and in competition with the poor white folks who want the same factory jobs. I just don't know what's to be done."

"I'm afraid I don't have any answers, either, except education, education, education. I will fight for the establishment of free schools and education for all people until the moment I take my last breath."

"And, if I know you right, you'll be havin' a talk with the 'Boss upstairs' about it right after!" Lang laughed, and Harriet and Joseph acknowledged with smiles the truth of it.

Their son William Fell died a few weeks later on January 4, 1874.

Just a few weeks later, Lang learned of the passing on January 22 of Rachel Morris of Doylestown, a venerable old lady who was the daughter of Peter Jackson, one of the first colored men to vote back in 1837, and wife of James K. Morris, the first to vote in Doylestown in the 1870 election. A widow by this time, she was living with the Schurz family in Doylestown and died suddenly while caring for the family's little two-and-a-half-year-old daughter Bessie while her mother worked in the house next door. She was buried with her husband at Buckingham graveyard.

On September 21, 1875 Caroline read an article in the *Intelligencer* that took both of them completely by surprise.

> On Saturday night last a young German who had been in the employ of Markley Rapp, on Aaron Fries' farm, at Bridge Point, suddenly left, taking with him fifty dollars

in money belonging to Jonas Wellings, another young man who worked for Mr. Rapp. The two men had been together in the room occupied by them in the early part of the evening, and on going down stairs Wellings thoughtlessly left the key in the trunk in which he kept his money. On returning to the room about eleven o'clock, he found the money had been taken out and that the man was gone. The thief is a young man about twenty-two years of age and had been in the employ of Mr. Rapp only a week, having worked for Walter Patterson, of Doylestown township, a short time before going to Rapp's.

Of course, Lang knew that Jonas had moved over to Fries' farm and was working for Markley Rapp, but Jonas hadn't said a word about the theft when Lang saw him the previous Sunday. He immediately went over to Bridge Point.

"Why didn't you tell me about your trouble, son? No wonder you was all down in the mouth last week."

"I don't know, Pop. I guess I was too embarrassed. That was pretty stupid of me to trust him. And I had no idea the paper was gonna get hold of it. The constable must've told 'em." He was tremendously disappointed, actually. This was all the money he had saved up looking forward to buying his own place some day.

"Do they know who the thief is, where he went?"

"Naw. They're not even tryin'. It's no use. He's long gone, prob'ly out west or to the city. I only got myself to blame, not trusting banks."

"Well, the only one I trust is the Doylestown Bank and that's only 'cause that's the one Dr. Cernea is involved with. Here, tell you what, son. I've got some savings here. Caroline and me don't need it, and I want you to have it." He reached in his pocket and brought out thirty dollars in Doylestown Bank notes.

"Oh, no, Pop! You shouldn't do that. You been savin' this for yourself. You might need it."

"No, I want you to have it. We got no need for money. And, 'sides, what's family for?"

"Gosh, Pop, I don't know what to say."

"Consider it your share of your mother's bequest. She really did love you, you know, and would want you to have it."

"Yeah, well…"

"John Balderston helped me understand that. 'The veil of illness clouded the eyes of love,' he said. You never knew your mother when she was young. By the time you come along, she was already gettin' sick. It's a real shame, and I'm sorry. And, then you had to go and lose Ruth Ann…" His voice trailed off in unspoken grief, and for a while the two just sat thinking, each remembering in his own way.

"Well," Lang finally said as he slapped his knees and prepared to get up and back to living, "I guess life ain't no guarantee of nothin' but hard work and heartbreak, as they say. So I got to be off to more of it!"

"Thanks, Pop. Really, I…"

"That's okay, son." He started to leave, then turned back. "I got one thing to ask you, though. If you don't mind, if anything happens to me, would you let Caroline stay in the house as long as she wants? I kind of promised to provide for her. You know how it is."

"Sure, Pop, of course. I been thinkin' about going to Philly anyway. Ollie Gibbs says that Mahlon and Elizabeth and the whole family are movin' there and I can come along with them."

"So I heard. Mahlon's talkin' about selling out and moving to the city. That'll leave me alone now that Andy's gone. Well, anyways, I talked with Elizzie about Caroline, and she agreed, too. She won't assert no rights to the property as long as Caroline is alive and wants to live there."

"Speaking of Elizzie, I'm worried about Billy. What does it look like to you?"

Lang wagged his head. "Not so good, I'm afraid. He's just not comin' up like a growing boy should."

"I was afraid of that. I noticed something, too. It's not so much his body, but his brain that ain't right, I think."

"It was the rock that hit him in the head in Lambertville. I know it. Everybody tells me it can't be proved that's the cause of his troubles, but I just know it in my bones. It's like his brain stopped developing that night. And Elizzie tells me he's subject to seizures, too. As if the poor girl ain't had more than her share of troubles in life…."

July 1876—the hundredth anniversary of the founding of the United States of America—was cause for more grieving than celebration for

Lang. On Saturday, July 1st, his old friend, William H. Johnson, passed away just two weeks after his eighty-second birthday.

Bill Johnson was one of the smartest, best educated men Lang had ever had the privilege of knowing, yet he was a compassionate and tireless worker for people of every color and social station. His whole life was spent in giving of himself to help, first, the downtrodden slave and, then, people whose lives and bodies were taken over by alcohol. There was hardly a cause for justice and education that Bill Johnson was not intimately aligned with.

It was said at his funeral in Buckingham Meeting House that the great number of friends and relatives in attendance felt as though "a father in Israel had departed from among them," and Lang could certainly agree with those sentiments. He, for one, would be forever grateful to Bill for personally bringing him home, lifting him out of the whiskey bottle and turning his life around forever more than thirty years before.

One by one, Lang was losing the people most dear to him since the days of his early adult life. Except for Joseph and Mahlon Gibbs and, he now realized, Dr. Cernea, it was getting so that Lang hardly had a friend left in this world.

And then, just days later, Lang learned that young Thomas Cernea, the architect, had died at his father's home in Buckingham at ten o'clock on the night of Independence Day. Lang knew that Thomas was not well. He had been in ill health for several years and had taken up painting partially as relaxation and a way to get good fresh air to strengthen his lungs and blood.

In Thomas' case, the legacy of his life's work was apparent every time one went to Doylestown and saw the buildings he had designed and built. And Lang had tangible proof for himself of the basic goodness and great worth of the short life of Thomas Cernea every time he looked at the photograph hanging over the red couch in the living room.

The last few years of Lang's life were spent fairly quietly, with two major exceptions, all of the "whoop-de-do" surrounding the Centennial celebrations being one. There were several meetings around the County. Although Lang did not feel comfortable attending the "tea drynke" at Solebury schoolhouse, where many antiques were exhibited and the people were dressed in period costumes, he did especially enjoy the gathering at Beaumont's Park where one of the speakers was Joseph's

son, D. Newlin Fell. Newlin, also a lawyer in Philadelphia like his
brother was before he died, gave a wonderful speech on "Women in the
Revolutionary War."

Then in July of the next year, Lang and Caroline were invited by
Joseph to attend the grand Centennial Celebration at Fairmount Park in
Philadelphia with the seventy-five children and all the teachers and staff
of the China Hall Orphans' School. Lang and Caroline drove down to
Bristol the night before and set out early in the morning with the group
on a train for Philadelphia.

A train! After near-about twenty years since the trains had been
coming to Bucks County, Lang finally got to ride on one of the huge
"iron beasts." He was so anxious he thought he was going to keel over.
His legs were wobbly, and the children, who had never known life without trains, giggled with delight to watch his nervousness.

But his fearfulness turned quickly to pleasure as the warm air
streaming in through the open window gently caressed his face, and the
countryside and then city scenes sped by as they traveled down the
tracks at, what, must be twenty, thirty miles an hour. Besides, he had
more to be afraid of outside the train than in, since far more people were
injured and killed when walking on tracks as were in derailments and
collisions with other trains.

The grand Bicentennial exposition was incredible to behold. There
was building after building filled with displays of machinery, art galleries, farm produce, fantastic new inventions. There were exhibitions
from foreign countries depicting the life of a typical citizen—France,
China, India, Germany, and more. There were horse and buggy races at
the grandstand and entertainments all over the park.

There was so much to take in they really should have planned to
spend a week there, not just a day, but unfortunately, there was no way to
house the group overnight without considerable expense. At ten o'clock
that night the bedraggled group made their way back to Bristol on the
last train of the evening.

This was really one of the high points of Lang's life, especially
seeing the children so happy and fortunate to have seen the exposition.
This was something they would remember their whole lives, and Lang
knew that Joseph and Capt. Marple and the others had paid for the whole
excursion out of their own pockets.

Then, in the summer of 1878, Lang was offered a job as coachman on one of the regular trips going back and forth to the New Jersey shore where the rich, and even some lucky working-class folks, went to the ocean to spend their summers. The trip to Atlantic City across the barren pinelands of Southern Jersey took several hours. It was late afternoon by the time the coach finally arrived, but Lang got at least two hours before sunset that night and then again early in the morning before the return trip to Bucks County to view the most magnificent, almost overwhelming sight of his life: The Atlantic Ocean.

His friends could not tear him away from the view. He sat a respectful distance, at least twenty yards away from the crashing surf, on a sand bank near where a large sidewalk made of wood was being constructed. The massive expanse of water and the crashing waves were at once frightening yet mesmerizing. He watched several people fishing along the shore and a couple of them showed him the bountiful fruits of their minimal labor.

"Why, it's almost as if the fish are jumpin' right into your sack," he commented in amazement.

He would have liked to continue going back, but he was getting nigh onto seventy years old now. It was becoming gradually harder to even get up in the morning let alone go to work at strenuous labor.

On a Saturday in early November 1880, Lang awoke as usual at four-thirty in the morning. He had lately taken to sleeping in the room off the kitchen so as not to disturb Caroline who slept until at least five-thirty. He dressed quietly and shuffled into the kitchen to stoke up the stove, which was kept burning day and night during the winter months, and pump some water for the coffeepot.

He ground up the beans in the coffee grinder and threw them into the pot, then went out to the pantry to the bread box that Caroline always kept filled with freshly-baked bread.

By the time his little breakfast was ready, Caroline was up and ready for coffee herself. Lang always had a hot cup waiting for her. He sat at the kitchen table, taking a smoke and a last cup of coffee before going out for the day.

His days now consisted mainly of tinkering in the barn, cleaning out the stables, feeding the animals, and doing handiwork around the house, although that was becoming less often. The arthritis was getting to him, especially today. His left shoulder and arm were hurting all the way down to the fingertips this morning.

"You goin' out today?" Caroline asked as she sat down across from him at the table.

"I was thinkin' about cleanin' up the churchyard this morning." He still went over to the Canada Hill church two or three times a week, although any more he would do a little work, then have to sit on the stone steps and rest for a while.

"Looks like it's gonna storm some time today," Caroline observed looking out the window.

"Aye. If I'm gonna do it, I'd best get at it."

He stood up and put his cup in the sink, then came back to the table and bent over to give Caroline a hug.

"Thank you for being my wife," he said and kissed her gently on the top of the head as he did every morning. And Caroline blushed as she did every morning.

They found him about two hours later, leaning against the embankment on Upper Mountain Road, clutching his chest and semi-conscious. Ironically, it was a dog that alerted the neighborhood that something was amiss. Some said later the dog's plaintive howling and barking could be heard a mile away.

He was brought home and put to bed in the little room off the kitchen. A doctor was summoned, who shook his head and said there was nothing that could be done.

Langhorn H. Wellings died just before midnight on November 6, 1880.

The Wind Storm on Saturday Night.

A miniature hurricane struck the buildings of Joseph Chapman, in Solebury, on Saturday night last, about midnight. Except the very high wind, the first intimation Joseph had of it were the stones from the chimney rolling down the garret steps. On further investigation he found the roof of his house literally torn to pieces. One side was slate, which had but recently been put on, and the rest shingle, and the two were mingled in utter confusion about the yard and road. His barrack, containing his hay crop, was blown down and the timbers, hay, &c. scattered in all directions. Two cows and calves imprisoned in the ruins were rescued by the neighbors without serious injury. The pig pen was also demolished, but fortunately his pigs were not hurt. The barrack of Phillip Larer was also overturned, and the roof of his barn scattered by the winds. The fences around adjoining fields belonging to R.H. Janney and Watson P. Magill were torn up. A large cedar tree on Mr. Magill's farm was twisted to pieces, and some other damage was done in the immediate vicinity.

[*Bucks County Intelligencer*, Tuesday, November 9, 1880]

DIED.

WELLING —November 6, 1880, in Solebury, Langhorn Welling, aged 69 years, 10 months and 11 days.

[*Bucks County Intelligencer*, November 27, 1880]

Epilogue

Elizzie Wellings Kohl's husband, Robert Kohl, died sometime before 1900; she is listed as a widow in the 1900 census of New Hope. William S. Cole died between March 17 and May 17, 1900 (the letters have worn away from the gravestone). He never married, and apparently Elizzie had no other children, as in the 1900 census she indicated she had given birth to one child who was not then living.

In 1887, the property at Canada Hill was sold by Elizzie Wellings Kohl and Jonas Wellings to Elizabeth Gibbs, Mahlon's wife, and, in 1906, Elizzie took it back, for some reason by way of Sheriff's Deed. Elizzie died on June 29, 1918, in the Canada Hill home, aged seventy-seven years, and is buried next to her sister, mother, father, and son in the Canada Hill cemetery.

Jonas Wellings moved to Philadelphia, met and married Winifred, last name unknown, an Irish immigrant, sometime between 1880 and 1887. They had four children: Charles, Joseph, Anna and Winifred Wellings. The entire family is listed as "white" on the 1900, 1910 and 1920 censuses. I believe Jonas and Winifred told their children and grandchildren that they were both immigrants from the British Isles. Some of the family are listed in the 1935 phone directory.

I don't know what happened to Caroline. I can find no record of her death or that she lived anywhere else. It could be she is buried at the Canada Hill Baptist cemetery and there is no stone and that she died before records were kept by the County or State.

Rev. Silas M. Andrews died on March 7, 1881, pastor to the day of his death at the Doylestown Presbyterian Church, as he had been for a month shy of fifty years, and key participant in almost every religious, charitable, and community service or event in Doylestown, Pennsylvania, during all of that time.

Dr. Arthur D. Cernea passed away quietly on June 30, 1883 at his home in Centreville, Buckingham Township. I am in touch with one of his great-great grandchildren, Daphne de Cernea.

Joseph Fell died at his home in Buckingham on March 11, 1887. One of his surviving sons, D. Newlin Fell, went on to become Chief Justice of the Pennsylvania Supreme Court and continued his father's work in education. There is a school in Philadelphia named after him. Another son, Edward Watson Fell, married a Kenderdine girl and settled on the old homestead. Joseph's daughter, Emily, married William T. Seal and moved to Philadelphia. A great deal of information about Joseph came to me through one of his distant cousins, David Fell, of Portsmouth, Virginia.

Judge Henry Chapman died on April 11, 1891, at his estate just north of Doylestown after retiring in November 1871 and taking the "Grand Tour" of the British Isles for a number of months with his family, among other travels.

(By then General) William Watts Hart Davis died on December 26, 1910, almost ninety years old. The last years of his life were spent actively involved as one of the founding members and president of the Bucks County Historical Society. His *History of Bucks County Pennsylvania From the Discovery of the Delaware to the Present Time* is still the definitive work of its type about the County.

Mahlon and Elizabeth Gibbs moved to Philadelphia sometime before 1900, and Mahlon passed away there before the 1910 census. I have identified fifteen possible children: Rebecca, b. 1848; Ajoina, b. 1849; Juliana, b. 1850; Oliver, b. 1851; Ruthann, b. 1853; Margaret, b. 1856; Rachel, b. 1856; Mahlon, Jr., b. 1860; Elmer, b. 1861; Ellsworth, b. 1863; Lincoln, b. 1864; Reading, b. 1867; Ulysses, b. 1869; Edwin, b. 1871; and Anthony B., b. 1874. There are four possibles listed on the 1910 census: George (who matches in age with "Ajoinah"), in Bucks County with wife Sadie (age 38), sons Sherwood (13), Oril (7), and Raymond (5), and daughter Efford Applegate (no age given). Grant (who matches in age with Ulysses and probably took his middle name), living with the Oliver Hagerman family at Langhorne Manor. Mahlon Y. Gibbs, who matches in age with Mahlon, Jr., in Bucks County, with wife Mary E. (53), born in New York, daughters Marion K. (11) and Mildred L. (6), and sons Herbert Y. (10) and Clarence H. (9). A woman matching Elizabeth Gibbs' age and color is shown living in Philadelphia with Levina Knonells.

As for the Hartless family, I know of no children, and I could not find any more references to Margaret Hartless, although there are several gravestones at Mt. Gilead close to Andrew's that are worn with age or vandalism.

Of Mary's surviving brothers and sisters, we know the following:

Elizabeth's three children, Elizabeth, Edward S. and Charles Height, signed Releases of Dower of their grandmother Mary Trullinger Stone's estate in 1864 and 1866. I was not able to find any more information on Elizabeth or her husband Aaron, although there were and still are many of the family Hite/Heit/Heidt/Height in the Bucks County area.

Sarah I know nothing further about other than she married a man by the name of William Page. If you've ever tried to search for "Page" and "William" in genealogical records on-line, you can imagine my frustration.

Jonas and Lydia had at least three children, Richard, Jacob and Margaret. The last I know of them is in May 1863, when Jonas, then residing in the City of New York, signed a Power of Attorney to Lydia to execute the Release of Dower of his mother's estate, which she did on May 11, 1863.

Eliza Ann and John German had four children: Tobias, Ralph, Anne and Esther. I know nothing more of them other than they signed what we call the "mass" Release of Dower, along with several brothers and sisters, in 1863.

Mahlon married twice that we know of: Mildred Pritchet, a widow, on January 25, 1856, in Merced County, California, and Amanda Hawkins, January 23, 1869, in Merced, by whom he had two daughters, Lillian Agnes (1873) and Alice (1878). He amassed quite a bit of property in Merced County, and died sometime between 1880 and 1883, when his widow, Amanda, married Louis M. Gillham.

Rachel and Aaron VanSant/VanSandt/VanZandt had three children: Mahlon married Felitia Jugrain/Jergan and died young, apparently childless. There is no further mention of Sarah. Aaron, Jr. married Mary F. Baxter on January 5, 1873, and moved to Sheridan, Worth County,

Missouri, where he worked as a very well-respected druggist and they raised nine children. He died there on September 15, 1930.

Aaron and his wife Mary Ann we know a great deal about because I have been in contact with two of his descendants, cousins Jackie and Rich. Aaron and Mary Ann had nine children, seven of whom survived to adulthood. Rich is descended from daughter Esmeralda and her second husband, Hawley Welch, and Jackie is descended from Mildred Mary and her husband, John Abel. Rich has done a tremendous amount of work on his great-great-grandparents, Aaron and Mary Ann Stone, and has identified over one hundred forty descendants thus far.

Amos died in Doylestown on March 6, 1887, the only one of the seventeen children of Jacob and Mary Trullinger Stone that we know of to be buried in the Doylestown Cemetery, alongside his only son, Thomas Chapman Stone, who died in the Civil War, and wife, Phoebe, who died at the home of her niece, Susan Augusta Stone Rorer, on March 22, 1901.

Chillian (or Killian), we have never been able to find any more information about. My only guess is that he changed his name; for example, on the 1860 Monterey County, California, census, there is a "Rocky Stone" born in Pennsylvania in approximately 1825, which is very close to Chillian's birth date of 1821, and he was living in close proximity to someone who could be his little sister and her family.

Harriet was dead by 1863 when her three children by John Hoff, Rutledge T., John Jr., and Daniel, were placed under the guardianship of Moritz Loeb (Jewish publisher). We have no further definitive information on Harriet or her husband. "Hoff" (also Huff/Hough) is a very common name in Eastern Pennsylvania. We do know that Rutledge served in the Civil War in both the 196th Pennsylvania and the 40th New Jersey Regiments. He married Elizabeth (last name unknown), ten years older than himself, and resided in Trenton in 1870.

Camilla and George Garren moved first to Kane County, Illinois (where brother Hiram Stone and his second wife Hannah lived), then to a western suburb of Chicago in Cook County. They had eleven children that we are aware of: Calvin, Samuel, Phoebe, Ella, Edward, Charles, George, Jr. ("Dode"), Frank, Ulysses, William, and Alice. Another humorous story about George Garren comes from Pliny A. Durant in his "Passing in Review: Reminiscences of Men Who Have Lived in St.

Charles," published in the *St. Charles Chronicle*, 22 May 1903, p. 1: "One of the best blacksmiths who ever wielded a hammer lived for years in St. Charles. His home was long on the corner now occupied by E.P. Phillips, and his shop was a busy place. He served in the Union army during the Rebellion and could tell some of the richest stories of southern experience of any man who returned from that wondrous service. He was a good musician and played a cornet in the old St. Charles band…. He had wind like his shop bellows, and was one of the strongest players I ever knew. He was the father of a large family of children, whose 'didos' [*sic*, dittos?] exasperated him sometimes beyond all account. When he thrashed one of them he performed the job in the same vigorous manner as he handled a piece of hot iron—and I think he never struck a blow amiss, for some of those youngsters were veritable fiends. They could think of more mean things, say more wicked words, and do more desperate deeds than all the rest of the town together. Yet I think they all grew up to be pretty respectable citizens. A man stopped at Garren's shop one day, and asked him how many children he had. The blacksmith wiped the sweat from his grimy brow, and counting on his fingers as he named them, answered, "Well, there's Calvin and Phebe and Sam and Ellen and Ed and Charlie and Dode—Oh,—! Go and count them yourself! There's ten or fifteen of 'em!"

Rebecca, on September 10, 1865, then a widow of Owen Swarts/ Swartz and living in Princeton, Bureau County, Illinois, married James C. Hubbard, a native of England. Rebecca had possibly five children with Owen Swarts: Hellen, Owen, Jr. (died young), Anna, Emma, and Ona, and by Mr. Hubbard she had one child, Ida May. The family moved for a while to Maple Township, Canadian County, Oklahoma, where James Hubbard died in 1903. Rebecca moved afterward to Texas County, Missouri, to live with daughter Ida May Hubbard and her husband, William Sitton, where she died sometime after 1920.

Hiram and second wife, Hannah, had eleven children in all: Ellwood, Flora ("Folly"), Anna, Charles, Albert, Jennie, Lillian, Helen ("Ella"), Walter, Frank, Woodrow. He died in Batavia, Kane County, Illinois, on November 17, 1913. I have been in contact with several of Hiram's descendants: Cousin Louise is descended from Hiram's first child, Susan Augusta. Brothers James and Jeffrey are descendants of

Hiram's son Frank Linton Stone. Clifford and his cousins, Sharon Stone (no, not *the* actress) and Linda are descended from Hiram's son Walter.

Emma, the baby, outlived all the others. She died in San Juan Bautista, San Benito County, California, on March 17, 1929, and is buried next to her second husband, Emanuel McMichael, and several of her children, in a cemetery on a hill high above the town. Her first husband had died at twenty-five in Chicago in 1856. By him she had Emma, George W., Jr. and Unknown. The last child apparently died young. Daughter Emma Rue died at nineteen in San Juan Bautista. With Emanuel McMichael, Emma had at least five children: Frank, Robert, Edward, Mary, and Anna. Frank died when he was only two years old and Robert died at six. Of the survivors, at least Edward and Anna never married and continued to live in San Juan Bautista until they died, Edward working as a bartender, and Anna serving as postmistress for the town for many years.

Last, but definitely not least in my estimation is my great-great-grandfather, **Reuben**. With the exception of Mary and Langhorn, Reuben is the one I know the most about since he is my direct ancestor. Reuben and his wife, Emily Black Love, had six children: (1) Emma Lydia Stone, b. 22 Oct 1850, m. William Anderson, d. childless 28 Mar 1931; (2) James Love Stone (my great-grandfather), b. 30 Mar 1854, m. Frances L. Goodenough, 17 Apr 1876, had two sons, James Johnson Goodenough Stone (my grandfather) and Edward Braislin Stone, d. 10 Mar 1937, Trenton, Mercer County, New Jersey; (3) Olive Griffith Stone, b. 17 Nov 1856, m. William Wilkinson, 2 Feb 1886, had six children: Clarence, William, Emily, Robert, Raymond, and Margaret, d. 22 Nov 1940, Philadelphia; (4) Rebecca Love Stone, b. 28 Feb 1859, m. Isaac L. Shinn, had seven children: Emily, Sallie, Willett, Reuben, Elmira, Emma, and Meribah, d. 29 Jan 1939, Burlington County, New Jersey; (5) Robert Love Stone, b. Dec 1862, m. Martha Evans, had two daughters, Helen and Marie, d. 6 May 1934; (6) Reuben Stone, Jr., b. 23 Jun 1867, m. Cora Sorter, had four children: John, Richard, Emily and Cora, d. sometime after 1900, Bronx, New York.

I have been in touch with several cousins from Reuben and Emily's children, including Alice, who is descended from Olive, and brothers Thomas and Edward, who are descendants, like me, of James Love Stone.

References

Bucks County Intelligencer, 1835-1880

Davis, Col. W.W.H., *History of Bucks County Pennsylvania From the Discovery of the Delaware to the Present Time*, Doylestown, PA: 1877

Doylestown Democrat, 1850-1880

Gattuso, John, *New Hope and Bucks County,* Stone Creek Publications, Milford, NJ: 1997

Litwack, Leon F., *North of Slavery*, The University of Chicago Press, Chicago: 1961

Lapsansky, Emma, *Black Presence in Pennsylvania—"Making it Home",* Pennsylvania Historical Association, University Park, PA: 1990

Ludwig, Ed; McNamara, Brooks; Strecker, Betty, for the Doylestown Historical Society, *Images of America—Doylestown—The County Seat of Bucks County*, Pennsylvania, Arcadia Publishing, Charleston, SC: 2000

Marshall, Jeffrey L., *Bucks County History: Fact or Fiction?*, Marshall Family Press, Newtown, PA: 1993

McNealy, Terry A., *Bucks County—An Illustrated History, Bucks County Historical Society*, Doylestown, PA: 2001

Oakley, Amy, *Our Pennsylvania—Keys to the Keystone State*, The Bobbs-Merrill Company, Inc., Publishers, Indianapolis-New York: 1950

Papers Read Before the Bucks County Historical Society, Vols. I through VIII, Bucks County Historical Society, Doylestown, PA

Richardson, John, *Solebury Township Bucks County Pennsylvania—A Short History of the Township and a Report on Township Officers and Affairs*, Offset Service Company, Philadelphia, PA: 1958

and the hundreds, if not thousands, of people who care so much about their subjects to post detailed information on websites—most of whom I will never be able to appropriately acknowledge.

Index

About the Author

Priscilla Stone Sharp has been involved in genealogy research for fourteen years. Her exploration into her family's roots uncovered this extraordinary American tale of love, survival, life and death, African and European Americans in pre- and post-Civil War America.